CARAVAGGIO STUDIES

Michelangelo Merisi da Caravaggio, after a drawing by Ottavio Leoni.

CARAVAGGIO STUDIES

BY WALTER FRIEDLAENDER

PRINCETON UNIVERSITY PRESS
PRINCETON, NEW JERSEY

TO MY STUDENTS
at the Institute of Fine Arts
New York University
from 1935 to 1955

PUBLISHED AS PART OF THE PROGRAM OF THE
INSTITUTE OF FINE ARTS OF NEW YORK UNIVERSITY

AIDED BY A GRANT FROM THE BOLLINGEN FOUNDATION

FOREWORD

No painter ever painted his own mind so forcibly as Michael Angelo Amerigi, surnamed Il Caravaggio. To none nature ever set limits with a more decided hand. Darkness gave him light; into his melancholy cell light stole only with a pale reluctant ray, or broke on it, as flashes on a stormy night. The most vulgar forms he recommended by ideal light and shade, and a tremendous breadth of manner.—HENRY FUSELI, *Lecture II*, 1801, p. 100

I N the past few years, Caravaggio's popularity with the public at large has increased astonishingly. Nearly all of his authentic works were brought together in the Milanese exhibition of 1951 and attracted thousands of visitors, some of whom had hardly known his name before. The rediscovery of the artist does not have the same character as the revival of El Greco, the Le Nains, and George de La Tour, because these were essentially provincial painters, and their works had no direct artistic progeny. By contrast, Caravaggio worked in the most important cultural center of his day, Rome, whence his ideas spread to the farthest corners of Europe and were recognized from the beginning by many artists as being something new and revolutionary. His influence, direct or more often indirect, is present in countless seventeenth, eighteenth, and nineteenth century canvases which display realistic or naturalistic features. The enormous impact of his art on later generations, in Spain and in Northern countries even more than Italy, is well known.

Nevertheless most art critics and academicians condemned the "vulgarity" of Caravaggio's paintings, at times even with moral indignation, from Bellori's biography in the seventeenth century, down to Burckhardt's *Cicerone* in the nineteenth. Being themselves committed to a standard of ideal beauty, they found his work no more than a base "imitation of nature" and charged him with having destroyed "good taste." Through two centuries this attitude prevailed, and Caravaggio was classified as a painter of low category. Nor could these opinions have easily been opposed, for the knowledge of his oeuvre was effectively obscured by the innumerable paintings in older collections which were labelled with his name, provided they were dark and realistic. Thus the Caravaggio research, especially the knowledge of his authentic work, was in a state of confusion.

The long and painstaking reconstruction of Caravaggio's oeuvre and the facts and circumstances of his artistic activity has been the work of many excellent scholars for the past forty or fifty years. As early as 1906, Wolfgang Kallab began his very advanced and comprehensive biographical work, which remained in fragmentary form because of his untimely death. The studies of Lionello Venturi, Matteo Marangoni, Herman Voss and Nikolaus Pevsner were among the earliest and most fundamental contributions to the investigations of Caravaggio's paintings. The practical value of the short monographs published by Leopold Zahn and Ludwig Schudt should not be underestimated, although they have not added considerably to our knowledge of the artist. The most prominent Caravaggio scholar today is Roberto Longhi, whose many years of rich and imaginative work paved the way for the marvelous Caravaggio Mostra in Milan. A large amount of new and important documentary material has been accumulated, giving our knowledge of Caravaggio a much needed precision. This material has been published by Orbaan, Lucia Lopresti, Aldo de Rinaldis, and others, as well as by Venturi, Longhi and Pevsner. The recent discovery of new documents by Denis Mahon revealed many interesting facts, particularly concerning the paintings which Caravaggio made for the church of San Luigi dei Francesi, and for Santa Maria del Popolo. Thanks to these and other investigations, we now have a fuller knowledge of Caravaggio's works than we have ever had before.

With the attention of the public focused on Caravaggio, with many problems of connoisseurship solved or at least brought to light and with our much enriched knowledge of literary and documentary sources, it has now become possible to write monographs on the artist containing all the available facts, composed and accentuated according to the individual aims of various authors. However, I feel that the time has not yet come to write a conclusive and comprehensive biography of Caravaggio. Such an undertaking should not be limited to recounting the facts of his life, to fixing the dates of his works and to establishing their sequence on the basis of documentary or stylistic evidence. It should also endeavor to explore the sense and significance of every painting in the context of the period, and to understand how the spiritual tenor of each differs from the conceptions of previous artists. More important, it should try to grasp the impression that Caravaggio's art made upon his contemporaries, not so much upon the intellectual art-connoisseur, as upon the average spectator.

It is true that many valuable investigations have been made about Caravaggio's artistic education. His apprenticeship as a very young boy in the shop of a rather mediocre Milanese painter was brought to light long ago by Nikolaus Pevsner. Much has been written about his artistic provenance and of the impressions which he received outside the shop of his provincial master from the surrounding world of North Italian art—from Savoldo, Lotto, Moretto, Antonio Campi and many others—impressions clearly reflected later in the works he executed in Rome. Roberto Longhi, in a famous and spirited article, propounded a theory of almost blood-and-soil character in which he tried to demonstrate Caravaggio's realism as being deeply rooted in the innate realism of Lombard art. Other scholars have vehemently attacked Longhi's Lombard theory as being too one-sided, and have stressed the purely Venetian-Giorgionesque influence on the artist. At present, most critics seem inclined to make a compromise between these two theories. The chapter here on the youth of Caravaggio reviews the many possibilities in Milan as well as in the Veneto which could have influenced Caravaggio's development, although it avoids generalizing conclusions.

Nevertheless, in analyzing Caravaggio's works, little distinction has been made between the impressions which the young artist received (partly subconsciously) from his artistic milieu, and the conscious selection from various paintings which the maturing artist made for the purpose of supplementing his own compositions. Not enough attention has been given to Caravaggio's own special brand of eclecticism, to his avidity in studying the formal details or the themes of many different painters. Observation of this kind is illuminating for the comprehension of Caravaggio's procedures and for the understanding of his personal accomplishment. For this reason it has seemed to me necessary to compare, much more than has been done, Caravaggio's representations (such as the *St. Matthew and the Angel* or the *Deposition*) with those of other painters in Italy and also in the North, not for purely iconographical reasons, but to show how original and even revolutionary his formal and spiritual solutions were.

The intention and meaning of Caravaggio's paintings—their semantics—have been even more neglected. Almost no attempt has been made to understand how his evocative stylistic innovations served as vehicles for the ideas he wanted to express. These devices should not be considered only from an aesthetic point of view but should be comprehended in the deeper sense in which they communicate a meaningful moral idea.

For whatever impressions we may have of Caravaggio's violent and neurotic personality, it is evident from his religious compositions that his artistic expression as a mature artist was dominated by an outspoken ideal. Caravaggio's flower and fruit pieces, half-figures of frivolous boys and musical scenes are extremely charming and amusing, and their loss would certainly be perceptible. However, it should not be forgotten that after the few years in which he produced these youthful, bohemian canvases, he turned his attention almost entirely to the creation of monuments of devotion, all of which are permeated with the same desire to realize the unrealizable, to bring the miracle within the immediate grasp and understanding of everyone.

Caravaggio's treatment of the supernatural as if it were reality, connects him, in my opinion, with the realistic mysticism of past centuries as it was still present in the religious prescriptions of Ignatius of Loyola's *Exercitia Spiritualia*. The essence of Loyola's religious realism was transmitted to Caravaggio through the circle of Rome's most popular and down-to-earth saint, Filippo Neri. As far as I know, no one has yet tried to understand the spirit of Caravaggio's religious art in this connection. He is the only painter who expresses, progressively and powerfully, the tendencies of this "low" church in the midst of the high Catholic hierarchy.

A more intense study of the religious movements which permeated the everyday life of the time would clarify to some degree the constantly repeated and often discussed classification of Caravaggio as a mere "naturalist." There is certainly a strong parallel between the direct and sometimes even coarse treatment of religious matters by San Filippo Neri, and the vulgarity in Caravaggio's provoking exhibition of a peasant's dirty feet in the painting of a Madonna, or the swollen body of the Virgin on her death bed. More significantly, Filippo Neri was blamed, despised and even persecuted by the regular conservative functionaries and professionals of the clergy just as Caravaggio was blamed by the high lords of the world of art.

To Federico Zuccari, president of the Academy of St. Luke and high priest of the divinely inspired Roman "disegno" (which included not only drawing but the entire learned procedure of art), Caravaggio's method of transferring "natura"—that is to say, the model— directly to the canvas without the medium of preliminary drawings must have seemed a kind of crime against the Holy Spirit. The Roman reactionaries' pretentious conception of art as a kind of transcendental metaphysic, was opposed by Caravaggio's simple, fanatical and almost religious postulate that art speak directly, using the easily understandable terms of the visible world. To the irritation of his rather simple-minded colleague and biographer,

Baglione, and to the astonishment of the much more clever and highly educated Bellori, Caravaggio created "arte senza arte," art without understanding what art is. Actually, while Caravaggio as a North Italian tended to think of nature in terms of color and chiaroscuro rather than disegno, as a professional active in Rome he had absorbed much of the structural element in Roman art. One of his most significant functions, in fact, was to bridge the long acknowledged schism between Roman disegno and Venetian colore. With the addition of the moral and social overtones of Caravaggio's painting, there resulted an artistic manifestation which was surprisingly new for Central Italy.

About 1600 one of the Flemish artists who frequented Rome reported to van Mander in Haarlem the emergence in the Roman art world of a curious young painter, who proclaimed loudly the new and rather subversive doctrine, that every work of art not made directly after life is child's play, not even excluding from this preposterous judgment the sacrosanct art of antiquity, or the "Divine Raphael." Such radical statements, though they were doubtlessly made "pour épater le bourgeois," probably gave rise to the assumption that Caravaggio was unable to draw or paint without having a model before him. This accusation, first used by Caravaggio's adversaries to discredit him and his art, later gained currency with such critics as Scanelli and Bellori, who used it to stamp him as a mere naturalist. In reality this derogatory classification, which so prejudiced the judgment of later centuries, was by no means valid, at least in an absolute sense. Caravaggio is quite obviously not a slavish imitator of visible objects, either in his early genre paintings like the *Fortune Teller* (which Bellori cites as an example of his painting directly after life), or in later works such as the *Martyrdom of St. Matthew*, with its stylized figure of the executioner, or the *Flagellation of Christ*. Caravaggio was certainly as well able to alter the appearance of the model or to draw a figure from memory as any of the maniera painters. Even assuming that as a boy he was a recalcitrant student in the shop of Peterzano—and this is not at all improbable—he had surely enough intelligence and ability to master elementary teachings. And to such schooling, "child's play," belongs the knowledge of the graduation of figures according to the distance from the foreground. It was therefore a kind of slander when his critics accused him of using a dark background simply to hide his inability to build up a real pictorial prospettiva. Quite to the contrary, Caravaggio needed this limitation of space to concentrate his composition. He used it to bring the miraculous event directly and persuasively before the eyes and into the heart of the worshiper. The real reason for Caravaggio's censure by the art critics of his day was not a lack of technical ability, but rather his conception of the relationship between the work of art and the worshiper who sees it. Caravaggio's offense was that he had challenged the whole God-given ideology of Roman art, drawing it down to earth from its higher spheres. In spite of these academic criticisms, it was just the directness of Caravaggio's art that brought him notoriety and even popularity. The impression which Caravaggio's paintings made on the populace of his day is difficult to estimate and explain because it is not only an art-historical problem, but a psychological and interpretative one. It involves not only a patient searching and understanding of every individual work but also a comprehension of the significance each work had for the community and for human feelings generally. This knowledge one cannot acquire by reading and interpreting the biographies of art writers of the seventeenth century. Most valuable and interesting though they are for the facts they contain concerning the life and works of Caravaggio, their authors are prejudiced—personally, or by their exclusively artistic or art-theoretical preoccupations. Of all these writers Bellori is the most spirited and erudite. By inserting a vita of Caravaggio in his selection of the most important artists of his period, he showed at least an awareness of the phenomenon "Caravaggio" and its significance from an art historical point of view. But he nevertheless condemns the naturalism of Caravaggio, according to classicistic-Poussinesque credo, as the "rovina della pittura," the "ruin of the art of painting."

Not for a moment did he try to investigate the deeper roots of this "naturalism," nor did he notice that the "colori poetici," "the colorful poetry," which he observed and admired in his idol, Poussin, are also present—though in a quite different way—in Caravaggio. It was not within the realm of an art writer of the seventeenth century to discover the poetic or dramatic force, and to understand the essence and magnificence of Caravaggio's realism. That would require a writer like Baudelaire. Men like Bellori, Mancini and Scanelli reflect, after all, the opinions of a relatively small circle of artists, literati, and collectors. They were forced to admire the technical novelties of the master, especially in regard to his color, but they did not understand the true intention of his innovations. It is characteristic that Mancini gives the same amount of attention to Giuseppe d'Arpino, the exponent of the late maniera, as to Caravaggio, the leader of the naturalistic school of painting. Similarly, the Marchese Vincenzo Giustiniani praises d'Arpino under the rubric "di maniera" in his somewhat naïve system of categories of painting, while he places Caravaggio (together with Annibale Carracci) in an only slightly higher position. These critics either did not see, or at least did not state, how far superior Caravaggio was as an imaginative artist.

Not one of the biographers explains why Caravaggio, in spite of his strange and individual personality and his violations of decorum, had so many commissions from important churches that he could scarcely carry them out. It is true that such commissions often came from wealthy individuals who wished to dedicate an altarpiece in a church as decoration for their family chapel. Some of these men may have chosen Caravaggio simply because he was in fashion, or because of his artistic skill, but others doubtless appreciated the religious impact of his paintings. Cardinal del Monte, Caravaggio's main protector, may have been one of these, but there is no real evidence to indicate whether this was the reason for his commissions. We have more information in the case of the abbate Giacomo Crescenzi, under whose supervision as trustee for the Contarelli legacy Caravaggio executed his famous paintings in San Luigi. The abbate was one of the closest friends and adherents of S. Filippo Neri in his last years. It would not, therefore, be surprising if he had favored Caravaggio because the painter's religious works corresponded in some ways to the sentiments of the Saint.

Thus it was surely not only Caravaggio's technique and method of painting which made so great an impression, but the spiritual content, the new concept of reality, which awoke first curiosity and then admiration. Such feelings may have played a part when the community of painters in Rome urgently requested permission from the agent of the Duke of Mantua to arrange an exhibit of Caravaggio's most moving painting, the *Death of the Virgin*, before it left Rome permanently. The purely painterly beauties of the work, the splendid red curtain and the oblique light traversing the auburn shadows, were of course of the greatest interest and most enjoyable to the professionals and connoisseurs. But more than anything else it must have been the emotional force of the composition which overwhelmed those who saw it. The painting had been opposed by the clergy of S. Maria della Scala allegedly because of the representation of the Mother of Christ in her death as a very poor woman, surrounded by barefooted old men. This social realism, however, tempered and elevated by a consciousness of the mystery of death and resurrection, must have evoked in many of the artists, priests, and laymen privileged to see the painting a feeling that their own emotions were expressed more eloquently by Caravaggio than they could have been by any other artist.

Such popular manifestations in favor of Caravaggio's art are rarely related, and even in the case of the *Death of the Virgin*, the motives and feelings of the spectators—apart from professional curiosity—were not written down and have to be reconstructed on the basis of our own impressions and our knowledge of the spiritual trends of the period.

This knowledge is still extremely limited. The time of the Renaissance has been (and still is being) investigated in many learned studies devoted to the cultural changes in society with respect to jurisprudence, economics, philosophy, and science, in order to gain deeper insight into the complex conception of the period. But very little has been done in recent times to illuminate the general situation in Rome from about 1580 to 1620, even though this period is of great interest for later developments. It began after the morose regime of the "pious popes" in the 1560's and 1570's had ended, when the narrow medieval spirit of the Spanish-dominated Counter-Reformation started to loosen its grip on Italy. Under Sixtus V and Clement VIII, a new western orientation began to make itself felt in papal politics, resulting in the reconciliation with Henry IV of France and accompanied by a broader and slightly more liberal mentality. Politically, however, the period cannot be considered as a final one, but rather as a time of growth and change which will culminate in the "ecclesia triumfans," the "magnificentia romana" of Urban VIII's reign. In art the situation is similar. The artists of the late sixteenth and early seventeenth centuries broke vigorously with the pallid late maniera, and attempted to restore the weight and substance of the High Renaissance. Nevertheless, even though the neoclassicism of Annibale Carracci's Roman works and the realistic chiaroscuro of Caravaggio are of fundamental importance for the main trends of seicento painting, the time was not yet ripe for the severe classicistic intellectualism of Nicolas Poussin, nor for the richly orchestrated illusionism of Pietro da Cortona's ceiling decorations.

The stylistic values of the visual arts of this period, particularly in painting, might be more clearly illuminated if they were compared with the cultural changes in other fields. The investigation of music, science, etc. in comparison with the painting, sculpture and architecture of the time has not yet been attempted. For example, there are the scientists like Galileo and Campanella, who were both near contemporaries of Caravaggio and based their studies, like the painter, directly upon nature, rather than upon previous conceptions of nature, and what is more, in nature sought evidence of the Divine. More immediately pertinent would be a kind of paragone between painting during the early Baroque period and the spectacular changes in contemporary music. The three great composers who made possible the flowering of Baroque music in Italy in the later seventeenth century, Monteverdi, Frescobaldi and Gabrielli belong to approximately the same time as Caravaggio. Popular music, adopted in the laudi and spiritual madrigals used in the circle of San Filippo Neri, was an integral part of the religious ceremonies which influenced Caravaggio's art so deeply.

Thus the foundations are not completely laid for a full and comprehensive presentation of Caravaggio's art and its significance in the context of his period. For this reason I have chosen to write a series of studies on the artist rather than the usual monographic biography. Studies can bring into focus general and specific problems, but they need not always arrive at concrete conclusions, and when they do, their conclusions are not necessarily claimed to be the only ones. In a word, studies are less definitive than a biography would be.

The chapters of this book were written over a long period of time and they therefore differ in style. My own conception of Caravaggio's art and personality also changed considerably in the course of writing. The views expressed may therefore sometimes seem at variance, and some repetitions proved unavoidable. It should also be noted that the subjects of the chapters were chosen in a somewhat arbitrary and associative way, so that each is conceived more or less as a separate essay. I have therefore endeavored to make the Catalogue Raisonné as extensive and readable as possible so that by studying it the reader will be able to follow Caravaggio's development in a detailed and analytical way. More specific information concerning the catalogue will be found in a special introduction which precedes this section.

Throughout the book I have relied heavily upon the literary sources as a basis for my study of Caravaggio. For this reason, Part III is devoted to a collection of all the known seventeenth century biographies and to the contemporary documents concerning the artist and his commissions. They are printed in English translations as well as in their original texts, and as far as I know, this is the first time that a collection of the written sources on Caravaggio has been published. Apart from their purely art-historical value, these writings—particularly the police records and letters of the agents of the Dukes of Mantua and Modena—provide an intimate and often fascinating picture of Caravaggio and of the society in which he lived. I hope, therefore, that this section of the book will have as much interest for the general reader as for the student of the seventeenth century.

The appreciation of Caravaggio's art has been discussed in the excellent Master's thesis by Margot Cutter: "Caravaggio: The Critical Reaction, 1600-1850," Institute of Fine Arts, New York University, 1940. (Excerpt: "Caravaggio in the Seventeenth Century," *Marsyas*, vol. I, 1941, p. 89.) For the influences of Caravaggio on the Netherlands, see the fundamental book by Arthur von Schneider, *Caravaggio und die Niederländer*, 1931, and, more recently, the catalogue of the exhibition, "Caravaggio en de Nederlanden," Utrecht and Antwerp, 1952.

There appeared in the wake of the Caravaggio Mostra, different books on the master, by R. Longhi, L. Venturi, and Roger Hinks—to mention only the most remarkable ones—see my reviews in the *Art Bulletin*, December 1953 and June 1954. I have used the more recent literature only sporadically because my text was already in print. For a complete bibliography on Caravaggio until 1951, see *Catalogo, Mostra del Caravaggiome dei Caravaggieschi*, Milan, 1951; also, L. Venturi, *Il Caravaggio*, Novara, 1951.

ACKNOWLEDGMENTS

In a sense, I consider the present book as a cooperative work. In my lectures on Caravaggio at the University of Freiburg, I had the opportunity to discuss the various Caravaggio problems with my students. This discussion was continued and emphasized during my activity from 1935 on at the Institute of Fine Arts of New York University. Especially the critical interpretation and the English translation of the biographies and documents are the result of repeated study of these texts with my students in seminars on Caravaggio. The patient and enthusiastic assistance of these young people contributed much to the progress of Part III. In the introduction to this section, I have expressed my thanks to the main contributors among my students and have added the names of the scholars in this country who revised a great part of these texts and gave much appreciated support.

I am most indebted to my assistants, Mary Anne Graeve, Irving Lavin, Richard Judson, Robert Rosenblum, and Iris Hofmeister for their constant help. I am especially grateful to William Crelly for his devotion to the work; he has spent over three years in close daily collaboration with me.

For their criticism and advice I am very thankful to Mr. Christopher Norris, Mr. Creighton Gilbert (who also placed at my disposal photographs which I would otherwise have been unable to obtain), and to Mr. Dennis Mahon, with whom I was in steady correspondence, as I am to my good friends Dr. Erwin Panofsky, Dr. Richard Offner, Dr. Richard Krautheimer, Dr. Jane Costello, and Professor Rensselaer Lee. For their help with the documents and biographies, I am also grateful to Miss Mirella d'Ancona, Mr. Dario Covi, Miss Patricia Egan, Mr. Kenneth Donahue, Dr. Jan G. van Gelder, Dr. William Heckscher, Dr. H. W. Janson, Dr. Richard Salomon, Miss Gustina Scaglia, Dr. Wolfgang Stechow, and Dr. Marco Treves. My friends in the Warburg Institute of London, Dr. Otto Kurz, Dr. Gertrude Bing, and the late Dr. Fritz Saxl, have continually shown a gratifying interest in the progress of the book. I am deeply grateful to Dr. Walter Cook, former director of the Institute of Fine Arts, whose tireless efforts have never ceased to aid and facilitate my work in every possible way. For the same indefatigable support and encouragement, I am thankful to the present director, Professor Craig Hugh Smyth.

I owe a special debt of gratitude to professors and directors of museums and other institutions: Professors Ainaud, dell'Acqua, Baumgart, Brandi, Heydenreich, Morassi, Sterling, and Wittgens. I have received help from the Uffizi Gallery in Florence, the Museum of the City of Genoa, the Thyssen Collection in Lugano, the Metropolitan Museum of New York, the Museum of Udine, the Borghese, Capitoline, and Doria-Pamphili Galleries in Rome, the National Gallery in Washington, the Royal Library of Windsor, and the Art Department of Princeton University. Princeton University Press has also facilitated my work on the book in a very generous way, especially through the constant understanding of Helen Van Zandt.

A large part of my work has been made possible by grants from the Simon Guggenheim Foundation Memorial and the Bollingen Foundation.

WALTER FRIEDLAENDER

CONTENTS

CONTENTS

PART III · BIOGRAPHIES AND DOCUMENTS

LIST OF PLATES

LIST OF REFERENCE FIGURES

BIOGRAPHICAL DATA

[1573]

September 28. Birth of Michelangelo Merisi at Caravaggio in Lombardy. His father Fermo Merisi was a master-builder in the service of the Marchese di Caravaggio.

[1584]

April 6. Contract between Battista Merisi, elder brother and guardian of Caravaggio after the death of Fermo, and Simone Peterzano, a painter in Milan with whom Caravaggio was to study during the subsequent four years. It is stipulated that a fee of twenty gold scudi be paid to Peterzano.

[1588]

April 6. Date on which Caravaggio's period of training in the shop of Peterzano was to have come to an end.

[ca. 1588-1591]

It can be assumed that Caravaggio left Milan some time after the expiration of his contract with Peterzano, after April 6, 1588. However, his arrival in Rome is not documented and it is not known if he went there directly from Milan. Bellori says that he went to Venice before going to Rome but this is only an assumption. Mancini's remark that Caravaggio went to Rome when he was about twenty years old is too vague to be reliable.

[ca. 1589-1596]

We have no exact dates concerning Caravaggio's early years in Rome. However, his biographers recount a number of interesting and noteworthy circumstances of these years:

——All of the biographers mention the poverty of Caravaggio's early years and Baglione says that at first he had so little success that some "gentilhuomini" of the profession contributed to his support.

——Baglione and Bellori (in a marginal note to Baglione) says that Caravaggio worked with a certain Sicilian painter named Lorenzo when he first went to Rome.

——Mancini speaks of a few months spent with the painter Pandolfo Pucci from Recanati ("Monsignor Insalata") for whom Caravaggio made devotional paintings which were sent to Recanati.

——Mancini also reports that during these years Caravaggio spent some time convalescing from an illness in the Ospedale della Consolazione, during which time he made some paintings for the prior of the Hospital, who sent them to Sicily (in another version: Seviglia).

——Mancini says that while recovering from an illness Caravaggio made the portrait of an innkeeper; it is not known if this was the same illness as that mentioned above.

——Mancini relates that Monsignor Fantino Petrignani gave Caravaggio a room in his palace in Rome, where he painted a Gypsy, a Flight into Egypt, and a Repentant Magdalene.

——In a marginal note of Bellori on the manuscript of Baglione's biography, there is mentioned

a period of time which Caravaggio spent with the painter Anteveduto Grammatica. This note, however, is crossed out, and the information is therefore unreliable.

——Baglione, Bellori and Mancini all say that Caravaggio spent a few months in the shop of Giuseppe d'Arpino, where he painted fruits and flowers. It has been assumed that Caravaggio worked in the shop of d'Arpino before the latter went to Naples at the end of 1589, but it is also possible that he met d'Arpino later about the time that d'Arpino received a commission for paintings in the Contarelli Chapel at San Luigi dei Francesi in 1591.

——Baglione and Bellori mention the painter Prospero Orsi (delle Grotesche) as a zealous advocate of Caravaggio's art. According to Baglione, Orsi had been a fervent adherent and imitator of d'Arpino before this.

——Caravaggio's close relationship with Cardinal del Monte is emphasized by both Baglione and Bellori. It is said that Caravaggio became acquainted with the Cardinal through Signor Valentino, an art dealer near S. Luigi dei Francesi. The artist seems to have been in rather desperate circumstances at the time, and the Cardinal took him into his own house. A document of 1600 (*see* Bertolotti) states that Caravaggio was living in the house of the Cardinal at this date, but he had probably been living there much earlier. Baglione says that Caravaggio obtained the commission for the Contarelli Chapel with the help of Cardinal del Monte.

Baglione says that the following paintings were made for the Cardinal: a *Concert of Youths*, a *Lute Player*, a *Fortune Teller*, a *Head of Medusa*, and a *Divine Love*. To these Bellori adds the *Cardsharps* and the *St. Catherine* (he does not mention the *Divine Love*).

——It is probable that the following paintings were also made during this period: The *Boy Peeling a Pear*; the *Fruttaiuolo* (?); *St. Francis*; the *Bacchino Malato*; the *Uffizi Bacchus*; the *Boy Bitten by a Lizard*; the *Judith and Holofernes*; and the *Portrait of Maffeo Barberini*.

——The date of the *First St. Matthew* is one of the most critical problems in reconstructing Caravaggio's chronology. It was certainly executed before the present paintings in the Contarelli Chapel, and stylistically it seems to belong to the first half of the nineties. The *First St. Matthew* was never accepted as the altarpiece for the chapel.

[1597]

Mention of Caravaggio as "celeberrimo pictore" in the testament of Don Ruggero Tritonio Abbot of Pinerola near Udine. This is the first dated reference to the painter after the contract with Peterzano. The reference is to a painting of St. Francis which had been given to the abbot by Ottavio Costa of Genova some time before.

[1598-1599]

——The two lateral paintings in the Contarelli Chapel (the *Calling of St. Matthew* and the *Martyrdom of St. Matthew*) were executed mainly between March of 1598 and April of

1599. However, their frames were not made until December of 1600. The *Second St. Matthew*, which is the present altarpiece of the chapel, was painted after the two lateral paintings, perhaps even considerably later since the frame was made for it in October of 1602.

——The following paintings probably belong to the second half of the nineties: The *Sacrifice of Isaac*, the *Incredulity of St. Thomas*, the *Supper at Emmaus* (Borghese), a *St. John* (probably that in the Doria Gallery) and the *Taking of Christ*.

[1600]

October 25. First mention of Caravaggio in the police records.

[1601]

February 7. Report of a reconciliation between Caravaggio and a certain Flavio Canonico, a captain of the Guards at Castel Sant'Angelo, whom Caravaggio had wounded with a sword.

May 5. Date of the inscription in the Cerasi Chapel; Tiberio Cerasi had died a few days earlier.

May 24. Date on which, according to the contract, the paintings in the Cerasi Chapel were to have been finished.

November 10. Date of final payment for Caravaggio's paintings in the Cerasi Chapel. According to Baglione, Caravaggio made two versions of these paintings, the second version in a different manner from the first. Baglione also says that the first version was taken by the Cardinal Sannesio.

[1602]

At the beginning of this year, or at the end of 1601, Caravaggio began to paint the *Deposition* in the Chapel of the Pieta at S. Maria in Vallicella. The painting was made for Pietro Vittrice, the friend of St. Filippo Neri.

[1603]

August 28 to September 25. Record of the libel suit of Baglione against Caravaggio, Onorio Longhi, Orazio Gentileschi, etc. because of offensive verses which had been directed against Baglione.

September 25. The Governor of Rome grants Caravaggio his freedom, after the intercession of the Ambassador of France, on the condition that he no longer offend Baglione and his company and that he does not leave his house without written permission from the Governor.

[1604]

The *Madonna di Loreto* in the Cavaletti Chapel at S. Agostino was painted between 1603 and 1605, probably in 1604.

January 2. Caravaggio at Tolentino in the Marche.

April 24. Report of Caravaggio's assault upon a waiter in the Osteria del Moro.

October 20. Caravaggio is in jail for throwing stones at the police.

November 18. Caravaggio insults a corporal who asks him for his license to carry arms.

[1605]

February 16. Caravaggio complains against a certain Alessandro Ricci concerning a rug.

May 28. Caravaggio arrested for carrying arms, but was immediately released.

July 20. Caravaggio is in jail for offending two women.

July 29. Complaint of the notary Pasqualone against Caravaggio, who had wounded him in the head. A few nights previously the notary had had an argument with Caravaggio concerning a girl called Lena "che sta in piedi in Piazza Navona."

August 6-24. Three letters of Fabio Masetti, the agent of the Duke of Modena, indicate that Caravaggio fled from Rome to Genoa after the above-mentioned assault on a notary, but that he was back in Rome by August 24.

——Masetti's letters also indicate that Caravaggio was already at work on a painting for Modena at this time; this is undoubtedly the *Madonna of the Rosary*.

August 26. Reconciliation between Caravaggio and the notary, Pasqualone.

September 1. Complaint of a former landlady of Caravaggio saying that the painter had thrown stones against her venetian blind.

October 12. Letter of Fabio Masetti in which he says that Caravaggio has asked him for a twelve scudi advance on a painting for Modena (the *Madonna of the Rosary*).

November 6. Letter of Fabio Masetti stating that Caravaggio has asked for another 20 scudi.

——The *Virgin and St. Anne* (*Madonna del Serpe*) for the Palafrenierei of the Vatican was probably painted in 1605. The painting was given to Scipione Borghese (made Cardinal in July of this year) for his growing collection which also included the *David with the Head of Goliath* and the *St. Jerome Writing*.

——The *Death of the Virgin* was probably painted in 1605/1606 (*see below*).

[1606]

May 29. Sunday evening: brawl over a ball game in the Campo Marzo which resulted in a duel between Caravaggio and a young man from Terni named Ranuccio Tomassoni. Ranuccio was killed and Caravaggio himself was severely wounded. A number of other persons were present including Onorio Longhi. On the following day the clerk of the criminal court visited Caravaggio in the house of one Andrea Rufetti and questioned him about his wounds. By May 31st, Caravaggio had fled Rome.

July 15. Letter from Fabio Masetti in which he complains against Caravaggio for not having finished the *Madonna of the Rosary*; he says that if the painting is not finished within one week he will not accept it.

——After leaving Rome Caravaggio spent some months in the Sabine Mountains (Paliano, Zagarolo, and Palestrina) under the protection of Don Marzio Colonna. During this period Caravaggio painted a *Magdalene* and a *Walk to Emmaus* (Mancini) both of which are known only in copies.

[1607]

——Caravaggio went to Naples either at the end of 1606 or early in 1607. Here he painted the *Flagellation of Christ* for S. Domenico, the *Seven Acts of Mercy* for S. Maria della Misericordia and four lost paintings, a *Resurrection of Christ*, a *Denial of St. Peter, Crucifixion of St. Andrew* (a painting in Toledo may be a copy of the *St. Andrew*), and a *St. Francis.*

September 15. Letter from Pourbus in Naples to the Duke of Mantua concerning the *Madonna of the Rosary* and the *Judith and Holofernes* allegedly painted by Caravaggio in Naples and for sale there at rather high prices. Pourbus seems not to have dealt directly with Caravaggio who was probably already in Malta or on his way there at this time.

February 17-April 28. A series of letters from Giovanni Magno, the agent of the Duke of Mantua, were written during the first half of 1607 and contain information concerning the *Death of the Virgin* which Caravaggio painted for Sta. Maria della Scala and which had been rejected. Rubens himself recommended the painting to the Duke of Mantua and seems to have held it in the highest esteem. In March the work was in the house of Magno and in April it was placed on public display for one week since it was "the talk of the town." Afterward it was taken to the house of Rubens who constructed a case for it and by the end of April it was on its way to Mantua.

May 26 and August 20. Two letters indicate that negotiations were under way to obtain a pardon for Caravaggio.

[1608]

——Caravaggio in Malta where he painted two portraits of the Grand Master, Alof de Wignacourt, a *Beheading of St. John the Baptist* for the Conventual Church at La Valletta, a *St. Jerome*, a *Magdalene* and a *Sleeping Cupid.*

July 14. Caravaggio was received into the Order of Malta at Cavaliere d'Obbediènza. According to Bellori, Caravaggio received a gold chain, two Turkish slaves and other tokens of the Grand Master's esteem for his work.

——In the early autumn of the year Caravaggio had a quarrel with one of his superiors in the order and was put into prison. By October 6 he had escaped and fled to Syracuse. For his disobedience in escaping, he was judged and finally expelled from the Maltese Order on December 1.

——In Syracuse Caravaggio painted the *Martyrdom of St. Lucy* for the magistrates of the city during the last months of 1608.

[1609]

——At the end of 1608 or at the beginning of 1609, Caravaggio left Syracuse and went to Messina where he was under the protection of the Lazzari family. For them he painted the *Resurrection of Lazarus* which was given to the Church of the Crociferi on June 10, 1609. Caravaggio also painted the *Nativity* for the church of the Capuchins in Messina at this time.

——From Messina, Caravaggio went to Palermo, probably in the summer of 1609. Here he painted a second *Nativity* (*Adoration with St. Francis and St. Lawrence*) for the Oratorio della Compagnia di S. Lorenzo.

——Caravaggio had returned to Naples by October 24, the date of a report received in Rome which states that he had been killed or wounded in Naples. This report doubtlessly refers to Bellori's account of an assault on Caravaggio by his enemies in the doorway of an inn which left him so disfigured that he was scarcely recognizable.

——It is possible that the *Salome with the Head of St. John*, mentioned by Bellori as having been painted to appease the wrath of the Grand Master of the Maltese Order, and the *Crucifixion of St. Andrew* mentioned above (copy in Toledo) which the Viceroy of Naples took to Spain in 1610, were painted in the last year of Caravaggio's life.

[1610]

——Caravaggio's second sojourn in Naples probably lasted about eight months. At about the end of June 1610, he left Naples by boat and somewhere near Port'Ercole was mistakenly arrested by the Spanish Guard and put into prison. He was released within a few days, but his boat, carrying his belongings, had already left. A few days later he died at Port'Ercole of a malignant fever.

——On July 29 and 31, two reports of Caravaggio's death reached Rome, one of which re-marked incidentally that he had been granted a pardon by the Pope.

——After his death, Caravaggio's belongings were taken into custody by the local Spanish authorities; among them was a painting of *St. John*.

PART I

CARAVAGGIO STUDIES

CHAPTER I

THE CONVERSION OF ST. PAUL: AN INTRODUCTION TO THE ART OF CARAVAGGIO

PLATE 33

THE story of the conversion of St. Paul is told in the Acts of the Apostles, chapter nine. Saul, as he was called before his conversion, was on his way to Damascus, "breathing out threatenings and slaughter against the disciples of the Lord." He had with him letters to the synagogues, authorizing him to bring bound into Jerusalem any Christians he found, whether they were men or women. "And as he journeyed, he came near Damascus: and suddenly there shined round about him a light from heaven: And he fell to the earth, and heard a voice saying unto him, Saul, Saul, why persecutest thou me? And he said, Who art thou, Lord? And the Lord said, I am Jesus whom thou persecutest: . . . And he trembling and astonished said, Lord, what wilt thou have me to do? And the Lord said unto him, Arise, and go into the city, and it shall be told thee what thou must do. And the men which journeyed with him stood speechless, hearing a voice, but seeing no man. And Saul arose from the earth; and when his eyes were opened, he saw no man: but they led him by the hand, and brought him into Damascus. And he was three days without sight, and neither did eat nor drink." In this way Saul, the bitter enemy and persecutor of Christianity, was transformed into Paul, the most zealous and successful propagator of the Christian faith.[1]

Before Michelangelo da Caravaggio's painting in Santa Maria del Popolo, made at the beginning of the seventeenth century, the greatest representation of this miracle was the fresco by Michelangelo Buonarroti which was painted about 1545 in the Cappella Paolina, the private chapel of Pope Paul III. In this grandiose composition it is not the figure of the fallen Paul which attracts our attention, so much as the rearing horse in the center. In the Acts there is no indication that Paul or his companions were on horseback at the moment of the miraculous conversion, and, correspondingly, no horses take part in the oldest versions of the scene, either in Byzantine manuscripts of the ninth century or in mosaics of the twelfth century. After the twelfth century, however, the conversion is regularly represented as an equestrian scene; henceforth, with few exceptions, we see the shock of the conversion manifested in the fall of the blinded and terror-stricken Paul from his horse. Sometimes the moment of the fall itself is represented: Paul hangs from his horse like an Amazon on an antique sarcophagus, his horse fallen to its knees. Sometimes the horse remains standing, arrested and a little astonished before its master, who lies on his back staring up at the heavenly apparition.

Like Paul, his companions are usually shown on horseback. In Raphael's tapestry of the *Conversion of St. Paul* horsemen fill the entire right half of the composition in a tightly compressed and agitated group. Opposite them Paul lies alone on a grassy slope bordering the road; his arms are outstretched and his beardless face with wide-open eyes bears a stunned expression. Behind him, his horse rushes wildly into the background as if thrown into panic by the dazzling apparition and the celestial voice. Two young servants run beside the horse, one pulling the reins in a vein attempt to check it.

[1] See Bibliography, p. 317.

Michelangelo's motif of the rearing horse held in check by the youth at its side probably derives from Raphael, although certain antique types, similar to the big horse in the Alexander mosaic, may have influenced both Raphael and Michelangelo. But in contrast to Raphael, Michelangelo gives a spectacular momentum to the scene by placing the horse in the center of the composition. The accompanying soldiers are without horses, perhaps because a multitude

FIG. I
Raphael, *Conversion of St. Paul* (tapestry). Rome, Vatican.

of horses would have diminished the gigantic volume of Paul's animal as it breaks through the center of the crowd, leaving behind it a narrow path, a kind of vacuum.

In Michelangelo's deliberately constructed scheme Paul's companions are divided into two groups of eleven figures each. They have the mechanical rigidity of lay-figures, functioning but not thinking; they have hardly any existence beyond that of basic bodily forms. They stand, lie, walk, and crouch in a great variety of elaborate poses, and they are related to each other by a precisely weighted balance of parallel movements which are intensified by repetition. Not even the protagonist is exempt from this sublime sterility. Paul lies with one leg extended and the other bent back, in the stereotyped pose of the fallen Heliodorus in Raphael's fresco.

According to the Biblical account Paul had journeyed to Damascus when he was relatively young. Raphael and Signorelli had therefore represented him in the conversion as a strong, youthful warrior. But in most other representations of the scene—in the mosaic of the Cappella Palatina in Palermo, in early manuscripts, in Beccafumi's *Altarpiece of St. Paul* in Siena—Paul's face with its rather long beard is that of an elderly man. In the Cappella Paolina fresco it bears a slight resemblance to Michelangelo's own features, perhaps implying the artist's identification

FIG. 2
Michelangelo, *Conversion of St. Paul*. Rome, Cappella Paolina.

of himself with the apostle in his acceptance of enlightenment and conversion. His eyes are tightly shut, his face empty of expression or expressing only a rigid passivity. His head does not turn directly toward the apparition, although he raises his left arm to protect his eyes from the sudden light, as in Signorelli's *Conversion* in Loreto. Instead the face is turned toward the spectator, or toward an indefinite point outside the picture. Michelangelo shows St. Paul already blinded and in that stupor which possessed him until the day when Ananias visited him in Damascus.

The passive impersonality of Paul and of the figures around him benumbs the greater part of the Paolina composition, as if at this given moment the whole turmoil, with its artificial attitudes and movements, were frozen into immobility. Equally inflexible is the space in which the composition is suspended. It is not the natural though idealized space of Raphael and the High Renaissance, in which logically constructed figures walk freely and breathe easily. It is certainly not the atmospheric space of the Venetians or of Correggio, nor is it the limited space in which the earlier figures of Michelangelo are imprisoned, the "carcere terreno" from which they struggle to be free. Rather the foreshortening of the horse moving toward the plain of Damascus and the distant hills indicates a remarkable extension into depth. The two little figures who emerge from nowhere, from below the lower margin, seem to push the composition back. Michelangelo uses these truncated figures only in his two Cappella Paolina frescoes, but they had appeared long before in the work of Pontormo, and are again to be found in the late-manneristic style of Greco. They are typically manneristic in the disproportion to the figures in the main groups, and by their dwarfish, ghostlike appearance they stress still more the unreality of the compositional space.

Nothing is said, in the Acts, of Christ's actual appearance at the moment when Paul, thrown to the earth by the shock of the light which suddenly shone around him, heard His mysterious and imperious voice. On the contrary, it is expressly stated that his companions were "speech-less" at hearing a voice but seeing no one. Nevertheless, except for the authors of some very early manuscript illuminations and of a group of paintings made in North Italy in the sixteenth century, the illustrators of the scene generally felt obliged to visualize the origin of the voice in the person of Christ. At first only the bust of Christ was introduced, and it was placed in the center of a circle in the sky from which beams of light radiated. Later Christ, speaking to Paul, was shown either in half or in full figure, now with, now without cherubim, sometimes in a prominent place, sometimes half hidden by clouds.

Michelangelo was the first to transform this rather simple apparition in the sky into a great celestial spectacle echoing the turmoil on the earth. The figure of Christ (which is, incidentally, a variation on a figure from Michelangelo's own *Last Judgment*) is shown rushing almost perpendicularly down from heaven. By this movement a narrow path or funnel is opened through the dense crowd of adoring angels, which parallels the path beaten by the big horse on the earth below. Through this funnel the celestial light shines down in the direction of the recumbent Paul. The host of angels on both sides, divided into different sections as in the *Last Judgment*, covers the whole upper part of the composition. Their figures, clumped together and swaying rhythmically, are even more dematerialized than those below. Dynamic power is concentrated exclusively in the Lord of Hosts.

Nothing could be more opposed in spirit and form to this conception of St. Paul's conversion than the representation of the same subject painted about half a century later for the Cerasi

Chapel in Santa Maria del Popolo in Rome by a young and revolutionary artist, Michelangelo Merisi da Caravaggio.

As is the case in the Cappella Paolina, the *Conversion of St. Paul* in the Cerasi Chapel has as its companion piece the *Crucifixion of St. Peter*. The two principes apostolorum and stories from their lives are often presented together. Unusual, however, is the combination of the conversion, the event which begins Saint Paul's Christian career, with the closing event of Saint Peter's life, his martyrdom. One might imagine that a more equivalent counterpiece, a representation of Christ giving the keys to Saint Peter, had originally been planned for the Cappella Paolina. Indeed, in the account of the Cappella Paolina in the first edition of his *Vite*, Vasari even assumes that this was the combination, correcting the error only in the second edition.[2] Michelangelo, or perhaps Paul III himself, may have chosen to juxtapose the Conversion with the Crucifixion of Saint Peter in order to symbolize the mystical death involved in both themes. Be that as it may, when Tiberio Cerasi, the consistorial attorney, desired to commission the decorations for his family chapel in Santa Maria del Popolo, the Cappella dell'Assunta, he selected as subjects for the side walls of this chapel the same unusual combination of events from the lives of Peter and Paul, in direct imitation of Michelangelo's arrangement in the private chapel of the Pope.

Possibly Caravaggio received this important commission because he had come from a Lombard town and was, therefore, a fellow-countryman of the Fratres Augustini Congregationis Lombardae, the owners of the church and of the convent of Santa Maria del Popolo. Moreover, the young artist, who was about twenty-seven years old in 1600, had already acquired sensational fame as a daring religious painter through his much-admired and much-attacked paintings in San Luigi dei Francesi. Even more than Annibale Carracci, whose highly original *Assunta* ornamented the main altar of this chapel, Caravaggio was the artist who could be trusted to compete with Michelangelo's treatment of the same theme, and at the same time to create something utterly different and new. Actually, Caravaggio's concepion of the miraculous conversion is rooted in a new spirit which is fundamentally opposed to that expressed by the rigorous abstractions of Michelangelo's last monumental painting in the Paolina. Caravaggio's *Conversion* is of special significance because it reflects, in concentrated form, the essential aspects of this new spirit.

The unprepared spectator who sees Caravaggio's *Conversion* for the first time would probably not be able to recognize at first glance what the painting represents. Even more than in the Michelangelo composition, the first thing to catch his eye would certainly be the enormous horse that fills more than three-quarters of the available space. It is a piebald, very bulky, and rather proletarian horse, quite different from that in the Raphael tapestry. A parallel to Caravaggio's horse need not be sought among antique or Italian traditions, but in Northern examples; this kind of animal, more a beast of burden than a saddle horse, is taken directly from Dürer's engraving of 1505, called the *Large Horse*. The muscular flank of Caravaggio's horse progresses in color from the dark brown of the croup through the lighter brownish yellow of the receding middle to the light yellow forequarters, very much as Dürer divided and modeled these three parts with the flexible strokes of his burin. Moreover, like Dürer, Caravaggio fills the picture area from frame to frame with its bulk. The volume of the horse is not placed parallel to the surface of the picture, but is turned at a slight angle into the background. Its plastic energy is strongly enhanced by this relatively slight foreshortening in the narrow space. The space itself, however, is in no way denied, as is more or less the case in mannerist paintings (including those of Michelangelo); but, emphasized by chiaroscuro, it fully preserves

FIG. 3
Dürer, *The Large Horse* (B. 97).

its pictorial value. In adopting this forceful approach to visible and tangible nature, Caravaggio strongly and deliberately rejected Michelangelo's esoteric ideals. In the naturalness of its form and conception, the horse in the Cerasi Chapel is far removed from that in the Paolina which expresses panic almost in the abstract. Nor is Caravaggio's horse modeled according to a canon based on idealized nature in the manner of the antique or the studied construction of Leonardo's standing horses. Caravaggio used Dürer's *Large Horse* as the direct model for his own in the *Conversion* because this heavy beast—so different in character from Dürer's Leonardesque *Small Horse*—corresponded to his own observation of common life and reality and was not an "idea fantastica."

Although Caravaggio's horse is the same realistic type as Dürer's, it has, nevertheless, quite a different character, being softer and not so pessimistically passive. It participates modestly in the action, lowering its big head with its black and white mane. A bearded old man, looking over the horse's head and holding it by the curb of the bit, replaces the figure of the soldier with a fantastic helmet and halberd in Dürer's engraving. Caravaggio is an excellent interpreter of the remote and confused understanding we sometimes see in the faces of animals. In his early *Flight into Egypt* he gave to the donkey listening to the music of the angel the same dumb but concentrated expression that appears in the face of the venerable Saint Joseph, who devoutly holds the notes of the canzone. In the *Conversion of St. Paul* the horse's lowered head and melancholy eyes correspond perfectly to the morose expression of the graybearded attendant with high, furrowed forehead who stands behind it. Both man and horse seem worried about something which they cannot fully understand, and hence they move slowly and cautiously. When Bellori criticizes the painting for its total lack of action, (questa storia è affatto senza attione) he is quite correct from the baroque point of view, which identifies action with movement. What Bellori does not understand is the inner psychological action which an attentive observer can divine in the hearts of the men and the horse, and which connects them more intimately with the advent of the miracle than would rearing horses and figures in torsion. The old man holds the bit in both hands, not because the horse needs to be kept from running away but because for some reason it looks troubled and is lifting its right foreleg. This is not a pose of high-stepping triumph as in some antique examples, nor the elegant pose, playful and impatient, of Leonardo's horses. Here the horse raises its leg for a very different reason: it shrinks from hitting the prostrate body of its master, an instinctive reaction which Caravaggio could have observed in any goodnatured horse anywhere.

Caravaggio has generally been dubbed a coarse naturalist. In reality he shows a surprisingly sensitive understanding which goes beneath the surface, bringing out with discretion and tenderness the half-hidden relationships between his figures, almost without the help of visible motion or emotion. The novelistic attitude which he had employed playfully some years earlier in his *Fortune Teller* is now developed with serious and universal meaning. Caravaggio leaves much to the onlooker's intuition, indicating only by subtle suggestion the delicate threads connecting the three figures—the horse, the attendant, and Saint Paul—to one another, and all three to the larger force of the miracle. This ability to fill his characters with a sensitive and stirring inner life, without classicistic idealization or manneristic abstraction, is one of the basic qualities of Caravaggio's art. Dürer's big horse is certainly interesting as an objective study of form, of type, and to some degree of character; but Caravaggio's horse has, if I may say so, a heart and takes a subjective and subdued part in the succession of events which Caravaggio has concentrated into his painting.

The intimate association of the horse with the miracle of the conversion is emphasized above all by an external element which raises this beast of burden above the realm of nature or of the imitation of nature. This element is the light which strongly illuminates most of its flank, from the ribs to the hip, and the raised foreleg, touching the lower part of the other foreleg and grazes the hind leg along its entire length. It also focuses on the old man's wrinkled forehead and upon parts of his bare legs; however, the fullest radiance is concentrated on the flank of the horse. From there it passes, by slow and subtle transitions into the darker half-tones, brownish-yellow, deep and warm, in which the head and hindquarters are submerged. The forceful plasticity and great volume of the horse are enhanced by the dark brown background. The horse is thus the principal recipient of the light, which strikes it so strongly that it seems almost to emanate from the hide.

There is no visible source of this light—no fire, not even torches, as in Raphael's *Liberation of Peter* or in Bassanesque night scenes, and although the light is sharp and the background very dark, it is not night. There is no indication of any natural source for the light; because it is a "magic light," and the sparse rays indicated in the upper right corner come from the celestial spheres. Our first impression that this is a realistic scene of a commonplace happening—a man fallen from his horse—vanishes before the realization that the light itself is the cause of the helplessness of the man lying before us, his arms outstretched, his eyes closed. It is the light of a miracle.

Light is the most powerful agent for transmission of the "magic realism" of Caravaggio. The history of painting affords a rich variety of works in which sacred persons and scenes are made prominent by the use of light from sources not always clearly indicated, as, for instance, in Masaccio's *Tribute Money*. Yet in such cases the light is not necessarily miraculous in itself, even though it illuminates sacred persons or scenes. When it has an essentially compositional purpose, as in Masaccio, it may not seem to come from a particular source at all, either natural or supernatural. But when light is given a psychological and dramatic impact, then the spectator is inevitably led to seek its source. Indeed, the effect of light may be so enhanced or exaggerated that objects struck by it seem to transcend natural experience, to be endowed with miraculous content. Tintoretto's lights, shooting obliquely through the spaces and between superimposed planes, heighten with sharp strokes the edges of angelic wings or by the radiance of a halo point out the small figure of Christ, forlorn in the misty background. They accentuate important points in their path in a surprising way, clarifying the different layers of the composition which accumulate like clouds, ambiguously interlaced. It is this ambiguity which brings a large part of Tintoretto's later work into the orbit of mannerism. The light of the earlier Tintoretto fuses with the surfaces of bodies in a more conservative way, creating an atmosphere of alternating darkness and clarity which pervades everything, figures as well as architecture and landscapes. This special kind of sfumato or chiaroscuro is still based on Titian, but almost from the beginning it is more abrupt and scattered than the characteristic lighting of most Venetian painting, and it inclines toward a darker tonality which tends to swallow much of the color without suppressing it. Titian never allowed his chiaroscuro to go so far toward darkness as to compromise the power of his color. Lodovico Carracci, in his two scenes of the Passion painted in the 1590's for the Certosa of Bologna (now in the Pinacoteca), continues the deep warm tonality of Titian, in which the colors are more deeply embedded than in the agitated flickering of Tintoretto's chiaroscuro. The Carracci were greatly interested in Tintoretto, although they certainly could not agree with the extravagances of his later work which seemed to them problematic, to say the least, and belonging to a mannerist past.

Caravaggio, who belongs to a still younger generation than the Carracci, does not subscribe to Titian's manner of making color triumphant over material; but, as an outspoken and belligerent antimannerist, he agrees even less with the antirealistic, eccentric, and spiritualized conception of Tintoretto's chiaroscuro and color scheme. In his handling of light and color he returns more to the manner of Giorgione, whose impact was felt during a great part of the sixteenth century, despite the importance of Pordenone, Palma, and the great followers of Titian. Federigo Zuccari judiciously observed this connection when he rather contemptuously characterized the *Calling of St. Matthew*, as being nothing else than the "idea" of Giorgione. "Pensiero di Giorgione" refers less to the few authentic works of the master than to the whole Giorgionesque current in the first half of the sixteenth century and even later, not only in Venice but also in the so-called terra ferma from Treviso to Brescia. Apart from its characteristic lyrical and bucolic subject matter, it is a style of clear and simple colors, of a rather melodious and undramatic sfumato, showing an astonishing amount of realistic observation of colors and textures. The main representatives, insofar as they seemed to have been of interest for the young Caravaggio, are Lorenzo Lotto, Romanino, Moretto, and Savoldo, whose works in Brescia, Bergamo, and Milan were easily available to him. (See Chapter II).

Girolamo Savoldo's paintings were certainly the most attractive of this group for Caravaggio as regards his approach to problems of light and shadow. As we learn from Savoldo's pupil, Paolo Pino, whose *Dialogo* appeared in 1548, the year of Savoldo's death, the connoisseurs of the time were interested in Savoldo's work primarily because of his sophisticated treatment of light. He was famous for his "auroras," morning scenes with reflections of the sun, as well as for certain scenes of "oscurità" of night and darkness. Pino goes so far as to say that the rather late works of Savoldo, with all their ingenious subtleties, give a more correct image of the truth (più vera imagine del proprio) than even the paintings of the Flemish school. In a similar way Caravaggio's own treatment of light and shadow was later acknowledged as evidence of his truthfulness to nature; and it is praised as one of his great achievements, perhaps the only one in the eyes of his early critics. It certainly shows some affinity with Savoldo: the way in which light runs along the crest of heavy folds in Savoldo's angel in the *Tobias* (Borghese) is similar to Caravaggio's treatment of the angel in the *First St. Matthew* (Berlin); the two are also allied by the strong material accentuation of the feathers in their unfolded wings. But the sentiment is utterly different: the sweetness of Savoldo's angel, still Leonardesque and in a Giorgionesque setting, is quite alien to the plump and girlish-looking angel in Caravaggio's work. Savoldo's chiaroscuro is warm, lyrical, and musical, but it is also scattered and in a sense affected, in contrast to the sober, precise, and extremely serious chiaroscuro of Caravaggio.

Of the local schools of Lombardy still active at the beginning of Caravaggio's life, that of the Campi in Cremona was the most important. Although the Campi no longer belong to the Giorgionesque group, some paintings of Antonio, the most interesting member of the family, are full of energetic, dark shadows and artificial lighting effects which are still related to the Giorgionesque blend represented especially by Savoldo. Antonio sets the scene of his *Execution of St. John the Baptist* (San Paolo, Milan) in a dark cellar-like room with deep shadows, partly lit by daylight coming through an open door and partly by the light of the big torch which plays over the forms. His fresco in Sant' Angelo in Milan representing the Empress Faustina visiting Saint Catherine in prison shows several sources of light—the flame of a torch illuminates the procession that emerges from the darkness and approaches the barred window of the Saint's cell; the cell itself, radiant with miraculous light; far behind, one has a glimpse of a vaulted hall; and high overhead, almost lost among the buildings, is a full moon.

But in spite of the impressions he might have received from such pictures during his youth in Lombardy, Caravaggio's treatment of light and shadow and, in this connection, his color scheme, are both materially and psychologically different from those of his Lombard predecessors. He is not interested in witty effects of sunbeams or in the flickering lights cast by torches, candles, or lanterns. Nor does he aim at luminaristic effects after the manner of Northern masters, as for instance, the Master of the Housebook in the Freiburg altar, who plays with torch flames, open fires, and a full moon all within a single painting. The face of Caravaggio's *Boy Bitten by a Lizard* is not vehemently lighted by a red, burning charcoal as are the faces of the boy, girl, and monkey in El Greco's early genre scenes. There is no candle on the table of his *Cardsharps* such as appears in similar scenes by Van Amstel of the Massys school. His work contains little of that willful excitement produced by a candle or a lantern so common among the later tenebrosi especially in the North, from Honthorst's flea-hunting scenes to La Tour's paintings of *Sebastian* or *Job* or Rembrandt's very early *Money Changer*. Caravaggio does not use light and shadow for sentimental or romantic purposes. He would not have introduced moonlight into a landscape—had he ever wanted to paint landscapes—as his follower, the romantic Elsheimer, loved to do, indulging in the exploitation of different light effects.

In Caravaggio's work there are, in fact, very few instances of light coming from an artificial source. Bellori mentions a painting of the *Taking of Christ* made for Asdrubale Mattei, which contained a lantern raised over the heads of the soldiers. A lantern is a rather rare detail for this scene in Italian painting, but it does occur in the North, for instance above the soldiers' heads in Altdorfer's painting of the *Taking of Christ* in St. Florian. There, however, the uncertain light flickering over the tumultuous scene comes not from the single lantern but from the many torches held by the soldiers. In Caravaggio's painting the only visible light-source seems to have been the lantern, as is confirmed by an old copy, recently discovered. Another lost painting, the *Denial of Peter* made for San Martino in Naples, is described by Bellori as "painted with nocturnal lighting" (colorito a lume notturno) and containing a fire, around which some soldiers warm themselves. But in the painting of this subject now in the sacristy of San Martino, which has replaced the original by Caravaggio, one can discover only a small chandelier partly cut off by the upper margin; the soldiers are playing dice and, despite the text of the Gospel (Luke 22:55), there is no fire at which they warm their hands. A third instance of artificial light, this time in an extant painting, is the flame of the torch held by the merciful man burying the dead in the *Seven Acts of Mercy* in Santa Maria della Misericordia, Naples. But the light of this torch occupies only a small part of the large painting, which is one of the most entangled, yet magnificent, compositions Caravaggio ever made. These examples comprise but a small portion of his considerable oeuvre. On the whole, Caravaggio's light and shadow, even when intensified to the strongest contrasts, are strictly, almost geometrically regulated, and the source of light almost never revealed.

In some of his earlier paintings Caravaggio indicated the entry of light by a rather sharply outlined triangular area coming from the upper right corner of the picture. In the *Magdalene* in the Palazzo Doria, or the *Lute Player* in the Hermitage, the small triangle in the upper corner interrupts with a cool and precise accent the warm uniformity of the brown background; at the same time it gives a kind of geometric explanation in abstracto for the sharp light which illuminates a great part of the figure and face as well as the flowers, jewelry, instruments, and other paraphernalia. The situation is surprisingly reversed in the *Boy Bitten by a Lizard*: the

FIG. 4
Altdorfer, *Taking of Christ*, St. Florian,
Stiftsgalerie.

triangular area above and behind the boy is dark brown, while the area below, penetrated by the light from the left, is of a light yellowish brown, which gradually darkens toward the lower right. In the *Calling of St. Matthew*, the impressive conclusion to Caravaggio's so-called Giorgionesque period, the lateral entry of light stretching along the wall produces, in addition to its compositional effects, a strong psychological impact. After the middle of the nineties, this initially rather small and confined area of invading light almost disappears. It is no longer present in the companion piece of the *Calling of St. Matthew* in San Luigi, the *Martyrdom of St. Matthew*. When it reappears later in the *Death of the Virgin*, it has lost its earlier sharpness of outline, is broader and softer, almost vaporous, although recognizable as a renewal of the earlier device by its diagonal passage, which lends such strong momentum to the grandiose design. But with or without this triangular beam, Caravaggio's method of conducting the light to the bodies is in principle the same. It penetrates the darkness obliquely from above, marking certain bodies or parts of bodies relevant to the understanding of the whole, leaving others in the darkness as irrelevant. It is almost as if Caravaggio had prepared his system of lights and half-lights first and then subjected the phenomena of the action to that system.

Bellori describes Caravaggio's post-Giorgionesque method in this way: "He never made his figures emerge into the open light of the sun; instead, he invented a method whereby he placed them in the brown air of a closed room. Then he chose a light placed high above, which falls in a plumb line on the principal parts of the bodies, leaving others in the shadow. In this way he attains a great force through the vehemence of his light and shade." The term "cellar light," later used quite generally and rather thoughtlessly for Caravaggio's kind of chiaroscuro, is already implied in Bellori's description; both are intended to lower the artistic value of Caravaggio's art in favor of the clear and serene quality of classicistic art from Annibale Carracci to Nicolas Poussin. But in spite of disparaging criticism, Bellori himself had to admit that Caravaggio's new method attracted almost all the young artists in Rome at the time. We see this in many examples: even painters who were later famous for their light, smooth colorism, like Guido Reni and Simon Vouet, during the first blossoming of their youth in Rome passed through a Caravaggesque period with dark shadows and strong highlights.

It is no wonder that artists who had become outmoded tried to suppress the popular movements growing up among the younger artists, or at least to disparage progressive tendencies, by saying they were nothing but old stuff in new form, that they were choses passagères or, as we would say today, only a fashion. But Caravaggio's art, and especially his treatment of light, was anything but a passing matter. Caravaggio and Caravaggism proved to be one of the most propelling forces in the history of art for centuries to come. The young artists who gathered in Rome from different parts of Europe were guided by a sound instinct when, as Bellori says, they not only admired Caravaggio's works "come miracole," but imitated him by "undressing their models and raising their lights" (spogliando modelli ed alzando lumi). They concentrated on Caravaggio because they saw in him a great and unique imitator of nature, (come unico imitatore della Natura) or of what they understood as nature. Perhaps more than his social realism, they admired his luminarism, by which he could transform nature into art.

Bellori (following almost literally a remark that Ridolfi had made about Giorgione) traces the "sweet and clear" coloring of Caravaggio's first Roman works to his study of Giorgione, who, in his opinion, had achieved the purest and simplest representation of natural forms in a few colors; he says that in his early years Caravaggio likewise used very few color tones and that his shadows were still moderate (veggonsi opere sue prime, dolci, schietta, e senza quelle ombre ch'egli usò poi). It was only after the pleasant, already very original and personal works of this early period that the artist steadily gained in fame because of the color innovations which he introduced. His palette, restricted to a minimum of tints and hues, ceased to be sweet and became "wholly intensified by dark shadows with a generous use of black to project the bodies into strong relief." This development from the smooth and more easily acceptable style to the unconditional seriousness of his tenebroso manner was naturally frowned upon by the academic critics. One is reminded of Vasari's censure of Pontormo when he speaks of the sweetness and grace of Pontormo's first works, those made in the best Florentine tradition. How could the man be so crazy as to spoil his charming color and the innate grace of his early works? The case of Caravaggio is similar, except that it proved more aggravating, for whereas Pontormo's later work in San Lorenzo was a formidable failure in the eyes of the public (to the satisfaction of Vasari) Caravaggio's "ignoble" manner had lasting and embittering success. Why did he not keep to his "sweet and neat" manner?

In Caravaggio's later works, the chiaroscuro sometimes obscures the solidity of forms (for example in the face of the man with the spectacles at the left of the *Calling of St. Matthew*), however it never completely destroys their contours. Its effect is rather to restrict the extension of the color areas and to diminish the splendor of the total surface. While Titian's tonality resounds in golden reflections, even in the shadows, Caravaggio eliminates transparency by the sober, thick opacity of his color areas and the heavy shadows which limit them. The luminary methods of Caravaggio, when adopted by others—the Italian Caravaggisti, and still more the foreigners from Ribera to Velasquez, from Honthorst to Rembrandt—were developed in different ways toward a gradual dissolution, in which the shadows first invade the edges and then destroy the solidity of forms.

When Bellori speaks of the "colorito" of Caravaggio, he is thinking of the treatment of light and shadow more than of the color scheme per se. However, color and light are almost always intimately interwoven. When Poussin wanted to write a treatise concerning the fundamentals of painting, he entitled it *De lumine et colore*. Light and shadow, in proportion to their strength, transform not the substance but the depth and force of color. Consequently, Caravaggio's early paintings, where the shadows are still "moderate," show large areas of uninterrupted, smooth color and their purity and simplicity remind us of Caravaggio's artistic ancestry in Lombardy and the terra ferma of such a work as Lotto's *Flight to Egypt*.

Caravaggio also inherited from Lombardy an extraordinary capacity for representing material values of texture. Recently the tactile rendering of the *Bacchus* in the Uffizi has been compared to Ingres' *Mme. Rivière* and even to Manet's *Olympia*. The reason the *Bacchus* appeared so modern upon its rediscovery was its flat sober treatment of the surfaces: the different whites in the tablecloth and in the sharp folds of the voluminous drapery; the yellowish grey of the cushion with blue-grey stripes delicately juxtaposed with the pink flesh tones; the dark colors of the red wine in the half-filled glass bottle, the blue grapes and the black hair, eyes, and thin-drawn eyebrows set off against the deep uniformity of the background. No slanting lights or form-destroying shadows have as yet appeared.

Caravaggio's warm feeling for the material value of the single object enabled him to be from the beginning a painter of the most intimate still-lifes. This too he may well have learned from painters of his native North Italy, for example Moretto. In many of his figure compositions we find musical instruments, flowers, fruit, bread, or pitchers, which are rendered with such an understanding of texture and with color values of such consonance that they are not inferior to Velasquez or to the fruits and orange blossoms of Zurbarán, which may themselves be indirectly dependent on Caravaggio. These still-life objects occur mainly in the early or relatively early works of the master. Like Velasquez he was much too concerned with greater problems in his later years to be interested in paraphernalia, although he never lost his passionate interest in tangible properties.

One of Caravaggio's greatest problems as his style progressed, therefore, was to make sure that the realistic foundation of his art would not be lost when subjected to the strongly supernatural and unsubstantial qualities of light. His great achievement was that he succeeded in this task by transubstantiating material through light, while at the same time preserving the solidity of the bodies through the physical assertion of the color. In his mature work socially inferior individuals, the kneeling peasants, the swollen corpse of a woman representing the dead Virgin, the common soldier in the guise of Saint Paul, all become exalted by the effect of the light. But simultaneously, the power of the color is not diminished, for despite the fact that the growing extent of the shadows reduces quantitatively the area upon which color can be spread, color gains in intensity what it loses in extent. The washed-out hues with which painters of the late maniera had covered large surfaces for merely decorative purposes are, of course, banished from Caravaggio's color scheme. The refinements in graduated shades of color seen in works of such aesthetes as Bronzino and, still more, Parmigianino have finally vanished. One looks in vain for the changeant tones of the Sarto school. The preciousness of Venetian color, the gold tones underlying Titian's system, are also missing. Nor would luxurious colors be consistent with the character of Caravaggio's art and its accentuated humbleness of content. To quote Bellori, Caravaggio banished "all prettiness and vanity" (ogni belotto e vanità) from his color. Gold, therefore, was excluded, as was ultramarine, a pigment made from expensive lapis lazuli and preferably used in thin transparent layers. The latter would have been of little use to Caravaggio anyway, since he did not need blue glazes in his paintings, where no sky or distant blue hills appear. Bellori even asserts that Caravaggio called blue (azzuro) "poison among the colors," and when he had to apply it, as to the robe of the Madonna or to a bunch of blue grapes, he toned it down. We know from Bellori's statement that the same is true of cinnabar, a sharp vermilion made from sulphur and mercury.

The most important place in Caravaggio's color scheme is given to the common but substantial earth color, ochre, which formed the basis of a great variety of shades, from a dark rusty brown to a light yellowish tan. The brighter colors, such as olive green, cerise, or wine red, sharp lemon yellow, or sap green, are limited for the most part, although not exclusively, to the figures. But they do not sink into the shadowy brown ground and sparkle out of the darkness like jewels, as in the late works of Rembrandt. Instead, they accentuate the substantial quality of material surfaces, adding corporeality to the figures by modeling their volumes in concert with the light. Colors which seem to penetrate objects or to make them recede, such as those used at the height of sixteenth-century Venetian painting, were of little value in the narrow stage of Caravaggio's settings. What he needed were colors and color-relations which would pull his figures and objects forward toward the spectator and give them weight and substance.

It can be said, in fact, that as a rule Caravaggio reverses the usual gamut of the color scale in order to stress the progress of forms projecting towards the spectator. He does not proceed from near to far, from the full heavy tones of fore and middle grounds to the thinner and lighter tones of the background. Instead, he tends to graduate this scale in opposite order—from the darkness of the background up to the brighter and lighter tones of the front. We often see in Caravaggio's paintings a bright sharp yellow used for an object of secondary importance which happens to be immediately in front, as in the trouser leg of the young dandy seen from the back in the *Calling of St. Matthew*, or on the breeches and coat of the little boy kneeling in the foreground before the *Madonna of the Rosary*. In the famous *Deposition* the jutting, almost menacing corner of the great slab supporting the compressed group of figures is vividly colored with bright yellowish grey on its receding side. The diagonal structure of the composition is pushed forward to the utmost limit of the pictorial space, a limit which is marked specifically by the brightness of the color. We no longer look into a fictitious world set apart by design, color, and light; the entire construction seems to come physically toward us as if entering step by step into our world. We are made the recipients of the miracle.

Although Caravaggio's color organization, like his handling of light, shows some reminiscence of his youth in Lombardy, there are fundamental differences between his approach and that of his countrymen. No doubt he had been greatly impressed by Savoldo's night scenes with artificial lighting which were in the Mint in Milan; the intensity of light and the density of shadow in these paintings must have lingered in his memory. In Savoldo's *St. Matthew* in the Metropolitan Museum, the background is dark and the brightest light and color are concentrated in the foreground on the glowing red cloth of the Saint's robe. However, the little lamp placed quite close to the surface sends its rays inward, thereby interrupting the outward movement. The dynamic force, the emergence from the pictorial setting, is therefore not nearly so strong in Savoldo's work as in Caravaggio's. Caravaggio employs every means within his power to bring the pathos of miracles closer and make them more immediate to the understanding of the simple man than Savoldo or any of his other predecessors had done. The humble spectator seeing the painting of the *Madonna di Loreto* in Sant' Agostino could easily identify himself with the bearded pilgrim or his worn-looking wife, who kneel before the floating and miraculous vision of the Madonna. (The kneeling peasants in van der Goes' Portinari altar likewise have a direct appeal, even though they are placed at a somewhat greater distance from the picture-plane.) Caravaggio's pilgrim, with the posterior of his bright yellow trousers and the dirty soles of his feet sticking out conspicuously, seems in attitude and expression, so nearly to inhabit the world of the worshippers outside the picture that he might be considered one of them. The miraculous Madonna, looking graciously down upon the two pilgrims, is almost close enough for them to touch her; she has only to take a step to mingle with the community of the faithful.

Caravaggio's new system of colors, which reinforces the pronounced forward direction of the compositional structure, brings the supernatural into the reality of the common world. At the same time, however, the miraculous light sets the sacred apart from the worldly. There exists, therefore, a kind of antinomy in the later works of Caravaggio: the figures and objects are by their arrangement made to reach out almost palpably to the immediate perception of the spectator, while the strong and inexplicable light fills them with a sublimity which keeps the worshiper in a state of humble awe. Although objects are given a powerful corporeality, they are at the same time enchanted, as if under a magic spell. This spell is not confined to a single body as in certain *Nativities* by Geertgen tot Sint Jans or Correggio, where only the holy body of the Christ-child radiates its splendor on surrounding persons.

Caravaggio's light comes from outside and transforms all reality. An excellent example of its dynamic force and supernatural quality is offered by the famous *Calling of St. Matthew* in San Luigi dei Francesi. On one side of the painting the multicolored and elegant company of the tax collector Levi, later called Matthew, sit around a table, counting money. This group is sharply illuminated and set off against the almost uniform darkness of the deep brown wall in the background. From the other side of the picture enter the two solemn figures of Christ and his apostolic companion, wrapped in simple brown robes, to call the tax collector to the apostolate. They are placed against an even deeper darkness, but the wall just over their heads, including the shining square window, is bathed in a bright light which floods in from the upper right-hand side and makes a sharp oblique line against the darkness. Compositionally, this opposition of dark and light, of brightly variegated color against the large expanse of brown wall, has a powerfully dramatic effect. Equally important, however, are the symbolic qualities involved in these contrasts. Darkness lies heavily over the colorful and worldly company around Matthew; while the light, abruptly penetrating the darkness, shines over the holy persons of Christ and the apostle, and with the voice of Christ it penetrates the heart of the sinner. It changes the tax collector Levi, addicted to money and luxury, into Saint Matthew the Evangelist, exactly as it changed Saul into Paul in the *Conversion of St. Paul*.

Rejecting the traditional full-view position, Caravaggio chose to present Paul's body from an unorthodox and subjective viewpoint, foreshortening it almost orthogonally. But the effect is far from the maximum set by the most famous example of such orthogonal foreshortening, Mantegna's *Dead Christ* in the Brera. Although the body of Paul is placed at a right angle to the horse, it is at a slightly oblique angle to the surface of the painting, corresponding to the slight turn of the horse toward the background on the right side. Nevertheless, the abrupt foreshortening of the body within a very shallow space evokes a reaction of shock and surprise. The body is seen from a totally unaccustomed view to which the conventional rules of proportion cannot easily be applied. Vasari in his third *Proemio* disapproved of forced and distorted views of the body which twist it out of its normal shape. This attitude is still implicit in Burckhardt's criticism of Caravaggio when he declares that the "higher laws of linear composition are almost unknown to the naturalists."[3] And indeed one sees here, as elsewhere in Caravaggio's work (cf. the left half of the Martyrdom of St. Matthew), a striking carelessness in the construction of the figures. The foreshortening of the upper right leg of St. Paul is rather awkward, and the hand and legs of the man in the background do not correspond at all logically to his head and shoulders seen above the horse. However, Caravaggio succeeded in giving drastic expression to a sudden happening, which is immediately realized even though it transcends normal experience. The motionless bulk of the horse, filling almost the whole background, looks more enormous than it really is; the body of the fallen soldier, with the help of rapid foreshortening, appears smaller than it is. The direction given by the length of the body cannot be carried visually beyond its own limit, for the bulk of the horse blocks any further extension into depth. It is this concentration of almost dialectically contrasted elements within an intentionally narrow and enclosed space which produces the explosive power of this *Conversion*.

Oblique foreshortening of a fallen figure is not without some analogy in earlier paintings. In Tintoretto's picture of the *Liberation of the Slave by St. Mark*, the slave, his knees drawn tightly together, lies prostrate on the ground, foreshortened in a similar oblique view and fulfilling the same perspective function as Caravaggio's Paul, although in an extended and open space. Another instance, where the situation is somewhat different, is the fresco by Signorelli, the *Signs of Destruction*, on one of the arches of the Cathedral of Orvieto. In the foreground the bodies of the dead or stricken form the end of a rushing movement from above which is so strong that the bodies are thrown out to the edge of the frame. One of these is foreshortened in a manner very close to Caravaggio's Saint Paul, his legs spread apart and his head directed toward the spectator. Caravaggio must have known the famous Tintoretto either through a drawing or an engraving or even directly from a trip to Venice (which is not so improbable as

FIG. 5
Tintoretto, *St. Mark Rescuing a Slave*
(detail). Venice, Academy.

FIG. 6
Signorelli, *Signs of Destruction* (detail).
Orvieto, Cathedral.

FIG. 7
Taddeo Zuccari, *Conversion of St. Paul*.
Rome, San Marcello.

has generally been thought), and he might very well have seen Signorelli's foreshortened man, since Orvieto would have been on his way to Rome. Another example of foreshortening which Caravaggio could not have overlooked is Taddeo Zuccari's *Paulus* in San Marcello in Rome. Zuccari's hero is young and beardless, dressed in Roman military costume with a helmet on his head. He hangs from his horse by one leg and, like Caravaggio's Paul, his arms are stretched out and he is strongly foreshortened. Nevertheless, the spirit of Zuccari's composition with its Michelangelesque tumult, is quite different from that of Caravaggio's painting.

Bellori and other art critics of the seventeenth century and later, who censored Caravaggio's art for being no more than an imitation of nature, did not realize that this stubborn "realist" learned and borrowed as unrestrainedly from past artists as the other two leaders of the baroque movement, Annibale Carracci and Peter Paul Rubens. Neither of these two started work under the domination of a single superior personality like Giulio under Raphael, Domenichino under Annibale or Van Dyke under Rubens, each of whose early works are often barely distinguishable from those of their respective masters. Instead, Annibale and Rubens, independent personalities from the beginning, studied various works of art from different periods, regions and styles, taking over whatever impressed them and using these borrowed bricks to build up or to support their own individual constructions. Malvasia in one of his unreliable, though often quite illuminating anecdotes attributes to Lodovico Carracci the sententious remark to his pupil and cousin Annibale, "to imitate only one master is to be secondary or merely a follower, but to look at everything, to select from others, is to become master and judge (caporione) over all."[4] This rather elastic attitude comes close to what was defined by eighteenth-century classicists as "eclecticism," a term originally referring to a derivative Greek or Roman philosophy which became especially applied to the Bolognese-Roman school, but was sometimes used to characterize the whole period, like the term "baroque," also a classicistic creation with derogatory connotations.

Nevertheless, this expression significantly refers to certain methods, if they can be so called, which contributed to the early baroque style. The reformers of this time found it necessary, consciously or unconsciously, in their struggle against the uniformity and the "idea fantastica" of the maniera, to study and use various artistic sources more extensively and intensely than was ever done either before or immediately after this era of stabilization. The "ritornare al segno," a return to solidity, objectivity and reason, restored nature as the primary teacher; in this regard Annibale and Rubens are different from Caravaggio only in the means and degree of application. Of equal importance for them are the models provided by classical antiquity and, beyond that, almost everything which was classical in the sense of exemplary, everything which was not Gothic, Manneristic, or Gothic-Manneristic. This included, among others, Leonardo, the great masters of the Renaissance, Raphael and (with some reservations) Michelangelo, as well as the illusionism of Correggio, the lyricism of Giorgione and Giorgionism, the dramatic colorism of Titian, the tenebroso realism of Bassano, the color refinements of Veronese and the fierce electricity of Tintoretto (again with reservations).

Caravaggio, despite his rough-spoken, slightly overemphasized pride in his individuality, was bound to practise a similar, though by no means identical, selective method as his more urbane antimanneristic colleagues, Annibale and Rubens. He had not the emotional and flexible mind of the young Annibale who could so easily compose a Madonna and Saints or an Assumption out of impressions he had formed while standing before Correggio in Parma combined with others he had received from Titian and Veronese in Venice. Neither did Caravaggio have the systematic, keenly-registering mind of Rubens who found no work of art beneath his dignity (not even Pulzone or Zuccari) as long as it possessed some feature which he could sometime expect to use. Caravaggio had not the same self-educating purpose, nor the wish to enlarge his pictorial horizon or deepen his understanding by learning from others; indeed, as we well know, he was rather belligerent towards the discipline of any standard kind of model. But perhaps it was just this attitude of disrespect, his rebuff of overidolized figures which allowed him to violate quite freely the spiritual property of others. He took over whole motives and particular poses from different masters and used them directly in his own work, for example in the *Boy Bitten by a Lizard*, the Doria *St. John*, the *Amor Victorious* and the *Martyrdom of St. Matthew*.

It is therefore not surprising that Caravaggio's St. Paul recalls earlier representations of foreshortened, prostrate figures, such as that in the lower left corner of Signorelli's *Signs of Destruction*, Zuccari's *St. Paul*, and especially the slave in Tintoretto's *Miracle of St. Mark*. Most significant, though, is the relation of Caravaggio's figure to Raphael. If we could turn Raphael's Saint Paul in such a way that his head would touch the lower frame and the length of his body would be directed more or less orthogonally inward, we would have a figure similar to that in Caravaggio's painting.

Raphael, like Caravaggio, saw Paul as a young soldier who has fallen from his horse, terror-stricken by the phenomena of the supernatural light and sound which surround him. As we have said, this conception deviates from the general one of Paul as an elderly man with a long beard and a bald head. Raphael may have seen Signorelli's painting in Loreto (the youthful type of Paul also occurs occasionally in Venetian painting), but he treats the young hero quite differently, not as a knight, but alla Romana. Saul, the Jewish warrior and agitator, was a Roman citizen by birth, a civis romanus, as he proudly declares himself in the Acts, chapter 22. It is natural that a High Renaissance artist should invest Paul with the classical guise of a Roman centurion, his face beardless, his costume outfitted with a Roman helmet and a short Roman sword. Raphael's novel, matter-of-fact representation of Saint Paul certainly attracted Caravaggio more than the morose spirituality in the greybearded physiognomy of Michelangelo's Paul. He therefore followed Raphael's example in this regard (as only Taddeo Zuccari had in some degree done before him). But there is a remarkable difference between the two, which seems to be indicative of Caravaggio's social point of view. Although Raphael's Paul is more robust and military than any of his artistic predecessors, he is still characterized as a distinguished and elegant man. Caravaggio possessed the insight to realize that the miracle of changing a man like Saul into Paul would be more strikingly effective if accomplished in a common man rather than in one of higher and more refined station. He therefore demoted Raphael's centurion to a soldier of the common rank and file.

Apart from this distinction in the social status, another 'important difference between the *Conversions* of Raphael and Caravaggio is the mode of communicating Paul's experience of the vision. The eyes of Raphael's Paul are wide open, staring fixedly, while those of Caravaggio's saint are tightly, almost convulsively closed. According to the most detailed narrative of the conversion, in chapter nine of the Acts, Paul realized he was blind when he got up from his fall and opened his eyes, but saw no one. It is to be assumed from this that he had closed his eyes because of "the glory of that light" which had precipitated his fall, and that his eyes had remained closed while he lay on the ground hearing and answering the voice of Christ. Nevertheless, notwithstanding Paul's explicit account of his blindness, most artists who have depicted the conversion have rendered Paul with open eyes as did Raphael. This is true in the *Cosmas Indicopleustes* (Rome Vat. 699) of the ninth century; and the master of the twelfth-century mosaic in the Cappella Palatina in Palermo shows the blinded Paul with wide, empty eyes during his fall, as well as when he is led away. The open eyes are frequent in the Umbro-Florentine tradition (Signorelli and Raphael) as well as in North Italian examples (Giovanni Bellini, Pordenone, Moretto, Parmigianino, Lodovico Carracci and others). Much rarer are

FIG. 8

Conversion of St. Paul. Cosmas Indicopleustes (Vatican Cod. Gr. 699, Fol. 83v).

FIG. 9

Conversion of St. Paul. Palermo, Cappella Palatina.

representations which stress the blindness. From later periods we find some scattered examples such as the beautiful composition in Beccafumi's *Altar of St. Paul* in which Paul lies on the ground sunk into an almost hypnotic sleep. In this respect as well as in others the most important representation previous to Caravaggio's is Michelangelo's, where Paul's eyes are shut to express the intensity of his response to the message of Christ. Subsequently, except for some minor artists in the wake of Michelangelo, like Taddeo Zuccari, only Caravaggio strongly emphasized the blindness of the Roman soldier. Caravaggio, who shows Paul at the beginning of the ecstatic trance leading to the conversion, stresses the inward process of conversion rather than the direct contact of Paul with Christ, when the fallen man, dazed by the light and

FIG. 10

Signorelli, *Conversion of St. Paul*. Loreto, Cathedral.

bewildered by the voice, recognizes in amazement the vision which appears in the sky. He could not accept this realistic and rationalistic interpretation of the conversion adopted by Raphael and most other painters. For him the miracle could only be effected beyond the realm of the visible, behind closed eyes.

If Caravaggio did not follow Raphael in the manner of interpreting Paul's reception of the miracle, he did in another point. Some of Raphael's predecessors, notably Signorelli and Bellini, represent Paul trying to lift himself up on his right elbow in order to look upward at the source of the voice and light, which is so strong that his other arm is raised to shield his eyes. This gesture was taken over by Michelangelo although his Paul does not look in the direction of the vision. The reaction of Raphael's Paul is much more pathetic; he has fallen on his back and, recognizing the Saviour in a flash, he raises both arms over his head almost in the orans gesture. Caravaggio took this expressive movement of the arms from Raphael. The whole attitude of Paul's body with raised arms calls to mind the idea of a man hanging from the cross and could therefore be understood as a kind of counterpart to the Crucifixion. However, in contrast to the ambiguous hyperintellectual symbolism of the maniera period, Caravaggio is here, as always, direct and natural in his approach to the miraculous. Paul's arms with the hands longingly raised and the fingers tensely spread apart seem to strive to encounter and embrace the celestial vision of Christ. This gesture is the only outward indication that Paul has felt and seen the divine apparition and that he contritely but joyfully responds to the powerful voice

FIG. II
Beccafumi, *Altar of St. Paul*. Siena, Museo dell'Opera del Duomo.

FIG. 12
Pordenone, *Conversion of St. Paul*. Spilimbergo, Cathedral.

FIG. 13
Moretto, *Conversion of St Paul*. Milan, Sta. Maria presso S. Celso.

penetrating his mind and body. The hands are not, as scientists and rationalists have suggested, the hands of an epileptic. In that case they would be clenched into fists which would open only by force. Before us is not a representation of a pathological case in the guise of a miracle, but of a profound psychological drama, the conversion of an obstinate soldier and hater of Christianity into the apostle of Christ.

Paul's features—the very low forehead fringed with curls of brown hair, the strong chin surrounded by a light beard—betray obstinacy, although the new experience seems to be already

FIG. 14

Parmigianino, *Conversion of St. Paul*. Vienna,
Kunsthistorisches Museum.

FIG. 15

Lodovico Carracci, *Conversion of St.
Paul*. Bologna, Pinacoteca.

FIG. 16

Rubens, *Conversion of St. Paul*. Berlin, Kaiser Friedrich Museum.

softening his rigidity. His expression is more individual than that of Raphael's helmeted centurion or the classic Roman face of Zuccari's warrior. It still contains characteristics found in Caravaggio's earlier physiognomical experiments, the *Bacchus*, the *Boy Bitten by a Lizard*, and the *Medusa* which are studies based on Caravaggio's own features and generally characterized by the low forehead, sharply drawn dark brows and a rather fleshy nose. The physiognomy of Paul is a development of this juvenile type, now a mature and robust young man whose expression has become blankly frozen by the shock of his unexpected calling. This coarse but impressive soldier's face personified the appearance of Saint Paul for Caravaggio exactly as the plebeian, flat-faced Socrates head had represented Saint Matthew for him in the first painting for San Luigi dei Francesi. It is part of the miracle, perhaps the part which most stuns the spectator, that such a wild and stubborn-looking man could have been overwhelmed by the grace of God and brought into His servitude. The deep concentration of Paul's soul is reflected in his face; he has heard the celestial voice and the outside world has momentarily disappeared for him; one sees that he has already willingly accepted the challenge of God. Caravaggio, like Raphael, shows Paul with outstretched arms and half-open mouth, for he too chose to represent the precise moment when Paul, subjugated, humbly answers, "Lord, what wilt thou have me to do?"

In trying to understand the psychology of Caravaggio's *Conversion* it is important to realize that the miraculous resides in the heart of man rather than in an external figure of the deity commanding from on high. As no source is indicated for the magic light, so there is no visible appearance of Christ; his presence can only be assumed. Every worshiper who entered the Cerasi Chapel, being acquainted with the story of Saint Paul, would understand, when he saw the fallen soldier together with the big horse, that the strong and inexplicable light reflecting on and from the horse's flank had caused the fall and that the voice, though not personified, had penetrated the heart of Paul and was accomplishing the conversion.

As has already been noted, nothing is said in the Acts of the Apostles about an apparition. However, most painters of this subject, both early and late, found no way to express the voice except by showing an image of Christ in the sky. This may be handled discreetly and remotely as in Signorelli's *Conversion* or with great expansion and turmoil as in Michelangelo's Paolina fresco. In the sixteenth century, however, a group of painters in North Italy, following the Biblical text more literally, entirely omitted the apparition of Christ and the hosts of angels. Pordenone was one of the first who dared do so, about 1524 in his painting on the organ wing of the Spilimbergo Cathedral. Here the miracle is manifested only by rays of light which cross the sky and strike Paul obliquely, causing him to fall from his horse just as he is about to lead his magnificent cavalcade through the high arch toward Damascus. However, Pordenone's original and forceful composition was not very well known. A painting of the scene which Caravaggio must have known was the *Conversion* which Moretto painted for the Mint of Milan (now in the choir of Santa Maria presso San Celso). In contrast to Pordenone's turbulent group of horsemen this scene consists of only two figures, Paul and his horse. The young warrior in the foreground is clothed rather like Raphael's centurion, in a cuirass with his legs and arms bare. He lies on his back propped up on his hands and looks upward in astonishment mingled with devotion at the dangerous-looking cloud overhead with its sharply lit edges from which emanates a single beam crossing the sky in his direction. This is the only sign of the supernatural in Moretto's painting. Behind Paul, almost leaping out of the composition, appears the enormous silhouette of the rearing horse. The whole conception comes surprisingly close to another painting of the *Conversion* recently ascribed very convincingly to Parmigianino (formerly credited to Niccolò dell'Abbate), and probably painted in Bologna about 1530 (now in Vienna). It is a curiously over-refined, typically manneristic composition in which the mysterious light, reduced to a few slight rays, breaks suddenly through the dark clouds. Finally, about ten or twelve years before Caravaggio's representation, Lodovico Carracci painted a similar large *Conversion of St. Paul* for the Zambeccari Chapel in San Francesco in Bologna (now in the Pinacoteca) in which the number of figures has again been increased. Here too the big rearing horse has a prominent place in the composition, though it is turned more sharply inward. In the foreground is the fallen figure of Saint Paul, his face turned upward and his left arm raised in startled surprise toward the sharp white light that extends over a greater part of the sky; but no apparition, not even a supernatural ray, is indicated.

Caravaggio might have seen any one or all of these representations of the *Conversion of St. Paul*, but Moretto's painting is by far the most important for his conception of the scene. There are basic elements in Caravaggio's composition—the preponderance of the horse's body and the reduction of the number of figures to two or three—which had been anticipated by Moretto's conception sixty years earlier. Nevertheless, when Caravaggio had finished the *Conversion* for Santa Maria del Popolo he had succeeded in creating a work essentially different from all precedents, including those from North Italy which had undoubtedly furnished him with the initial idea for the composition. Here there is nothing of the playful mannerism of Parmigianino nor of the rather tumultuous baroque of Lodovico. Neither is there any trace of Moretto's academic romanticism. The type of *Conversion* without a painted vision, propagated in North Italy during the sixteenth century, is brought to its definitive conclusion by Caravaggio. One could hardly go further either in the reduction of figures or in the secularization of the miraculous content. From Pordenone to Lodovico, the divine apparition is never actually present, but its emanations are spectacularly manifest: either artless, oldfashioned beams of light directly connect divine and human beings or the dazzling illumination of the sky gives an unnatural appearance to the atmosphere. In Caravaggio's *Conversion* there is no sky and only a faint spray of light entering from the upper right corner, yet one feels immediately that the light flowing around the man and the horse comes from heaven with Christ as its source, that it is the light of Paul's revelation.

No one before Caravaggio—and no one after him—made in this sense a truly human experience of Paul's conversion without sacrificing its supernatural value. No one had even seriously attempted to do so, for formerly the conversion had always remained in the realm of singular experience. All were interested in a more or less documentary rendition of the exciting event or in the psychophysiological effect of sudden and intense light being thrown upon men and horses or in the distribution of masses between earth and sky. Caravaggio deliberately avoids the rearing horses and all the turmoil and excitement provoked by the fall of Paul and its attendant phenomena. In sharp contrast to the full baroque development of Rubens who painted his two *Conversions* almost as if they were grandiose and colorful cavalry battles, Caravaggio's is of the utmost calm and restraint. There is almost no movement except for the slow upraising of Paul's arms. The model for the horse, Dürer's *Large Horse*, the most phlegmatic animal Caravaggio could have found, would not dream of rearing or running away even in the face of startling lights and sounds. Any loud movement, any vehement gesture would have diverted attention from the inward process of the conversion. In this way, by excluding every overt indication of the supernatural, Caravaggio was able to present within a purely human sphere a new and profound interpretation of the miracle.[5]

THE MARTYRDOM OF ST. PETER

PLATE 34

BAGLIONE tells us that both of the paintings in the Cerasi Chapel replaced previous versions of the same subjects and that these earlier versions had been executed in a different manner (questi quadri prima furono lavorati da lui in un altra maniera). Since they had not pleased the patron (non piacquero al padrone) they were taken by the Cardinal Sannesio. Until recently nothing has been known about these first versions. However, two paintings have now been published which afford us at least a general idea of their compositions, a *Crucifixion of St. Peter* in the Hermitage and a *Conversion of St. Paul* in the Odeschalchi-Balbi Collection in Rome. Naturally it is difficult to make an absolute judgment on the basis of these rather disputable paintings, but they do indicate that the first versions were more loose and awkward and lacked the monumental concentration of forms which one sees in the final paintings.

We can only guess at Caravaggio's reasons for painting the second versions. The first paintings for the Cerasi Chapel could hardly have been disliked and refused because they were too insolent, too vulgar; or because they offended the feelings of the Church. If this had been so, how could one explain their being bought by Cardinal Sannesio? This venerable priest and candidate for the Papal throne was in no way comparable to that young and independent collector of modern art, the Marchese Giustiniani, who avidly bought the refused first version of the *St. Matthew and the Angel*, probably just because it was so young, fresh, impudent and charming. When the Cardinal bought pictures they certainly had to be impeccable in form as well as in content, and most probably could not deviate too much from sacred convention. One suspects, therefore, that Caravaggio himself considered the two earlier paintings too conventional and, realizing their lack of finality, decided of his own accord to repaint them.

The Raising of the Cross of St. Peter is, of course, intimately connected with the Raising of the Cross of Christ. In the sequences of the Passion of Christ, however, the Elevation of the Cross is not illustrated. The very complete *Small Passion* of Dürer, for instance, shows the nailing of Christ to the cross as it lies flat on the ground, and immediately afterward there follows the Crucifixion.[6] The intermediate stage of mechanical raising is omitted because it did not belong to the accepted narration of the Passion, like the Descent from the Cross. We find, therefore, only some scattered examples of the Elevation, particularly in German woodcuts and paintings of about 1500, and later in the circle of Altdorfer and Wolf Huber, which were prevented by their isolation from forming any special iconographical tradition. In Italy in the sixteenth century, representations of the scene were even more rare. A *Raising of the Cross of St. Philip*, by Filippino Lippi, in Sta. Maria Novella from the beginning of the century (certainly influenced by Northern models), and the raising of the cross of a thief in the great *Crucifixion* in S. Rocco, painted by Tintoretto in the mid-sixties, seem to be the only remarkable Italian examples of Elevations. There is not a single Raising of Christ's Cross of any importance in the Italian painting of the sixteenth century, in spite of the growing interest in

FIG. 17
Filippino Lippi, *Raising of the Cross of St. Philip*. Florence, Sta. Maria Novella.

FIG. 18
Tintoretto, *Crucifixion* (detail). Venice, Scuola di San Rocco.

motion, as manifested in the more and more abundant Descents from the Cross from Filippino and Rosso, through Salviati and Daniele, and finally down to Barocci and Cigoli.

It may be that the frequent controversies in Jesuit literature at the end of the sixteenth century, especially in France and the Netherlands, over such points as whether Christ was crucified on the cross already erect, or spread out on the earth, were reflected in the new choice of preliminary stages of the Crucifixion as subjects for painting.[7] In any event, it is characteristic that the first *Raising of the Cross of Christ* on Italian soil was made by a foreigner, Rubens, working on a foreign commission for a Roman church, Sta. Croce in Gerusalemme, and that it was painted at just about the time when Caravaggio, and Guido Reni, made their *Raisings of the Cross of St. Peter*. Rubens' painting was still the work of a beginner, but in it is the genius of the artist who eight years later found the solution for the theme in his grandiose painting for the Cathedral of Antwerp where he shows and develops what he had learned in Italy, perhaps even from Caravaggio's first and imperfect version of the *Crucifixion of St. Peter*.

If the Raising of the Cross of Christ lacked a regular iconography, it is no wonder that the Raising of the Cross of St. Peter, too, had no fixed scheme. The first step was taken by Filippino Lippi, who is in general remarkably advanced, and interested in introducing action into Crucifixion scenes. In the main group of his big fresco of the *Crucifixion of St. Peter* of 1484 in the Brancacci Chapel, three men are raising the cross bearing St. Peter by a pulley. But as Filippino

FIG. 19
Reni, *Crucifixion of St. Peter*.
Rome, Vatican.

Lippi's scheme is here consciously Masacciesque, there is no great difference in the effect from the older representations of the crucified St. Peter, as for instance, those by Giotto and his school in St. Peter's or by Masaccio himself in Berlin. It was not until the forties of the sixteenth century that an entirely new conception of the Raising was finally created by Michelangelo in his monumental *Crucifixion of St. Peter* in the Paolina. There, five or six men try vehemently to shove and lift the lower end of the great cross into the previously prepared hole. The cross is not yet raised to its full height, so that although the body of St. Peter is fastened head downward, it no longer appears in rigid immobility, but is still alive, moving, and being moved.

After Michelangelo no artist of any importance tackled the problem for more than half a century. It remained for Caravaggio to give it his own modern interpretation different from the imposing, but frozen, stylization of the Paolina fresco. Caravaggio reduced the number of figures to four and shaped them into a deliberate pattern. He constructed a kind of wheel, whose center is the middle of the cross and whose spokes are formed by the bodies of the saint and the three men. It is open and flexible, in this respect not unlike the circular composition of Jacopo Tintoretto's *Forge of Vulcan* and similar paintings of the end of the seventies in the Antecollegio of the Palazzo Ducale. One has the feeling that the wheel, with its living spokes crossing each other diagonally, might start to turn, that there is constant implicit motion. It is

FIG. 20

Filippino Lippi, *Crucifixion of St. Peter* (detail).
Florence, Carmine, Brancacci Chapel.

FIG. 21

Masaccio, *Crucifixion of St. Peter*. Berlin, Kaiser Friedrich Museum.

no longer a display of mere activity, as in so many *Descents from the Cross*, where the almost acrobatic movements of the many figures climbing up and down the ladders have little to do either with the awesomeness or the sanctity of the event. Even in Michelangelo's lofty work the figures are remote schemas, particles of a symbol, not immediately interested in their various actions of holding, shoving, or lifting. Caravaggio's three men are made to work hard seriously and with concentration. Each of their movements is basically necessary for the final result, the raising of the cross bearing St. Peter.

The three men labor impassively, as at some mechanical project, like forces of nature, and just as inevitably. They are so direct, so intense, so close, that we feel almost forced to follow their operations, and to participate in their terrible work. The first, standing behind the cross and seen from the back, is leaning and pulling energetically on the rope, which is attached to the lower part of the cross. The second, with deep furrows in his rugged face, embraces the near end of the heavy cross with both arms, holding it up with all his might to support the upward movement caused by the rope. The third man, kneeling on the earth, is lifting and bracing the center of the cross from beneath with his left shoulder. The tension of his body must be strong, for his light yellow trousers are pulled taut around his hips which, like his cramped feet, stick out toward the spectator.

The men are still at the beginning of their work. The cross is as yet raised no higher than the level of our eyes. We look straight into its lower right angle, so that by a curious trompe l'oeil the transverse bar on which the left arm of St. Peter is nailed appears to be almost a continuation of the main bar, which is covered with his body. In this way the whole conception of Caravaggio's second version is brought into contrast with other raisings of the cross, in a formal, as well as in a psychological way. The body of the saint is no longer seen upside-down, in an indecorous position which allows neither approach nor response. Caravaggio's St. Peter follows the slanting movement of the cross; his feet and bent knees are higher than his head, but the deviation from the horizontal is not so great that it is disturbing or distorted. He is still actively conscious, and able, to a certain degree, to move and to communicate with us. With a last effort of his will he has turned his broad chest around as far as possible and raised his shoulders, so that one is given a full, though partly foreshortened, view of his muscular white body.

This rather daring and unusual construction allows a direct approach into the core of the action. Even Michelangelo did not think of altering the position of the saint so radically and still shows him with his feet high in the air. It should be noticed, however, that he is here in an oblique rather than a vertical position; his body, too, is no longer rigid and straight, but bent and flexible; even more, his head is turned around toward the spectator. So too is the head of Caravaggio's *St. Peter*, which is a very dignified head with a grey beard and expressive features and surely from the same model used for the *Second St. Matthew*. He looks out of the picture as if he might speak to the people, asking, by his personal appeal, for their close attention to the glorious example of his indestructible faith.

It often happens that second versions become to a high degree defined and precise, concentrated and conclusive; they get a touch of finality which allows of no further omissions or additions. One can call them "classic" in the sense that they represent the highest peak of their kind for generations. Poussin's *Shepherds in Arcadia* or his *Education of Jupiter*, in their first versions are charming and colorful in style, loose and informal, but not until their second versions do they reach the height of classic stylization accepted as the final crystallization of the problem. In a similar way the second version of the *Crucifixion of St. Peter*, as we see today in Sta. Maria del Popolo, is a masterpiece of condensation; when one looks at it, one feels that no clearer or more precise form could have been found to describe the essential action and to bring it as close as possible to the attention of the community.

There was nothing, however, in either painting which could be regarded as contrary to the prescriptions set down in regard to art by the Council of Trent. Unlike the *First St. Matthew* and the *Death of the Virgin*, there was nothing which would give offense to sacred usage

FIG. 22
Michelangelo, *Crucifixion of St. Peter*. Rome, Cappella Paolina.

(costume), nor anything which would abuse the dignity of the saint represented. Both paintings were, in spite of their radically new and unaccustomed conceptions, perfectly fit objects for devotional meditation. The miracle of the conversion of St. Paul, as well as the miracle of the faith of St. Peter, are not remote spectacles, far separated from the spectator. They speak directly to him, on his own level. He can understand and share their experiences: the awakening of faith, and the martyrdom for the faith. Like St. Thomas, whose incredulity Caravaggio also painted in a humble and moving picture, he can put his finger into the wound.

CHAPTER II

CARAVAGGIO'S YOUTH IN LOMBARDY

CARAVAGGIO is a small town in Lombardy. It is about four miles from Treviglio which is located at the junction of two important roads, one coming from Milan and the West, the other from Bergamo and the North. Neither of these towns is more than twenty miles away. The road from Milan runs eastward through Brescia and Verona, ending at Venice; the one from Bergamo runs southward through Cremona, Parma, Bologna, Florence, and finally to Rome. A youth born and reared in Caravaggio in the 1570's, finishing his education in Milan in the 1580's, had ample opportunity to enrich his eyes and his memory with significant works of art by the masters who had worked in this region, local or foreign, older or contemporary. When his temperament drove him beyond the limitations of his province, the way stood open to him to the two most important art centers of our civilization at that time: Venice and Rome.

The way to Rome was perhaps the better paved for the family called Amerighi, Merigi, or, with the characteristic North Italian sibilant, Merisi da Caravaggio. At least we find frequent references in Roman archives of the 1530's, 40's and 50's to the name of an "architetto" Giulio Merisi, who, like other artisans and craftsmen from this little town, worked in various places in Rome. We know also that Lombard architects, masons, and decorative painters were much in demand there.

Here in this little town of Caravaggio was born Michelangelo Merisi, the great painter to whom Mancini says his century owed so much—and, we may add, not only his century. We are able today to fix Caravaggio's birthdate with remarkable exactness as September 28, 1573, on the basis of an "epitaph," birth certificates being found only rarely in North Italy at this time. His father, Fermo (named after the local patron saint), seemed to have followed the traditional profession of the family; he is said to have been a mason (muratore), a "builder of houses," or as Mancini puts it, the "maestro di casa ed architetto del Marchese di Caravaggio." It seems probable that Mancini was right, and that he actually was in the service of this noble family (a branch of the Sforzas) as superintendent of their buildings. This family still had a good deal of prestige at the end of the century, although all Milanese territory had been a domination of the Spanish crown since the death of the last duke in 1535. About 1590 a Marchesa di Caravaggio is respectfully mentioned in various Lombard chronicles.[1] One must, therefore, acknowledge that Michelangelo Merisi da Caravaggio was descended from a moderately well-to-do family of honorable artisans, called "assai honorati cittadini" by Mancini. Even after the death of his father, which occurred when Michelangelo was still a boy, there was enough money available in the family to pay twenty-five gold scudi for his board and education. His brother, Baptista, replacing his father as head of the family, signed the contract giving Michelangelo as an apprentice into the custody of Master Simone Peterzano, a painter of some limited importance in Milan. He did not, therefore, enter the profession of his father. The document is dated April 6, 1584, when the boy was not much more than ten and a half years old, and carried an obligation to stay for four years, that is until 1588. We must remember that there was nothing uncommon about beginning an apprenticeship at such an early age.

Bellori fabricates the story that Caravaggio carried hods of mortar into buildings under construction, and only by chance discovered his inclination for painting, by preparing plaster for some of the fresco painters. This legend makes the beginning of Caravaggio's career more colorful and at the same time more humble. Actually, everything seems to have proceeded at this stage in quite a normal and bourgeois way. The boy had probably shown remarkable gifts in painting; judging from his early productions in Rome, one can assume that he was rather precocious. Nor was it uncommon for citizens of Caravaggio to make their fame and fortune as painters: Fermo (Ghisoni) da Caravaggio, Giulio Romano's assistant in Mantua, and Polidoro (Caldara) da Caravaggio, the celebrated decorator of façades and painter in chiaroscuro, are examples. So there was nothing unusual in making the young Michelangelo Merisi apprentice to an approved painter. Because there was no good painter in his small town, he was sent to Milan, the capital of Lombardy, which even under Spanish domination was still flourishing to some degree, in spite of all the disasters it had undergone.

However, there was no great choice of experienced painters at this time, even in Milan. The post-Leonardesque movement of Luini, Boltraffio, and so on, had long since disappeared; so too had the curious late-Gothic art of Gaudenzio Ferrari. Neo-Giorgionism had played a short but, as we shall see, significant part in the development of art in Milan, through the work of Savoldo there in the 1530's, but this movement was extinguished by his departure. Some time had still to elapse before the new evolution which was to bring Milanese painting into line with the countermanneristic tendencies of the great reformers of Italian painting— the three Carracci in Bologna, Cigoli in Florence, and Annibale and Caravaggio in Rome. The protagonists of this remarkable movement were still in their early youth when Caravaggio came to Milan as an apprentice: Cerano (Giovanni Battista Crespi), Morazzone (Pierfrancesco Mazucchelli), Giulio Cesare Procaccini, who created, partly in collaboration, the new style in Lombardy, were all born in the 1570's, a few years before or after the birth of Michelangelo da Caravaggio. All received their artistic education outside of Milan and Lombardy, in Rome, Venice, or Bologna.

Simone Peterzano, Caravaggio's teacher between 1584 and 1588 (if the contract was carried out) is perhaps best characterized, in a contract with the Barnabites of 1580, as a "not unlearned painter" (pictor non ineruditus).[2] He was a man of considerable experience and knowledge, but not much more. The praise lavished on him by Paolo Lomazzo in the *Idea del Tempio della Pittura* is understandable only if we realize that Peterzano was his Milanese colleague receiving commissions from the Duca di Terranova, Governor of Milan. Simone Peterzano calls himself "discipulus Titianus" when signing his late paintings, such as the *Deposition* of 1591 in San Fedele, and in 1585 we find him also called "Simon Venetianus," although his native town was Bergamo and in earlier documents he is always called "Bergomatus." It seems, therefore, that in the period of his later style, which includes the apprenticeship of Caravaggio, he liked to publicize his artistic relationship to Venice and to Titian. One can occasionally discover a painting, such as the *Paul and Barnabas* in San Barnaba in Milan, which is obviously based on a work by Titian, in this instance, the *Descent of the Holy Spirit* in Santa Maria della Salute, but he exaggerates Titian's visionary composition into a wildly excited, typically manneristic painting. On the whole very little of his uneven production manifests a vital understanding of any phase of Titian's work.

Through a contract with another apprentice before Caravaggio's time we know that Peterzano gave instruction in painting ornament and portraits (dipingere la rabesca e far

FIG. 23
Peterzano, *Paul and Barnabas*. Milan, S. Barnaba.

FIG. 24
Titian, *Descent of the Holy Spirit*. Venice, Sta. Maria della Salute.

ritratti), although his main work was in the grand manner. Paintings for organ wings and altarpieces, with many figures in violent movement, are preserved to us, and we know of enormous decorations in fresco which he made for the Certosa di Carignano, a famous sanctuary not far from Milan. In the workshop of this versatile and efficient master the young Merisi certainly had a solid technical education, laying the basis for the painstaking execution which distinguishes most of his later works. A youth leaving the studio of Peterzano after four years of apprenticeship was surely saturated with practical knowledge in various fields, in drawing and painting in oil and fresco, in perspective and foreshortening (di sotto in sù), and also in the more advanced studies of light and shade (chiaroscuro), motion and emotion (moti ed affetti). These aspects of craftsmanship had been extensively treated in the most famous treatise of the manneristic period, Lomazzo's *Trattato della Pittura* of 1584.[3] This author, a friend of Peterzano, was also a painter, collector and art writer. However, it must be remarked that treatises on art, though intended for the use of coming generations, are often extremely retardataire. Almost by definition such a work sums up the experiences of a lifetime and by the time it appears it has been superseded by the opinions of the younger generation. A boy like Caravaggio, precocious, stubborn, and independent (as we know from his later life), could only become more and more antagonistic toward the schoolmasterly doctrines of Lomazzo, and the equally schoolmasterly paintings of Peterzano.

Although the young apprentice undoubtedly had to prepare the ground for his master's large fresco enterprises, the technique of fresco in general, with its rather flat modeling and diffuse light, could not express his or his generation's feeling for reality. Caravaggio later despised working in fresco; other leaders of the antimanneristic movement—Cerano, Morazzone, Giulio Cesare Procaccini, and notably the young Rubens—had more or less the same attitude. The common bond of this generation of painters was basically their antipathy to the maniera and its principles, though of course some residue of the old style lingered to varying degrees in their works, especially their earlier ones. The factors inherent in Procaccini's art—adequate space for every substantial object, and density for the bodies themselves—are much more easily achieved by oil technique than fresco. Cerano's early work is still in the wake of Gaudenzio Ferrari's spirituality, but his mature work unmistakably documents the new feeling for presentation by the almost Shakespearean stage-presence of the figures in his brilliant scenes of the life of San Carlo Borromeo, in the Cathedral of Milan. The same is true of Caravaggio; the angel seen from the back in his early *Rest on the Flight* retains a slightly manneristic attitude, dependent on Peterzano, although St. Joseph and the ass behind him, in the solidity of their bodies and expression, are corporeal in an utterly unmanneristic way.

One may therefore wonder if the young Amerighi could have been seriously attracted to the contorted figures and excited flickering light of Peterzano's *Paul and Barnabas*. It is still less likely that he could have been satisfied with his master's *Resurrection* and *Ascension of Christ* in the presbytery of Carignano, those paragons of the bloodless late maniera as it had been formulated by Vasari and Alessandro Allori. Apart from the technical training, the profit which the young Caravaggio derived from his apprenticeship in Peterzano's studio was a stimulus to oppose him—a preparation standing him in good stead in his later career.

There were, however, certain works by an artist living in Milan which must have corresponded very well to the ideals taking shape in the mind of the growing artist during these four years. These paintings were produced in the critical years of the 1580's virtually before the wide-open eyes of the young boy from Caravaggio, who certainly absorbed everything new and exciting around him. Anyone who is curious to discover the sources of Caravaggio and Caravaggism, and enters the rather unspectacular church of Sant' Angelo in Milan, will find a partial solution to his problem in the large painting in the first chapel on the right, a striking proto-Caravaggesque work. It was painted by Antonio Campi in 1583, and represents the *Visit of the Empress Faustina, accompanied by her General Porphyrius, to St. Catherine in her Prison*. This strange and fantastic composition differs from almost everything else produced in the period, certainly from the pale and eclectic manner characteristic of Lombard painting during the second half of the century. The difference lies not so much in the excellence of color or draughtsmanship (the bad condition does not allow closer observation in this respect) as it does in the whole invention—the mixture of spiritual and worldly elements, of supernatural, artificial, and natural light, the strong chiaroscuro in which the multicolored figures move, and the utterly romantic scenery with enormous stone walls, half-open against the sky and crowned

FIG. 25
Peterzano, *Ascension of Christ.*
Milan, Certosa di Caregnano.

by a large bust of the Emperor and a statue of Justice. The young apprentice from Peterzano's shop must have been stunned by the audacity of the new feeling expressed in this composition, comparable to nothing he had ever seen in contemporary art.

However, although the painting was surely a kind of novelty for the period in which Caravaggio grew up, it was not completely original. There can be no doubt that it is based on a work of Antonio's much older brother Giulio, the *St. Agatha in Prison* in the church of S. Agata in Cremona, which was painted in 1537. This older painting also represents a visit by night to a female martyr in prison and shows several sources of light: the moon and torches. Giulio Campi must have studied the *St. Peter in Prison* of Raphael in Rome or a copy. His painting, as well as the three others in the series of the life of St. Agatha, is rather stiff. Antonio has made a successful effort to loosen the composition and to introduce a more realistic light

FIG. 26
Antonio Campi, *Visit of the Empress Faustina to St. Catherine in Prison*. Milan, Sant' Angelo.

and space. Yet such paintings remain exceptional in the work of both brothers. Most of their productions are an eclectic mixture of classicism and mannerism, with none of the imagination shown here.[4]

Another influence might possibly have awakened or reinforced Antonio's consciousness of the vital problems of realism and chiaroscuro: the Milanese works of Girolamo Savoldo. At the time of Savoldo's death in the middle of the century, his relatively few works were not yet appreciated as fully as they deserved, according to Paolo Pino, his pupil, whose *Dialogo di pittura* appeared in 1548 (Savoldo . . . ha ispeso la vita sua in poche opere, e con poco pregio del nomę suo). But in 1568 Vasari, in the second edition of the *Vite*, praises highly four nocturnes by Savoldo, "quadri di notte e di fuochi," in the Zecca, the Mint of Milan, and warmly commends those "capricious and sophisticated" works.[5] One might almost suppose that a revival of Savoldo took place in the latter part of the century, possibly connected with the renewed interest in the problems of light and shadow based on Leonardo's studies as documented in Lomazzo's *Trattato*. Savoldo had been influenced by Leonardo's chiaroscuro, but as has been recently suggested, only during his maturity and especially in his works for the Milanese Mint. Perhaps a similar phenomenon may be assumed in the relationship of Antonio Campi to Savoldo with respect to Savoldo's chiaroscuro and illumination by means of several lights. Campi too seems to have discovered very late the artistic value of the "hundreds of exact subtleties of Savoldo's chiaroscuro" (Pino) which made the four pictures in the Mint so remarkable. In Antonio's *Death of the Virgin* in S. Marco in Milan, probably a work of the mid-1570's, we can distinguish, in spite of the very bad preservation, the figure of an apostle facing us, sitting at a table and reading the litany from a book illuminated by a candle; this figure reminds us immediately of the corresponding figure in Savoldo's impressive and colorful painting of *St. Matthew* now in the Metropolitan Museum. Though the motive of the artificial light could also have been derived directly from Romanino's *St. Matthew* in Brescia of 1521, (which was probably the source for Savoldo's *Matthew*) the similarity between the two figures is so evident that one must assume that Antonio Campi was familiar with Savoldo's painting. From this one may conclude, first that the *St. Matthew* of the Metropolitan Museum belongs to the series of the four paintings "di notte e di fuochi" which Vasari mentions as being in the Milanese Mint, where a representation of St. Matthew, the former money-changer, would be very appropriate; second, that in his last years Antonio was inspired by Savoldo's capricious and luminous style, especially of his paintings in the Mint, to produce paintings which impressed the young Caravaggio. The shadows become heavier and darker, as one can see even in the illustrations of his *magnum opus*, the *Cremona fedelissima* of 1585—the allegories of the titlepage, or the battle scenes with the famous "carroccio" (engraved by the young Agostino Carracci). A really Savoldesque feature appears in his paintings of this time. For instance, in the very impressive *Beheading of St. John* in S. Paolo in Milan, about 1580, the illumination of the dark dungeon by a brightly burning torch, and the view into a lighted doorway at the back where two women appear, are related to Savoldo's *St. Matthew*. Savoldo's rhetorical splendor has been changed by Antonio into a more sombre and dramatic mood with sharper contrasts of light and dark. The realistic, almost Flemish character of Antonio's composition, which Caravaggio certainly admired very much, may still have been in his mind when he painted the *Beheading of St. John* in La Valletta in Malta almost at the end of his life, although the arrangement of the figures is very different and the composition is infinitely superior. Likewise the most important production of Antonio's last years, the *Visit to St. Catherine*, would be still less understandable if one did not assume his knowledge of Savoldo's "capricious and sophisticated" inventions in the Mint. Such effects in Campi's painting as the view through the darkness into brightly illuminated smaller rooms, in which small figures move, repeats the use of similar luminous inserts in the background of Savoldo's *St. Matthew*. But again, one observes that Antonio filled

FIG. 27
Giulio Campi, *St. Agatha in Prison*. Cremona, S. Agata.

FIG. 28
Antonio Campi, *Beheading of St. John*. Milan,
S. Paolo.

FIG. 29
Savoldo, *St. Matthew*. New York, Metropolitan Museum.

the composition with a realistic liveliness which gives the painting a very different character from any by Raphael or Savoldo, making it "modern" in the sense of the coming generation, particularly of Caravaggio. If, like Zuccari, one considers the painter of the *Calling of St. Matthew* to be an imitator of the manner of Giorgione, or influenced by the partially Giorgionesque manner of Savoldo, it must be realized that the presumed Giorgionism or Savoldism was seen through the temperament of Antonio Campi's last works. To take one instance: in the refined circle of Giorgionism we would never encounter a pair of dirty soles confronting the spectator. But we find this kind of boldly realistic presentation in Antonio Campi's *Nativity* in S. Paolo (1580). The dirty feet of the two peasants in Caravaggio's *Madonna di Loreto*, which so offended the feeling of cultivated art critics like Bellori, were as such really no novelty.

Antonio Campi's *Visit to St. Catherine* was painted in the church of Sant' Angelo virtually before Caravaggio's eyes. If we should hear that he had helped Antonio as a garzone in this work, it would not surprise us in view of his later development. We can certainly assume that the young painter, apprenticed in a maniera workshop, sided passionately with the modern trend taken up by the Campi. He consequently became interested in the revival of the artistic personalities belonging to the generation of his grandfathers, whose ideals of reality and lyrical chiaroscuro contrasted sharply with the inflated emptiness of the Milanese school as represented by Gaudenzio's pupils, Lomazzo, Peterzano, and others. This late sixteenth-century revival of the so-called Giorgionesque art of Lotto and Romanino, certainly awakened the strongly anti-manneristic tendencies which we find evidenced in Caravaggio's later works.

But one must not exaggerate the "Giorgionesque" influence on him—nor of what has been called the Lombard tradition. It was early recognized as one of the components of his art and became indisputably associated with him, but it is not the only solution or explanation of the Caravaggesque phenomenon, which quite naturally changed according to the character of his time and as his own personality developed. This must be taken into account when speaking of Caravaggio's relationship to Savoldo. We do not know enough of the subjects of Savoldo's "capricci," with the probable exception of the *Saint Matthew*, to measure the degree of influence they could have exercised on the late work of Antonio Campi, and through this on Caravaggio. In any case, as we have tried to prove, he must have seen the *Matthew*, which at this time was probably still in the Mint; this may explain the general affinity between his own *First St. Matthew* and Savoldo's, which of course has not escaped the sagacity of various critics. Possibly Caravaggio recalled the way in which the deep, dark background of Savoldo's painting serves as a foil for the luminous group of the Evangelist and the angel, and this is reflected in his own work. But the difference in sentiment and execution prevail; Caravaggio's conception of a miracle as a psychological act in a lower-class milieu leaves no room for Savoldo's lyrical and shining beauty and visionary rhetoric.

Savoldo's representation probably depends on the painting by Girolamo Romanino of 1521 in S. Giovanni Evangelista in Brescia, which shows *St. Matthew and the Angel* illuminated by the light of a candle (FIG. 67). Romanino's picture, however, has a much heavier effect, and therefore seems to approach Caravaggio's conception more closely. It may be that other works by this gifted contemporary of Savoldo in Brescia, particularly his secular decorations with their sometimes surprising freshness and directness, also impressed the young Caravaggio. The likelihood that he knew Romanino's frescoes in the Cathedral of Cremona from childhood increases this possibility, but no precise indications of such an influence are to be found in his later work.

In addition to the Giorgionesque painters of the early sixteenth century, Caravaggio was also interested in the works of another Brescian: Moretto.[6] The proof of this is Moretto's *Conversion of St. Paul* at Sta. Maria presso S. Celso (FIG. 13). It is a striking fact that this picture, which reminds us of Caravaggio more than any of Moretto's other works, was presumably the only one for a Milanese church. Caravaggio was not so much impressed by its glowing splendor and capricious illumination as by the simplicity of action, reduced to the two figures of the gigantic rearing horse and the man lying on the ground. Formally and psychologically he altogether changed the composition, taking over for his own *Conversion* only the iconographical scheme. It is therefore a misleading exaggeration when one of the most spirited writers on Caravaggio calls Moretto "Caravaggio avant la lettre." Neither in his artistic intentions nor in his methods of construction, is Moretto a precursor of Caravaggio, who was to revolutionize almost the entire artistic world by his conception of light and color, and of iconographic content. Moretto's figures have a noble, rather academic attitude, very far from the intensely human feelings expressed by Caravaggio's figures; his classicistic compositions often display a rigid symmetry and purity which Caravaggio would have been neither able nor willing to continue. Among Moretto's numerous paintings in the churches of Brescia, which the young boy had presumably visited, there is not one which shows a direct relationship in spirit or in construction to any later work by Caravaggio. For example, Moretto's *Nativity*, formerly in Sta. Maria della Grazie, is a carefully symmetrical composition of isolated figures, while in Caravaggio's late painting of the same subject in Messina, the rustic people are heaped up in a diagonal and most unacademic composition and are bound inexorably together by the deep chiaroscuro. Nothing could be more different than the whole conception (tutto il pensiero) of these two works. Nevertheless, in contrast to the jumbled compositions of Peterzano and his companions, Moretto's monumental classicism and Raphaelism were an impressive example of artistic wisdom for the young Caravaggio; even though he did not follow it closely, it helped to prepare him for the classical style which he met in Rome. Also he was probably attracted by the simplified color system of Moretto, in which everything partakes of a silvery chiaroscuro, and still more by his sober and

FIG. 30
Moretto, *Nativity* (detail). Brescia,
Pinacoteca.

exact representation of material objects. The basket of towels in Moretto's *Nativity*, or the fish-head and tablecloth in his painting of *Christ in the House of Simon* in Sta. Maria in Calchera, have the same kind of density and sincerity as Caravaggio's still-lifes, such as that in his *Supper at Emmaus*. On the whole, one can assume that Moretto's part in the education of Peterzano's young disciple was limited to showing him one more way of escape from the confusion and artificiality of the maniera.

The Merisi family must also have had many friends and relations in Bergamo, the town so close to Caravaggio. Bergamo was, moreover, the birthplace of Peterzano. The young Michelangelo Merisi probably often had the opportunity to go there and to see a number of works by Lorenzo Lotto in the churches and perhaps also in the palaces of the town.[7] Lotto, a descendant of an old Bergamasque family, had worked there almost continuously between 1513 and 1525. He was the most versatile, the richest in invention, and consequently the most influential of the Venetian-Lombard group. Less capricious than his contemporary Savoldo, and much more imaginative than the considerably younger Moretto, Lotto with his strong lyrical feeling can also be associated with Giorgione and Giorgionism. In his *Trattato* Lomazzo praises him, and also the Dossi, for the luminous landscapes in the backgrounds of their paintings; in the *Tempio*, of the same author, he is described as a master in creating effects of light (maestro di dar il lume). The color system of his earlier works is, like that of Giorgione, based on a few clearly distinct and pure colors, in contrast to Titian's richness and golden luster. Bellori says that when the young Merigi first began to look at nature he reacted in the same way as Giorgione, using colors which were "sweet, pure, and without the shadows of his later period"; his statement is correct, but only in a limited sense. It would have been more accurate if, instead of Giorgione's name he had used Lotto's, whose colors and light the boy could study at his leisure when he was in Bergamo. Moreover, there were other peculiarities in Lotto's paintings of the Bergamasque period (or a little later) which the young Merisi must have admired greatly. Lotto's *Holy Families* lie relaxed under shadowy trees, display such intimacy in the relationship of the figures, and are so well attuned in their grouping that their charm could not escape the sensitive mind of the young artist who subsequently, in his early Roman years, tried to evoke it in his own work.

In Lotto's charming painting, the *Marriage of St. Catherine* of 1523, both the Madonna seated on one side and St. Catherine kneeling on the other bend their heads down toward the Christ child between them. This movement not only exhibits gracefully the long lines of their shoulders and necks, but binds the whole group closely together with a very tender and delicate feeling. The motive probably goes back to the *Virgin and St. Anne* by Leonardo, the painting which Leonardo took to France in 1517 but which came back to Milan, or some other place in Lombardy, soon after his death. Here too we find the long uninterrupted shoulder-line, the head of the Virgin bent toward the child in a way intimately connecting the two figures. One can therefore be almost sure that Lotto saw the original or one of the numerous copies after this famous work, and that he constructed the whole left part of his composition after this model, with characteristic modifications. The difference consists principally in the psychological motivation of the movement: the pose of the Virgin in Leonardo's painting is wholly determined by her concentration upon the Child; on the other hand, the movement of Lotto's Madonna and of his St. Catherine, who turn their heads toward the spectator, is less organic, more abstract, and even more mannered. The movement of Lotto's Madonna also recalls Michelangelo Buonarroti's conception of such figures as the young woman in one of the lunettes of the Sistine ceiling who combs her hair, bending her head far down to one side in a similar attitude. One should not forget that Lotto was in Rome during most of the time that

FIG. 31
Lotto, *Holy Family*. Vienna, Kunsthistorisches Museum.

Michelangelo was working on the ceiling, and that he may have become interested in the strained and tense movement of some of the figures in the *Ancestry of Christ*, whose spirited realism is so exceptional in Michelangelo's work. However, it is more likely that he adopted the motive from Leonardo, using it in his own gentle way for some of his compositions of the Bergamo period. He does not restrict its use to the subject of the Madonna and Child, but uses it also to indicate the intimate relationship of the kneeling Christ to his mother as he takes leave of her (1521, Berlin). The young Caravaggio was apparently attracted by this tender motive. However, he does not use it so much in Lotto's way, for compositional purposes, as for single or even isolated figures, such as the Madonna bent over the Child in the *Rest on the Flight*, or the *Magdalene* (both very early paintings) to express by this almost resigned gesture the humbleness and helplessness of the women. He later repeats the motif in the *Madonna di Loreto*, bringing the Virgin close to the adoring peasants by this gesture of humility. He again approaches the sentiment of Lorenzo Lotto in the expressive bending of the head of the young adoring shepherd on the left side of the very late *Nativity* in Palermo. Even the extremely accentuated shoulder and neck of the executioner in the *Martyrdom of St. Matthew,* and of Christ in the *Flagellation* in Naples, may go back to this first impression, although in the meantime other works, principally Sebastiano del Piombo's *Flagellation* in S. Pietro in Montorio, had perhaps exercised a more immediate influence on Caravaggio in this respect.

One of his first paintings in Rome, the charming *Rest on the Flight,* shows plainly how much he was indebted to Lotto's lyrical and sensitive compositions. The Madonna seated beneath a tree, her head heavy with sleep, bent on her shoulder protecting the Child in her

FIG. 32
Lotto, *Marriage of St. Catherine* (detail). Bergamo, Galleria Carrara.

arms is a Lottesque conception. The angel may also be found in several variations in Lotto's paintings. To account for the stronger and more realistic feeling which pervades this early painting, one must of course allow for the vigorous individuality of Caravaggio, so different from Lotto's.

There is another possible source for the composition, at least for the upper part, which may be the result of a boyhood impression. The Ambrosiana in Milan owns a painting by Jacopo Bassano also representing the *Rest on the Flight into Egypt;* the upper part, with the marvelously painted profile of a donkey and the leaves of a tree sharply silhouetted against a fragment of landscape, is surprisingly similar to Caravaggio's painting. Also comparable are the flowers, and the realistic texture of the clothes and other accessories. Bassano's painting was formerly in the possession of the Archbishop of Milan, Cardinal Federigo Borromeo, who presented it to the Ambrosiana in 1618. Probably it was owned by the Borromeo family long before this date. If so the young Caravaggio would certainly have seen it when he was an apprentice in Milan, probably even before he studied the paintings of Lotto in Bergamo. The *Rest on the Flight,* one of Jacopo Bassano's main works, painted about 1560, has an obvious relationship, especially in the main group, to some of Lotto's Holy Families. It would therefore have been relatively easy for the young Caravaggio, when he composed his *Rest on the Flight* in Rome, to combine the realistic features in the upper part of Jacopo's painting with certain lyrical and intimate aspects taken from Lotto. The result was not an eclectic combination, but a fresh and youthful composition, full of invention and charm.

From Lotto the young Caravaggio could also learn the significance of the hand as a key to the interpretation of a human being. Lotto's hands are not of the beautiful and aristocratic sort

FIG. 33
Jacopo Bassano, *Rest on the Flight into Egypt*. Milan, Ambrosiana.

created by Leonardo, nor are they like those in some portraits by Titian or van Dyck, but rather common, broad, and short-fingered. Because they bring out vividly the reality of the person to whom they belong, Lotto gives them a prominent place in the composition, for example, in his *Betrothal* in the Prado, the double portrait of Messer Marsilio from Bergamo and his bride united by a roguish Cupid. In his early genre painting of the *Fortune Teller*, Caravaggio repeats Lotto's "jeu de mains" using it to express the subdued relationship between the boyish cavalier and the shrewd young gypsy. The importance of the hands as an expression of individual consciousness rather than merely as instruments of active gesture had been utterly neglected in the period of the maniera, when an absorption in eurhythmy, symbolism or empty decoration gave no opportunity for such psychological interpretation.

Caravaggio is probably the first and certainly the most insistent painter of his period in the use of gestures to express the feelings of the common man. This is not only true of his early works, when the influence of Lotto is obvious; in almost all of his compositions hands play an important part, most conspicuously in the very last work which he made in Rome, the *Madonna of the Rosary*. The strong hands of St. Dominic holding the miraculous rosary, and the hands of the kneeling men and women raised to the Madonna, again recall Lotto's painting of the same subject in Cingoli, although Caravaggio's greatly exceeds in scope the modest devotional work of Lotto. Caravaggio, who seems to have been connected with the projected decoration

FIG. 34
Lotto, *Betrothal*. Madrid, Prado.

FIG. 35
Lotto, *Madonna of the Rosary*.
Cingoli, S. Domenico.

of the Casa Santa in Loreto about 1600, may have seen Lotto's painting in nearby Cingoli, on the occasion of a visit from Rome to Loreto.

Savoldo, Lotto, Romanino and Moretto were all more or less connected with the region of Michelangelo Merisi's birthplace. But there were other great Northern Italian painters who made a sufficiently strong impression on the young artist's mind for us to detect their traces in works he painted later. The question of whether Caravaggio was in Venice during his youth has been rather heatedly discussed. Did he have an opportunity to see the marvels of High Renaissance Venetian art in the churches and palaces of Venice, and the frescoes on the Fondaco dei Tedeschi? Did he study the great works by Titian: the *Assunta* and the *Madonna di Pesaro* in the Frari, the dramatic foreshortenings of the *Sacrifice of Isaac* in Sto. Spirito, or in the same church, the *Descent of the Holy Spirit*, in a miracle of magic light? Did he stand in SS. Giovanni e Paolo before the *Assassination of St. Peter Martyr*? Did he see the noble decorations of Veronese in S. Sebastiano, or his marvellous *Marriage of St. Catherine*, finished at about the time Caravaggio was born? Was he by chance in Venice when Tintoretto was still working on the most daring and advanced creation of the second half of the century, the frescoes in the Scuola di San Rocco? All these works, and many others by these and other masters of the Venetian school, contributed at the end of the century either directly or indirectly to the formation of the early Baroque, to which Caravaggio's art belongs as an integral part. The language of their forms was used, consciously or not, as a kind of vocabulary, just as the classic language of Leonardo, or the idiom of Raphael and Michelangelo, had been adopted by the generation which followed them. In this general sense the overwhelming splendor of the great period of Venetian art penetrated to some degree the artistic life of the neighboring districts, and inevitably formed part of Caravaggio's artistic education. But in very few cases can one state with certainty that he has taken motives directly from any of the great Venetian masters. One cannot say of any of his works that it is even approximately in the manner of Titian or Tintoretto or Veronese, as one can say that his *Rest on the Flight* is Lottesque or, as Federigo Zuccari said of the *Calling of St. Matthew*, that it is "Giorgione's idea." Nothing in Caravaggio's work is comparable to the two Passion scenes of Lodovico Carracci in the Certosa in Bologna from the beginning of the 1590's, which are frankly in the style of the late Titian, or to Lodovico's *Preaching of St. John* from the same period, where the boatman and the trees are unmistakably Tintorettesque. Never did Caravaggio come as close to a High Venetian master, or to any other master, as Annibale Carracci comes to Veronese in his *Crucifixion* of 1594, now in Berlin.

Bellori, without any traditional or documentary basis, constructs a sojourn in Venice for the young Caravaggio, in order to explain the Giorgionesque element in his early works. Dramatizing Mancini's rather casual remark on the boy's already unstable character, he draws conclusions about Caravaggio's youth from what he knew of his turbulent life in later years. He invents a brawl into which the quarrelsome boy is supposed to have been drawn, and makes this the cause for an alleged flight to Venice. By this device Caravaggio's way is made open to the works of Giorgione, whom, Bellori says, the youthful artist enthusiastically took from then on as a kind of "escort" in his "imitation of nature" (se lo propose per iscorta nell'imitazione). Thus Bellori connects the formation of Caravaggio's art, not with the great stress of Venetian painting which was still continuing in the time of his youth, but exclusively with the calm, lyrical art of Giorgione, and principally with his color. But the Giorgionesque element or style which Caravaggio's contemporaries recognized, or thought they recognized, in his early works was not necessarily derived directly from the few authentic works of Giorgione in Venice and its immediate neighborhood; it could be found quite as easily and abundantly in Caravaggio's own region. Giorgionism, under which heading are grouped various currents more or less loosely connected with the pastoral mood and the devices of light and color invented by Giorgione, had become a movement of secondary importance in Venice itself. It was more at home in the smaller towns and territories outside Venice; the city itself remained the natural place for the main current, the dramatic art of the later Titian and Tintoretto. If we could discover more traces of this urban Venetian art in Caravaggio's later work, we too would probably find it worthwhile to insert a sojourn in Venice into the already crowded chronology of Caravaggio's youth. As it happens, we know of only one instance when Caravaggio borrowed from an important work of art in Venice; the main group of Titian's *St. Peter Martyr* (FIG. 79) is taken over almost without alteration for his *Assassination of St. Matthew* in San Luigi. But the fact that it appears in reverse makes it highly probable that he took it from one of the many engravings of Titian's famous work, rather than directly from the painting. His use of Titian's motif in this form seems to speak more against than in favor of a sojourn in Venice.

Yet Venetian art of this more monumental type was far from being unknown in Milan and its environs. As we have seen, Peterzano, Caravaggio's teacher, proudly calls himself "Titiani discipulus." Although his works fall short of so high a standard, his young apprentices undoubtedly found studies and sketches and engravings by or after Titian in his studio. Moreover, a great work of the 1550's, Titian's most mature period, was in Milan: The *Crowning with Thorns*, which Titian had made for Sta. Maria della Grazie and which was only taken away in Napoleonic times to its present location in the Louvre. One may imagine that this powerful work made a strong impression on the youthful Caravaggio, as it did on everyone who saw it; we have, however, no direct trace of it in his works. The *Crowning with Thorns* in the Cecconi Collection in Florence, which is considered a copy after the painting by Caravaggio mentioned in the sources, has only a slight and general affinity to Titian's work, certainly less than Lodovico Carracci's *Crowning with Thorns* for the Certosa. On the other hand, the strong chiaroscuro of Titian's painting, in addition to that of Savoldo, was certainly not without influence on Antonio Campi's late style, and through him, also on Caravaggio. There was another outstanding work by Titian within Caravaggio's reach, the *Resurrection* altarpiece of about 1520 in SS. Nazzaro e Celso in Brescia. With its famous *St. Sebastian*, based on the Laocoon as well as on a Michelangelo slave, Titian had introduced the Roman High Renaissance into North Italian and Venetian territory. The elaborate construction of the figure became a model for later artists, including again Lodovico Carracci, who imitated it in his own *St. Sebastian* in the Doria Gallery. So it could also have prepared the young Merisi to understand the contrapposti and torsions of Michelangelo's gigantic figures in Rome. His relationship to Titian may have been similar to his later attitude toward Michelangelo: one of the greatest respect, probably even of admiration, but tinged from the beginning with a certain antagonism. He could borrow motives from him or, as we have seen, whole groups, but never would he emulate the noble spheres in which Titian's figures move, nor try to compete with him in the brilliance of his colors. Titian's compositions are always full of implied dramatic movement; the movement of Caravaggio's figures is from the outset designed for arrested representation, corresponding to the reforming and neo-Classical tendencies of the period around 1600, such as the later work of Annibale Carracci. This is one of the fundamental differences between the art of Titian and that of Caravaggio: Titian leads to the full Baroque movement of mass and color in Rubens and Delacroix, whereas Caravaggio's Giorgionism prepares the way for the restrained art of Velasquez, and Manet.

The astonishingly proto-Baroque and dramatic art of Pordenone, who was Titian's early competitor, is even more remote from the character of Caravaggio's works.[8] The young boy, spending his childhood in Caravaggio, must have known Pordenone's emotional Passion scenes in the Cathedral of the neighboring town of Cremona. It may very well be that he recalled the terrifying tortures in Pordenone's *Crowning with Thorns* when he later painted in Naples the

FIG. 36
Titian, *Crowning with Thorns.*
Paris, Louvre.

FIG. 37
Titian, *Resurrection Altar* (detail, S. Sebastian). Brescia, San Nazaro e Celso.

two almost grotesque executioners in his *Flagellation of Christ*. The maniera magnifica, as well as the robustness of Pordenone's compositional style, may even have prepared the way for such compositions as the *Madonna of the Rosary*. There is, however, not a single painting by Pordenone which in my opinion can be connected more than vaguely and indirectly with any work by Caravaggio, in spite of the enthusiastic efforts of the most recent biographer of Pordenone to prove such a connection. It seems to me significant that Pordenone's brilliant

Conversion of St. Paul, with the wild horses rushing through a dark arch, had no influence whatever on Caravaggio's composition, but that instead he chose Moretto's much cooler and more simplified composition for his model, although both belong to the same general type of the Conversion without apparition. It was Rubens, not Caravaggio, who understood the precociously Baroque element in Pordenone's art, exactly as he understood the magnificent and Baroque dissolution of color in the very late Titian.

At the time when Caravaggio was learning the art of painting from Peterzano in Milan, the three great masters of the second flowering of Venetian art in the sixteenth century, Jacopo Tintoretto, Jacopo Bassano, and Paolo Veronese, were still living, although all were at the very end of their careers. However, none of the really outstanding works of these masters was, as far as I know, in Milan or its vicinity at the time of Caravaggio's apprenticeship. The political and financial situation in Lombardy in this period did not allow for the giving of large commissions to outside artists. But smaller or less important works by these three artists, the most progressive of their time, must certainly have come to Milan, and their styles were known to the artistic circles of the town through copies, sketches and engravings. By means of these, Caravaggio was able to study the foreshortening of the slave in Tintoretto's famous *Liberation of the Slave*, as he did in the case of Titian's *St. Peter Martyr*, and to use this knowledge for his figure of St. Paul.

It is doubtful, however, whether he would have come very much under the influence of Tintoretto's art, even if he had seen a greater number of his important works in his youth. With the exception of Rubens, in a few works made after his return to Antwerp in which he was experimenting with different styles, very few artists of his generation did feel Tintoretto's influences. The witty remark allegedly made by the sarcastic Agostino Carracci, that Tintoretto was sometimes better than Titian, sometimes worse than Tintoretto, is quite characteristic of the change of taste between the older generation and the extremely serious-minded reformers. Lodovico, the oldest of the Carracci, was the closest to the mannerists, and therefore still willing to make concessions to Tintoretto's manneristic tendencies. But for his younger cousins, for Agostino, the sober and almost pedantic engraver, and his brother Annibale, the future leader and ancestor of Seicento classicism in Rome, Tintoretto was "good" only when he was to some degree following the path laid down by Titian and the Venetian High Renaissance. The young Caravaggio probably grew up in the same spirit, as he was still an apprentice in Milan when the two brothers visited Venice. He was certainly attracted by some works of Tintoretto, such as the *Miracles of Saint Mark*, but his feeling for reality and simplicity would have been repelled by the chromatic mannerism of Tintoretto's later works, his fantasies of space, color and light in S. Rocco and S. Giorgio Maggiore, just as he would have been aghast if he could have seen the mystical mannerism of Tintoretto's follower Domenico Theotocopuli, El Greco.

The relationship of Caravaggio to Paolo Veronese is even less positive. Veronese's wonderful art is not dramatic like Titian's, not exciting and urgent like Tintoretto's, but thoroughly self-contained and almost motionless. The most refined color surfaces, tempered by diffuse silvery light, correspond to the equally tempered and restricted emotion of his figures, in strong contrast to the spiritual movement and the burning life beneath the apparent calmness of

Caravaggio's compositions. Yet there are some paintings or drawings, most of them attributions to Veronese or made with the help of his studio, which make us think of various compositions by Caravaggio, or of his compositional method. Veronese's *St. Cristina* series made for Torcello, (now in the Academy of Venice) contains a prison scene showing St. Cristina visited and fed by angels, in which the almost bare, brownish walls on one side are juxtaposed with a colorful group of figures on the other, bringing to mind the *Calling of St. Matthew* and even more, the *Decapitation of St. John the Baptist*, Caravaggio's late work in Malta. Furthermore, in the Russell Collection there is a very spirited drawing in black chalk, formerly ascribed to Veronese,

FIG. 38
Veronese, *St. Cristina*. Venice, Academy.

representing a Negro boy sitting at a table and greedily biting into a pear. It is this kind of genre figure which could have inspired the young Caravaggio to produce the half-figure painting of a boy peeling a pear, mentioned by Mancini, and preserved only in copies. We cannot, of course, draw any definite conclusions from these facts. The refined and aristocratic art of Veronese, which played a rather important part in the formation of the art of Annibale Carracci, was of almost no importance in the education of Caravaggio, Annibale's younger and much more radical rival in the reconstruction of a solid art of painting.

It is much more difficult to define Caravaggio's relationship to the Bassani, either positively or negatively.[9] In the art of Jacopo da Ponte and his many assistants and followers, most of them members of the family, there appears a realistic trend which is nowhere else so pronounced in late Venetian painting. Even in the seventeenth century, Ridolfi praises Jacopo for having abandoned the customary manner and for forming his own style "forcefully based on nature." The popular and simple attitude of the Bassani becomes evident when one compares it with the magnificence of Titian, with the noble refinement of Veronese, or the exhibitionistic violence of Tintoretto. The material treatment of humble figures, the warm chiaroscuro with clear but not brilliant or over-refined hues, the night scenes and artificial lighting in some of their works must have caught the attention of the boy who later became the leader of the European realistic movement. Such paintings by Jacopo as the *Rest on the Flight* in Milan, the large *Nativity* in Bassano, the *Adoration of the Shepherds* in Dresden, the *Entombment* in Padua, and the *San Rocco* in the Brera have, as a whole or in part, a definitely Caravaggesque appearance, although stylistically they are the antecedents of the works of the Caravaggisti (Honthorst, for example) rather than of those by Caravaggio himself. Some of the works of Jacopo's son Francesco, especially the Giorgionesque *Boy with a Flute* in the Vienna Gallery, whose head is wreathed

FIG. 39
Veronese (?), *Boy Eating Fruit*. Formerly London, Russell Collection.

FIG. 40
Francesco Bassano, *Boy with a Flute*. Vienna, Kunsthistorisches Museum.

with wine leaves like a young Bacchus, remind us of similar Caravaggesque figures by Terbruggen. With the exception of the Ambrosiana painting already discussed, we cannot recognize any specific painting by the Bassani which has directly influenced a work by Caravaggio. A general affinity between the Bassani and Caravaggio exists, however, in their common serious determination to bring transcendental and miraculous subjects into the humble sphere of earthliness and humanity.

This survey has tried to present a cross-section of the artistic material available to Michelangelo Merigi da Caravaggio when he was a painter's apprentice in Milan between 1584 and 1588. Only those artists have been discussed whose works can with a degree of probability be assumed to have attracted the lasting attention of the youth. Of course one cannot know what kind of art, good or bad, old or new, filled the boy's heart with delight, or what he rejected as he advanced toward maturity. To this latter category probably belongs Gaudenzio Ferrari, the most important artist of the post-Leonardesque period in Milan, whose curiously retardataire production is a hybrid of late Gothic and manneristic elements. The same is true of the even more clearly manneristic production of painters quite well-known in their time, such as Trotti Malosso, a number of whose paintings the young Caravaggio had certainly seen in Cremona during his childhood. For the young man who, as Bellori puts it, had chosen Giorgione (or Savoldo or Lotto) as his guide, this provincial mannerism undoubtedly became, after a while, unendurable.

Caravaggio's relationship to Leonardo, the greatest master ever to work in Milan, must be reconstructed somewhat differently. If he so desired, Caravaggio could have seen daily Leonardo's greatest work, the *Last Supper* in Sta. Maria della Grazie, although it was already in an extremely damaged condition; it is not impossible that Leonardo's psychological grouping of figures finds some reflection, however indirect and diluted by the intervening developments, in Caravaggio's *Calling of St. Matthew*. Caravaggio's early studies of physiognomy as in the *Medusa*, also undoubtedly depend upon the interest in modes of facial expression, which essentially began with Leonardo and was still very much alive in sixteenth-century Milan. As an apprentice of Peterzano, the friend of Lomazzo, in whose writings the glory of Leonardo had been evoked, he was surely encouraged to develop the deepest respect for the art of the great master. But Leonardo's discoveries concerning the construction of the human body and the harmonies of light and dark had become common property by the end of the sixteenth century. The young student did not have to turn to the original source, not to the derivatives of Leonardo's school; he could study some of Leonardo's effects modernized, and therefore much more interesting to him, in Savoldo's art, and the effects of Savoldo on the most up-to-date productions of his time, those of Antonio Campi.

There were certainly some other works of art in Milan and its environs, more than we can know, which made a passing impression on the young boy. Rather early in Milan, as in Venice, collections were formed which included Northern painters such as Bosch and Massys. About 1530, the *Anonimo Morelliano* mentions a painting of half-figures in the Casa Lampogniano, representing a patron making his account with his agent, ascribed to van Eyck or Memling.[10] Such northern genre paintings with half-figures may have had some influence on Caravaggio's early productions in Rome. It would be interesting to know whether the young man had seen other genre paintings of this kind by the Venetian or Lombard school, for example *The Venetian Lovers* (or *The Seduction*), a well-known painting by Paris Bordone of the 1540's, which came to the Brera from a Milanese family. Genre motives like these must have attracted the young artist in Milan, even before he painted the *Fortune Teller, The Cardsharps*, the *Boy Peeling a Pear*, the *Boy Bitten by a Lizard*, and others. A drawing once attributed to Veronese has already been mentioned in connection with the *Boy Peeling a Pear*. There is, however, a still more striking example whose motif Caravaggio certainly used: a drawing by Sophonisba Anguisciola, in her time a rather famous woman painter from Cremona, representing a little boy whose finger is being pinched by a crayfish in a basket, and a young girl putting her arm around him and smiling at his terror. This motive was found very amusing, and copies were made of the drawing (Tommaso Cavalieri, the friend of Michelangelo Buonarotti, sent a copy of the drawing to the Grand Duke of Tuscany); one of these may well have come into the hands of Caravaggio, perhaps through the Campi, as Bernadino Campi was Sophonisba's teacher. Baldinucci mentions another anecdotal drawing by Sophonisba in which a young girl makes fun of an old woman who is studying an alphabet on a children's blackboard with great attention.[11] It is interesting to discover that the genre scenes which Caravaggio introduced into Roman art about 1590 could have grown out of his youthful impressions in Lombardy.

The time which Caravaggio spent between his eleventh and fifteenth years was certainly not lost for his artistic education. Whether for some reason he left the atelier of Peterzano

FIG. 41
Paris Bordone, *The Venetian Lovers.*
Milan, Brera.

FIG. 42
Sophonisba Anguisciola, *Child Pinched by a Crayfish.*
Florence, Uffizi.

prematurely, or whether he stayed there the full four years stipulated in his contract, is not of great importance. His independence from the Milanese maniera was probably already quite clearly marked by the end of the four years. Proof of this is that his first works in Rome, two or three years later, show Giorgionism and realism in the special sense just discussed, rather than traces of North Italian mannerism. Caravaggio never forgot the deep, rich impressions of his youth; we can discover reminiscences of very different works of art which he had seen and admired in this early period in many of his paintings, even the later ones. But when this part of his education was finished, there was little left in his own region for him to learn or observe. His high-strung mind refused, of course, the ridiculous idea of entering the guild of Milanese painters, or of offering his services to the court of the Marchese di Caravaggio. There were, as I indicated at the beginning, two ways open to him: the way to Venice, and the way to Rome. It was the choice of Rome which decided his historical mission.

CHAPTER III

CARAVAGGIO AND THE ARTISTIC MILIEU OF ROME

A CCORDING to the contract, Caravaggio's apprenticeship in the studio of Peterzano was to have ended in the spring of 1588. Since there is no evidence to the contrary, we can assume that the stipulated term of four years was fulfilled. We may also assume that shortly thereafter he left Milan for Rome, at the age of fifteen or sixteen. It is possible that he spent a short time in other towns on the way, which would not contradict Baglione's statement that Caravaggio went to Rome "hereafter" (dapoi), i.e. after his apprenticeship was finished, and began to learn painting in earnest (se ne venne a Roma con animo di apprender con diligenzia questo virtuoso essercitio). We do not know whether he was sent to Rome by his family, because it was in the tradition of the Merisi and other artisans from Caravaggio to look for work there, or whether he was running away from his family and especially from his brother who had brought him to Peterzano. The latter possibility is intimated in Mancini's story: how years later a priest, claiming to be Caravaggio's brother, called at the home of the Cardinal del Monte, and asked to see Caravaggio, who was then living there. To the dismay of the entire household, the already famous painter not only refused to see him, but categorically denied having a brother at all. In all likelihood, therefore, Caravaggio did not travel to Rome in the manner of the youthful Parmigianino, escorted by relatives, but rather like Benvenuto Cellini, who at the age of sixteen ran away from his father's home in Florence. With all the elasticity of a carefree youth, Caravaggio must have journeyed southward from town to town, climbed the passes of the Apennines, and finally reached the Via Flaminia which led him straight to Ponte Molle and Porta del Popolo. In any case, in 1589 or shortly thereafter Caravaggio was in Rome, the city of his achievement.

In spite of some possible connections with compatriots in Rome, the young Merisi had to endure the usual privations of a struggling young artist. His miseries are suggested by the often very colorful accounts of Mancini, Baglione, and Bellori, which in spite of their dissimilarities, provide a roughly accurate chronology of his various periods of servitude. It was natural, of course, that he should seek employment in his craft, and his first opportunity was with a certain Lorenzo, a Sicilian painter "of very crude works" (di opere grossolane). His situation did not improve much when he stayed with Pandolfo Pucci, holder of a benefice from St. Peter's, who required of him "services which were beneath him," and whom he later dubbed "Monsignore Insalata," as if he had fed him nothing but salad greens; for him he painted devotional pictures which Pucci then sold in his home town of Recanati. A short time later he was given lodging in an inn, where he made a portrait of the innkeeper. It is not surprising that he finally took sick (perhaps in 1591 when Rome was ravaged by a terrible plague and famine) and, having no resources, was taken to the Ospedale della Consolazione where shortly before (1585) provision had been made to take care of inn servants in case of illness (as is recorded in Totti's *Ritratto di Roma*, 1638, p. 418). While convalescing he made many pictures for the prior, who took them either to Sicily or Seville, according to variant manuscripts of Mancini. Advancement of a kind came when he entered the services of the painter Giuseppe Cesari Arpino, later his enemy; for him he painted still-lifes and flowers. Probably while in this studio he met Prosperino Orsi, a painter of ornament (grottesche), who later became one of Caravaggio's greatest advocates, and also an enemy of Arpino. Shortly thereafter, he tried to make himself independent. A certain Monsignore Petrignani gave him a room and there he painted many pictures. But success was not immediate. He remained in desperate circumstances until the art dealer Valentino finally succeeded in selling some of his pictures to the Cardinal del Monte, who took him into his house and became his protector. The years of tribulation were now ended, and the tragic situations in the remainder of Caravaggio's life were produced not by external conditions, but by his own impetuous temperament.

From an historical point of view, Caravaggio's arrival in Rome occurred at an uncommonly opportune moment. The Franciscan Felice Perotti, cardinal of Montalto, had been elected Pope, in the spring of 1585, and had taken the name of Sixtus V. It is hardly an exaggeration to say that in his five pontifical years this extraordinarily active, clever, and deeply religious man set the stage for an ecclesiastical, political and artistic centralization such as Rome had not seen since the time of Julius II.[1]

The dome of St. Peter's had just been completed, including its lantern. In the middle of St. Peter's Square stood the obelisk from the circus of Nero, transported and raised by the energy of Sixtus and the technical ability of his architect Domenico Fontana, an enterprise held a generation earlier to be almost impossible. On the base of the obelisk are two inscriptions: the first praises the laborious transfer of the obelisk, formerly dedicated to the "impious cult of the Gods of the Gentiles," to the "threshold of the apostles"; and the other consecrates the obelisk, now cleansed of "impure superstition," to the "undefeated cross." Both inscriptions emphasize the conversion of a pagan monument to the Christian faith, which is symbolized by the golden cross on its summit. To be sure, when Sixtus preserved and reestablished these and many other antique monuments in this way, he did it not for the sake of art, or with any archeological or humanistic sentiments, but exclusively "in majorem Dei et Ecclesiae gloriam," for the greater glory of the Catholic Church triumphant over paganism, the "ecclesia triumphans" which is celebrated in the greatest poem of this period, the *Gerusalemme Liberata* by Torquato Tasso.

The great era of humanistic research, archeological discovery and the welcome reception of classical learning—the times of Julius II and Leo X—had passed. Every effort was now concentrated on stabilizing the deeply shattered structure of the Church by executing the inner and outer reforms prescribed by the edicts of the Counter-Reformation at the Council of Trent. Everything which was contrary to the "una et sancta ecclesia catholica," or which could distract the mind of the faithful worshipper, was damnable. This implicated the Turks, the heretics in France and elsewhere in Europe, as well as the temples of the pagan gods which still stood among those "seven churches" which were the "mirabilia," not only of Christian Rome, but of all Christianity. Only in the time of the Barberini pope Urban VIII and his successors, when this period of transition and struggle was over, when the affairs of the Church were settled and a limited victory had been won, could the luxury of humanism and archeology be fully enjoyed.

Sixtus V, however, was a shrewd and practical governor. He had no iconoclastic intentions in his destruction of old monuments, but he felt that of course they should not be allowed to interfere with his vast enterprise of creating functional thoroughfares, paths of communication from one end of Rome to the other, but instead should be used as quarries for his many buildings, aqueducts and other constructions. This was the case, for instance, with the famous and decorative, but utterly useless Septizonium, which Domenico Fontana demolished, with the Pope's permission, down to the last stone. In this way even the pagan stones could be made to serve his thorough reconstruction of Christian Rome. The baptized obelisks could be used as landmarks or termini for public roads and squares. Like them the Fontana Felice, named for Sixtus (Felice was his Christian name) and the other monumental outlets of the aqueducts lent a personal and distinctive note to his sober, but magnificent city planning.

Nevertheless, there were still many collectors of Roman antiquities, many enthusiasts for the ancient heritage connected so indissolubly with the glory of Rome. The antiquarian Pirro Ligorio had died only a few years before, leaving unpublished his immense inventories and researches on ancient art. Sixtus therefore met even from within the circle of his cardinals some opposition and protest against his policy of simultaneous tearing down and building up. But on the whole the young Caravaggio found a rather unfriendly attitude toward classical art and humanism, which had not changed essentially during the reign of Clement VIII, who followed Sixtus to the papal throne.

Sixtus' deep religious feeling went well with his eminently practical good sense. In combining these qualities he differed from his predecessors, the "holy popes," the zealous Paul IV, the ascetic and saintly Pius V, and especially the pious but ineffective Gregory XIII, with whom Sixtus, as a cardinal, had been in open disgrace. Though Sixtus was a rather erudite man, as evidenced by the edition of the writings of St. Ambrose which he made with Carlo Borromeo, his religiosity was less ascetic or mystic than pragmatic. Thus, upon his entrance into the Roman world, the young Caravaggio, did not become involved in the abstract, allegorical speculation on religious and secular matters of the previous generation. To realize the change which had taken place one has only to look at the symbols or allegories in the decorative paintings of the Vatican Library commissioned by Sixtus, which, in open contrast to the complicated and erudite allegories of the manneristic period just passed, are of an almost touching simplicity and directness. "Morality" is symbolized by a procession of "dowered brides," referring to the dowries distributed by the pope on special occasions; "Safety" is illustrated by a lion, the heraldic animal of Sixtus V, charging a wolf, referring to Sixtus' success against the brigands; "Thriftiness" is represented by the same lion guarding a safe, an allusion to the treasures which Sixtus collected by his wise economic measures and stored in the Castel Sant'Angelo, piece by piece, so that by the end of his pontificate he had become one of the wealthiest sovereigns in Europe.

By this direct and realistic approach to almost all aspects of his rule, Sixtus succeeded in stabilizing the power of the Church and the papacy, politically and spiritually. Against the wishes of mighty Spain, which had dominated his predecessors, he inaugurated a policy favoring Henry of Navarre, the future King Henry IV, which when put into effect by

Clement VIII resulted in France's remaining in the Church rather than turning to Calvinism. He liberated Rome from the tyranny of the local barons who protected the brigands, annihilating this almost insupportable plague by the most rigorous and even cruel methods. He not only made Rome and its environs safe, so that the faithful adherents of Christianity could visit the city unmolested, but in the five years of his pontificate he changed her appearance almost completely by his buildings, viaducts and roads. Henceforth Rome began again to be a center of European and Christian culture, and to regain her old splendor. But it was not yet the Rome of the seventeenth century; the exuberant and brilliant "Roma barocca" of Urban VIII and Alexander VII, epitomized by the full Baroque buildings of Bernini and Borromini. The period inaugurated by Sixtus V is marked, on the contrary, by a rather pedestrian uniformity, solidifying and realizing the often reactionary aspirations of the decades of the Counter-Reformation. The general tendencies of this period, extending through the reign of Clement VIII and into that of Paul V, correspond to the art of the "early Baroque," or perhaps better "pre-Baroque," which begins with the rationalistic "reform" of the Carracci and has as its nucleus of realism the works of Caravaggio.

The period of the maniera had definitely passed—the time in which it was possible in 1573 for the Venetian Inquisition to accuse Paolo Veronese of having abused holy subjects by introducing musicians and fools into his big painting of the *Feast in the House of Levi*; and when, about ten years later, the old Florentine sculptor, Ammannati, published his famous "pater peccavi" letter, expressing his remorse for having made so many nudes during his lifetime. Such occurrences demonstrate that the rigorous and puritan spirit of the Council of Trent toward the arts was still alive at the end of the maniera period. However, it was obviously no longer influential in the 1590's, when Annibale Carracci painted in the house of one of the highest dignitaries of the Church, Cardinal Odoardo Farnese, the most luxurious work of art since the Renaissance: the ceiling of the Galleria Farnese, celebrating the loves of the pagan gods in the water, in the air, and on earth.

It is therefore not astonishing to find that the extensive theological literature on the use and abuse of works of art in the service of the Church and with regard to general morality, is restricted to the maniera period. To cite only the most famous of these publications, Johannes Molanus' *De Picturis et Imaginibus Sacris* appeared in 1570, Cardinal Paleotti's *Discorso Intorno le Imagini Sacre et Profane* in 1582. Nothing of this kind came out after 1590. Even more surprising, and—as far as I can see—never fully realized, is the fact that not only ecclesiastical writing, but the fundamental writings on art after Leonardo, were a product of the maniera period. With the general decay of visual values in large parts of artistic production and with an often exaggerated appreciation of sophisticated and allegorical content, there coexisted the most flourishing and most important literature on art ever seen. Between 1550 and 1590 there is a great concentration of famous and important biographies, topographies, and systematic or theoretical treatises, which became the models for later writers. The fifties began with Giorgio Vasari's world-famous *Lives of Painters, Sculptors and Architects*, and there followed Condivi's *Life of Michelangelo* (1553) and Lodovico Dolce's well-known dialogue on painting, *Aretino* (1557). In the sixties appeared the first book of Vincenzo Danti's *Treatise on Perfect Proportion* (1567) and Benvenuto Cellini's two treatises on goldsmith's work and sculpture (1568). To the sixties or the beginning of the seventies belong the great treatises on architecture by Vignola (1562) and Palladio (1570); at the beginning of the eighties appeared Francesco Sansovino's *Venetia Città Nobilissima* (1581), the first compendious description of a town including its works of art, and in the same year, 1581, Bocchi's *Beauties of the Town of Florence*. Raffaele Borghini's *Riposo,* the maniera continuation of Vasari (1584), is also a work of the eighties; and in this decade there appeared also the basic, general and theoretical treatises on painting, Armenini's *Precepts of Painting* (1587) and, still more important, the two works of Lomazzo, the friend of Caravaggio's teacher Peterzano, the *Treatise on the Art of Painting* (1584), followed by a kind of appendix: the *Idea of the Temple of Painting*, which appeared in 1590—the last book of its kind for a very long period.[2]

From the nineties on, literary utterances on artistic topics seem to have been wiped out almost completely. It appears that connoisseurs and art lovers had become surfeited with literature on art of all kinds; that people left the artists to themselves to solve their new and exciting problems by practice, rather than by theory. In any case, it is a significant phenomenon that for at least half a century, from about 1590 to about 1640, hardly any books directly connected with painting and theory were published in Italy. It is characteristic that there was no demand at all for biographical works on artists—the third edition of Vasari was not published until 1647, about eighty years after the second. There was no publication of the *Considerations of Painting* by Giulio Mancini, the physician of Urban VIII, and one of the most interesting art writers of the time, which contain most valuable biographical and critical notes (some of them on Caravaggio). There was, it seems, no further need for prescriptions as to the best way to become an artist or painter, and certainly not for systems and theories. The contrast with the loquacious period of the maniera is indeed amazing, in this respect as in others.

Caravaggio's artistic career in Rome coincides almost exactly with the pontificate of the Aldobrandini pope Clement VIII. About the time of Clement's election in January of 1592, Caravaggio began his independent career in Rome; and it was in the year after Clement's death in 1605 that he was forced to leave the city.

Caravaggio arrived in Rome during a progressive period in which his special talents could develop freely and rapidly. The difficulties which he met had deeply personal causes and did not affect the reception of his art. As soon as he had overcome the usual beginner's troubles he was considered extremely promising. It is not astonishing that Caravaggio's new and bold art quickly made a deep impression on the avant-garde of young artists and connoisseurs. But it is surprising that after he had executed the important commission for San Luigi dei Francesi so many Roman congregations and churches sought to obtain his paintings—Sant' Agostino, Sta. Maria del Popolo, Sta. Maria in Vallicella, Sta. Maria della Scala, and the Palafrenieri of St. Peter's. It was known that improprieties were to be expected in his paintings, that their decorum (costume) was not always acceptable and might cause remonstrances. Yet he could never complain of being neglected or repudiated because of the boldness and novelty of his art, even though it was so obviously opposed to everything with which the Romans were familiar.

Caravaggio would have found it more difficult to reach the top so quickly had he stayed in Milan or some other smaller, provincial community. In Bologna, for example, the two young Carracci had great trouble at first in competing with the closed shop of the old school; the masters of the maniera, "this rabble," as Annibale complains, "were after them as if they were assassins."[3] Rome was, or became in the time of Sixtus and Clement, too international for this kind of provincialism. In spite of the guilds and the Academy of St. Luke, life was not narrow; an artist could develop freely and independently, and could quickly attract the attention or admiration of connoisseurs. Since the great programs of Sixtus V in building and city planning were stirring up wide activity, a young artist coming to Rome could easily fill a need. Furthermore, he could quickly attract the interest of circles of advanced taste, provided he introduced something unknown and exciting. It was also Caravaggio's good luck that through the successful financial policy of Sixtus, Rome was becoming a rich city. Enough money circulated to encourage important commissions, especially in churches, even for such a difficult person as Michelangelo da Caravaggio.

Surely he was a strange personality, difficult to control. It is Cardinal del Monte, his patron, who characterizes him as a "cervello stravagantissimo." But this is already the beginning of the period when an artist was granted the right to his individuality, even though this individuality might cause him to diverge from the conduct of life appropriate to a good artisan-citizen. This new attitude may be connected with the changing social position of the artist in the course of the sixteenth century, and to the interest which was taken not only in his work, but in his personality as well. The loosened ties with the guilds, whereby the painter had been forced into a community with pharmacists, "medici," and "speciali," and the creation of academies on an essentially artistic basis, emancipated the artist and reinforced his self-consciousness. So the ecclesiastical officials for whom Caravaggio worked cared not at all that the young Lombard painter whose works were causing so much excitement lived a wild and unbridled life. And Cardinal del Monte, a personage of high distinction (personaggio di gran nobiltà), prefect of the "fabbrica di San Pietro" and protector of the academy of painters, seemingly had no scruples about giving him shelter in his palace for years, even though his explosive character must have been evident long before it was formally documented in police records.

The start of Caravaggio's career was well timed from another point of view. The great activity of Sixtus V, and to some extent of Clement VIII, in giving commissions for building and rebuilding, restoring and adapting, decorating with paint and sculpture, had created a need for the services of many new artisans and artists in Rome. But the painters and sculptors who painted the decorations in the Vatican and the Lateran, or carved the statues and reliefs for the different chapels or the monumental fountains, were almost without exception mediocre and unoriginal. There was hardly a forceful personality among them, and this paucity was realized at the time. For example, the colossal statue of *Moses Striking the Rock*, by one Prospero Bresciano, at the outlet of the Acqua Felice was considered a complete failure. The construction of the most imposing enterprise of Sixtus V, the Cappella Sistina in Sta. Maria Maggiore, was a notable event but an artistic failure. The same may be said of two flat tombs for Sixtus and Pius V in this chapel; compared to the exuberant mid-century tomb of Paul III by Guglielmo della Porta, they are reactionary in style. Flemish sculptors who were brought to execute these works introduced into Rome the malerisch style of the Low Countries, which may have been of some importance for the later development of sculpture in Rome. But their works show only a fraction of the talent and imagination displayed by their countryman Giovanni da Bologna in his sculptures in Bologna and Florence.

The general level of official or semi-official painting was correspondingly low. Certainly in its quality it offered no particular competition to the young Caravaggio. Post-Classical painting in Florence, during the whole of the sixteenth century, had maintained a certain unity, from the anticlassical revolt of Pontormo and Rosso to the over-refinement of the Studiolo painters. The same was true of Bologna, from Niccolò dell'Abbate and Pellegrino Tibaldi to the early work of Lodovico Carracci. In Roman painting, however, there was no continuity after the Sack of Rome and the consequent exodus of most of the Renaissance painters. Individual artists or small groups did not lead to the formation of a local Roman school; one can speak of a specific Roman school or schools only after the beginning of the seventeenth century, when the followers of Annibale Carracci and Caravaggio had formed coherent groups. The *Last Judgment* by Michelangelo was too gigantic and overpowering, and had too much the character of a stylistically final phase to become influential as a whole on the local production. His isolated works in the Cappella Paolina, made in the 1540's, were likewise without much influence, since they remained practically unknown. Of the work by painters in his inner circle, Sebastiano del Piombo's grandiose and colorful compositions caused no reverberations; Daniele da Volterra's *Descent from the Cross* in Sta. Trinita dei Monti was later included among the greatest masterpieces of painting, equaled only by Raphael's *Transfiguration*, but its influence on Roman painting was also negligible. For a time Roman painting seems to have become almost an appendix to Florentine maniera. The big commissions fell to Florentines—to Vasari, who executed the life and deeds of the Farnese pope, Paul III, in the Cancelleria, and to Salviati, who in a more refined and elegant way also painted the history of the Farnese, and ended his mural enterprises with the striking and witty Bathsheba frescoes in the Palazzo Sacchetti.

Florentine painters displayed their typically late-manneristic style principally in those Roman churches and oratories which were connected with Florence, such as the oratory of S. Giovanni Decollato, whose congregation was Florentine. Cardinal Ferdinando de' Medici, later the Grand Duke of Tuscany, gave a commission to Jacopo Zucchi for allegorical paintings in the Palazzo Firenze which are stylistically close to those of the Studiolo in the Palazzo Vecchio in Florence. The Florentine branch of the maniera, changed and moderated in part by local Roman influences, stretches far into the century. Jacopo Zucchi's last work, *Amor and Psyche*, in the Galleria Borghese, is dated 1589, on the eve of the young Caravaggio's arrival in Rome.

Roman "drawing" (disegno), as opposed to Venetian "color" (colore) is the old slogan repeated again and again by Vasari. No one can deny that Central Italian artists were more interested in the outline and structure of objects, than were North Italians, especially Venetians, whose primary concern was with painterly values. Yet that does not mean that Rome and

Venice, the main centers of these opposite trends, had no communication with each other. In spite of their deep antagonism on artistic principles, they had many points of contact and possibilities of mutual influence. It is true that when Salviati and Vasari, both protagonists of "disegno," worked in Venice around 1540 they could not gain a firm standing in the stronghold of "colore." But it is at least significant that they could work there at all, and their decorative and complicated style even awakened some interest in certain Venetian circles, perhaps influencing the early works of Tintoretto. Conversely, when the two Florentines returned to

FIG. 43
Zucchi, *Amor and Psyche*. Rome,
Galleria Borghese.

Central Italy they brought back with them something of their artistic experiences in Venice. In this way a small measure of the principles of Venetian or North Italian art was available to painters of the next generation, for example to the Zuccari.

But along with these sporadic communications, there was, to a greater extent than we recognize, a direct influx of Venetian or Northern Italian art into Rome. It is true that Titian, who painted his heroic *Danäe* in the Belvedere on his visit to Rome in 1545, was more interested in "ancient stones" than in his Roman colleagues, and apparently made not the slightest impression on their activities. However, a much more modest painter, Girolamo Muziano of Brescia, settled permanently in Rome, and there had a prosperous career, displaying in his comparatively few works the influence of Moretto, of which his famous example is the altarpiece in Sta. Maria degli Angeli, *St. Jerome Preaching to the Hermits*. Although he recalls in some respects Sebastiano del Piombo, the Michelangelesque Venetian, Muziano was not devoted to Michelangelo's art. There is relatively little mannerism in his work. In contrast to most of the maniera painters working in Rome at this time, he had a typically North Italian sensitivity to landscape, and was famous for his scenes of saints and hermits seated or standing in broadly painted natural settings. Under Sixtus' predecessor, Gregory XIII, Muziano became one of the most prominent and highly regarded artists active in Rome, and was chosen in 1565 by Cardinal Contarelli to paint his chapel in S. Luigi dei Francesi, which he never began. The creation of a higher social position for artists was in great part achieved by his influence at the papal court. It was he who prepared the way for the foundation of the Academy of St. Luke, which Federigo Zuccari later inaugurated. During his first years in Rome, Caravaggio must certainly have known Muziano, who died in 1592, or at least have seen him pointed out as an important figure. Many features of his work could have aroused the young artist's sympathies, although there was little in them which he could not have learned at home. Some of Muziano's more mannered productions, such as his *Descent of the Holy Spirit*, could have reminded Caravaggio of Peterzano's painting of the same subject, but the latter was executed in a much more excited style than Muziano's Romanized version of Titian's painting.

Muziano was superintendent of all the big decorative enterprises in the Vatican—the Galleria Vaticana, the Cappella Gregoriana, etc.—through the 1570's and into the 1580's. Yet despite his important activities and undeniably excellent craftsmanship, his artistic personality was not strong enough to attract a school of younger painters. His pupils, Cesare Nebbia, Paris Nogari, G. B. Ricci da Novara, and the two Alberti, who worked under Sixtus V and Clement VIII, were for the most part well-trained craftsmen and quick fresco workers, but they were insignificant as artists. To the young Caravaggio, their innumerable works, exhaustively listed by the seventeenth-century guidebooks, were surely a negligible quantity from a dead past. All of these men were thirty to forty years older than Caravaggio, although some of them were still working long after his death.

The most conspicuous artist of the last three decades of the sixteenth century was certainly Federigo Zuccari. He tried to dominate the artistic scene in Rome, just when the vigorous and substantial art of the young Caravaggio was definitely attracting attention. Born at the beginning of the forties and therefore belonging to an older generation than Caravaggio, his character, his aims and his talents are decidedly antithetical to Caravaggio's whole personality and to everything he stood for. Not that he was a bad artist, in the usual sense of the word. He mastered his métier quite adequately—Caravaggio himself, in his enumeration of good and bad artists of his acquaintance, gave him credit for being a "valenthuomo" and a "buon pittore" along with Pomarancio, Arpino, and even Annibale Carracci.[4]

Federigo began his career about 1550, at a very early age, by assisting his brother in painting facades in Rome. This brother, Taddeo, had grown up in the Roman tradition of Perino del Vaga and Polidoro da Caravaggio, but had also introduced North Italian and especially Correggesque elements into his compositions. A typical example is his much praised fresco cycle (now rather damaged) on the vault of the Mattei Chapel in Sta. Maria della Consolazione, the church belonging to the hospital in which the young Caravaggio was later treated. In most of his numerous frescoes in the palaces in or around Rome, a kind of moderate maniera prevails. The torsions and contraposti are taken from Michelangelo, but they are displayed in a well-ordered structure derived from Raphael and his school. Vasari praises Taddeo's "dolce e pastosa" manner; he was considered the better and more original artist, though the difference between him and Federigo seems small.

Taddeo died at the age of thirty-seven—"like Raphael," says Vasari—and was buried by Raphael's side in the Pantheon. Federigo followed in his footsteps at Caprarola, as well as in

FIG. 44
Muziano, *Descent of the Holy Spirit*. Rome, Vatican.

the Sala Regia and elsewhere. To the already rather eclectic style of his brother he added new elements, picked up on the extensive travels which led him as far as England. Certainly he was very well acquainted with Venetian painting. About 1580 he even had the great honor of replacing a famous work by Titian in the Palazzo Ducale: the big historical fresco, *The Emperor Barbarossa Kneeling before Pope Alexander III*. In his enormous *Last Judgment* for the dome of the Cathedral in Florence, he tried to revive the late-Florentine mannerism of his predecessor, Vasari, by introducing some devices of the chromatic mannerism of Tintoretto. He certainly also enlarged Taddeo's rather limited repertory by new "inventions" of an allegorical or literary character, as for instance, the *Angels Adoring the Name of God*, a painting he made about 1590 for a chapel of the Gesù. Even more characteristic, however, are the frescoes in the "artist's mansion," still known as the Palazzo Zuccari. They not only show scenes from the life of his family; they express his whole artistic philosophy. In their pretentiousness and spiritual arrogance they go far beyond the rather modest though equally mediocre illustrations designed for his house in Arezzo by Vasari (here as in other cases Zuccari's model). In his not very numerous writings, too, Federigo is much more strained, dogmatic and scholastic, than the prolific Vasari, whose main interest is in the artist, not the "idea of the artist." Federigo Zuccari, on the contrary, is personally and emotionally involved in the emphatic definition and proclamation of the "artist" as something godlike, as an emanation of the Divine Wisdom. Zuccari's vanity is not naive, childlike, and open, like that of Vasari and other similarly active and efficient personalities, but is of an almost impersonal conceit, and therefore much more

FIG. 45

Federico Zuccari, *Angels Adoring the Name of God*. Rome, Gesù, Cappella degli Angeli.

FIG. 46

Federico Zuccari, *The Glorification of the Artist*. Rome, Palazzo Zuccari.

dangerous; he feels that he is the bearer of a sacred mission. The apotheosized artist painted in one of his frescoes in his house is not himself as an individual, but as he felt himself—the earthly incarnation of this image.

With such ideals in mind he established the Academy of St. Luke, whose first Principe, or President, he was, and whose initial sessions in 1593 he directed. Zuccari did not limit the aims of his new organization to the raising of the social standing of artists and the promotion of their talents, as other corporations had done. The academy he dreamed of was to be the stronghold of an extremely high conception of the artist's value and mission, and at the same time was to serve as a bulwark against vicious modernistic and individualistic novelties. The statutes proposed by Zuccari, and recorded by the first Secretary of the Academy, Romano Alberti, were therefore of extreme rigor: absolute obedience was postulated for the members, as if they belonged less to a free association of artists than to a militant religious society like the Society of Jesus. "No one in the Academy," one reads under the heading *Prohibitions*, "shall dare to act otherwise than in a virtuous and modest way; one shall be quiet and peaceful, and shall in no manner provoke trouble or grumble" (che non sia alcuno che nell'Accademia ardisca far azione men che modesta . . . e che debbe esser pacifico e quieto e non attizzare nè mormorare). Every offender against this law was to be immediately expelled—"at the will and pleasure of the President" (a volontà e gusto del Signor Principe); moreover, whoever acted contrary to a command given by the Principe should be imprisoned on the Capitol "on simple order of the President." Although Caravaggio's name is mentioned in Missirini's list of *professori* of the Academy, one can hardly imagine that he would have voluntarily subjected himself to the narrow-minded suppression of his individuality. However, the draconic laws set down by Zuccari were probably only on paper and not really enforced.[5]

The young painter certainly was not in the least interested in speculations about the origin and essence of art, nor in the relation of the "disegno interno" to the "disegno esterno" and so on, in which Zuccari indulged and with which he sought to fill the new Academy. Caravaggio, in his life as well as in his art, was too earthbound to perceive in his work the spark of Divinity ("scintilla della Divinità") ignited in him through the medium of the angels, and preceded by the "disegno interno" or the "idea." For him the "disegno" was not, as in Zuccari's sophisticated etymology, a "segno di Dio" (a sign of God), but something which one had to do, rather than to talk about. Zuccari's neoscholastic terminology, based partly on doctrines of Thomas Aquinas, corresponds thoroughly to the medievalism postulated by the Council of Trent and to the reactionary ideas of the Counter-Reformation movement under the Holy Popes. But toward the end of the century the fundamental stabilization of the Catholic Church and faith seemed to have been assured. When the church recognized the converted Henry of Navarre as King Henry IV of France, the predominant Spanish influence was broken, and the medievalistic and retrospective tendencies began gradually to decline.

This fundamental change in intellectual cast made Zuccari's theories appear anachronistic even when they were first put forward at the Academy in 1593, and still more so when they came out in print in Turin in the first decade of the new century, at the end of Zuccari's lifetime. They have, to be sure, a certain acumen, and are often not without originality. Nevertheless, the whole schematic and theoretical spirit of Zuccari's *Idea* was just as negligible to the younger generation as the spirit and style of the works which he had produced during his long lifetime. It appeared as a kind of revenant from a dead past in the period of Annibale and Caravaggio, when all positive forces were concentrated on overcoming the "Gothic" features of mannerism—in form as well as in feeling—and when a resolute approach to nature and human experience was opposing abstractions and generalizations of every kind.

Yet, as the sponsor and first president of the Accademia di S. Luca, and as an honorary citizen and patrician of Rome, Federigo Zuccari was an outstanding figure in art politics. In many parts of Italy, and even more abroad, he had long enjoyed the reputation of being one of the best painters in Italy. He had been called to Spain to paint large frescoes in the Escorial; in Elizabethan England he had made portraits of the Queen and the most prominent personalities of the court. Some of his works, especially his *Last Judgment* in Florence, seem to have been influential in the formation of the late-manneristic generation in the Netherlands. Otto van Veen, the teacher of Rubens, had studied under Zuccari in Rome in the late seventies; Hendrick Goltzius had paid him a respectful visit in 1591; and the academic encyclopedist Van Mander was closely connected with him.

It is true that his artistic reputation had suffered appreciable setbacks in the later years of his life. His most pretentious enterprise, the decoration of the inner shell of Brunelleschi's Dome in Florence, had been condemned from the first by the Florentines, who (as the satirist Lasca writes in one of his madrigals) would never cease complaining if it were not whitewashed one day (non sarà mai di lamentarsi stanco, se forse un dì non le si da un bianco). His frescoes in the Escorial, as we know from a letter of the Austrian Ambassador in Madrid, were much disliked by the Spanish King and Court, though very well paid. In his satirical painting, the *Porta Virtutis*, he had inconsiderately given vent to his resentment toward some Bolognese critics by representing them with asses' ears. This typical manifestation of an inflated but impotent artist had earned him disgrace and temporary banishment from the Bolognese Pope, Gregory XIII, so that he could hardly finish his frescoes in the Cappella Paolina, his last official work in Rome. Under the following popes he was given no more official commissions. Nevertheless, even long after his death, Baglione calls him a "grand' huomo" and the "most fortunate painter of his time, who made a very considerable income and was more loved and honored by princes than anybody else."

The aging Zuccari found himself, therefore, in a rather precarious position: on the one hand he was spoiled by his successes and overconscious of his mission as the chosen preceptor of art, while on the other, he became extremely touchy toward any criticism, and certainly suffered from the younger generation's total disrespect for his art and personality. He could not afford to overlook the revolutionary products of Caravaggio and even less their subversive influence on public taste. This fully explains the vicious utterances of the old academician against the young genius, which, although contained in letters of very dubious authenticity, are so much in character that they should not be neglected.[6] Just as every professor of an academy would do, he calls the "extravagance" of Caravaggio's paintings—not to speak of his character—a "more than sufficient" explanation for the great number of his admirers and protectors. "The richer and more important gentlemen are, the more they feel themselves connoisseurs, and find everything beautiful which has an air of novelty and which takes them by surprise." He had tried early to devaluate even the novelty in Caravaggio's work, exclaiming before his masterpiece, the *Calling of St. Matthew* in S. Luigi, that he saw nothing but the conception of Giorgione and did not understand why so much fuss was made about it.

The understandable prejudice of the Principe dell'Accademia against the rising star had no effect; Caravaggio's new art was too powerful, and the admiration for it too widespread, even in the highest and most influential circles. The recognition of his superiority as an artist had so strengthened his position with the noble patrons of art in Rome, the Cardinal del Monte, the

Mattei, the Crescenzi, and especially, the Marchese Vincenzo Giustiniani, that even his social misbehavior could not weaken it, whereas Federigo Zuccari seems to have been persona non grata at the Court and in the circles of Clement VIII. This, and his inability to compete with the powerful forces of the new Renaissance in Rome, of Annibale and of Caravaggio, probably decided Federigo to look for honors and fortune outside Rome, in spite of his interest in the education of artists and in the Accademia di S. Luca. After finishing the frescoes in the Casa Zuccari, and making it the seat of the Academy, he left Rome for good in the first years of the new century. After many peregrinations to Venice, Lombardy, and Piedmont, he died in Ancona in 1609—the same year as Annibale, and a year earlier than the upstart who had supplanted him, Michelangelo da Caravaggio.

Zuccari and Caravaggio represent two opposed patterns of personality and social status as well as of style; Zuccari is the organizing and academic artist almost in the French sense, while Caravaggio is the completely independent Bohemian artist. Both types come clearly into view at this date for the first time, and both are equally accepted by the public: Caravaggio as a good painter despite objections to his personal behavior; Zuccari as a person of official distinction despite the dubious quality of his painting. It is just Zuccari's significance as a countertype of Caravaggio which makes him important for the present discussion.

Cristoforo Roncalli also belongs to the generation which immediately preceded Caravaggio. During Caravaggio's sojourn in Rome Roncalli was closely associated both with the "most noble" Crescenzi family, and the Marchese Vincenzo Giustiniani. As we know from Baglione's *Vite*, he taught painting and drawing to the Crescenzi brothers, and was on terms of great familiarity with Monsignore Crescenzi, later the cardinal. At the same time he was advisor to the Marchese Vincenzo Giustiniani on artistic matters and made trips at the Marchese's expense or in his entourage to all parts of Italy and to France, England and Germany. Although Roncalli was born in Pomarancio, near Volterra, his family came from Bergamo and he evidently still felt himself a Bergamasque. Considering the close connections between Bergamo and the town of Caravaggio, it would be quite natural that he should have wanted to help his young compatriot by fostering the interest of the Crescenzi and the Marchese Giustiniani in the prodigy from Caravaggio. It seems possible that Roncalli helped to persuade the Marchese to buy Caravaggio's paintings, and it would speak well for Roncalli's taste and understanding if he undertook the protection of the young artist, even though he himself represented a different current, that of idealistic monumental painting. Caravaggio in turn acknowledged the good qualities of Roncalli, calling him, together with two other prominent painters, a "valenthuomo," and adding that he not only understood the craft of painting (pittore valenthuomo che sappi dipingere bene et imitar bene le cose naturali) but that he was also a competent judge of painters (valenthuomini come quelli che si intendono della pittura e giudicaranno buoni pittori).[7] It is interesting to remark that Rubens recommended a painting by Roncalli to the Duchess of Mantua in 1607, the same year in which he recommended Caravaggio's *Death of the Virgin* to this lady.

Roncalli's teacher was Niccolò Circignani, the older Pomarancio, who must here be mentioned only for his notorious scenes of torture and martyrdom in Sto. Stefano Rotondo, the venerable church given by Gregory XIII to the Jesuit-dominated Collegium Germanicum. These gory displays, unprecedented in Italian painting, were designed as examples for young priests, to prepare them to endure torture and death for their faith with constancy of soul. Most of the paintings of this cycle were made by the older Pomarancio, who also painted a similar series in the chapel of the English College in Rome representing the deaths of the English martyrs. These frescoes are remarkable documents of a direct and compelling approach to the spectator, and as they were produced in the 1580's, just before Caravaggio came to Rome, they could hardly have escaped his attention. And in spite of the mediocrity of their execution and their old-fashioned style, their directness could have exercised a certain influence on Caravaggio, although he himself mostly abstained from any display of exaggerated cruelty, even in his few representations of martyrdoms. As we will see, the scene of St. Thomas à Becket, who was murdered by soldiers before his altar, may have been in Caravaggio's mind when he planned the similar scene of the Martyrdom of Matthew.

Cristoforo Roncalli, the "Cavaliere delle Pomarancie," broke away rather quickly from the superficiality and the diluted color of his teacher. In the great altarpieces of his mature years, in and outside Rome, he tried to build up his compositions in full, warm colors with relatively few figures. We find in his painting traces of Venetian or North Italian art, as is often the case with Roman painting of this period. He also reverted to the rather classical construction of Giulio Romano's Roman works, and even the monumental style of some of Beccafumi's figures may have affected him when he worked in Siena (as Bellori noted in the margin of his Baglione). Thus, like other minor painters of his generation such as the Florentine Domenico Passignano who had worked with him in the Cappella Clementina, Roncalli marks a kind of transition from the maniera to the academic current of the Seicento. He was a contemporary of Annibale Carracci and Cigoli (who were born in the fifties), and he long outlived these artists. However, unlike them, he was not a strong enough personality to produce a decisive break with the traditional artistic conceptions of the time and he cannot have been of any considerable importance for the revolutionary art of Caravaggio.

As we know from Baglione, Caravaggio did not long maintain good relations with Roncalli. Allegedly he participated about 1600 in a competition for the decoration of the Casa Santa in Loreto, which Roncalli won. The latter was then attacked by a "Sicilian traitor" and slashed in the face with a knife. Caravaggio was naturally suspected, according to Baglione, perhaps only because he was later marked in the same cruel way in Naples.

It has been suggested that a direct connection exists between the art of Scipione Pulzone and that of Caravaggio, especially with respect to portraits. Such a connection is, in my opinion, difficult to substantiate. Pulzone, born about 1550 in Gaeta, between Rome and Naples, was still alive in the 1590's when Caravaggio worked in the Contarelli Chapel. His fame is founded principally on his portraits, which are sober, direct and unstylized, and may have had some influence on the neoclassic school of Carracci (e.g. Domenichino). Unlike many other North Italian painters, Caravaggio certainly did not have the ambition to become a great portraitist. The few portraits which we have from his hand or which are attributed to him (and most of these are not undisputed) do not contribute very greatly to his fame. It is nevertheless quite possible that in some instances Caravaggio permitted himself to be influenced by the very respectable but rather dry manner of Pulzone's portraits. For example, there are certain general stylistic affinities between Pulzone's *Portrait of Cardinal Spada* and the portrait of *Paul V* attributed to Caravaggio; and the portrait of Maffeo Barberini, which is now usually considered

FIG. 47
Pulzone, *Portrait of Cardinal Spada*. Rome,
Palazzo Spada.

an early Caravaggio, was formerly even called a Pulzone. There are also a few religious paintings by Pulzone which, because of their clear form and sharp silhouette, may possibly have attracted the young Caravaggio, as they attracted Rubens, but for this we have no real evidence.

Giuseppe Cesari d'Arpino, later the "Cavaliere" d'Arpino, was only five years older than Caravaggio. Spiritually, however, he is far away from the reform movement of the last decades of the sixteenth century which, in creating the "Early Baroque," provided the basis for the varied developments of the coming century. In contrast to Annibale Carracci or Caravaggio, Arpino did not stand resolutely against the diluted maniera trends of Zuccari and others, but mingled them with academic, eclectic elements, partly Venetian, but for the most part deriving ultimately from the Raphael School. A skillful and by no means tasteless artisan, he lived a long life (1568-1640), and, in his own time, he was considered by the art critics to be a leader—

though only of the "ultima maniera." Mancini (about 1620) uses Arpino to exemplify a school of painting which is distinguished by a certain ease and correctness and by good and graceful compositions, but which is not founded on the exact observation of nature, as is the school of Caravaggio, and does not have the gravity and solidity of the Carracci. However, he adds that Arpino's paintings have a kind of beauty which at once attracts and delights the eye of the spectator. Later in the century Pietro da Cortona expressed an opinion which is similar to Mancini's[8] about the working methods of Caravaggio and Arpino. It is interesting to remark that this great master of the illusionistic Baroque tried to do justice to two earlier currents in Roman painting which were as opposed to his own ideals as are the "naturalism" of Caravaggio and the polished "late maniera style" of Arpino. Cortona praises Caravaggio's "marvellous" paintings, especially those of San Luigi, as the highest perfection obtained by observing nature (osservò il naturale in dipingere). But at the same time, he finds Arpino a remarkable personality because he followed his own genius and, in his graceful works, reached the highest degree of perfection in a manneristic style (e s'avanzò all' eccellenza d'uno stile manieroso). As an example of Arpino's gentle style Cortona cites his frescoes in the Contarelli Chapel, and as examples of his expressive style his paintings of military combats (surely the famous frescoes representing scenes from Roman history in the Palazzo dei Conservatori).

It is not surprising that Caravaggio and Arpino, who were men of such different character and who had directly opposed concepts of art and its meaning, should have been on bad terms from the beginning; their personal relations did not improve with time. However, the antagonism between them was probably exaggerated by the biographers who were delighted to ornament the real situation with colorful anecdotes. For example, Sandrart tells of a meeting between Caravaggio and Arpino in which Caravaggio challenged Arpino to dismount from his horse and fight him. Arpino refused to fight because he was a Cavaliere and this was taken as the reason for Caravaggio's visit to Malta, that he, too, might become a Cavaliere. Actually, there is no evidence which indicates that Arpino, who was the acknowledged favorite of Clement VIII, used his papal connections to intrigue directly against Caravaggio. The only certain thing we know about the relationship between the two men is that Caravaggio had worked in Arpino's shop when he was young. Arpino is known to have been a shrewd man in matters of business who, as Bellori says, well knew how to advertise his merchandise (il cavaliere era astuto e sapeva dar martello et vendere la sua mercanzia), and it is possible that he exploited the young Caravaggio's talent for painting "fruits and flowers." On the other hand, Caravaggio seems to have acknowledged the skill and ability of Arpino, because he mentions him first among the "valenthuomini" in his deposition during the lawsuit of Baglione.

Although Arpino's contemporaries classified him as the leader of an important late maniera style which extended far into the seventeenth century the words "maniera" or even "manieroso" did not have the same connotations which modern criticism has given to them. Arpino's maniera is far removed from the manneristic style of the 1530's and 40's in Florence, Rome and Parma and later in the Studiolo. On the contrary, even the early works of Arpino, the ceiling frescoes of San Martino in Naples and later those in the Cappella Olgiati in S. Prassede, are almost intentionally opposed to the flattened foreshortenings, the complicated contortions, and the unnatural proportions which characterize the mannerism of the earlier Cinquecento. Arpino's works, like those of Roncalli, have a calm monumentality and are closer to the conceptions of Cigoli and the Carracci than to mannerist paintings. What they lack is stylistic incisiveness. They are, if I may say so, too inoffensive and too passionless to capture the interest

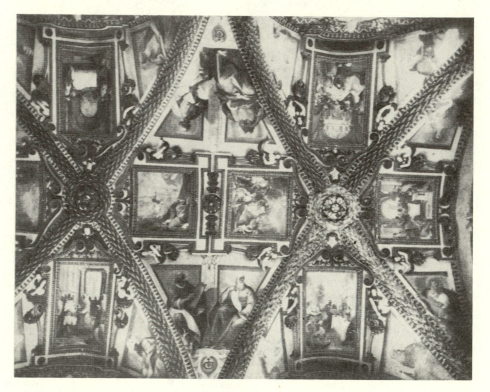

FIG. 48
Giuseppe Cesari d'Arpino, *Ceiling Frescoes*. Naples, Certosa di San Martino.

of the spectator. However, they existed in great number and, possessing a certain delicacy and clarity, they are representative of a general taste for elegant and easily understandable paintings. On the whole, the Cavaliere d'Arpino presents an aspect of efficient mediocrity in the vocabulary of the conservative late maniera, and as such he marks the middle ground between the radical artistic parties of Caravaggio and the Carracci.

One of Caravaggio's strongest personal adversaries in Roman artistic circles was Giovanni Baglione, who was two years older than he, and who is known to posterity almost exclusively through his very sober and reliable *Vite de' Pittori*, published at the end of his long lifetime. His animosity toward Caravaggio is shown in almost every line of his biography, and our knowledge of his antagonism is increased by the records of his suit for libel against Caravaggio and some of his colleagues. (DOCS. 5-13). From these records we learn that he was despised and derided by Caravaggio's clique, which consisted, in the first years of the new century, mainly of Orazio Gentileschi, Onorio Longhi, the architect, and Caravaggio himself. They delighted in circulating long and very coarse poems satirizing Baglione and spoke contemptuously of his

FIG. 49
Giuseppe Cesari d'Arpino, *Ascension*.
Rome, S. Prassede, Cappella Olgiati.

paintings, and he, in turn, accused them of slander. He was especially adamant toward Caravaggio, who, he said, was just envious because he, Baglione, had received the commission for an *Ascension* in the Gesù. As an artist he was, strangely enough, a follower of Caravaggio, especially in his use of light and dark—a fact which, according to his other biographers, Caravaggio did not very much appreciate. Baglione was strongly criticized for a *Divine Love* (FIG. 61) which he had made in competition with Caravaggio's *Victorious Amor*, but it is characteristic that Baglione's painting was later considered a Caravaggio. He himself published a long list of his works at the end of his autobiography in the *Vite*, but in spite of some very interesting performances, he never really developed a consistent and expressive artistic personality.[9]

{75}

Artistically, all these painters of stylistic compromise, with their quite respectable but rather empty compositions, had little to offer the young and intransigent Caravaggio. It was only when Annibale Carracci came to Rome in 1595, to paint the famous frescoes of the Galleria Farnese, that Caravaggio met a really worthy rival. For about eleven years, from 1595 to 1606, Annibale and Caravaggio lived in Rome. The community of artists was rather small, but nothing is known of any personal contact between them. Annibale was perhaps the most respected and sought-after painter in Italy, next to his cousin and teacher Lodovico Carracci, who had preferred to stay in Bologna, where he had gathered as his pupils some of the most important Italian artists. Annibale entered the service of the powerful Cardinal Farnese and brought with him a staff of collaborators, notably his brother Agostino, whose fame as a painter and especially as an engraver equaled his own. Caravaggio was patronized by the Aldobrandini circle, the Francophile party of Clement VIII, against whom the Farnese as partisans of Spain were in open opposition. This perhaps explains why Annibale, in spite of his excellence as an artist, never received an official commission from Clement VIII, and also why Annibale and Caravaggio had no contact. Moreover, Caravaggio, who was so much younger, was still a beginner when Annibale arrived, although already very conspicuous among younger artists and art-lovers for the startling novelty of his paintings. Certainly Annibale paid serious attention to the art of the young innovator, although possibly not without a presentiment of danger because of the strong impression which his temerity had begun to make on the younger members of the Carracci school, even in Bologna. The possibility that Annibale was himself directly interested in the chiaroscuro experiments of his younger colleague is suggested by an engraved *Crowning with Thorns* which he made in 1606 and which is comparable to Caravaggio in its realistic approach to the figures as well as in its use of dark shadows. Conversely, it is possible that the change in the compositional style, which we note in Caravaggio's paintings after the *First St. Matthew*, as for example in the *Supper at Emmaus* and the *Doubting Thomas*, depends somewhat upon impressions received from the grand manner of Carracci.

The similarity between Caravaggio and Annibale Carracci consisted in their common challenge to the "idea fantastica" of the maniera through a return to "nature." On this basis it is possible to place these otherwise very different artistic personalities into a single group, as was done by Vincenzo Giustiniani. In his letter to Teodoro Amideni, Giustiniani classifies the art of painting into twelve categories.[10] Near the end of his enumeration he makes a sharp distinction between painting "di maniera" (no. 10) and "di natura" (no. 11). The first of these categories is typified by the painter who, with a long experience in drawing and coloring, puts into a painting that which is in his imagination, without using a model. The second is typified by the artist who works with real objects before him and who is a man of practical experience and, more than that, of natural instinct—a gift, says Giustiniani, granted to very few artists. In his tenth category he places such painters as Federigo Barocci and Giuseppe d'Arpino, giving as examples the frescoes made by the latter in the Capitoline. In category number eleven he names the Spaniard Ribera, and Dutch and Flemish painters like Honthorst, Hendrick Terbruggen and, surprisingly enough, Rubens. The twelfth and last of his categories is the most perfect and at the same time the most difficult because it combines both the "di maniera" and the "di natura" categories. Here he includes the painters whom he ranks highest, but with the distinction that some are more inclined to paint from their imagination, and others more from nature. In this way he aligns the manner of Caravaggio with that of Annibale Carracci. Even though one sees clearly Giustiniani's wish to reserve the highest place for his own favorites, it is remarkable that Caravaggio is here for the first time exempted from the damnation of being called a "mere imitator of nature," and that he is given the same credit as the great idol

FIG. 50
Annibale Carracci, *Crowning with Thorns.*

of the period, Annibale Carracci. It is true that the "idealist" Carracci has a strong naturalistic bias, as is witnessed by his early drawings, which often show an extraordinarily fresh and objective interest in everyday figures and scenes. But this realism is not carried through into his paintings; rather it constitutes a kind of substratum, out of which he is able to create a more convincing idealism. As a social attitude this suggests an interest in dignity, decorum and the suppression of common life, in contrast to Caravaggio. Furthermore, it is significant that these realistic drawings vanish almost entirely when Carracci enters the atmosphere of Rome, and there develops his monumental style in the great classical tradition. On the other hand, it is also true that Caravaggio is not a pure naturalist, as he was characterized by the intellectuals and classicists. He too was caught in the current of structural monumentality. However, judging from their intentions, both artistic and social, as embodied in their finished products, the old "idealist" and "realist" distinction between Annibale and Caravaggio still retains, when taken with a grain of salt, an essential truth.

The fundamental difference between the art of Annibale Carracci and Caravaggio was emphasized by Bellori, the fervent advocate of Nicolas Poussin and of his ideology. Bellori was able to make a sharper and clearer distinction between the two artists than were the "dilettanti" Giustiniani and Mancini, because he was a professional esthetician and art historian (one of the first of his kind, in fact) and because, living later, he had a clearer perspective of the period. In my opinion, the much discussed question of whether Annibale's merit lay in his imitation and revival of the classical ideal of Raphael and the antique or in his own artistic originality, is rather superfluous. One cannot consider Jacques Louis David, the painter of the *Sabines*, simply as a neo-Poussinist without missing the complexity of his artistic character and his historical significance. Bellori, however, goes too far in his artistic partisanship when he denies Caravaggio every relationship to the great masters of the High Renaissance and the antique and when he tries, with the help of old-fashioned anecdotes, to show Caravaggio as a stubborn and uneducated antagonist of the art of the past. It is quite possible that the arrogant Caravaggio often boasted of his artistic independence from traditions, as young artists of his temperament often do. Nevertheless, he surely studied the works of Raphael, as did Savoldo and Titian. Indeed, the paintings which Caravaggio saw in the Sistine Chapel, the Stanze, and the Farnesina were incomparably more decisive for the formation of his art than were any of the works of the lesser artists whom we have discussed in this chapter. However, the artistic ideas which Caravaggio took over from the High Renaissance are only compositional and formal ones, and in spirit his art is extremely different from that of Michelangelo and Raphael—more so than is the art of Annibale. Still there is a definite revival of the formal aspects of classical art in the works of both Annibale and Caravaggio, the strongest protagonists of the anti-manneristic movement. Thus it is just as correct to consider their art as a continuation and expansion of the High Renaissance as it is to call it an early phase of the Baroque.

CHAPTER IV

SOME SPECIAL PROBLEMS CONCERNING CARAVAGGIO'S EARLIER ROMAN WORKS

JUVENILIA

PLATES 1-13

A<small>N ENGRAVING</small> by Ambrogio Brambilla, published in 1582, some years before Caravaggio came to Rome, consists of many tiny sketches illustrating the "Cries of Rome." It shows that not only snails (lumache a cento), figs, garlic (il bel aglio), crickets (ecco grilli da cantare), old iron and hundreds of other articles were sold by ambulant vendors on the streets of Rome, but also paintings on wood (i bei quadri in tavola) and paintings on canvas (i bei quadri in tela). Although we know from various sources that most of these were certainly devotional pictures fabricated en masse, it may be assumed that products of popular art like still-lifes, landscapes, and genre scenes, or illustrations of stories (le bell'istorie) were also available, to be purchased by anyone at a modest price.

It is entirely probable that some of Caravaggio's very early products were sold on the popular market, or were intended for it. We know from various sources that Giuseppe Cesari, the future Cavaliere d'Arpino, took the young Caravaggio into his house. Bellori elaborates upon this fact by saying that Cesari required the boy to earn his keep by painting flowers and fruits for him. By coincidence we happen to know that a group of paintings still in the Villa Borghese in Rome came in a rather curious way from Cavaliere d'Arpino into the Borghese collections. For one reason or another, probably for debts, the Papal treasury, at the beginning of the reign of Paul V, had confiscated part of the estate of the Cavaliere. With it went a collection of about a hundred objets d'art which the Pope presented in 1606 to his art-greedy nephew Scipione Borghese.[1] Apart from some small paintings by the Cavaliere himself, the collection consisted mainly of anonymous works of a particular character: landscapes with shepherds and ruins, still-lifes, or figures of boys or girls with baskets full of fruits or flowers. The popular subject matter of these paintings suggests the possibility that they represent a special class of art work which was produced in Arpino's studio in his early years. Being at the time almost exclusively a fresco painter, Cesari had very little use in his own work for the genre figures, fruits and flowers contained in his collection. It is therefore quite possible that he kept Caravaggio and other young artists to paint popular subjects for him which he could profitably sell.

Two paintings in the Villa Borghese, from this group originally belonging to Arpino, have been listed in several inventories and catalogues of the collection under the name of Caravaggio, and later scholars have generally accepted them as two early paintings made in his shop. One is the half-figure of a boy (ragazzo satiresco) crowned with ivy and holding a bunch of grapes in his right hand, with some fruit lying on a table before him; the other is the well-known boy with a rather saccharine expression holding a round basket filled with blue and yellow grapes and other fruits with their leaves. Whether these two paintings are early originals by Caravaggio (earlier, it has been said, than the Uffizi *Bacchus*), or joint productions in which he did only the still-lifes which seems quite possible, they are of special interest as examples of the type of painting which may have been made in Arpino's shop for the popular market.

To judge from these two paintings, it was the combination of genre figure and fruits and flowers which corresponded to the popular taste of the time, rather than arrangements of flowers and fruits alone. Some pure still-life was developing by the end of the sixteenth century, but neither in the Netherlands nor in Spain, and decidedly not in Italy, had it attained the full legitimacy as a separate branch of painting which it was to reach in the first half of the seventeenth century. However, van Mander tells us of a painter, Lodovyck van den Bos, working just after the middle of the sixteenth century, who painted flowers not only on the backs of portraits or other paintings, as we sometimes find in that period, but also painted isolated still-lifes of flowers in vases.[2] In the same way, and probably deriving from such Northern models, some painters specialized in flowers and fruits in Italy, even in Rome and even in the time of Caravaggio. Baglione mentions at least one, Mao (Tommaso) Salini, as the "first to arrange and paint flowers with their leaves in vases." His flower compositions were not simply objective, but contained "various whimsical and odd devices" (con diverse invenzioni molto capricciose e bizzarre). Whether Mao's inventiveness, which Baglione praises so much, was limited to the arrangement of flowers alone, or whether he combined still-life with a figure, as in the half-figure paintings of the d'Arpino collection, we cannot know. Such work was certainly sold anonymously, with or without the intervention of a commission, among the "bei quadri in tela."

Whether Caravaggio painted isolated fruit and flower pieces in his youth is equally debatable. It is true that Bellori, speaking of Caravaggio's activity in the service of Giuseppe d'Arpino, seems to think of still-lifes in the modern sense, without figures, for he conjectures that one reason why Caravaggio left Cesari after some months was that he was not allowed to paint figures. On the other hand, the only example given by Bellori to illustrate this special kind of Caravaggio's work is a carafe of flowers reflecting the light from a window. However, this exquisitely painted still-life is not an independent painting, but stands, as Baglione had previously described it, on the table in Caravaggio's *Lute Player* (in the Hermitage), contributing its special charm to one of the most delightful of his early half-figure paintings. Except for the *Basket of Fruit* in the Ambrosiana, which is now generally agreed not to be a very early work, no authentic isolated still-lifes by Caravaggio are preserved. This does not exclude the possibility that they once existed, only to disappear among the anonymous products for the popular market. We do know of early works which have vanished, such as the small devotional pictures painted or copied by the boy for Pandolfo Pucci, the beneficiato of St. Peter's, or for the prior of the Ospedale della Consolazione.

Bellori commented that it was only through Caravaggio's superior craftsmanship that the painting of flowers and fruits attained the high degree of beauty so fully appreciated in Bellori's own time. But what really accounts for the fame and influence of Caravaggio's early works, even more than the novel and refined treatment of still-life, was the entire rendering of the early half-figure compositions and the conception of individual character contained in them. These early paintings, with or without their gay accompaniment of flower vases and fruit-laden baskets, are so imbued with witty invention and technical excellence that they rapidly outgrew the level of popular art and attracted the attention of connoisseurs, even finding entrance in some instances into the palaces of the "gran signori."

This recognition of genre art as an independent and respectable branch of painting signifies an evolution of taste within Caravaggio's generation which affected even Rome, the domain of the traditional painting in the grand manner. The popular market, by giving painters a chance to exhibit in the open the products which they hoped to sell to the bourgeoisie, may partially have prepared the ground for a growing appreciation of works in the petite manière. But it was largely due to the invasion of Rome by Northern artists who, though on the whole of second-rate quality, brought with them their native taste for textural finesses, physiognomical studies and landscapes. The prolific Flemish painter Paul Bril, for example, helped pave the way for the rise of landscape painting which later culminated in Claude's lyrical works and Poussin's grandiose views of the Roman Campagna. The Northerners, predominantly Flemish, also transmitted to Rome their innate fondness for the popular scenes which had long been the fashion in their own country. Some paintings of this kind had already found access to Italian collections—tavern scenes often disguised as the "Prodigal Son," card players, money changers, kitchen and market figures—by such artists as Lucas van Leyden, Quentin Massys, Marinus van Roymerswaele, Jan van Hemessen, Pieter Aertsen and Joachim Beukelaer.

Seen against these special currents in late sixteenth-century art in Rome, the genre character of Caravaggio's early works is less extraordinary than it appears at first glance. Furthermore, it had long been the custom in Central Italy to turn to subalpine territory for artists skilled in handicrafts which were less highly developed at home. Thus Rome welcomed many artists whose work contained transalpine affiliation and who filled the demand not only for crafts, especially masonry and decorative sculpture, but also for the painting of ornament and genre. The young Caravaggio, coming from this subalpine region to Rome, arrived with his trade in hand, so to speak, and could make his living more advantageously by work of this kind, which was either indigenous or familiar to his own province, than by joining the great masses of fresco painters. He did not practice this métier for long; evidently as soon as he felt free to do so, he turned to the great figure compositions of religious import which became his real vocation.

The juvenile paintings of secular subjects are relatively few, to judge from the lists in the sources. However, without positive knowledge to the contrary, one is justified in assuming that originally there were more. Although a few reached great art collections and have thus been preserved for us, others may well have been sold inconspicuously and have had less chance of survival. The biographers mention the following single half-figures: a *Bacchus*, a *Lute Player*, a *Boy Peeling a Pear*, and a *Boy Bitten by a Lizard*. In addition to these are mentioned the following compositions containing two or more half-figures: the *Cardsharps*, the *Fortune Teller*, and a *Musica* of several youths. Bellori characterizes the whole group as "Sweet, smooth, and without those shadows he later used" (dolci, schietti, e senza quelle ombre ch'egli usò poi). This description corresponds very well to the visual appearance of the *Fortune Teller*, in the

Louvre, the *Cardsharps*, formerly in the Sciarra Collection, and the *Concert of Youths*, in the Metropolitan Museum.

The artistic public of Rome toward the end of the sixteenth century had not yet become accustomed to the half-figure composition with secular subject matter, and was therefore attracted by its novelty. However, it was by no means an invention of the young Caravaggio. Almost from the beginning of the century Flemish painters had used the limited frame of the half-figure painting to display as closely and shockingly as possible the facial expressions and significant gestures of their low-class figure types, mostly two or three figures of money changers, drunkards, lecherous old men and whores. The young Caravaggio had certainly seen half-figure compositions similar to the *Ill-Assorted Lovers* by Quentin Massys, and Jan van Hemessen's *Loose Company* during his youth in Lombardy, or in central Italian collections; he may actually have seen the *Money Changer and His Wife* by Marinus van Roymerswaele in Florence. However, Caravaggio, in his *Cardsharps* and *Fortune Teller*, shows not the slightest didactic or moralizing tendency; nothing of the satirical and defiant mood of the Northern artists can be found in these works. They are tempered by his Italianism, not only in style, but also in a certain humanism.

Yet the works by Caravaggio have their own flavor and character. Even such an Italian half-figure painting as the *Two Lovers* by Paris Bordone is still in the Venetian tradition of the pictures in which each figure relaxes in its own existence: each only loosely connected with the other by a kind of lyrical harmony, by the melody of the color and by extremely reserved gestures indicating the intimacy of their relationships. On the other hand, the Northern paintings, where everything is loud, imposing and unequivocally coarse, contain nothing which implies a real story of narrative sequence. We see a man behind a table counting his money, while his wife, rather bored, looks into an illuminated book, or a young woman caressing an old fool with one hand, while with the other she gives the purse she has stolen from him to the procurer hidden in the background. All these are characterizations, almost caricatures of well-known types, not casual players in an unfolding story with whom we can sympathize.

Bellori borrows an anecdote, which Pliny had used in connection with Lysippus, and applies it to Caravaggio: the young Caravaggio, rebuked for not studying classical statues by Glykon, Phidias, and such old masters, pointed to the people in the street and boastfully exclaimed, "Nature gave me these as teachers." To prove it, he picked out a gypsy girl, took her home, and made a painting of her. But this study "after nature" resulted in a composed and refined illustration of a story, not in a realistic portrait. A quite special atmosphere of trickery and eroticism is created by the two figures in Caravaggio's painting—the sly pretty fortune teller, and the naive young dandy, who seems a little embarrassed by the girl's approach. There is little indication of this inner movement in the action, but enough to enable the amused spectator to guess at the romance just beginning.

In another incident, which in a novel would be an episode similar to the *Fortune Teller*, we meet the same seemingly very innocent young nobleman, deeply involved in a game of cards. It is not the amiable society game depicted in the frescoes of the Palazzo Borromeo in Milan or in those by Niccolò dell'Abbate in the Palazzo Poggi in Bologna, but a game arranged by rather disreputable characters, obviously planning foul play. Their unwary victim, soberly and expensively clad, probably on his first escapade away from home, is cheated in a well-known manner: the situation represented before us has reached the moment of highest tension, when the decisive card which the youth is about to play is revealed to his opponent by a sign from his partner. Of the two cardsharps, the one giving the signal, bearded and in a light green jacket with black-and-yellow-striped sleeves, looks very much like the professional ruffian; the

FIG. 51
Massys, *Ill-Assorted Lovers*. Paris, Collection Pourtalès.

FIG. 52
n Hemessen, *Loose Company*. Karlsruhe, Gemaeldegalerie.

FIG. 53
Van Roymerswaele, *Money Changer and His Wife*.
Florence, Bargello.

other, only slightly older than his dupe, with a long pink feather hanging from his hat, has more the appearance of an occasional adventurer.

The Northern examples of cheating figures correspond in many ways to the typological satires of Erasmus in his *Praise of Folly*, or to similar Northern literature. The mood of the scenes represented by Caravaggio, wherein the elegant and frail youth is cheated by professional cardsharps or by a sweet young gypsy, has likewise a literary parallel: in the *Novelas Ejemplares* of Cervantes we find similarly insignificant events in the lives of adventurous young cavaliers, who have run away from home and made friends with gypsies, treated in this same gentle and romantic manner, smilingly and ironically. In this sense Caravaggio's *Fortune Teller* and *The Cardsharps* are "novelistic." They are not literal "imitations of nature" but are scenes which he might have visualized in his imagination, after reading a story.

Out of studies and observations of his own features—laughing, terrified, grimacing—and of his torso, which he apparently saw in three-quarter length in his mirror, Caravaggio invented his imaginary portraits of the smooth and unctuous Bacchus, of the frightened effeminate boy bitten by a lizard, of the calm androgynous lute-player, the curiously nostalgic and erotic boys of the *Musica* and the most pathetic *Medusa* with her wreath of snakes. Even in his mature period, the odd so-called *St. John* and the triumphant and impudent *Amor* continue this series, which is full of personal allusions and ambiguous problems.

There is nothing exactly like these witty and passionate single figures by Caravaggio, even in Northern countries. To account for the tendency in these works to relay complex reactions by an expressive play of physiognomy, one can only refer to Leonardo's physiognomical studies. That interest in psychophysiological relationships was still alive in the Milan of the sixteenth century is indicated by the attention given to this subject by the great scientist Gerolamo Cardano, whose father was a friend of Leonardo. Through Lomazzo, who quotes Leonardo profusely in his *Trattato*, the young apprentice of his friend Peterzano could very well have been influenced and interested in physiognomical studies.

Bacchus and *Boy Bitten by a Lizard* PLATES 7, 9

The first of these mirror-images, a Bacchus, was for a long time identified as the one in the Uffizi. Here too North Italian reminiscences underlie the thematic conception. On his way to Rome Caravaggio might have had the opportunity of visiting the Castle of Ferrara, where he could have seen a curious painting by Dosso Dossi (now in the Modena Gallery) belonging to a series representing the five senses. It shows the bust of a man, his head wreathed with vines, holding a glass of wine and staring out at the spectator. It is conceivable that this dignified yet comical-looking gentleman, dressed as a God of Wine, left an impression on the adolescent; perhaps the direct gaze and appurtenances of still-life in the *Bacchus*, echo something of Dosso's drinker. But Caravaggio's figure is a very different person; he is no longer homely, and the conception is refined and lyrical. Instead of Dosso's bust-length figure, he chose the more elegant and elongated form of a half-figure, a form which is mainly used in the sixteenth century for portraiture and decorative painting, such as Niccolò dell'Abbate's series of *Musicians* in three-quarter length, now in Modena. But the direct record of natural appearance produced by

Caravaggio's mirror-image is in marked contrast to such purely decorative works. The general Giorgionesque influences which play a part in much of Caravaggio's youthful painting are also to be found in this picture.

Despite Bellori's indignant reproach of Caravaggio for his antagonism toward antique art, this painting shows a definite acquaintance with classical sculpture. The intention was obviously to compose in a classical spirit: *Bacchus* leans in a leisurely attitude against his couch, which is padded with a cushion and covered with a white cloak, as if on a triclinium; his full shirt is

FIG. 54
Dosso Dossi, *Bacchus*. Modena, Gallery.

pushed off the left shoulder in toga fashion, "all'antica." His regular, fleshy features bring to mind the sensuous idealism of certain Hadrianic representations of Antinous or Bacchus, or a combination of both types.

The *Bacchus* is an early work, perhaps one of the earliest, to judge by the rather awkward, still untutored handling of the torso. When it first emerged from the store room of the Uffizi in 1925, in rather bad condition, the public was startled by its fusion, both ingenious and ingenuous, of refinements of texture and color with a curious spiritual wantonness. Michelangelo Buonarroti, in contrast to antique prototypes and to the slightly later interpretation by Sansovino, characterized his Bacchus by the facial expression of a sloven, stupid with drunkenness. The features of Caravaggio's Bacchus, on the other hand, are personalized despite their almost classical regularity, and are overlaid only with a sullen superciliousness.

The most outstanding instance of physiognomical research occurs in the *Boy Bitten by a Lizard*, which is so progressive in its presentation of facial and bodily contortions, and so accentuated in its chiaroscuro, that it should be dated considerably later than the smooth and shadowless *Bacchus*. The extraordinary energy of transitory movement displayed by Caravaggio in the contraposto and the facial expression of the frightened boy is almost unparalleled in any

FIG. 55
Niccolò dell'Abbate, *Musician*. Modena, Gallery.

previous painting. El Greco's *Boy Blowing on a Coal* is quietly retained within its own plane, as is characteristic of the Venetians, especially the Bassanesque school, and lacks Caravaggio's explosive force. Sophonisba Anguisciola's much-coveted drawing of a girl holding a crying child who has been pinched by a crab (FIG. 42) is, compared to Caravaggio's picture, like an illustration from a children's book—intimate, anecdotal, and with a playfulness similar to the eighteenth-century sentiment of Greuze. Next to this gentle comedy, Caravaggio's version appears infinitely ambitious; it shares none of that mild humor, but records a set of violent reactions caused by the startling discovery of a lizard hidden among the fruits, which has fastened upon the boy's finger. Although the situation cannot be called humorous it is certainly ludicrous, even ambiguous, revealing a handsome youth, a rose behind one ear, squeamishly repelled by so harmless an animal as a lizard! But petty as this situation is in reality, it takes on an over-whelming force through its intensification by the closely restrictive frame of the bodily and spiritual commotion; it is a piece of trickery suggestive of the close-up device in moving pictures, which succeeds in turning an absurd drama into something convincingly shocking.

A third single half-figure, mentioned only by Mancini, is the *Boy Peeling a Pear* (un putto che mondava una pera con il coltello). We no longer have an original, but as far as we can judge from the copies the attitude of the boy is neither emotional nor expressive. It is rather atypical for Caravaggio, and closer to Venetian masters, as we have observed in comparing this picture to the drawing of a Negro eating a pear.

Head of the Medusa

PLATE 14

Physiognomic expression is also strongly emphasized in Caravaggio's singularly interesting head of the *Medusa* in the Uffizi, painted on a roundel of wood (sopra una rotella rapportata). Behind the distorted features one can still perceive the family resemblance of this snake-haired demon to the face of the Bacchus, for here too Caravaggio has transformed the reflection of his own face in a mirror into a fantastic image in mythological guise. This is not, therefore, the comely Medusa with classical features found in late antique monuments and the later Renais-sance (cf. Cellini's *Perseus*), whose one deformity is her hair changed into snakes by the vengeful Minerva. Caravaggio's *Medusa* is based on the ugly grimacing type of earlier antique and Etruscan exemplars, supplanted in the Middle Ages by the hideous face of the Arabic demon Al Gol. His sense of experimentation in the expression of physiognomy, already spectacu-larly manifested in the *Boy Bitten by a Lizard*, is here climaxed by convulsive muscular action making the eyes bulge, furrowing the bridge of the nose, and opening the mouth in a scream. Leonardo as a youth had painted a Medusa head with a headdress of knotted serpents, called "the most queer and extravagant invention" by Vasari.[3] But he had also made on a round panel of wood, like Caravaggio's, an object which was so horrifying to look upon, according to Vasari, being composed of lizards, snakes, bats, etc., collected by Leonardo in his studio, that it reminded one of a Medusa. This "Animalaccio" was allegedly sold to the Duke of Milan by Leonardo's father.

Milan also claimed the famous armorer Piccinino, one of whose masterpieces was a round parade shield centered by a gorgon, presented in 1552 to Charles V. Caravaggio might easily have seen a similar piece, or even a model or copy of it, since Piccinino's shop was still in operation while he was serving as Peterzano's apprentice in Milan.

Representations of the Medusa-head on oblong or, in a more antique manner, round shields were not uncommon in the fifteenth and sixteenth centuries. In all the examples the head of the Medusa plays its classical role as a direct "apotropaion" whose petrifying effect will intimidate and repel the enemy. In a symbolic-philosophic sense, the enemies of man are within himself, and Ripa, in his *Iconologia,*[4] therefore defines the head of the Medusa as a symbol of the victory of reason over the senses, the natural foes of "virtu," which like physical enemies are petrified when faced with the Medusa. Thus *Philosophia*, as we see in a small engraving from a series ascribed to Mantegna, can be represented as Minerva holding a shield with the head of the Medusa as a weapon of wisdom intimidating the senses.[5]

Perhaps it was this sophisticated allegorical explanation of the Medusa which tempted Cardinal del Monte, Caravaggio's first Maecenas, to acquire the rotella. Yet when the Cardinal

FIG. 56
Philosophia (engraving ascribed to
Mantegna).

gave it in 1608 as a wedding present to Cosimo, the future Grand Duke of Tuscany, he may have presented it either in this edifying spirit, or merely as one of the currently fashionable parade shields which were often painted or repainted by fairly reputable artists. Years later Cavaliere Marino, in his small book *Galeria Distinta,*[6] dedicated a short poem to Caravaggio's "Head of the Medusa in the Palace Gallery of the Grand Duke of Tuscany," in which the shield is praised solely as an apotropaion having the power to change the Duke's enemies into "cold marble" at the sight of the "proud and cruel Gorgon, to whose brow, most horribly, numberless vipers lend a terrible and squalid pomp" (Quel fier Gorgone, e crudo, / Cui fanno horribilmente / Volumi viperini / Squallida pompa, e spaventosa ai crini?). At the end of the poem, evidently unaware of Ripa's allegorical interpretation, Marino reaches the edifying and at the same time flattering conclusion, so typical of him, that the real Medusa, the true protector of the Duke, is his own valor (la vera Medusa è il valor vostro).

One may wonder how the conception of the painting came about in the first place. We have seen that Caravaggio as an adolescent entertained himself by drawing his contorted face from a mirror. This time, by embellishing his study with a headdress of snakes, he turned it into a fanciful rendering of a Medusa. Cardinal del Monte was undoubtedly impressed by its exceptional combination of objective realism and passionate expression. Not since Leonardo had an artist been able to render so strongly the spurting blood and the metallic luster of the greenish patterned snakes, and at the same time to capture the horror in the face of the decapitated Gorgon. Perhaps, remembering Vasari's description of Leonardo's monstrous contraption in a round frame, the Cardinal had transferred it (Baglione uses the word "rapportata") to a sixteenth-century convex tournament shield, probably already in his possession, as an emblem of spiritual and bodily strength.

The obvious exploitation of the physiognomy in the work itself, in addition to the facial characteristics of the thin dark brows and short stubby nose, relate the Medusa head to the earlier phases of Caravaggio's production. Yet its vigorous plasticity and forceful realism place it after the *Boy Bitten by a Lizard*, closer to the Giustiniani *Amor*, the Michelangelesque *St. John with a Ram*, and not too far from the *First St. Matthew*. The facial type of the earlier works, although differing in mode and complexity of expression, is basically always the same because it is Caravaggio himself who masquerades behind the changing images.

TWO CASES OF PERSIFLAGE DIRECTED AT MICHELANGELO

Saint John the Baptist
PLATES 25, 26

The spirit of mischievousness running through the early works occurs again in two paintings of Caravaggio's mature period. In both cases the parody is at the expense of the greatest genius of the sixteenth century, Michelangelo Buonarroti. By the end of the century, the impact of his monumental works had considerably diminished. However, every young artist coming to Rome must still have found the art of the great master an object of tremendous awe, though not necessarily of love. Caravaggio, evidently possessed of a curious but understandable desire to display his spiritual independence of the "terrible," vented his feelings in travesties of two of the master's great works: the ignudo above the *Erythraean Sibyl* on the Sistine Ceiling, and the sculptured *Victory* in the Palazzo Vecchio.

The first of these is a painting in the Doria Gallery generally called *St. John the Baptist*. Apart from deliberate changes dictated by his new conception of space and light, Caravaggio took the general posture from Michelangelo's ignudo. But he replaces the head of this awesome and passive figure with a head recalling in its smiling boyishness the previous images of himself, his constant protagonist. Is this painting really a Saint John? The young boy, confidently smiling, turns his broad face toward the spectator over his outstretched arm, affectionately embracing a large, gentle-eyed ram. I know no previous Saint John whose companion is a crumple-horned sheep rather than an innocent white lamb, the Agnus Dei. Actually the ram is no more the invention of Caravaggio than is the posture of the naked boy; it too comes from the Sistine Ceiling. We find, in close proximity to the ignudo near the *Erythraea,* the scene of *Noah's Sacrifice,* where in the lower left corner a nude man holds a ram

FIG. 57
Michelangelo, *Sacrifice of Noah* (detail).
Rome, Sistine Chapel.

FIG. 58
Michelangelo, *Ignudo.* Rome, Sistine Chapel.

FIG. 59
Leonardo (?), *St. John.* Pa
Louvre.

which is awaiting slaughter. Combining the ignudo with the sacrificial ram, Caravaggio arrived at a very unconventional composition.

At the start he perhaps had no other intention than to render the Michelangelesque figure as a youth seated on a rock with his pet animal, a kind of genre figure conceived in a vein similar to his *Boy Bitten by a Lizard.* Indeed, when in the 1620's Gaspare Celio saw the painting, together with other works by Caravaggio, in the Palazzo of Ciriaco Mattei, he saw the naked youth as a shepherd, identifying him in his *Memoria* as a "pastor friso." Frisus, or Phryxus, is a legendary figure, who, with his sister Helle, escapes a sacrificial death in Boeotia by flying to

Colchis on the back of a miraculous ram with a golden fleece, which he later sacrifices on the altar of Zeus or Mars. Since Frisus is invariably mentioned as a prince, not a shepherd, this learned interpretation of the painting by Celio is probably based on a rather vague association, evoked by the combination of the ram with the naked boy. But it shows that at that early time the painting was not always considered a Saint John.

On the other hand, the seated youth could very well be passed off as a young Saint John in the Desert, even though he lacks any other telling attributes, such as the cross, book or banderole. The isolated plant in the lower right corner, with its broad, hard green leaves, could conceivably have been designed as a desert plant; the small bird in the upper left corner, which is somewhat difficult to distinguish, may be a dove, although this holy apparition is usually associated with a later episode in the Saint's life, the Baptism of Christ. Certainly the ram, so tenderly and protectively embraced by the boy, has a sacrificial connotation, although it is difficult to see in it a symbol of the sacrifice of Christ, replacing the Agnus Dei. It is true that none of these features, taken singly or together, could change a worldly nude shepherd boy into a holy young Saint in solitude. Yet the fact that in Basel and in the Villa Borghese, we have several examples of similar Giovannini from the immediate circle of Caravaggio, indicates that the interpretation of the naked boy with a ram as St. John in the Desert must have existed in Caravaggio's own time, probably with his approval. Baglione, who was certainly well informed about Caravaggio's works, unreservedly calls the Mattei painting a "San Giovanni Battista," and by the middle of the seventeenth century the composition of the Doria painting and its replicas were labeled *Saint John the Baptist* without question.

Caravaggio, moreover, was not the first or only artist to render an alleged Saint with such ambiguity. As in the case of the *Medusa*, Caravaggio could again have found a precedent in Leonardo. The famous Leonardesque *St. John* in the Louvre shows a naked youth seated in a landscape, and the ambiguity which this figure must have displayed from the beginning probably explains why, shortly after it came to Fontainebleau, it was overpainted to represent a Bacchus. A similar situation persists in the Doria painting; one is startled by a most curious mixture of sculptural stylization, mocking Michelangelo, and the boy's extremely sensuous expression and gesture, which conveys a sharp and testy spirit of persiflage and equivocal mockery.

Amor Victorious

PLATE 32

Caravaggio's second playful adaptation of a work by Michelangelo is his *Victorious Amor* in Berlin. By reducing the *Victory*, Michelangelo's most manneristic and elongated figure, to stocky boyish proportions, the *Amor* must have appeared as an outrage bordering on sacrilege to those still adhering to Michelangelesque canons. The posture of his lower limbs, one leg extended and the other bent back at almost a right angle to the body, clearly imitates Michelangelo's figure; the only difference is that the *Victory* crushes between his legs the pathetic head of a bearded old man, like Mithras killing the bull, while Cupid's left leg rests casually on the table which is covered with white drapery. Above the waist, however, nothing remains to recall Michelangelo. The sturdy torso and insolent, lively expression, totally alien to the athletic beauty of Michelangelo's figure with its spiraling torsion and empty face, might have been drawn from a street urchin. Like the *St. John in the Desert*, this brazen boy is still related in spirit to the early transmutations of Caravaggio's self, now wittily exalted beyond those youthful disguises to the position of a demon who laughingly dominates the whole world: *omnia vincit amor*. Never before was the reputed mischievousness of Cupid so pointedly stressed. The whole attitude of Caravaggio's figure lends an air of uncompromising travesty to the Platonic implications of Michelangelo's tragic masterpiece, and in fact to the whole Renaissance ideal of love. In keeping with the jest, the heavy dark eagle- or vulture-wings, which contrast markedly with white swan-wings (like those of the angel in the first *St. Matthew*) seem rather loosely attached to the boy's back as if they did not belong to him, although the boy obviously takes wholeheartedly to his role of Cupid. As a sign of his office he triumphantly raises two arrows in his right hand, one tipped with a red point and the other with black, indicating, perhaps, the two wounds of love accepted and love rejected.

Caravaggio's half-stylized and half-naturalistic, partly satirical and partly serious "Earthly Love" was counterbalanced in the collection of Vincenzo Giustiniani, by an earnest and rather prudish painting of *Divine Love* by Giovanni Baglione, dedicated to Cardinal Giustiniani, Vincenzo's brother. In this diligent work the *Divine Love* is shown with a sword raised in one hand, taking menacing steps over the fallen and naked body of the young Earthly Love and a satyr representing worldly lust. Furthermore, this challenging Amor is vested like a Saint Michael in shining armor from neck to toe, which seems to have provoked criticism from some of Baglione's contemporaries. Orazio Gentileschi, in speaking of this painting, remarks reprovingly that an Amor should, properly speaking, be a "putto e nudo"'; Baglione evidently found it necessary to take heed of this comment, for he made a second version in which the Amor retains the same very Zuccaresque pose, but wears less clothing. The bold nudity of Caravaggio's boy seems like an open retort to the overstressed propriety of Baglione's first version, and it may even be intentional that the lower right corner of Caravaggio's *Amor* is so conspicuously filled with plates of cast-off armor. On the whole the confidence of Caravaggio's boy is so overwhelming as to put on the defensive any bearer of divine heraldry, especially the weak and uninspired *Divine Love* of Baglione.

Earthly Love now triumphs over symbols of the moral and intellectual world. At his feet, unobserved and despised, are objects alluding to everything associated with the highest human values from the time of Plato's *Republic*: science and art, literary fame and martial glory. Geometry and music, two of the seven liberal arts often closely associated, portentously fill the greater part of the left side; the usual tokens of geometry, the compass and triangle, are in the foreground with their sharp points directed at the spectator, while music is prominently represented by two magnificent stringed instruments, the recently invented Cremonese violin with the bow slung over the finger board, and the more conventional lute with its pegbox sharply bent back. A part-book, showing four systems each of five staves is spread out beneath the instruments. Portions of a blue globe with gold stars are visible behind the right leg of Cupid. Altogether these features constitute three parts of the scholastic formula of the quadrivium:

music, geometry ånd astronomy. Only arithmetic appears to be missing, unless possibly it is present in the prominently displayed lute with its pegs suggesting the graduations of tones. The objects on the right, however, do not complete the scholastic classification with representations of the trivium. Rather, the symbolism is loftier and more meaningful. Oddly correlative with the numerous paintings of *Vanitas* of this period, where death in the form of a skull mocks at the empty pleasures of vanity, the "puer lascivus" here smilingly annihilates the

FIG. 60

Michelangelo, *Victory*. Florence,
Palazzo Vecchio.

FIG. 61

Baglione, *Divine Love*. Berlin, Kaiser
Friedrich Museum.

creations of the ambitious, triumphing over the branch of laurel with its red berries and evergreen leaves, the usual symbol of immortal fame. A big volume, negligently tossed aside, lies behind Cupid's left leg, perhaps the magnum opus of some great master, its open pages revealing lines scribbled with the long white quill. Equally belittled is military glory, defamed and discredited by the useless cuirass and empty pieces of armor. As the final humiliation, the crown and sceptre are almost hidden among the folds of white drapery on the table.

The automorphic images reflecting different aspects of Caravaggio's own self, spiritually as well as bodily, which started during his high-spirited adolescence, reach a climax in the *Victorious Amor*. Here he reverts for the last time to the characteristics of his youth, simultaneously replacing the early Giorgionesque lyricism with a more mature and subtle power. The Giustiniani painting was made about three years before his final departure from Rome;

with the aid of the corroborative evidence brought out in Caravaggio's trial in 1603, and on the basis of stylistic comparison we can establish the date of the painting within this year.

The conceit of the *Victorious Amor* could very well have been worked out by Caravaggio himself, but the detailed symbolism was probably invented by the learned circle of the Giustiniani. In any event we may be sure that it was not merely the lowbrow delight on the face of the boy god, which was new and daring and modern for the period, but also the degradation of those values symbolized by the special choice of objects. No one before Caravaggio had been able to depict the devil in the flesh or carnal love so freely and naturally as a matter of triumph and joy. Such a liberal outlook could only have been accepted by a progressive circle, one of realistic, rather sophisticated, urbane taste, which no longer found it necessary to repudiate the potential power of the senses over the spirit. It is not surprising, therefore, that Vincenzo Giustiniani, the collector and connoisseur with the most advanced tastes of his time, regarded the *Amor* with such deep affection and amusement that, as Sandrart relates, he covered it with a green curtain, in order to make grand finale on visits to his collection. However, more conservative onlookers were doubtless shocked by its audacity, and it may also be that Giustiniani employed the green curtain to avoid offending the less broadminded of his friends.

TWO RELIGIOUS FIGURES RELATED TO THE GENRE-PAINTINGS

Magdalene

PLATE 15

In the Olympian altitudes of Tuscan and Roman art it was considered quite improper to demote dignified saints and venerable apostles by depicting them in such a way that without their attributes one would take them for ordinary people. It is not surprising that the average conservative was shocked by the young painter who dared to represent Saint Mary Magdalene as a plump girl in her teens, completely indistinguishable from anybody else, except for her jewels, her fancy dress and her ointment jar. Equally disturbing to these people, as we will see, must have been the reputation Caravaggio earned a few years later by representing the usually very formal Saint Matthew as a kind, poor, and illiterate elderly man with a Socrates head, his coarse legs crossed and exposed to the spectator. But among the younger generation quite a few were delighted by the audacity and charm of this precocious gamin, whose pugnacious wit had already revealed itself in the early paintings of secular subjects. Caravaggio's lowering of saints from their pedestals, with a slight vulgarity, was not displeasing, even to certain members of the clergy and their adherents who had heard coarse and jocular expressions in the conversation and religious lectures of San Filippo Neri.

Here too Caravaggio is an iconographical pioneer only if one's point of view is limited to Roman art. In the North and in Caravaggio's homeland of Lombardy it was quite customary to give religious figures an ordinary, bourgeois appearance. Savoldo's *Magdalene* (London and elsewhere), for instance, is identified as a saint only by the dimunitive ointment jar in the lower left corner; otherwise she might be a romantically veiled beauty whom one could have seen in the streets of Venice. In Flemish art the Magdalene is frequently represented as a young matron or as a young nun in a simple, almost portrait-like manner. Caravaggio's *Magdalene* in the Doria is comparable to the seated *Magdalene* in the National Gallery in London, attributed to Roger van der Weyden. Although the latter is only a fragment and its background completely overpainted, it certainly suggests the possibility that Caravaggio could have seen a composition in an Italian collection which repeated the general form of this work. From such an example Caravaggio may have received his idea of representing the Magdalene like a sitter for a photograph, in a half-formal pose, silhouetted against a neutral background. But, granted the remarkable similarities of form, the psychological impact is utterly different. The young woman in the

FIG. 62
van der Weyden, *Magdalene*. London, National Gallery.

FIG. 63
Savoldo, *Magdalene*. London, National Gallery.

FIG. 64
Correggio, *Deposition* (detail, Magdalene). Parma, Gallery.

Flemish painting might be a beguine of patrician family; her clear-cut features are serene and gentle as she meditatively and patiently studies her illuminated missal. Caravaggio's *Magdalene* sits forlorn in dreamy repentance. The somnolent and sluggish posture of her body expresses her humble submission. Her plump young figure seems unsuitably garbed in the over-lavish dress with its rich damask pattern; the precious gems which had formerly adorned her peculiarly innocent-looking figure are scattered over the floor as if thrown down in disgust. It is the moment right after her conversion, and the consuming effect of this experience is shown by her exhaustion and by the painful frown which disturbs her brow. This display of physical humility as the result of religious emotion creates a new type of Magdalene, which not only diverges from the prim spirit of Northern prototypes, but also from such openly demonstrative and excited Magdalene figures as that by Titian in the Pitti.

The special flavor of Caravaggio's *Magdalene* in the Doria originates from the same inquisitive interest in character that sometimes manifests itself in the juvenilia. Still in the vein of the early works, the *Magdalene* because of her vulnerability is the most touching among them. It was just the emphasis on simplicity of feeling and attitude which was misunderstood by the critics and literati of the seventeenth century. Bellori in describing this work expresses his disapproval of letting a girl who is obviously doing nothing but sitting and waiting for her hair to dry (in atto di asciugarsi li cappelli) stand for Saint Mary Magdalene simply by virtue of an oil flask and jewels. Scanelli in his *Microcosmo della pittura*[8] is sharper in his criticism: he confronts Caravaggio's *Magdalene* with the Magdalene in Correggio's *Pietà* in Parma, declaring that, compared with the natural and sorrowful spirit of Correggio's figure, the naturalism of Caravaggio is superficial, that his *Magdalene* is without grace and completely lifeless (in ogni parte morta). Scanelli ignores the fact that the situations of the two figures are not in the least comparable. Correggio's Magdalene participates in the action of mourning over the dead body of Christ and shows her grief and desperation in her face and gesture. Caravaggio does allow for a strong physical sign of emotion in a similar scene of bereavement in his *Deposition* in the Vatican, where one of the grieving women at the top of the composition, probably the Magdalene, raises her arms in the traditional gesture of lamentation. The Doria *Magdalene*, on the other hand, is isolated, motionless, and outwardly unaffected. But she is far from being "morta."

First St. Matthew

PLATE 28

The undeniably coarse conception of the Saint in Caravaggio's first version of *St. Matthew and the Angel* for San Luigi dei Francesi evoked the displeasure of the purists and conventionalists in Rome even more than the *Magdalene*. Only there or in Florence would the reaction of shock and distaste have been so marked that, as Baglione said, "nobody liked" the painting. Caravaggio's homeland did not so obsequiously conform to the proud standards of Central Italian conventions. We find relatively early examples from Lombardy of Saint Matthew represented as a low-class "type" looking as if he were a cobbler or a blacksmith. Datable about 1521 is a very characteristic Lombard *St. Matthew and the Angel* in San Giovanni Evangelista in Brescia, by Romanino (FIG. 67); here St. Matthew sits very close to the threshold of the frame, his legs crossed and his bare feet protruding. With a sense of ponderousness he writes in the book which he holds in his lap. Assisting him by holding a candle is a small wingless angel (at least, the wings do not show) looking like a young choirboy, dressed in a violet-colored gown with a lace collar. The light from the burning candle casts a glow which intimately encircles the two figures, making the spectator feel their strong kinship in the task. Dependent on this is the monumental and more spectacular work in the Metropolitan Museum by Savoldo, already mentioned (FIG. 29) as probably being one of his works for the Mint in Milan. Savoldo's *Matthew* is really one step up the social ladder from Romanino's. But his shiny and subtle elegance is induced more by the splendor of Savoldo's fulminating color and light than by his social characterization. If we look beneath the glossy surface we see that this Matthew is also a rough man, with his heavy black beard and low forehead not very different from northern types, as in paintings by van Hemessen. A third example from the end of the century by Vincenzo Campi shows a similar conception; it is, however, rather conventional and antiquarian in setting, and awkward in composition.

Caravaggio's *St. Matthew* is, on the whole, closest to Romanino's, but is considerably more secularized. In this regard it is also significant that the undignified motif of the crossed legs in Caravaggio's figure finds its closest precedent in the Venetian area, for example in a drawing in the Uffizi, no. 1772, attributed to Domenico Campagnola. This shows a bearded old man seated, with his bare legs crossed and protruding toward the spectator in a position remarkably similar to Caravaggio's saint. But it is quite possible that he had seen in Milan the interesting series of sketches by Ambrogio Figino (preserved in his sketchbook at Windsor), the same artist whose figure composition Caravaggio directly imitated in the *Madonna del Serpe* (see Catalogue Raisonné). The sketches of Figino are obviously inspired by the prophets and sibyls of the Sistine Ceiling. Of these forty-odd studies for a Saint Matthew, several have a great similarity to Caravaggio's composition, both in the spatial relationships of the two figures and in the pose of the saint, often with crossed legs. They could very well have been in Caravaggio's memory when in Rome he began to work on his own *First Matthew*, and in part they also prepared him for seeing the Sistine Ceiling. But the Michelangelesque attitude in Figino's drawing was changed significantly and given warmth when the young Caravaggio saw Raphael's charming and sensuous spandrel fresco in the Farnesina, the group of *Jupiter Kissing Cupid*, which undoubtedly impressed him by the closeness of the young body to the vigorous man.

The democratization of saints like Matthew on the part of Lombard artists probably was rooted in a general religious disposition to return to the supposed simplicity of the early Christian apostles. Ranke[9] refers to Protestant and related tendencies which would have favoured such popular feelings, flourishing in Lombardy near the Swiss border at the time of the Reformation; the famous inquisitor Ghislieri (later Pius V) was sent to Bergamo and other towns of this region, and had the greatest difficulty in extirpating them. Caravaggio, reared among these local currents and perhaps not untouched by them, introduced this popularized conception of St. Matthew as a simple scribe to the Roman public. He could expect some sympathetic response from at least part of the population in Rome, for as we have noted the circle around Filippo Neri also put forward ideals of simplicity and humility, though in accordance with the Catholic reform following the Council of Trent.

Ancient and Byzantine examples of the inspiration of an author or evangelist, even down to Poussin's *Inspiration du poète* are extremely refined and dignified. Caravaggio's inspired saint, however, is deliberately shown as a clumsy man, almost in caricature. It is no wonder that voluntarily or otherwise, Caravaggio had to withdraw his first conception of the saint, which he had created in the exuberance of his youth. No one would have understood how the well-dressed gentleman Levi-Matthew, as shown in the *Vocation*, changes into a peasant, shabbily dressed and so uneducated that the angel must gently lead his calloused hand when, many years after his Calling, he writes his Gospel.

It seems natural that this simple and humble Matthew, as the young Caravaggio saw him, would not write in the elegant Greek that his colleagues Mark, Luke, and John used, but in

FIG. 65
Figino, *Sketches for a St. Matthew*. Windsor, Library.
By permission of Her Gracious Majesty, The Queen.

FIG. 66
Campagnola (?), *Drawing*. Florence, Uffizi.

FIG. 66A
Peterzano, *St. Matthew and the Angel*.
Certosa di Garegnano (Milan).

the language of his people, Hebrew, or even in the vernacular Aramaic spoken by Christ and his disciples. According to tradition the gospel of St. Matthew was originally written in Hebrew, not in Greek as were the other three. Consequently, on the open page of the big book held on his knees we see the first words of his Gospel—verse 1 and part of verse 2 of the *Liber Generationis*—in Hebrew and in Hebrew characters, retranslated from the Greek text or from the Vulgate. Of course the young painter himself was far from knowing anything of

FIG. 67
Romanino, *St. Matthew*. Brescia, San
Giovanni Evangelista.

FIG. 68
Raphael, *Jupiter and Cupid*. Rome,
Villa Farnesina.

these erudite distinctions. However, it seems that he painted his *First St. Matthew* in the palace of the Cardinal del Monte, who had just accepted the promising painter as a member of his entourage. One can therefore assume that either the Cardinal or one of his ecclesiastical family supplied Caravaggio with the information, buttressing in this subtle way Caravaggio's popular conception of St. Matthew.

The saint has no halo, as the later *Matthew* has; in its place is a small strip of the white-feathered wing which serves, together with the girlish round face of the angel, as a foil setting off the large bald head of Matthew. He sits heavily on a scissor-shaped chair of the so-called Savonarola type over which he has laid his pinkish-brown coat. He concentrates very hard, so that he can follow the dictation of the angel and write it down; his tense expression reveals his anxious attention. The girl-angel also takes her mission very seriously; her round and open mouth seems to articulate every syllable of the text, but, not trusting the saint's capacity for understanding, she has laid three fingers of her plump and childlike hand upon his enormous one, which apparently is more accustomed to heavy manual labor than to literature. In this way she leads Matthew's hand with the quill held awkwardly between the fingers, from right to left, according to the method of Semitic writing.

The maidenly figure of the angel contrasts pleasantly with the roughness of the masculine St. Matthew, whose obvious awkwardness and inability are touchingly opposed to her efficiency. Both figures, gently but closely knit together, form a kind of sculptural group in which humbleness combines with grace, and where dull matter is animated by celestial inspiration. Here in *St. Matthew and the Angel* Caravaggio approaches his goal of presenting the miracle by earthly means. The Saint has been demoted, but the angel too has been deprived of her official heavenly rank; she appears in a very human shape as a young girl of charming and rather sensuous vitality—she could very well be the adolescent sister of one of Caravaggio's boisterous young companions. Compared to the anemic angel in the Doria *Flight*, who is still rooted in the Milanese maniera, the very natural body of this angel shows the young master's courageous advance toward an earthly reality. No trace remains of St. Joseph's grandfatherly mildness and dignified simplicity in the proletarian figure of the Evangelist. There is not the slightest concession, either in color or in features, to "dignity and beauty" in the old sense. The Giorgionesque lyricism and musicality which so charmingly pervade the *Flight into Egypt* are now definitely left behind.

CHAPTER V

THE CONTARELLI CHAPEL[1]

PLATES 28-31

THE focal point of Caravaggio's artistic activity was for many years the French National Church of Rome, San Luigi dei Francesi, located between the Pantheon and the Piazza Navona in the old quarter of Sant' Eustachio. In the immediate vicinity of the church were the palaces of a number of Grand Signori who favored, protected, and, as Caravaggio's adversaries claimed, spoiled the young and already very temperamental artist in spite of—or perhaps just because of—the novelty and audacity of his painting. Unlike the old-fashioned professors and academicians such as Federico Zuccari, these collectors and art enthusiasts early recognized and came to value the progressive force of Caravaggio's genius. By far the most important of them was the Cardinal Francesco Maria del Monte to whom the young and struggling artist was introduced by a certain Valentino, a French art dealer connected with San Luigi. As the official representative of the Grand Duke of Tuscany in the College of Cardinals, del Monte resided in the Palazzo Madama, one of the Roman palaces belonging to the Medici, located right next to San Luigi. The cardinal was a protector of the newly-established Academy of St. Luke, and was a kind of ecclesiastical minister of the arts in Rome. He took Caravaggio into the Palazzo Madama as a pensionnaire and bought quite a few of his paintings, among them such early works as the *Concert of Youths* and the *Fortune Teller*, and it was the Cardinal del Monte who was probably most instrumental in obtaining the Contarelli commission for Caravaggio. Of almost equal importance for the artist was the patronage of the Marchese Vincenzo Giustiniani (the brother of Cardinal Giustiniani) who was one of the most prominent art collectors of his day. His rich collection of antique sculpture and contemporary painting was housed in his splendid palace, located across the street from San Luigi in the via Dogana Vecchia. Giustiniani was to become the most enthusiastic collector of Caravaggio's work and in his famous letter, written after the death of the artist, he ranks him with the best of his contemporaries. Another family which seems to have been associated with this circle of art patrons was the family Mattei, which also had a palace in the neighborhood of San Luigi. Two sons of this family, Asdrubale and Ciriaco, owned paintings by Caravaggio at a relatively early date and it was Ciriaco Mattei whom Baglione criticized for falling under the spell of Caravaggio's renown. More directly connected with the French National Church were the Crescenzi, an old patrician family whose palace was not far distant from the church in the salita dei Crescenzi. As will be seen, certain of the Crescenzi were in charge of the decorations for the Contarelli Chapel and were directly responsible for the fact that Caravaggio received the commission. It was in these surroundings that Caravaggio's advanced artistic ideas were encouraged and first given public recognition. And it is certainly not by chance that almost all of these patrons, through their families, were associated with the liberal political faction which had advocated the election of Clement VIII, the pope who had finally concluded a peace with France by acknowledging Henry of Navarre. In these very same years

Annibale Carracci and his helpers were at work for the Farnese, who were among the staunchest supporters of the political interests of Spain.

Although the foundation stone of San Luigi dei Francesi was laid by Cardinal Giulio de Medici, later Pope Clement VII, as early as 1518, the massive and impressive facade (probably the work of Giacomo della Porta) was not finished until seventy years later, in 1589—just about the time when Caravaggio came to Rome. It was another member of the Medici family, Catherine, Queen of France, who provided most of the funds for the decorations of the interior of the church and for the construction of the facade. Among the other benefactors of the church, Moroni in his excellent and comprehensive *Dizionario Ecclesiastico* mentions especially Mathieu Cointrel, a French nobleman from Anjou, who contributed money for the facade and donated 10,000 scudi for the decoration of the high altar. Cointrel, better known as Matteo Contarelli, held the important office of papal datary (the person in charge of ecclesiastical grants and dispensations) under Gregory XIII, and he was raised to the cardinalate in 1583, only two years before he died. In 1565 he endowed the chapel in San Luigi which bears his name and in which, at the end of the century, Caravaggio executed the paintings which made him famous. Contarelli must have intended to begin the decoration of his chapel immediately after he acquired it, because in the same year he made a contract with the painter Girolamo Muziano from Brescia, in which he set out an elaborate program for these decorations. According to the contract the chapel was to be decorated with various scenes from the life of his patron, St. Matthew, the apostle and evangelist. On the lateral walls were to be the two most important events of the saint's life, his Vocation and Martyrdom, the beginning and end of his evangelical career. The three divisions of the vault were to carry scenes of minor events from the saint's later activity in Ethiopia, and four prophets in the corners. All of the decorations were to be in fresco, except for the altarpiece of St. Matthew and the Angel writing the gospel, which was to be painted in oil. It is almost exactly the program which we see in the chapel today.

Muziano apparently never even began the work in the chapel, and, for reasons which we do not know, the program was not carried out during the lifetime of Cardinal Contarelli. However, the original plan was by no means abandoned; when Contarelli died in 1585, he had not forgotten to set aside a fixed sum of money in his will for the work in the chapel and to give specific instructions regarding it. As heir and executor of his will, he named not a member of his own family, but an Italian, Virgilio Crescenzi, who later retired from the trusteeship and was succeeded by his son, the abbate Giacomo Crescenzi. One can well imagine that under these circumstances tensions arose between the Contarelli and the French clergy, on the one hand, and the Roman administrators, the Crescenzi, on the other, which hampered the smooth progress of work in the chapel. According to Chéramy, the will of the Cardinal was even contested by his natural heirs, and this resulted in a lawsuit which lasted for a number of years. Furthermore, under the severe reign of Sixtus V an inquiry was made to find out how Contarelli, as a papal datary, had come by his great fortune. Even though he had been a favorite of Gregory XIII, the cardinal was at times suspected of having amassed his fortune through simony. Such difficulties as these may account for the fact that Virgilio

Crescenzi, as official heir, placed the memorial inscription on the floor of the chapel only in 1590, the year of Sixtus' death.

The only step which was taken to commence the work for the chapel in the time of Sixtus turned out to be a complete failure. Probably not on the initiative of the Crescenzi, who were quite experienced in matters of art, but rather on that of the nephews of the Cardinal ("i Contarelli," as Baglione calls them) a contract was made with a poor Flemish sculptor, Coppe Fiammingo, for a statue of St. Matthew and the Angel to be used instead of the altarpiece originally planned. Since this statue was already blocked out (abozzato) at the time of the contract, it would seem that Coppe had been chosen for the work some time earlier. This "sculptor," whose real name was Jacob Cornelisz Cobaert, was accustomed only to small metalwork and copying from the antique, and, as Sandrart and Baglione say with derisive contempt, was totally unable to model even a hand, let alone such a large-scale work in marble as was needed for the chapel. Instead of the four years which he was given for the work, Coppe spent "his whole lifetime" (tutto il tempo di sua vita) on the statue and still never finished it (the angel was finally added by another sculptor). When the Contarelli inspected it they found it extremely dry (una seccagine) and there was surely no question of placing it on the altar of the chapel.

After Virgilio Crescenzi had asserted himself as the official heir of the Cardinal by including his own name in the inscription, he made a resolute beginning of the work in the chapel; in 1591 he concluded a contract with Giuseppe Cesare d'Arpino, who in spite of his youth—he was only twenty-three at the time—had achieved considerable renown as a fresco painter. Arpino, who had just returned from Naples where he had been working for S. Martino, executed the frescoes on the vaulted ceiling of the chapel—the scenes from the life of St. Matthew, the Sibyls and Prophets. Even though they are very badly preserved, it can be seen that they are of a rather mediocre quality—neither good nor bad, as is usually the case with Arpino's work. After finishing the vault, Arpino stopped working in the chapel, and in the two years which were given to him for the completion of the work he did not even begin the two most important parts of the program, the Calling and the Martyrdom. Even van Mander, who is very well informed about the artist, cannot explain Arpino's failure to complete the work; he only says that there were special reasons. Arpino's name was, nevertheless, associated with the Contarelli commission much later.

After this brief activity in the chapel, there seems to have followed another interval of almost complete inertia, and finally the negligence caused such a stir that an official complaint was brought against the Crescenzi by the clergy of San Luigi. As has been remarked, tensions probably existed already between the Contarelli family and the Crescenzi, and it is more than likely that the action of the clergy was instigated by or made in concert with the nephews of the Cardinal. This would explain the viciousness of the attack which was levelled against the Crescenzi. The clergy complained that the Crescenzi made only empty excuses about difficulties with the painter and the sculptor, and that meanwhile the chapel remained boarded up and could not be used for masses. The Abbate Crescenzi was himself accused of prolonging his trusteeship of the large sum of money with which the chapel had been endowed, and it was even suggested that he had made financial speculations with the funds which should rightfully have been used for the glorification of the Cardinal's name and the absolution of his soul. Whether or not these suspicions and accusations were justified is extremely difficult to say, even when one studies the rather complicated documents concerning the affair. Giacomo Crescenzi is known to have belonged to the most intimate circle of San Filippo Neri in his last years and seems to have been a man of considerable respect and trust in this circle. And indeed his defense of the supervision of the work is not without a certain amount of justification. He asserts that the chapel has been finished for many years and at great expense—as anyone who looked at it could see—and adds that only the two lateral walls remained to be painted, which was no fault of his, but rather of the painter who had agreed to complete the work, and had not done so. In any event, the complaints of the clergy resulted, in 1597, in a papal investigation (the painter, of course, was Arpino) of the finances of the chapel, and the pope placed the entire endowment under the control of the Fabbrica di San Pietro, the pontifical agency which supervised the building and property of St. Peter's and of other Roman churches.

After the intervention of the Fabbrica the work in the chapel began to progress quickly. As we know from a promissory note, the sum of 400 scudi was set aside in July of 1597 for Arpino. This money was obviously intended as a payment for the paintings on the lateral walls of the chapel, which had remained untouched until this year. The note itself was to be valid for only one year. Taken at face value, this promissory note would indicate that Arpino had again been asked to finish the work which he had originally been commissioned to do. However, there is also the possibility that it was only a legal formality intended to insure the administrators against liability toward him. Since Arpino was at this time overburdened by other commissions (for example the series of large battle scenes in the Palazzo dei Conservatori which he had begun in 1596), there was little or no chance of his actually undertaking the extensive work yet to be done in the chapel. Also it was shortly after this time that he went to Ferrara in the retinue of the pope.

In spite of the considerable information which we have concerning the Contarelli Chapel it is still not possible to say exactly how and when Caravaggio became associated with the work there. However, even a cursory examination of the documents makes it evident that two accounts which were generally accepted in the older Caravaggio literature have to be rejected. First, Caravaggio's paintings for the chapel were certainly not made at the time of the memorial inscription, around 1590, and not by a precocious boy of seventeen or eighteen years, but rather by an artist who was already mature. Second, the story which Bellori gives is a falsification or at least a distortion of the facts. He says that Caravaggio was introduced to the Crescenzi by the famous poet, Giambattista Marino, a friend of the Crescenzi and of Arpino, and that the work was divided between the two painters. However, Marino was in Naples during the 90's and his friendship with the Crescenzi began only after he came to Rome in 1600. Baglione, who is the most reliable source concerning these years, indicates that Caravaggio's association with the Contarelli Chapel began with the *First St. Matthew*; he says that after the Contarelli became displeased with the work of Coppe, Caravaggio was asked to make a painting to replace the statue. This, however, does not altogether clarify the problem, because even though Coppe's contract was to have ended in 1591, it is quite possible that he was not dismissed from the commission until later. Moreover, as we have seen, the altarpiece seems always to have been treated separately from the other decorations in the chapel. Thus the *First St. Matthew* can be dated only approximately and on the basis of its style. The spirit of the painting recalls the simple and intimate scenes of Caravaggio's youth; however, in many respects its style looks forward to the works of his mature Roman years. The articulation of the two figures is more complex and subtle than we have hitherto seen, and, in contrast to the earlier works the color is richer, warmer and more painterly. Most important, though, is the plastic weight of the figures which is forcefully emphasized by the forward projection of the limbs—particularly of St. Matthew's left leg—and by the rather delicate torsion of the poses. There is also a new concentration of the forms within the picture space which is enhanced by the sharp frontal lighting. The *First St. Matthew* is the first instance of this powerful concentration of plastically projecting forms which Caravaggio takes up again in such paintings as the *Deposition* and the *Crucifixion of St. Peter*. Although the work must be placed before the two lateral paintings in the chapel, it is a rather advanced work, and was probably painted sometime between 1595 and 1597. According to Baglione the altarpiece which Caravaggio made pleased no one, and on the basis of this remark, the imaginative Bellori invents an interesting psychological situation in which the young Caravaggio was put to shame at the very outset of his career because the pious priests removed his first great masterpiece from the altar of the chapel. Only through a deus ex machina, the Marchese Giustiniani, was Caravaggio saved from lasting disgrace—the Marchese took the painting and paid for another to replace it. Much of this has the air of pure romance. Even Baglione, who had reason enough to be hostile toward Caravaggio, makes no mention of the priests rejecting the painting, and if there had been any gossip, the chattering Sandrart would surely have picked up the details when he was in Rome. Thus the *First St. Matthew* was probably not officially refused, although it was naturally criticized by the more conventional-minded. When Caravaggio had conceived the *Calling* and the *Martyrdom*, he must have realized that the personality and appearance of the saint in the earlier version was not congruent with the protagonist of the laterals. And when one compares the *First St. Matthew* with these laterals, it is at once evident that the earthy and simple saint is quite out of keeping with the elegant and wealthy gentleman of the *Calling* and also with the old patriarch of the *Martyrdom*. It is even possible that Caravaggio voluntarily withdrew the *First St. Matthew* with the promise to make a new version (which would not have been an isolated example in his career, cf. the Cerasi Chapel) particularly if the Marchese Giustiniani was eager to acquire this delightful painting for his own collection.

The valuable documents concerning the Contarelli Chapel, which were recently published by Mr. Denis Mahon, have made it possible to date the lateral paintings, the *Calling* and *Martyrdom of St. Matthew*, with a reasonable amount of certainty. Since there was still a possibility of Arpino finishing the work in the chapel as late as November 1597, Caravaggio could not very well have received an official commission before this date. However, this does not exclude the possibility that he had been unofficially considered for the commission sometime earlier. Baglione remarks that Caravaggio received the commission through "il suo cardinale" and this is confirmed by the fact that the Cardinal del Monte was a prefect of the Fabbrica di San Pietro and was thus in a position to influence strongly the choice of his protégé. In any event the documents seem to indicate that the lateral paintings were still missing from the chapel in the spring of 1598. On the first of May 1599, the governing body of San Luigi finally resolved that the Contarelli Chapel should be opened for services, and two chaplains were appointed for the celebration of masses in the chapel. It can be assumed that at this time the lateral paintings were more or less finished, or at least well under way. Caravaggio would have had about one year to work on these laterals before the opening of the chapel (if he began to paint them as late as 1598), which is a rather short time for such a large undertaking. Caravaggio's name is mentioned in connection with the affairs of the church as late as June of 1600, and long after the chapel was officially opened, he may very well have continued to work on the *Martyrdom*, which he changed a number of times. The final altarpiece, as we will see, was certainly painted later than the laterals.

Caravaggio's representation of the *Calling of St. Matthew* is extraordinary both in execution and in the way in which the scene is conceived. In Italian examples of the scene from the late fourteenth and early fifteenth centuries, like that by Jacopo di Cione in his *St. Matthew Altar* in the Uffizi and later the one by Carpaccio in the Oratorio degli Schiavoni in Venice, the saint is shown stepping out of the countinghouse to receive the benediction of Christ. In the paintings by Niccolò di Pietro Gerini at Prato, he is shown seated at a table with an assistant. In Northern examples from the sixteenth century, the atmosphere of the scene is very much changed and degraded; in fact, the act of the Vocation can be so reduced in importance that it is used merely as a pretext for a scene of coarse carousing, as in the many versions of the subject painted by Jan van Hemessen and his followers (e.g. his painting in the Metropolitan Museum of New York). Caravaggio's composition is closer to the Northern examples than to earlier Italian ones, but it certainly has none of the vulgarity of a van Hemessen. It seems quite likely that Caravaggio used Northern models for several details in the group of figures seated around the table in his painting. Sandrart, in his life of Holbein, remarks that a woodcut of this master was the source of one of Caravaggio's figures in the *Calling of St. Matthew*, and indeed the young man at the left, bent over the table in Caravaggio's composition bears a striking resemblance to the corresponding figure in Holbein's woodcut of *The Card Players* from the *Dance of Death* series (edition of 1545). Another curious comparison is the position of St. Matthew's hands and those of the man in Marinus van Roymerswaele's painting, *The Money Changer and His Wife*, FIG. 53, which was probably in Florence even in Caravaggio's day.

Caravaggio depicts Levi with a full well-kempt beard and fine dress, as is natural, since his profession was a lucrative one. One can well believe that this same man held a great banquet in honor of the Savior shortly after he was called to the apostolate (Luke 5:29). The small company of young men around St. Matthew is neither drinking nor dicing nor playing cards as Sandrart, who certainly had the cluttered examples of his own time in mind, would have it. The group is not composed of mere vagrants, but of upper-class playboys who sit quite peacefully and slightly indifferent around a simple, oblong table, the top of which is

FIG. 69
Niccolò di Pietro Gerini, *Calling of St. Matthew*. Prato, San Francesco.

FIG. 70
Jacopo di Cione, *St. Matthew Altar: Calling of St. Matthew* (detail). Florence, Uffizi.

FIG. 71
Carpaccio, *Calling of St. Matthew*. Venice, Oratorio degli Schiavoni.

bare except for a few scattered coins, an ink-pot, an open account book and a small bag of money. The costumes of the young men, with their rich damask doublets, their garishly striped sleeves and their dapper plumed hats, are extremely elegant and colorful. These costumes are certainly not the everyday dress of Caravaggio's time, and the explanation of them as the livery of pages (perhaps the pages of the Cardinal del Monte or of the Marchese Giustiniani) which has recently been put forward is most convincing. Saint Mat-

FIG. 72
Van Hemessen, *Calling of St. Matthew*. New York, Metropolitan Museum.

thew, as he counts out the coins, is startled by the sudden appearance of Christ and his heavenly companion. The gesture of Christ's summoning hand at once calls to mind that of God the Father in Michelangelo's *Creation of Adam*. However, the X-rays of the *Calling*, which show the left side of the composition almost unchanged, reveal an extremely interesting pentimento on the right side. For the figure of Christ, who is at first represented unaccompanied, Caravaggio does not use the gesture of command as in the definitive version, but rather one of inviting; it is the characteristic Italian gesture of beckoning with the fingers of the hand turned downward. Perhaps Caravaggio found the first gesture too casual for the Savior and decided to use the more dignified and eloquent gesture from the Sistine Chapel. The psychological interrelation of the participants in the scene is expressed with the most careful and dramatic penetration; Christ's sudden appearance is like a flash of spiritual light in the midst of this worldly and rather suspect gathering. The expression of Matthew is one of embarrassed astonishment; he looks thoughtfully in the direction of Christ and points to himself as if to say, "Do you mean me"? The bespectacled old man with the Rembrandt-like face and the brooding boy on the left do not yet seem to be aware of the momentous event which is taking place, but the two boys on the right look at the approaching figures with somewhat empty expressions, disturbed by the intrusion which they are unable to comprehend. One of these rather ambiguous boys, the one seen from the back, according to the colorful, but not very trustworthy account of Malvasia, is a portrait of the Bolognese painter, Lionello

FIG. 73
Holbein, *Dance of Death Series:
The Card Players* (edition of
1545).

Spada, who was allegedly so attached to Caravaggio that he served him as a model. The elegant sword hanging so conspicuously at his side could conceivably be associated with the name.

The group of boys seated around the table continues both formally and psychologically the genre paintings of Caravaggio's early period. The questionable atmosphere recalls, for example, *The Cardsharps* in which the young cheat seen in profile even has a certain affinity with the so-called "Spada." In these early paintings Caravaggio had limited himself to single figures or small groups. Thus the *Calling* represents the first use of such a group in a large-scale history painting charged with religious emotion. The momentary tension through which Caravaggio had made his everyday episodes interesting has now become a crisis affecting all humanity. To this end the stage, though still strictly limited, is now enlarged so that it no longer serves exclusively to display mere physiognomical studies but provides a greater amplitude for the development of the drama. Caravaggio divides the surface of the painting horizontally into two parts which balance each other, the lower part filled with rich and colorful figures, the upper part almost empty. The bare wall is interrupted by a large high window permitting only a subdued light to enter through its oilskin pane. This division of space, which Caravaggio uses here for the first time, is of great importance for his own later work and for the painting of following centuries—one sees such a spatial arrangement for example in one of David's greatest compositions, the unfinished *Jeu de Paume.*

The second lateral painting in the Contarelli Chapel is the *Martyrdom of St. Matthew*, a scene which is not frequently represented. The martyrdom of the saint occurred after he had solemnly forbidden the marriage of Hirtacus, King of Ethiopia, to Iphigenia, the daughter of the former king, who had been converted to Christianity. Hirtacus, overcome with rage, sent his henchmen into the church to slay the saint. They found him just ending the celebration of the mass and, without respecting the sanctity of the church, they stabbed him repeatedly until he fell dead on the altar steps. As far as I know, there are no Northern examples of the scene, and the main Italian ones are in the series which were mentioned in connection with the *Calling*. In the fresco by Gerini in Prato, which may be taken as representative, St. Matthew is shown kneeling before the altar and is stabbed in the back by a warrior. The other half of the scene is filled by a host of men led by King Hirtacus, who directs the execution. A young acolyte appears running away in horror—a figure, frequently used in such scenes and one which plays an important role in Caravaggio's painting. Of course Caravaggio could have seen later parallels to this figure in representations of other stories, such as Donatello's *Feast of Herod* (Siena Fount) and Lotto's *Martyrdom of St. Peter* (S. Alonzo Maggiore).

A parallel subject to the *Martyrdom of St. Matthew* is the murder in the cathedral of St. Thomas à Becket. The martyrdom of St. Thomas was well known in Italy at the time because of the great excitement caused by the murder of Catholic priests in England around the middle of the sixteenth century. Circignani (Pomerancio), the artist who had painted the great series of martyrdoms in S. Stefano Rotondo in Rome, had also executed a series of paintings for the English College of Rome showing the martyrdom of saints who had met their death in England. Among these was, of course, the *Assassination of St. Thomas*, which is known to us only in an engraving. Caravaggio certainly knew this painting, and there is even a certain similarity between the warrior who slays St. Thomas and the executioner in Caravaggio's painting.

The composition of the *Calling of St. Matthew* seems to have been the result of a single artistic impulse; but this is not the case with the *Martyrdom*. The reason for this is probably that the *Calling* is in a sense the continuation and the perfection of the suave and lyrical paintings of Caravaggio's youth, whereas in the *Martyrdom* he was confronted with the problem of representing a turbulent and violent action. This problem seems to have caused Caravaggio considerable difficulty. Bellori relates that he remade (rifacce) the *Martyrdom* two times, and this information is confirmed by the excellent and informative X-rays which have recently been made at the Istituto del Restauro in Rome (PLATES 29D and 30F). Judging from the X-rays, Caravaggio's first projects for the *Martyrdom* were much more in keeping with the quiet and restrained composition of the *Calling*. However, the formal conception of the scene is very different. It was quite possible for Federico Zuccari to associate the *Calling* with Giorgione, but such a thing could never have been said of the first projects for the *Martyrdom*,

FIG. 74
Niccolò di Pietro Gerini, *Martyrdom of St. Matthew*. Prato, San Francesco.

FIG. 75
Jacopo di Cione, *St. Matthew Altar: Martyrdom of
St. Matthew* (detail). Florence, Uffizi.

FIG. 76
Martyrdom of St. Thomas à Becket
(engraving after Circignani).

because they are decidedly in the classical tradition of Roman painting. It is evident here that Caravaggio had made a careful study of Raphael's Stanze. The man seen from the rear in the center of the X-ray is a standard sixteenth-century figure which is related to the executioner in the *Judgment of Solomon* on the ceiling of the Segnatura; and the running man with the sword, on the left, is taken almost literally from the *Battle of Ostia*. There seems also to be a

<table>
<tr><td>FIG. 77
Caravaggio, Martyrdom of St. Matthew (reconstruction on basis of X-rays).</td><td>77A.
Raphael, Battle of Ostia. Rome, Vatican</td></tr>
</table>

tendency in these first projects to arrange the figures in a kind of oval grouping in a way which is similar to that of the *Battle of Ostia* and which is, moreover, extremely different from the final composition. Raphael's figures are derived from antique sculptures and this is probably also true of the boy-angel with the outstretched arm, holding the Gospel of St. Matthew on the right side of the X-ray. In the first projects for the *Martyrdom*, the figures are placed much lower on the canvas than in the final painting, and the upper part was to have been empty except for a large architectural backdrop in a severe classical form. The X-rays indicate that Caravaggio changed the positions of the main characters of the scene, St. Matthew and the executioner, a number of times before he arrived at his final solution. The large repoussoir figures, which play such an important role in the completed composition, have not yet been introduced into the first projects, and the shrieking boy is also absent, but the child between the legs of the central figure seen from the rear in the X-ray may be a first idea for this boy.

Evidently Caravaggio felt that this severely classical composition was inadequate to express the vehement drama of the event. He may also have felt that the earlier composition did not represent the action clearly enough, and in fact in the first project Saint Matthew is almost lost in the turmoil of moving figures. An earlier painting of the same subject and one with which Caravaggio must have been familiar, did exist in Rome: Muziano's painting (in

FIG. 78

Muziano, *Martyrdom of St. Matthew*. Rome, Sta. Maria in Aracoeli.

FIG. 79

Titian, *Death of St. Peter Martyr* (engraving after a destroyed painting).

tempera on canvas) in the Mattei chapel at the church of Sta. Maria Aracoeli. However, even though there is a remarkable similarity between the pose of Caravaggio's executioner and Muziano's, Caravaggio did not find an acceptable solution to his problem in the Roman tradition (nor in the work of Giorgione). Rather, he turned to Titian's *Death of St. Peter Martyr* for the Frari (now destroyed), one of the most impressive representations of the assassination of a saint that he could have known. He takes his central group, consisting of the executioner, St. Matthew, and the shrieking acolyte directly from Titian's painting, and arranges them in a square, using the altar front with the Maltese Cross as the center of the background. From this center the figures scatter centrifugally outwards with an almost explosive force. A limited space is created by an additive series of planes marked by the repeated horizontal lines of the body of the saint and the altar steps, the rhythm of which is terminated in a kind of compositional coda by the extended right leg of the angel hovering above. A forceful though somewhat artificial tension is created by the balance between these horizontals and the obvious verticals in the arms and bodies of the other figures. The use of geometric configurations in the building up of the composition shows that in the final painting Caravaggio had not altogether abandoned the classical and intellectual method of Raphael, as it is seen, for example, in the arrangement of the *Death of Ananias*. However, this classical

FIG. 80
Raphael, *Death of Ananias* (tapestry). Rome, Vatican.

element in the composition is counterbalanced by the over-all crossing diagonals, one sweeping from the right, the other from the left, less well defined, but serving to point out the illuminated face of King Hirtacus. This kind of composition in a grand style, with its emphasis on receding diagonals, is in some way related to the incipient development of the Baroque style of painting as seen for example in the famous and extremely advanced *Martyrdom of San Vitale* (Brera) by Federico Barocci. The repoussoir figures in the lower corners are much more vital to the arrangement than those in the foreground of Tintoretto's *Last Supper* in San Rocco, and the compositional bravura of the *Martyrdom* points in the direction of Caravaggio's more complicated and more subtly constructed compositions such as the *Seven Acts of Mercy*.

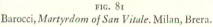

FIG. 81
Barocci, *Martyrdom of San Vitale*. Milan, Brera.

FIG. 82
Tintoretto, *Last Supper*. Venice, San Rocco.

As was said earlier, the *First St. Matthew* may never have been placed on the altar of the Contarelli Chapel, and to complete the old program which had been outlined by the Cardinal, Caravaggio had to make another altarpiece. The second painting of *St. Matthew and the Angel* which he made is conceived in another spirit and executed in a strikingly different style from the first. It is also much taller than the first one. Perhaps it was to satisfy the clergy of San Luigi that Caravaggio painted this much more conventional painting. In contrast to the *First St. Matthew*, the saint is here characterized as a dignified, deeply inspired, and rather remote patriarch with a long gray beard and a partly bald head. He wears a small, thin halo which was not present in the first version. There is no longer the intimate relationship between the saint and the angel which is so touching in the earlier painting; here the angel is suspended in the air and foreshortened to such a degree that only the upper part of his body is visible. This is not an appealing adolescent girl, but rather a kind of gamin whose mischievous face recalls the *Amor Victorious* in Berlin. The work is no longer painted with the forceful but painterly plasticity which drives the forms forward toward the beholder, but is so arranged as to keep the composition strictly behind the picture plane. In general the painting is much more severe than the first version, and the only capricious note in the scene is the stool which totters precariously over the edge of the platform on which the saint stands—in a way which recalls the basket of fruit in the *Supper at Emmaus*. In its style the *Second St. Matthew* is the most advanced of the three paintings in the chapel and has therefore been placed at the very end of the years in which Caravaggio worked at San Luigi. In 1603 Caravaggio was under the protection of the French ambassador, and it is possible that he was still working for San Luigi at this time. The similarity between the angel in this painting and the *Amor Victorious* would suggest a rather late date for the work. (See also DOC. 44 A-D.) The same is true of the surprising similarity between the head of St. Matthew and that of St. Peter in the Cerasi Chapel. Doubtless the date of the *Second St. Matthew* is later than the consecration of the Contarelli Chapel in 1599. It should also be said that if this is the case, one must not absolutely reject the possibility of a later date for the second version of the *Martyrdom*.

We know from Federico Zuccari's comments about the Contarelli Chapel that the completed work made a considerable stir in the Roman artistic society of the day. However, perhaps because of the bad light in the chapel, these paintings never had the popularity of such works as the *Deposition* in the Chiesa Nuova and the *Crucifixion of St. Peter* in the Cerasi Chapel. The *First St. Matthew*, of course, being in the private collection of the Marchese Giustiniani, was not considered as a part of the series, and of the paintings which were to be seen in the chapel only the *Calling* seems to have been very well known. Sandrart refers to the *Martyrdom of St. Matthew* as an "expulsion from the Temple" which he certainly would not have done had the painting been a famous one; the composition was not influential except in isolated examples, such as Simon Vouet's *Clothing of St. Francis*—which, as has recently been remarked, seems to be a kind of compositional summary of the two laterals in the Contarelli Chapel. The *Calling*, on the other hand, did make a strong impression, especially—and this is not surprising—on Northern painters such as Hendrick Terbruggen, who uses parts of Caravaggio's composition for his own very different interpretation of the scene. It is characteristic, though, that Terbruggen is interested mainly in the genre elements of the painting, and that he misses a most Caravaggesque feature—he uses only the lower half of Caravaggio's composition and leaves out the dramatic empty space above the figures. When the paintings from the Contarelli Chapel were shown for the first time in the Mostra del Barocco in 1923, they came as a revelation of the profundity of Caravaggio's religious and psychological expression. Although these paintings mark the beginnings of the artist's mature artistic career, they do not yet show the complete and perfect formulation of style and expression which we see in his great Roman altarpieces—rather they mark a turning point toward his most mature and impressive religious paintings.

CHAPTER VI

CARAVAGGIO'S CHARACTER AND RELIGION

WHEN Caravaggio left the shop of Peterzano in Milan and settled in Rome he was still only a boy. Of these early years the literary sources say almost nothing. For knowledge of his character and the development of his personality through this time we are restricted to an inevitably subjective interpretation of his early works, the automorphic features in such paintings as the *Bacchus* with wine and grapes, the head of *Medusa* garlanded by living snakes, a *Lute Player* near a splendid bouquet of fresh white flowers, or the boy wearing a pink rose behind his ear terrified by the bite of a lizard. Only by trying to understand the spirit of these youthful productions is it possible to reconstruct a plausible image of the "artist as a young man." In them Caravaggio appears as a young and very gifted painter, of great vivacity, slightly depraved, perhaps even vicious, not at all illiterate, though by no means given to literary or theoretical studies, and musical by nature, with his head full of madrigals and canzoni. His image based on these pictures is that of a very intelligent and interesting youth who observed himself and the world around him keenly and sharply, with sensibility and even tenderness, though sometimes with a strongly satirical approach, and who as a whole enjoyed life and youth intensely in spite of his struggle for existence and his basically melancholy nature.

The high and often presumptuous spirits of the young master which we are inclined to discover in the early half-figures and genre paintings are only rarely to be felt in his middle period, after the *First St. Matthew*, and they disappear almost totally from the works which he painted after 1600. Austere seriousness penetrates the monumental creations of his "maniera magnifica," for instance in the *Death of the Virgin*, where even in the accessories no prettiness is tolerated ("niente bellotto," as Bellori says). The fruit basket on the table of the London *Emmaus* displays wilted leaves and worm-eaten apples instead of the glistening fruit of the early *Bacchus*. No trace of a satirical or ironical mind can be found in his later paintings. It has not been emphasized enough that the relatively few profane genre paintings of Caravaggio are the work of a very young painter, and that from the beginning of his maturity his artistic activity was almost exclusively dedicated to altarpieces, which express his religious persuasion. The marked change in the character of his expression might be taken as an indication that something happened, in his outward life or his inner experience, which influenced and altered the natural development of his personality, but we have no evidence as to what it might have been.

Caravaggio was not the type of artist who is closely attracted to literary groups. While his contemporary Rubens conducted his whole life in the full glare of publicity, we have no letters by Caravaggio (if he ever wrote any) and no allusions to him in letters of contemporaries. Such letterati as Bellori would have dismissed him to obscurity if his powerful and revolutionary art had not scandalized them by its novelty, and alarmed them by its enormous success. They take Caravaggio's tenebroso manner, the dark shadows which he used after the pure and sweet colors of his first period to be an expression of his turbulent nature, and they suggest that his whole physiognomy and appearance, his dark complexion, black eyes, hair and eyebrows—in short, his whole black character—is reflected in his later paintings. Baglione could have given us much more intimate information about Caravaggio since, unlike Bellori, he was his contemporary, working in the same city and sometimes for the same patron, Giustiniani. But unfortunately he had a personal grudge against him, and not at all without reason, as we know from his suit for slander against Caravaggio and his friends in 1603. To Baglione, Caravaggio was a satirical, haughty, and terribly conceited person, who said nothing good of past or present painters, and who appreciated exclusively himself and his own work. These accusations are in part confirmed by van Mander (or his informants in Rome) before 1603, when he says that while Caravaggio did not praise his own works openly, he did refer to those of others as "bagatelli" because they did not follow nature. To a certain degree these accounts of Caravaggio's arrogant behavior may have been founded upon fact, and they were certainly true with respect to his judgment of Baglione's painting. On the other hand, we have Caravaggio's very noble declaration before a judge, in which he explains what he means by a competent artist (a "valenthuomo") and which painters among his colleagues in Rome he considers to be such. With surprising moderation he includes among this number not only Annibale Carracci, but also painters who worked in a manner directly opposed to his own, such as Zuccari, d'Arpino, and Pomerancio. The hatred of the deeply offended Baglione, however, follows Caravaggio beyond the grave, and he concludes his account of his lamentable death in Port' Ercole with the words, "he died miserably, just as he had lived." Mancini, who may not have known Caravaggio personally, although he writes about him only nine years after his death, says nothing about his character in general, but gives an extremely verbose story about Caravaggio and his brother, which is obviously intended to show the artist's total lack of human feeling. He makes it appear that Caravaggio had broken a most sacred familial bond, by refusing to recognize a priest who claimed to be his brother, and by stubbornly denying that he even had a brother. The Cardinal del Monte and his entourage were horrified by Caravaggio's behavior, the more so since it was well known that he did have a brother. Provided the story is true (Mancini is the only writer who gives it), it would explain the bitterness which had been accumulating in Caravaggio for a long time, and which was caused by his loneliness and lack of family attachment.

All the literary sources—Baglione, Bellori, Sandrart and Passeri—agree in pointing to Caravaggio's violent and quarrelsome temperament and to his extremely disorderly behavior, which is fully confirmed by the numerous police records concerning the painter in the State Archives of Rome. His spirit of bravado and the pleasure he took in playing the swordsman—at least in his later years—must have been very conspicuous. With the large sword which he always carried, he walked through the streets of Rome looking for adventure and trouble in the company of rather wild companions, like his old friend Onorio Longhi, the architect, or with professional soldiers, like the captain from the Castel San Angelo. Of these nightly excursions the police records often relate only trifling incidents, small disturbances of the peace and the like. Caravaggio throws stones against the blinds of a former landlady with whom he has quarreled; on another occasion, sitting in an inn, he hurls a plate of artichokes at a waiter's head and threatens him with a sword because he has given an insolent answer. He is arrested by the constables whom he has insulted for daring to ask for his license to carry arms. But there are also more serious accusations against him in these records, among them an assault made upon a notary on account of a woman, Lena from the Piazza Navona (Lena chi sta a piede a Piazza Navona), Caravaggio's girl at this time. Finally he got into still more serious trouble with the law when, in a kind of duel, he killed one Ranuccio Tomassoni from Terni, with whom he had played ball and quarreled. As a result of this he was banished from Rome, but this experience by no means reformed Caravaggio. Later in Malta, he was again unable to restrain his hot temper; he offended a Cavaliere di Giustitia, his superior, and was thrown into prison.

There are two factors to consider in this astonishing accumulation of violent acts committed by Caravaggio. First, they all occur after 1600—or at least we have not a single record of misbehavior before this date. His more or less criminal actions as revealed to us in the police records start, it would seem, only after he was twenty-seven—well after the irresponsible years of his unprotected youth. One would expect that at this age, when he was almost at the peak of his fame, had a promising future, and was living in the security of well-paid commissions, he would have settled down to the life of an established and highly regarded artist, like his colleagues Annibale Carracci and Arpino. Just the contrary happened; the last decade of his life from 1600 to 1610 is full of turbulence and violence. As one reads the accusations made against him from month to month and from year to year, one gets the impression that he had a headstrong disregard for his own safety. Secondly, none of his misdemeanors and offenses was committed for personal gain. Rather, they served as outlets for an unbridled temperament which in an obviously pathological way could be excessively irritated by the smallest incident, with no regard for himself or others. The real character of Caravaggio, however, cannot be judged only on the basis of his irresponsible actions—the most significant facts about his personality are to be seen in his works, and we should not be prejudiced by Baglione's personal hatred and Bellori's artistic antagonism toward him.

The years from 1600 to May of 1606, in which so many records of Caravaggio's violent actions are reported, are also those of his greatest artistic productivity and his most concentrated power of creation. In these six and a half years, he painted in an uninterrupted sequence seven of his largest and most important religious compositions: the *Crucifixion of St. Peter* and the *Conversion of St. Paul*, the *Deposition* for the Chiesa Nuova, the *Madonna di Loreto* for Sant' Agostino, the enormous *Madonna with St. Anne*, the magnificent *Death of the Virgin* for Santa Maria della Scala, and finally the *Madonna of the Rosary* for the Duke of Modena. In addition to these major masterpieces he painted various other pictures during this period, for example the *St. Jerome Writing* and the beautiful *David with the Head of Goliath*, in the Borghese. The mere quantity of his production during these years is impressive.

Nor did the quality of his work suffer from the unbalanced temperament and impatient irritability shown in his personal affairs. Caravaggio's manner of painting, from the beginning, is fundamentally opposed to the fa presto procedure so characteristic of the fresco painters of the maniera, even though, as has already been remarked, he was sometimes careless in the construction and coordination of figures. In his early years he painted fruit and flowers, and the time-consuming objectivity of the still-life painter is deeply rooted in him. It is true that all the accessories displayed in his earlier works, for example those seen in the *Supper at Emmaus*, in London, disappear from his paintings after 1600 in favor of a much broader and larger treatment of the whole. Still his feeling of responsibility toward the tactile values of the surface continues undiminished—in curious contrast to his irresponsible behavior as a member of the community.

The union of the sublime and the humble, of the monumental and the spiritual, make Caravaggio's paintings of these last years in Rome excel everything that he did before or after. Even his masterpiece from the end of the preceding period, the *Calling of St. Matthew*, still seems to have much Giorgionesque charm, much "vanity" in the color and interest in the particular and the narrative, when compared to the austere and direct works of his later Roman period. On the other hand, the works made after his flight from Rome, in the Sabine mountains, in Naples, Malta and various Sicilian towns were often painted in haste and anxiety, and are therefore uneven in execution and badly preserved. They are of admirable conception and real grandeur, but on the whole they lack the decisive finality of the monumental Roman works. In their realization of religious expression, these works overshadow everything painted by Caravaggio's contemporaries, even by such a sensitive and noble artist as Annibale Carracci. Since Masaccio's works in the Brancacci Chapel, nothing had been created in Italian painting of such monumental sobriety and directness. Raphael's space and figure compositions were certainly influential for Caravaggio's art, but Raphael's expression of religious ideas has nothing in common with the completely unhumanistic and unphilosophical conceptions of Caravaggio. The sense and the aim of religious painting for Caravaggio were not the raising of the worshipper to a transcendental and idealistic sphere as in Raphael's *Transfiguration*, but rather a direct communication between the human being and the divine through faith.

Through the centuries, Caravaggio has been called a mere imitator of nature. His most important and efficient detractor, Bellori, asks the rhetorical question: how a man like Caravaggio could seriously "aspire to art without understanding what art really is," art being understood as the expression of a preconceived idea. Because in the opinion of the classicistic critics and theorists Caravaggio's art lacked an ideal, there arose a tendency to believe that his religious paintings were nothing but documentary representations of religious events expressed in a commonplace and realistic manner, and without being inspired by any real religious feeling. Nothing could be less true. "Realism" in Caravaggio's works means not so much detailed accuracy in rendering the natural object, as a bringing of the object—the supernatural included—near to the spectator, almost to the degree of physical tangibility. Caravaggio's religious expression has a very special character which, though it does not show the naïveté of a Fra Angelico, the almost fanatical spirituality of a Pontormo or Parmigianino, or the sensuous ecstasy of a Bernini, it is surely as sincere and perhaps more revolutionary than the religious expression of these and other artists whose works reflect the religious ideas of their centuries. In the same way, Caravaggio's realistic mysticism is the strongest and most persuasive interpretation of the popular religious movements of the period in which he lived.

Mystery and realism are by no means contradictory. When, in the *Madonna di Loreto*, Caravaggio places the radiant figure of the Virgin so close to the kneeling peasants that they could easily touch her robe, the perception of the supernatural through the senses is for the spectator perhaps a greater mystery than the abstract vision of a host of angels adoring the name of Christ as painted by Federigo Zuccari. This feeling can be traced to the devotional books of the fourteenth and fifteenth centuries, for example Rudolf of Saxony's *Vita Christi* or Thomas a Kempis' *Imitatio Christi*, expressions of the deepest pietistic mysticism which try to direct the human spirit toward perfect harmony with the transcendental order of the universe. In order to achieve this aim, or at least to approach it—because the highest perfection seems unobtainable on this earth—one must be in close contact with the divine by physical means, through the senses. Therefore in these writings the miraculous and transcendental are not emphasized; there is little or no mention of visions or of miracles of the saints, of the Assumption of the Virgin, etc. It is rather the relation of the individual to God that receives stress, and the representations from the life of Christ are intended as models for all mankind. Ignatius of Loyola's *Exercitia Spiritualia* are to a large extent based on these earlier pietistic and mystical doctrines.[1] Here too one finds a great simplification of devotion; there are no visions, no ecstasies, no adoration of the saints or of their relics; the main interest is centered in the individual and his contact with God. St. Ignatius objected strenuously to abstract and scholastic reasoning and to the visionary aspects of medieval theology, which persisted in the more conservative factions of the Counter-Reformation. Instead, he wished Christian mysteries to be contemplated in terms of the actual and tangible. He teaches in the *Exercitia* how to obtain spiritual understanding through the use of the senses, demanding that the exercant "see with the eyes of the imagination the corporeal place where the object which he wishes to contemplate is found" (Paragraph 47). In another passage, he urges that the exercant "see the persons with the eyes of the imagination, meditating and contemplating in particular their circumstances," and that he imagine them through the other senses also, to "touch with the interior touch, as, for example, to embrace and kiss the places where such persons trod or sat," (Paragraphs 122 and 125). He asks him to contemplate "the place or cave of the Nativity, how large or how small, how low or how high, and how it was prepared." (*Exercitia*, second week, first day, 2nd Contemplation.) The mysteries of the Passion are to be contemplated in the same concrete and perceptible manner; for example the road along which Christ had to carry the Cross to Golgotha, how heavily the cross weighed upon his shoulders, etc. Such an historical or traditional event, known through the gospels, is to be perceived in the imagination of the exercising disciple by means of the senses as though it belonged to the actual, tangible world. However, since the event is a part of Christ's Passion, it has a decidedly supernatural connotation and must therefore be contemplated as a mystery; indeed such events are referred to as "mysteries" in the *Exercitia Spiritualia*.

Caravaggio represented the *Conversion of St. Paul* with the same kind of sober observation, with the same close sensuous grasp of the factual and tangible, which St. Ignatius would have demanded from the imagination of the exercant. In composition too the space is strictly limited and precisely measurable. The miraculous light is powerfully visualized without the indication of an ethereal source, and the celestial voice can almost be heard by the spectator, even without the image of Christ who utters it—exactly as it would be heard by the exercant in his overstimulated imagination. Caravaggio's *Conversion* is a realistic mystery just as are the contemplations of Saint Ignatius, and it is significant that, in the contract of 1600, Tiberio Cerasi specifies this painting, which he ordered, as "the Mystery of the Conversion of St. Paul." Caravaggio's representation of the mystery in completely human terms corresponds closely in spirit to the contemplation of the mysteries in the *Exercitia*; both make the supernatural tangible and understandable to man's spiritual intelligence with the help of the senses.

When the Virgin is mentioned in the *Exercitia*, it is more with regard to her earthly life as the Mother of Christ than as Queen of Heaven, just as in the gospels and the devotional books cited above. Similarly Caravaggio's oeuvre does not include a single representation of the Assumption of the Virgin, in sharp contrast to the great number of Assumptions painted by most of his contemporaries, the three Carracci, Cigoli, Barocci, Rubens, and others. When Caravaggio paints the Madonna, he places her in closest communication with human beings; for instance in the *Madonna di Loreto*. In the *Madonna del Serpe*, he projects the three over-lifesized figures of Saint Anne, the Virgin and Christ so close to the spectator and gives so much substance to the boyish body of Christ and to the large snake that the allegorical mystery can be grasped immediately and factually. In accordance again with the practice of the *Exercitia*, Caravaggio is very restrained in the representations of saints and visions. Even the prayers and ecstasy of Saint Francis—among the most favored subjects in Central Italy at this period (cf. Barocci, Cigoli, and others)—do not appear in Caravaggio's mature work, although the personality of the "saint of the poor" was certainly close to his heart.

The affinities between Caravaggio's mature religious conception and the *Exercitia* by no means prove or even suggest a direct affiliation of the artist with the Company of Jesus. The kind of art which the Jesuits were later to use as a special kind of propaganda fidei is closely connected with the flamboyant baroque style of Rubens and Bernini, of Baciccio and Padre Pozzo, and hardly adapted to the expression of the sober and mystic realism of Saint Ignatius and Caravaggio. Clement VIII, who was Pope during most of Caravaggio's career, was no great friend of the Jesuits. Caravaggio never worked for the Gesù or for other Jesuit churches, but for the Augustinians, the Carmelites and later for the Dominicans, the old adversaries of the Jesuit order. He was most closely connected with the French, through his work at San Luigi dei Francesi, the French national church, and as late as 1603 he was under the protection of the French Ambassador. However, in spite of a certain anti-Jesuit feeling in Rome at this time, the religious ideas and practices of Saint Ignatius' *Exercitia* had become very popular—probably because they gave a precise formulation to older popular feelings and mystic sentiments. Carlo Borromeo, the great Archbishop of Milan, practiced the *Exercitia*, as did Filippo Neri, Rome's most popular saint. In his early years, Filippo had even been asked by Loyola to enter his Society, but had refused because he disagreed with many aspects of its procedure and policies.

The rigorous and rational opinions of St. Ignatius about the relationship between the human and the supernatural were probably introduced to Caravaggio in the informal atmosphere of the spiritual life created in the second half of the sixteenth century by Filippo Neri.[2] The influence of San Filippo himself, or of his Congregation, upon Caravaggio's religious painting

FIG. 83
Death Mask of San Filippo Neri. Naples, Oratorio.

is not easy to define because of its general and emotional character. Nevertheless it is surely as important as the influence of the *Exercitia Spiritualia* since Filippo Neri played such an overwhelming part in the religious situation which Caravaggio encountered when he came to Rome. In my opinion, the character of Caravaggio's later works cannot be fully understood without considering Filippo's principles and religious activities. Together with other similar movements in Italy (for example the Barnabites and the Theatines), the Filippini formed a kind of "low church" in Rome which had an immense popularity. From the pietistic movements of earlier times they had inherited a simplicity of faith and a mystic devotion which gave each individual a direct and earthly contact with God and His Mysteries. In this respect the Filippini and other such groups were close to Protestant creeds which had originated from similar sources. They were even suspected—especially during the pontificate of Pius V—of heresy, and it was said that the "Lutheran Pest" lay behind their private gatherings, their sermons by laymen and their singing in the vernacular. The vice-governors of Rome even threatened to suspend Filippo's community because of the new ideas which he was introducing to the people and because of the "insolence" of the discourses which he permitted his pupils to deliver in public. However, the community was never suspended, because of its unshakable fidelity and obedience to the Pope and to the dogmas of the Church. Filippo never defended himself but always obeyed official orders, and he seemed almost to welcome humiliation. Moreover, he always had the support not only of his many fervent adherents, but also of high ecclesiastical figures such as his good friend Carlo Borromeo who successfully dissuaded the Pope from discontinuing Filippo's Oratorio. In 1575 Gregory XIII confirmed the constitution of the Filippini and gave them the church of Sta. Maria in Vallicella, which was totally re-built and was thereafter called the Chiesa Nuova—the church for which Caravaggio later painted his famous altarpiece. At different times the Cardinalate was offered to Filippo, but he always refused it; he did not want to be a dignitary and hated pompous and empty ceremonies to such a degree that whenever he was forced to participate in them, he tried openly to ridicule and debase his part in them. Many amusing stories have been told about him in this respect: at the solemn occasion of the inauguration of the Chiesa Nuova, in which he had to represent his community, he stood on the steps of the church among the highest dignitaries of Rome and suddenly pulled the beard of the tall and stately Swiss Guard who was standing next to him. On another occasion, when the Pope had ordered him to move from his modest lodgings in San Girolamo to new quarters in the Oratorio, he and his com-panions carried his miserable furniture, kitchen pots, etc. through the streets of Rome in a kind of mock procession. St. Bernard's maxim, "Spernere se ipsum," the despising of oneself, was deeply rooted in Filippo's character. His great popularity with the people of Rome was gained through his charity, his independence, and his easy and jocular behavior with everyone from the poorest pilgrim to the highest official. His extraordinary human attraction drew men to him "as a magnet draws iron." Thus great numbers of people frequented the gatherings of the community in the beautiful and holy places of the city, where, after informal sermons and disputations, they sat down together for a modest meal and listened to musical performances. The people, however, were not only amused and entertained by Filippo's unpredictable actions; they not only admired his humility and his effectiveness, but they began to attribute miraculous powers to him. Tales were circulated in Rome about his predictions and his cures; in short, he was already considered a saint in his own lifetime. However, Filippo mistrusted super-natural visions and ecstasies in himself as well as in others. It is true that he felt himself possessed by the Holy Ghost and his hypersensitivity and passion were so strong that he was often unable to finish a sermon or a mass because of the trembling of his body. Nevertheless, he always discounted the idea that he possessed supernatural powers and was capable of working miracles, because for him the greatest virtue was humility.

Such an extraordinary personality as Filippo Neri could hardly have escaped the attention of the young Michelangelo Amerighi when he came to Rome about five years before the death of the Saint. Filippo was then an ailing old man, confined to his room in the Chiesa Nuova for long periods. He could no longer take part in the delightful gatherings of his followers in the gardens and vineyards of Rome, but he was still able to fill the hearts of young people with a "religion of joy," as it was called by Cardinal Valiero in his treatise, *Filippo, ossia dialogo della delizia cristiana*, which was written during Filippo's last years. The impression which the "dried up, thin, and emaciated" saint made on the population was undiminished and probably even stronger than it had been before: "no ecclesiastic" says Cardinal Cusano, "whether religious or secular had been held in greater veneration by people of all classes, common folk as well as nobles—courtiers, cardinals and popes."

Even though it is improbable that the young Caravaggio ever belonged to the inner circle of San Filippo, some relations with the Filippini can be traced during his early years in Rome. Several members of the Crescenzi family, some of whom were associated with S. Luigi dei Francesi and with the administration of the Contarelli Chapel belonged to the most intimate circle of San Filippo's friends during his last years. The abbate Giacomo Crescenzi, the same man who, as we know from recently published documents, was suspected of fraud in the administration of the Contarelli Chapel (DOCS. 40-43), had been one of the "spiritual children" of San Filippo and was one of the few to be called to his deathbed. Roncalli (called Pomarancio), who was the drawing teacher of the Crescenzi family and who (as has been remarked in Chapter III) must have been somehow related to Caravaggio, painted a portrait of San Filippo, and after his death decorated the chapel of the saint. However, there was a more direct connection between Caravaggio and the Filippini through Pietro Vittrice, whose life had once been saved by Filippo and who was one of the saint's most important friends at the Papal Court. It was Pietro Vittrice who commissioned Caravaggio to paint the *Deposition* in the Chapel of the Pietà for which he, as one of the founders of the Chiesa Nuova, had obtained special privileges. Caravaggio surely knew Pietro Vittrice long before he was commissioned to paint the *Deposition*. According to Mancini, a very early painting by Caravaggio, the *Buona Ventura*—for which he received only eight scudi—was in the possession of Alessandro Vittrice, a Roman nobleman, probably the same nephew of Pietro mentioned in the records of the Chiesa Nuova (DOC. 49). Thus the impact which the spirit of San Filippo and his congregation made upon the young man should not be underestimated.

A lively and impressionable young artist like Caravaggio was certainly full of enthusiasm for the saint and probably seized every opportunity to see him and study his appearance. When Caravaggio painted the *First Saint Matthew* and gave the humble figure of the saint a Socrates face, it is not impossible that he had San Filippo (not bodily but spiritually) in mind, for in his circle of intimates the saint was at this time called a "Christian Socrates." Throughout his life Filippo had been especially friendly to young people. In his last years he was full of affection for his young friends, the children of the Vitelleschi and the Crescenzi families, as though he were "their father in blood"; he even enjoyed it when they played ball in the corridors or anteroom of his chamber and he did not allow them to be chased away. Thus, if they liked, Caravaggio and his young friends could have had easy access to the part of the Oratory in which Filippo lived. Also, the part which music played in the services of the

Filippini, inside and outside the church, must have attracted the young artist whose paintings—especially the early ones—show his enthusiastic devotion to music. Long before Caravaggio came to Rome, Palestrina had participated in the musical life of the Filippini and almost from the beginning another composer, Giovanni Animuccia, who was a fervent adherent of Filippo, had composed his laudi, motets, and spiritual madrigals for the use of the congregation. One can imagine that young friends of Caravaggio, or even he himself, had participated in the singing of such motets and madrigals whose texts, incidentally, were no longer written in Latin, but in Italian.

Filippo Neri never taught anything really new; he never created a system into which he inserted older religious conceptions as did Loyola in his *Exercitia*. There is nothing in his preserved sermons, letters or notes which could have given Caravaggio a basic idea for the composition of any one of his paintings. The realistic approach of the individual worshiper to the mystery of the supernatural, as expressed so impressively in Caravaggio's paintings, does not necessarily show an exclusive influence of the ideas of the Oratory, but is more probably related to the principles of St. Ignatius, even though, as has been remarked, Caravaggio may have been introduced to these principles by the Oratorians. Filippo mitigated and loosened the severe and rigid prescriptions of the Spanish Loyola and made religious devotion more human and accessible for everyone. He reanimated the spiritual life of Rome more than anyone else by making it more intimate and natural than it had ever been before. These qualities of naturalness and intimacy, of "familiarità e domestichezza," in the teaching of San Filippo account for his immense popularity with the Roman populace and surely made an indelible impression on the young Caravaggio, which is reflected in his mature paintings.

The profound honesty and directness of Caravaggio's religious expression is very well exemplified by the various ways in which he represented the Madonna, and in some respects his treatment of this subject indicates how close he is to the religious and social feelings of San Filippo. In some instances, Caravaggio clothes the figure of the Madonna in elegant, modish and even indecorous costumes. In the *Madonna di Loreto* the fine costume of the Virgin and the nobility of her countenance are necessary to indicate the impression which her divine presence makes upon the poor and humble pilgrims who kneel before her. In the *Madonna del Serpe*, the role of the Virgin is to substantiate an abstract religious idea—the church triumphant over heresy; here she appears as a divine heroine who, with her young son, crushes the head of the hideous snake beneath her foot, and a humble costume would have been quite inappropriate. On the other hand, in the *Death of the Virgin* and the *Nativity*, the two scenes which Caravaggio painted from the Madonna's life on earth, the depiction of her poverty and humility is not only permissible but is demanded by the Gospel and by the Apocrypha (from which the story of her death is drawn). The *Death of the Virgin*, from Caravaggio's late Roman years, with its portrayal of profound grief and the heavy silence which pervades the group of humble, mourning apostles, is the most outstanding example of the artist's penetration into pure human emotion, stripped of all Quintilian rhetoric. The poverty and the nakedness of the bed on which the swollen corpse of the Virgin has been laid, and the marvellous expression of peace in death on her face are in full accord with Filippo

Neri's supreme demands for humility and simplicity. Savonarola, whom Filippo so greatly venerated that he spent a whole night in Sta. Maria sopra Minerva praying that his writings might not be placed on the *Index Librorum Prohibitorum*, had objected to the representation of the Mother of Christ as if she were an elegant courtesan. It is interesting to note that about a hundred years later, when Caravaggio painted the Virgin, in Sta. Maria della Scala, as an extremely poor woman of the people, he was accused of having portrayed his mistress, a girl of the slums. However, this is no common woman who lies with her bare legs crudely projecting over the end of the bier, mourned, as it were, by the elders of the congregation, but it is the Mother of the Savior in the full majesty of her death. Caravaggio has translated a familiar scene of death and grief into the most awesome expression of a Christian mystery. One of his latest works, the *Nativity* at Messina (a painting which is very different from the more conventional *Adoration of the Child* in Palermo) is unsurpassed in its expression of Filippine simplicity, poverty and humility. The Messina painting is a direct antithesis to such works as the brilliant and elegant *Nativity* by Correggio from which Ruben's altarpiece for the Filippini in Fermo is derived. It is difficult to imagine a more desolate place than this poor and half-ruined stable where the pathetic figure of the Virgin is seen on the ground, reclining against a wooden manger and pressing the Infant tightly against her body as though she were protecting Him from the nocturnal cold. On her face is an expression of calm and pensive humility, which has a moving psychological countertheme in the dumb wonderment of the shepherds and of St. Joseph. The placement of the Virgin directly on the ground recalls the low-seated *Madonnas of Humility* from the Trecento and the corresponding figures in some *Nativities* from the same period, and brings to mind the scholarly etymology that derived the word "humilitas" from "humus," earth.[3]

The Chiesa Nuova was built over a long period: in Caravaggio's time the supervisor of the work was the father of his good friend Onorio Longhi. The church does not at all reflect Filippo's religious principles either in its architecture or in its decoration. When it was first proposed that the vaults of the church be covered with ornamental stucco, Filippo insisted that they be whitewashed instead, and they remained whitewashed until Pietro da Cortona covered them with his brilliant decorative frescoes. The present church is a sumptuous early baroque structure and the paintings which adorn its chapels reflect the general artistic taste of the time. There are paintings by Pulzone, Muziano, Barocci and the famous altarpieces by Rubens, none of which—although they were all by competent or excellent painters—has anything in common with Caravaggio's serious and thoughtful representation of the *Deposition* for the Cappella della Pietà (now in the Vatican), which was immediately considered his masterpiece. It has been observed that this painting does not simply represent the carrying of the body of Christ to the tomb, as does, for example, Raphael's famous *Deposition* in the Borghese. The figures of the composition—the grief-stricken woman and the two men who support Christ's body—are placed together on the great stone of the tomb in an almost sculptural group. The stone itself is set obliquely so that its corner projects emphatically toward the spectator, bringing him into direct contact with the pathetic scene. This emphasis on the corner of the stone certainly has a symbolic meaning. It is an allusion to the special significance which in the Old Testament was attached to the cornerstone of the house and figuratively to faith, and which in the New Testament was applied to Christ who is the foundation of the Church. "The stone which the builders rejected, the same is become the head of the corner" (Matthew 21:42). The large stone may also refer to "the stone of unction" (see Catalogue Raisonné) on which Christ's body was anointed. In this sense it would be a symbolic reference to the sacrament of extreme unction, made particularly significant by the fact that San Filippo

FIG. 84
Roger van der Weyden, *Entombment*. Florence, Uffizi.

devoted a large amount of his energy to the revival of the practice of the Holy Sacraments in Rome. A remarkable similarity to Caravaggio's use of the stone is found in Roger van der Weyden's *Entombment* in the Uffizi, which was probably known both to San Filippo and to Vittrice, who commissioned the painting for the Cappella della Pietà. In fact, in the iconographic context of the dedication of the chapels (which were devoted to the Mysteries of the Virgin) Caravaggio's painting has more the character of a *Pietà* than of a simply narrative *Deposition*. Caravaggio's combination of plastic realism in the figures with the subtle symbolism of the stone shows a depth of religious reflection unequalled by any of his contemporaries and which is entirely in keeping with San Filippo's religious intensity.

We have seen that Caravaggio's paintings—particularly the eloquent and monumental works of his mature years—express an astonishingly original and intense religious feeling bearing the imprint of the popular religious movements of his time: the precise spiritual rationalism of St. Ignatius and the informal mysticism and humility of St. Philip. Within this framework, Caravaggio developed his individual religious ideology, dominated by a strong social consciousness. It is probable that the circumstances of his life, the poverty of his early years and other personal difficulties, caused him to rebel against convention and gave him a sharp awareness of the spiritual needs of the individual, whatever his social rank. Again and again in his paintings, Caravaggio shows a deep sympathy for people who are materially poor—for example the poor peasants kneeling before the *Madonna di Loreto* or the simple people at the feet of the *Madonna del Rosario*.

The spiritual language of Caravaggio's paintings did not find an immediate continuation in the works of any other painter. The so-called Caravaggisti were concerned almost exclusively with other aspects of his art, his chiaroscuro effects, his genre subject matter, his color and composition, and they seem to have been unable to comprehend the full meaning of the psychological and social elements of his religious paintings. Such painters as Gentileschi, Saraceni, Manfredi and even Borgianni cannot be called religious painters in the same sense as Caravaggio.

Nor did the religious implications of Caravaggio's works have a very extensive influence outside of Italy. The association of commonplace and familiar figures with sacred events in a few of the early works of Velasquez, such as the *Kitchen Maid* and *Mary and Martha*, remind one of Caravaggio, but they are essentially genre paintings with religious overtones. Much more interesting and significant is the comparison with Rembrandt. Just as Caravaggio was influenced by the ideals of Filippo Neri, Rembrandt was, in his later years, inspired by the doctrines of the Mennonites. An interesting parallel can be drawn between the Filippini and the Mennonites, in so far as both were popular religious movements and in a sense spiritually opposed to formalistic and abstract official churches, the one in Holland being the rigid and dogmatic Calvinist Church. In spite of their fundamental differences, both the Filippini and the Mennonites believed in a strict adherence to the Gospels and emphasized the Christian virtues of humility and simplicity, as do all popular pietistic movements. Numerous late religious works of Rembrandt were directly influenced by Mennonite texts and principles in their spiritual content as well as in their subject matter. However, even though both Caravaggio and Rembrandt were men of great spiritual sensitivity and were influenced by similar religious values, their conceptions of religious scenes are fundamentally different. The significant differences between their religious paintings are partly the result of the reasons for which they were painted. Almost all of Caravaggio's religious works, beginning with the San Luigi series, were altarpieces designed for the worship of the Christian community and its members, whereas most of Rembrandt's religious paintings were made not on commission, but as private expressions of his own imaginative impulses, there being no place for paintings in Calvinist churches. Rembrandt could thus treat Old and New Testament subjects in the same impressive manner that he employed for such nonreligious paintings as the *Oath of Julius Civilis* or the

Homer, and he did not have to take into account the spiritual relationship between the worshiper and the sacred scene. Conversely, the principal purpose of Caravaggio's great altarpieces was to depict Christian mysteries so that the worshiper could grasp them in terms of his own life. Rembrandt's aim was not to show miracles in terms of this earth, but to express the radiance of his inner visions. He substantiates these visions in his paintings through his amazing interpretations of human psychology, and, perhaps more, through his spectacular effects of light. In Caravaggio's works the supernatural is always implicit in the actuality of the scene; his light, falling upon the physical objects, evokes from them the supernatural.

It is curious to remark that in France, where there existed a religious atmosphere comparable in many ways to that which San Filippo Neri had created in Rome, almost none of the important artists of the time—Vouet, LeSueur, Philippe de Champaigne—even approached Caravaggio's religious expression. Only in a profane work such as Louis Le Nain's *Repas de Paysans* do we find an expression which is comparable to Caravaggio in its profound piety.

FINIS

VAN MANDER tells us that Caravaggio went from one ball game to another and was always ready to draw his sword and engage in a brawl. On Sunday evening, May 29, 1606, in the Campo Marzio, near the palace of the Grand Duke of Tuscany, Caravaggio was playing palla a corda—a kind of tennis—with his old friend Onorio Longhi, a certain Captain Antonio from Bologna who was stationed at the Castel' Sant' Angelo, and Ranuccio Tomassoni, a well-bred young gentleman from Terni. As frequently happens in such games, a quarrel arose over ten scudi which Ranuccio won from Caravaggio, and the two men came to blows with their rackets. As he later asserted, Onorio intervened and tried to reconcile the two opponents, but his efforts were in vain; they resorted to arms and fought a kind of duel in which Caravaggio received serious head wounds and Ranuccio was knocked down and killed. Caravaggio was seconded by the Captain Antonio, who was later arrested; Onorio was banished from Rome and went to Milan, whence he petitioned the Pope to allow him to return to his wife and five children. Caravaggio escaped and found temporary refuge in the house of a certain Andrea Ruffetti near the Piazza Colonna where a clerk of the Criminal Court (notaio de'Malefizi) visited him while he was still in bed recovering from his wounds. When the clerk asked him who had wounded him so severely in the throat and on the left ear, he replied that he had fallen down in the street, wounded himself with his sword, and that no one had been present. Caravaggio was not arrested at once, but was forbidden to leave the house under penalty of a five-hundred-scudi fine. It would almost seem that certain influential persons did not want the famous artist to be put in prison and be judged as a common criminal. On the very next day after the visit of the "notaio de'Malefizi" a news-report (avviso), dated May 31, related the whole affair with the remark that Caravaggio's whereabouts were unknown. On the same day Fabio Massetti, the Duke of Modena's agent, wrote in a report that Caravaggio was a fugitive and was on his way to Florence. Caravaggio had left Rome, but he had not set out for Florence and Modena as Massetti supposed. Instead he fled into the Sabine Mountains, to

Palestrina, Zagarola, or Pagliano, where he was under the benevolent protection of Duke Marzio Colonna; there he was beyond the reach of the pontifical courts but was still able to remain in contact with his friends in Rome, who might have been able to obtain a quick pardon for him from the Pope. To judge from Massetti's letters it would seem that Caravaggio's case was not considered hopeless, because the crime which he had committed was not premeditated and because he had himself been wounded. However, the pardon was not granted until much later; it was still being negotiated in August of 1607, when Massetti wrote to Modena about the advance of thirty-two scudi which he had given Caravaggio toward the price of an altarpiece. Caravaggio painted only two relatively small works while he was in the Sabine Mountains, a *Magdalene* of which we know at least two copies and a *Christ at Emmaus*.

It is not known exactly when Caravaggio left the Sabine Mountains and went to Naples, but considering the amount of work he did there, it could scarcely have been later than the end of 1606 or the beginning of 1607. Having grown tired of waiting for a pardon from the Pope, and being in need of funds (Bellori says that he left Rome "without a penny") he went to Naples, where many large and lucrative commissions awaited him. The most impressive and beautiful work which he painted in Naples is the large altarpiece representing the *Seven Acts of Mercy* which he made for the Confraternity of the Madonna della Misericordia. This work, which combines seven separate episodes into a single unified scene, is ample proof that Caravaggio's energy and power of creation had in no way been diminished by his recent misfortune; in fact, he seems to have set to work in Naples with renewed enthusiasm and determination. The *Seven Acts of Mercy* continues the rich and virile religious expression of his late Roman years, demonstrating again his sympathetic understanding of human compassion and suffering. His unequaled ability to represent the deepest meaning of Christian humility is, here as before, completely in harmony with Filippo Neri's religious principles. Another important work which Caravaggio painted in Naples is the large altarpiece of the *Flagellation of Christ* for a chapel in San Domenico Maggiore. Most of the other works which he painted are lost or unknown. Bellori mentions a *Denial of St. Peter* for San Martino and Mancini speaks of two paintings for Sta. Anna dei Lombardi, a *Resurrection* and a *St. Francis*. Two more paintings by Caravaggio are mentioned as having been in Naples at this time; one is the famous *Madonna of the Rosary* and the other is the *Judith and Holofernes*. In my opinion neither of them was done during Caravaggio's sojourn in Naples even though the painter Pourbus, who offered to buy them for the Duke of Mantua, says that they were. The *Madonna of the Rosary* is probably the painting which the Duke of Modena had ordered through Massetti and which was still unfinished when Caravaggio fled from Rome. Both of these paintings were for sale in Naples at rather high prices, but they were sold by agents rather than by Caravaggio himself. (The prices show how famous Caravaggio was by this time.) When he went to Naples no really important painter had been active there for many years. Arpino's frescoes at San Martino were pleasant but did not make a great impression on Neapolitan artists, whereas Caravaggio's uniqueness was at once recognized, especially by the younger generation. Caracciolo, who worked at the Miseracordia immediately after Caravaggio, was the most important artist to propagate the spirit of Caravaggio's art in Naples.

It is not known exactly when Caravaggio left Naples, but the fact that Pourbus was negotiating (not with Caravaggio himself, but with agents) for the purchase of the *Madonna del Rosario* would indicate that the artist had already left Naples by September of 1607—the month in which Pourbus' letter was written—and it can be assumed that he was in Malta or on his way there at this time. In any case, the amount of work which Caravaggio did in Malta—he painted two portraits of the Grand Master, a *Beheading of St. John, a St. Jerome, a Magdalene* and a *Cupid* there—would have required about a year's time and he left Malta in October of 1608. According to the garrulous Sandrart, his only reason for going to Malta was that he wanted to become a Knight of St. John in order to equal his rival, Giuseppe d'Arpino, who seven years earlier had been made Cavaliere di Cristo by Clement VIII. Such an honor was surely a kind of triumph for Caravaggio and he may have felt that it would compensate in part for the misdeeds which he had committed in Rome. However, the most reasonable explanation for his trip to Malta is that there was a great need for artists to decorate the new Conventual Church in La Valletta. When the Grand Master heard that the famous Caravaggio was in Naples he may have sent his emissaries there to persuade him to come to Malta.

Caravaggio was introduced to the Grand Master, Alof de Wignacourt, shortly after his arrival on the island. Wignacourt, a French nobleman, at once commissioned him to do his portrait. According to Bellori, Caravaggio made two portraits of this high dignitary. One shows him standing in full armor, carrying his staff of office, with a page holding his plumed helmet at his side. The other is a less formal portrait which shows the Grand Master seated and wearing the robe of his rank. The first of these portraits, which Bellori says was in the Armory of Malta, is probably the painting which is now in the Louvre. Wignacourt is said to have been greatly pleased with these portraits, and it was not long before Caravaggio was given the Cross of Malta. He was officially received into the order as Cavaliere di Grazia (Obbedienza) on July 14th, 1608. In addition to making Caravaggio a knight in the order, the Grand Master favored him with a gold chain, two Turkish slaves and "other signs of his esteem for the painter's work."

The largest and most important painting made by Caravaggio during his stay in Malta was the *Beheading of St. John* for the church of San Giovanni. It is possible that Caravaggio had not entirely finished it when he left Malta, for Bellori remarked that "the canvas showed through the half-tone," and it is today so blackened that one can see only the remains of an admirable work of art. By drawing the figures together into an almost geometric form, a half circle, setting them apart and to the left on a cross-lit stage, and contrasting them to the sober rectangularity of the prison wall behind, Caravaggio achieves a monumental grandeur and restrained drama. It is as if he had once again come to the solutions that Masaccio had found in the *Tribute Money*.

Caravaggio's stay in Malta was successful at first. Bellori says that he was delighted by the honor of being received into the Order of St. John, by the esteem in which his works were held by the Grand Master, and by the abundance of his life. Accustomed to more or less bohemian ways, he found here the opportunity to live almost as a nobleman. His enjoyment of these advantages was, however, to come to an abrupt end because of his incorrigible tendency to get into trouble. In spite of his many past experiences, he quarreled again, this time with a Cavaliere di Giustitia, and was put in prison. The cause of the quarrel is not known, but in the eyes of the strictly military Order of Malta an offense to a superior was a serious matter. Caravaggio then made a daring and dramatic escape from the Castel' Sant' Angelo at night and set sail to Sicily on a barque. To the Order, his escape constituted desertion, a capital crime. On October 6, 1608, on the order of the Fiscal Procurator, Don Hieronymo Varayz, a Criminal Commission was set up by the Grand Master and was instructed to collect all evidence concerning Caravaggio's escape. On November 21 the council voted to deprive him of his habit. The final action was taken on December 1, when Caravaggio was solemnly "expelled and thrust forth like a rotten and diseased limb from the Order and Society" (tanquam membrum putridum et foetidum–DOC. 30).

Caravaggio stayed in Sicily, probably awaiting the time when he could return to Rome. He undoubtedly left Malta penniless and was obliged to find commissions in various Sicilian towns in order to earn money for his return to Italy. The fact that the powerful order of Maltese Knights had affiliates and representatives everywhere, particularly in a city like Syracuse, the port nearest Malta, may have made Sicily dangerous for Caravaggio, and this too may have been a reason for his movement from place to place on the island. In Syracuse, where he must have arrived shortly after his escape in October, he painted the *Burial of St. Lucy* for the church of Sta. Lucia located outside the city by the sea. He must have received the commission almost immediately upon his arrival, since he remained in Syracuse for only a few months. Yet in this time he executed the picture, on a monumental scale, and showing a grandeur of composition that seems in its very greatness to express the strain and hazard in which it was made.

By the end of the year 1608, according to Susini, a Sicilian writer of the early eighteenth century, he had been forced to leave Syracuse after a brawl with a schoolmaster who was suspicious of the attention the artist paid to the young boys under his tutelage. Caravaggio spent a longer time in Messina than he had in Syracuse, working under the protection of the Lazzari, a family of wealthy Genoese merchants whose headquarters were in Messina. For their family chapel in the recently built church of the Crociferi, Caravaggio painted a *Resurrection of Lazarus*, overpowering in its depth of feeling and illuminating in its masterful concord of light and forms. The humble and miraculous *Nativity* for the church of the Cappuccini is of the same high quality. During the months of his stay in Messina Caravaggio is still called "Miles Gerusalemitanus" in a document concerning the donation of the *Lazarus* to the church of the Crociferi, even though he had been ousted from the order of St. John of Jerusalem months before. It seems that Caravaggio's expulsion from the order was not made public; even the documents relating to his death refer to him as a Knight of Malta.

Caravaggio left Messina and went to Palermo some time during the summer of 1609. The church of the Oratorio of San Lorenzo in Palermo contains his *Adoration of the Child with St. Francis and St. Lawrence*. It is a painting of very different character from the scene of the *Nativity* in Messina, and lacks its simple and unpretentious expressiveness. The composition is conventional, and the figures of the praying saint and the angel flying down from above recall ideas which Caravaggio had exploited earlier. The conservatism of the picture in thought and feeling is utterly unlike the forceful creativeness of the others made by Caravaggio during these troubled months, as if the painter had been seriously hampered by the demands of less advanced patrons.

Caravaggio sailed from Palermo to Naples with the hope of returning soon to Rome. He probably knew that Cardinal Gonzaga (whose brother, the Duke of Mantua, had bought the *Death of the Virgin*), was trying to arrange a pardon for him from the Pope. Meanwhile, Caravaggio attempted to placate the wrath of the Order of Malta. According to Bellori, he made a painting of *Salome with the Head of St. John* for the Grand Master, probably the very impressive composition to be seen in the Escorial. But instead of improving, his situation grew worse. An avviso published in Rome on October 24, 1609 states that in Naples "the famous painter," Caravaggio, had been either killed or disfigured. This certainly refers to the episode described in greater detail by Bellori and Baglione, who report that the artist was caught by his enemies in the doorway of the Hosteria del Ciriglio, and so severely slashed in the face that he was almost unrecognizable. Whether this was an action privately taken by the Cavaliere with whom Caravaggio had quarreled in Malta, an official punishment by representatives of the Order, or an expression of offense by persons unknown, it was certainly an act characteristic of vendetta.

The circumstance of Caravaggio's last months can be pieced together only with some difficulty. The wounds inflicted upon him by his enemies must have required a considerable length of time to heal. The eight or nine months which he spent in Naples after the attack would have given him enough time to execute several paintings after his recovery. In 1610 the Count of Benevente, Viceroy of Naples, took to Valladolid a *Martyrdom of St. Andrew* by Caravaggio. A copy, apparently after this picture, exists in Spain, and it is possible that the original was painted by Caravaggio during these months. The posthumous inventory of Caravaggio's belongings mentions a *St. John the Baptist* which may also have found its way into the possession of the viceroy, since a letter from his office requests that a painting of this subject be sent to him. Certain paintings now lost, such as the *Resurrection* for Sta. Anna dei Lombardi in Naples, may possibly have been made during this second sojourn there.

About the end of June 1610, Caravaggio, with his belongings, boarded a two-masted ship, a felucca, and set sail from Naples, bound for some unidentified port to the north. It is curious that he did not follow the usual land route that leads from Naples to Rome, by way of Terracina. He may have felt safer traveling by sea than by land, although it is unlikely that he should still have been pursued by his enemies, since they had already so successfully wounded him. Caravaggio by-passed Civitavecchia, the regular port for Rome, and continued north, a circumstance that might even be taken to indicate that he did not intend to go directly to Rome, but rather to some other city like Florence, Mantua or Genoa. An avviso of July 31, 1610 announced that he had already been granted his pardon by His Holiness, but it is not certain whether he had received the news during his voyage. Caravaggio went ashore somewhere near the small town of Port'Ercole, on the promontory of Monte Argentario in southern Tuscany, a part of the coast which was at this time under the jurisdiction of the

Spanish Viceroy of Naples. Bellori relates that the Spanish Guards, mistaking Caravaggio for another Cavaliere for whom they were lying in wait, arrested him and threw him into prison. He was released after a few days only to find that the felucca had sailed without him, carrying off all his belongings. Bellori's account seems not to be altogether complete, since it is known that after Caravaggio's death his property, including the *St. John* mentioned above was taken into custody by the local authorities who, assuming that he was still a Knight of Malta, offered it to the Prior of Capua. It was after the prior had refused to accept it that the Viceroy of Naples asked to have it forwarded to him.

Caravaggio was released by the Spanish Guards, in a state of utmost desperation and fury. He started out on foot along the beach in the terrible heat of July—beneath the "sforza del sol Lione," as Baglione calls it. When he came to Port'Ercole he was ill and exhausted, and within a few days he died of a malignant fever, in all probability the malaria perniciosa that pervades this region. A few days later two avvisi dated July 28 and 31, 1610, announced to Rome the death of one of its most celebrated painters:

1610, July 28

Word has been received of the death of Michelangelo da Caravaggio, a famous painter, eminent in the handling of color and painting from life, following an illness in Port'Ercole.

BIBLIOGRAPHICAL REFERENCES

CHAPTER I

1. E. Dobschütz, "Die Bekehrung des Paulus," *Repertorium für Kunstwissenschaft*, L (1920), p. 57 ff.
2. G. Vasari, *Le Vite di Michelangelo Buonarroti*, edited by Carl Frey. Berlin, 1887, p. 172.
3. L. Burckhardt, *Cicerone*, Collected Works, III (1933).
4. C. Malvasia, *Felsina Pittrice*, I (1678), p. 388.
5. Cf. W. Friedlaender, "Der Anti-Manieristische Stil um 1590 und sein Verhältnis zum Übersinnlichen," *Bibliothek Warburg*, VIII (1928-29).
6. Bartsch: nos. 39 and 40.
7. E. Mâle, *L'Art Réligieux après le Concil de Trente*, 1932, p. 267.

CHAPTER II

1. For the historical background of North Italy see C. Cantu, *Grande Illustrazione del Lombardo et Veneto* V (1857), p. 1041.
2. A. Morassi, "Simone Peterzano," *Bolletino d'Arte* (1934), p. 103.
   N. Pevsner, "Eine Revision der Caravaggio-Daten," *Zeitschrift für Bildende Kunst*, 1927-28.
   R. Longhi, Quesiti Caravaggeschi—I. Registro dei Tempi.—II. I Precedenti, *Pinacotheca*, 1928-29, pp. 17-33 and 258-320.
3. See also, Lomazzo's *Idea del Tempio della Pittura*, 1590.
4. Cf. A. Perotti, *I Pittori Campi da Cremona*, Milan.
5. C. Gilbert, "Milan and Savoldo," *Art Bulletin*, XXVII (1945). A full study on Savoldo by Mr. Gilbert has just been completed.
6. See G. Gambosi, *Moretto da Brescia*, Basel, 1943.
7. See B. Berenson, *Lorenzo Lotto*, London, 1901, and L. Venturi, *Giorgione e il Giorgionismo*, Milan, 1913.
8. See G. Fiocco, *Giovanni Antonio Pordenone*, Udine, 1939.
9. See E. Arslan, *I Bassani*, Bologna, 1931.
10. M. Michiels, *Anonimo Morelliano* (edited by Frimmel, 1896), p. 54.
11. F. Baldinucci, *Notizie dei Professori del Disegno* (edited by Ranelli) Vol. II, p. 633.

CHAPTER III

1. On Sixtus V see J. A. Hübner, *Sixte V*, Paris, 1870 and L. Pastor, *History of the Popes*, vols. XXI-XXII.
2. W. Friedlaender, "Zuccari and Caravaggio," *Gazette des Beaux-Arts*, Vol. XXXIII (1948), p. 31 ff. and D. Mahon, "On some aspects of Caravaggio and his times," Metropolitan Museum Bulletin, October, 1953. Cf. also J. Schlosser, Die Kunstliteratur (Book VI: Die Kunstliteratur der Manieristenzeit), Vienna, 1924.
3. Malvasia, *op. cit.*, I, p. 366.
4. See Part III, Document no. 11.
5. Cf. Missirini, *Memorie per servire alla storia della Romana Accademia di San Lucca*, 1823, p. 32 ff.
6. Cf. D. Mahon, *Studies in Seicento Art and Theory*, 1947, p. 180 ff.
7. See Part III, Document no. 11.
8. Mancini, Trattato, Marciana Manuscript, Venice, fol. 145r. Pietro Berettini da Cortona (Britio Prenetteri) and Ottonelli, *Trattato della Pittura*, Second edition, Venice, 1696, p. 26 (first edition, Florence, 1652).
9. For more complete information on Muziano, Zuccari, Roncalli, Pulzone and Arpino, see Baglione's *Vite* and H. Voss, *Die Malerei der Spätrenaissance*, Berlin, 1920.
10. Bottari, Lettere, IV (1768), p. 247 ff.

CHAPTER IV

1. A. De Rinaldis, "D'Arpino e Caravaggio," *Bolletino d'Arte*, 1935-36, pp. 577-80.
2. van Mander, *Das Leben der Niederländischen und Deutschen Maler*, edited by H. Floerke, I (1906), p. 143.
3. Vasari, *Vite* (ed. Milanesi), IV (1879), p. 25.
4. Edition of 1593, p. 233.
5. R. van Marle, *Iconographie de l'Art profane au Moyen-Age et à la Renaissance*, II (1932), p. 263.
6. 1620, p. 28.
7. See Part III, Document no. 12.
8. 1657, p. 277.
9. *Die Römischen Päpste*, 1899, p. 230.

CHAPTER V

1. For the literature concerning the Contarelli Chapel, see Catalogue Raisonné.

CHAPTER VI

1. *Exercitia Spiritualia*, Rome, 1548; English translation by W. H. Longridge, London, 1919. See also Gothein, *Ignatius von Loyola und die Gegenreformation*, 1895, and L. Zarnke, *die Exercitia Spiritualia des Ignatius von Loyola* (in Schriften des Vereins für Reformationsgeschichte, No. 151), 1931.
2. The main source of my discussion of San Filippo is the excellent and comprehensive work by Ponnelle and Bordet: *St. Philip Neri and the Roman Society of his Times*, English translation by R. F. Kerr, London, 1932.
3. Cf. Meiss, *Painting in Florence and Siena after the Black Death*, Princeton, 1951, pp. 132-156.

PART II

CATALOGUE RAISONNÉ

ABBREVIATIONS
IN THE CATALOGUE RAISONNÉ

SOURCES AND PERIODICALS FREQUENTLY CITED

Baglione—Baglione, G. *Le vite de' pittori* . . . , Rome, 1642

Bellori—Bellori, G. P. *Le vite de' pittori* . . . , Rome, 1642

Bertolotti—Bertolotti, A. *Artisti Lombardi a Roma*, Milan, 1881

Malvasia—Malvasia *Felsina Pittrice*, Bologna, 1678

Mancini—Mancini, G. *Trattato della Pittura*, Venice, Bibl. Marciana, Ms. It. 5571; and Florence, Bibl. Naz. cod. Pal. 597

Manilli—Manilli, J. *Villa Borghese discritta*, Rome, 1650

Orbaan—Orbaan, J. A. F. *Documenti sul Barocco in Roma*, Rome, 1920

Passeri—Passeri, G. B. *Vite*, ed. Hess, 1934

Sandrart—Sandrart, J. von *Teutsche Academie*, Nuernberg, 1675

Seannelli—Seannelli, F. *Il Microcosmo della Pittura*, Cesena, 1657

Scaramuccia—Scaramuccia, L. *Finezze de' pennelli Italiani*, Pavia, 1674

Van Mander—Mander, K. Van *Schilderboek*, Alkmaar, 1604

Mostra—*Mostra del Caravaggio e dei Caravaggeschi*, Milan, 1951

Prec., Borghese—Longhi, R. *Precisioni nelle gallerie italiane R. Galleria Borghese*, Rome, 1928

Anales—Ainaud, G. *Anales y Boletin de los Museos de Arte de Barcelona*, 1947

Arch. Stor. Mes.—*Archivio Storico Mesenense*

Art Bull.—*The Art Bulletin*, The College Art Association of America

Boll. d'Arte—*Bolletino d'Arte*

Burl. Mag.—*The Burlington Magazine*

Gaz. d. B-A—*Gazette des Beaux-Arts*

Internat. Studio—*International Studio*

J. d. K.—*Jahrbuch der preussischen Kunstsammlungen*

Par.—*Paragone*

Pin.—*Pinacoteca*

Prop.—*Proporzioni*

Rass. d'Arte—*Rassegna d'Arte*

Riv. d'Arte—*Rivista d'Arte*

Z. f. b. K.—*Zeitschrift für bildende Kunst*

INTRODUCTION TO THE CATALOGUE RAISONNÉ

THE basis for the Catalogue Raisonné is the description of Caravaggio's works found in the literary sources of the seventeenth century. The most important of these is the biography of Giovanni Baglione, Caravaggio's contemporary and competitor. Since Baglione was only a few years older than Caravaggio and worked in Rome during the entire time that Caravaggio was there, he is the only one of the biographers who was able to observe Caravaggio's activities at close range. In spite of the enmity which existed between the two painters, Baglione's account of Caravaggio's works, especially those which he made in Rome, is usually sober and reliable. The most extensive and best known biography of Caravaggio is that of Giovanni Pietro Bellori. Although Bellori supplements the account of Baglione in many instances, he is more concerned with the interpretation of Caravaggio's art than in giving a factual account of his works. On the other hand, Bellori is much better informed about Caravaggio's post-Roman years in Naples, Malta and Sicily. Much less systematic than the biographies of Baglione and Bellori are the writings of Giulio Mancini, the physician of Urban VIII, whose manuscripts nevertheless give some very valuable information about paintings by Caravaggio which is not found elsewhere. Other writers, such as Scanelli, Malvasia, Passeri and the two foreigners, van Mander and Sandrart, do not contribute to our knowledge of what Caravaggio actually painted, even though in some cases they give additional information about his works.

By limiting Caravaggio's work to paintings mentioned in the three principal sources— Baglione, Bellori and Mancini—and identifying them, in so far as it is possible, with corresponding works in churches and collections, we have a solid foundation for the reconstruction of Caravaggio's oeuvre. In fact, almost every painting which is attributed to Caravaggio and which is not mentioned in the sources can, in my opinion, be eliminated. Of course there is always the possibility that certain paintings by Caravaggio may have escaped the notice of his biographers. As is usually the case, this is especially true for his earliest works. Until now, however, no undisputed painting is known which is not mentioned in the sources. Even such an attractive painting as the *Narcissus* in the Corsini Gallery, which was still shown as a Caravaggio in the recent exhibition at Milan and which is nowhere mentioned in the sources, cannot, in my opinion, be accepted as a Caravaggio.

Because the catalogue is based almost completely upon the literary sources, it does not follow the customary arrangement. The consideration of each of Caravaggio's works begins with a quotation or paraphrase in English of the reference or references in the literary sources. There follows a discussion of the paintings which correspond to these references. Documents pertaining to the paintings and commissions of Caravaggio are also noted and discussed in the catalogue, as is the modern critical literature.

Certain problems arise when one tries to coordinate the information given in the sources with the paintings which are known. Frequently, a choice must be made between a number of paintings whose subject matter corresponds to particular passages in the sources. Quite a few paintings have been associated with Baglione's rather scanty description of Caravaggio's

Bacchus, but only those in the Borghese and Uffizi seem to be accepted as a Caravaggios. It is well known, however, that the artist painted certain subjects more than once. For example, we know from the sources that he made several paintings of the young St. John. Because of such problems as these, it has seemed advisable, in some instances, to group paintings of the same subject together under a single heading. In this way attributions which come close to Caravaggio are discussed in connection with accepted paintings of the same subjects.

After we have decided which particular paintings correspond to the references in the sources and have eliminated those which do not, we may still be faced with the question: Is the chosen painting actually from the hand of Caravaggio, or is it simply a repetition of one of his compositions? Is the painting an original or a copy, and if it is an original, how well is it preserved—how much remains of the original surface? A copy of a painting, even if it is only a pale reflection of the original, can frequently be of very great value, especially when it preserves a composition which is mentioned in the sources and which would otherwise be unknown to us. The rather poor copy of the *Taking of Christ*, which was brought to light through the efforts of Roberto Longhi, affords us a glimpse, however nebulous it may be, of one of Caravaggio's most powerful works. The better a copy is and the closer it comes to our idea of what the original looked like, the greater is its value. I would even go so far as to say that an excellent contemporary copy can be of greater documentary value than a badly preserved and often repainted original. As early as the 1590's there were copies of the *Doubting Thomas* in Bologna which were very much admired by Bolognese painters.

Where it was possible the problem of preservation has been discussed in the Catalogue Raisonné. However, the results of the scientific investigation which is being carried on are as yet quite incomplete. The works which Caravaggio painted after he left Rome—in Naples, Malta and Sicily—are in a particularly bad state of preservation. In some cases, notably in the *Martyrdom of St. Lucy* in Syracuse, scientific restoration has removed the overpainting so that we are at least able to see the general conception of the original. With the help of X-ray and careful visual examination, it has frequently been possible to detect pentimenti beneath the present surfaces of paintings and thus to see how Caravaggio corrected and altered details such as the position of an arm, a head or even a whole figure. The reason pentimenti are so often found in his paintings is that he worked directly upon the canvas, using it almost as other painters use their sketchbooks. He did not make detailed preliminary drawings, but this, of course, does not exclude the possibility that he used small compositional sketches. The scientific investigations of Caravaggio's paintings which have only recently begun (mainly by Professor Cesare Brandi's Istituto del Restauro in Rome) will undoubtedly reveal a much more precise notion of the way in which he worked.

With some exceptions, the paintings treated in the Catalogue Raisonné are arranged in chronological order. For the most part, the chronology of Caravaggio's works is not particularly complicated, although the dating of the paintings made during the early years of his Roman period is somewhat problematic. A stylistically homogeneous group of smaller paintings, mostly genre and half-figure compositions, belongs, as we are told by Baglione and Bellori, to the artist's early years in Rome. As is the case with most artists, the precise dates of these early paintings are difficult to discover. Formerly it was generally accepted that this group of paintings was begun in about 1589, soon after Caravaggio's Milanese apprenticeship, but more recently it has been suggested that they were begun later, about 1591/1592. The difference, however, is only a matter of a few years, and it does not greatly affect our understanding of Caravaggio's development. Baglione tells us that the early single and half-figure paintings were drawn after Caravaggio's own reflection in a mirror, and the fact that the boys in the *Musica* and the *Bacchus* are from sixteen to eighteen years of age would indicate a correspondingly early date for the beginning of Caravaggio's artistic career, around 1590. The documents which were recently published by Denis Mahon have made it possible to date the two lateral paintings in the Contarelli Chapel at the end of the century, but other works of Caravaggio's early maturity such as the *Supper at Emmaus* and the *St. Thomas* cannot be exactly dated even though they belong to a stylistically homogeneous group of paintings which are close in time to the Contarelli Chapel. Thus Caravaggio's early work can be divided only into general chronological groups, and in order to fit the individual paintings into these groups we must rely heavily on visual judgment. It should also be kept in mind that the limits of these groups cannot be strictly defined; the transition from Caravaggio's first style to that of his early maturity is especially uncertain.

The groups into which the paintings in the Catalogue Raisonné have been divided are the following:

I. Still-life Paintings.
II. Early Paintings: about 1590 to 1595.
III. Early Maturity: about 1595 to 1600.
    A. Smaller Religious Paintings.
    B. Contarelli Chapel.
IV. The Monumental Roman style: 1600 to 1606.
V. Post-Roman Paintings: 1606 to 1610.
    A. Paintings made in the Sabine Mountains and during Caravaggio's first sojourn in Naples.
    B. Paintings made in Malta and Sicily and during the second sojourn in Naples.
VI. Portraits.
VII. Paintings mentioned in the sources for which neither original canvases nor undisputable copies are known.
VIII. Paintings mistakenly attributed to Caravaggio in the literary sources.

STILL-LIFE PAINTINGS

1. PAINTINGS OF FRUIT AND FLOWERS

SOURCES

Baglione, 136: describes the still-life in "a painting of a youth playing a lute" in which there is "a carafe of flowers filled with water in which one can easily distinguish the reflections of a window and other objects in the room. On the flowers is fresh dew which is rendered with exquisite accuracy."

Bellori, 202: gives almost the same description as Baglione, but does not relate it to any particular painting. "He was employed by him, Arpino, to paint flowers and fruits, which he made so well that they attained the high degree of beauty so fully appreciated today. He painted a carafe of flowers in which he showed the transparency of the glass and of the water and in which one can see the reflection of a window in the room; the flowers are sprinkled with the freshest dew drops. He also made other excellent paintings of this kind, but he worked on such subjects with reluctance, feeling great regret at seeing himself kept away from figure painting."

Letter of *Vincenzo Giustiniani*, Bottari, *Raccolta di Lettere sulla Pittura*, 1768, vol. VI, p. 247: Giustiniani quotes a statement made by Caravaggio that "it required of him as much craftsmanship to paint a good picture of flowers as one of figures." (Tanta manifattura gli era un quadro buono di fiori, come di figure.)

PAINTINGS

PLATES 9, 13

A. Although Baglione refers specifically to the *Lute Player*, his description seems closer to the still-life in the *Boy Bitten by a Lizard*, in which the reflection of the window and the dewdrops on the flowers are more prominent than in the Hermitage painting. Bellori's description is certainly based on that of Baglione, but he forgets to mention the *Lute Player*. Both of these accounts are very similar to van Mander's description of the still-lifes of the painter Lodovyck van den Bos, who worked in the second half of the sixteenth century. He also painted ". . . fruits and flowers in a glass with water, with such accuracy and patience that everything was quite natural, showing the heavenly dew upon the flowers." (see van Mander, ed. Floerke, 1906, vol. I, pp. 142/143). It is not impossible that Baglione knew van Mander's description; in any case, it is very probable that Caravaggio had seen paintings similar to those of van den Bos. The reflection of a window in a glass had been a feature of Northern painting since the period of the van Eycks; the element of still-life in Caravaggio's paintings undoubtedly has an ultimately Northern derivation, though of course the result is very different.

B. *Basket of Fruit*. Milan, Ambrosiana, 45 x 59 cm. Mostra No. 11.   PLATE I

In 1607 this picture is mentioned as belonging to a group of paintings which formed the first gift of the Archbishop Federico Borromeo to the Ambrosiana. Later (1618), Federico describes this work in his *Museum*: "nec abest gloria proximae huic fiscellae, ex qua flores(?) micant. Fecit eam Michael Angelus Caravaggensis, Romae. . . ." In a letter of 1596 to Federico

Borromeo, Cardinal del Monte thanks him for presents which he had received and adds that he had wanted to reciprocate with paintings; he asks the archbishop to excuse the delay because "I am dealing with persons with whom I have to arm myself with patience" (quoted by Roberto Longhi, *Pin.*, I, 1929, p. 31). It might very well be that this is an allusion to his protégé Caravaggio, who, as we know from other sources, was not an easy person to treat with. If this is the case, the date of 1596 would show that the Ambrosiana painting does not belong to the very early period, as was once supposed. The strongly tectonic composition of the work separates it chronologically from the more freely arranged still-lifes of his early youth. The painting is close to the fruit basket in the London *Supper at Emmaus*, which can also be dated 1596/1597, although it is not an immediate study for it.

The question of whether or not Caravaggio painted independent still-lifes remains somewhat problematic; Bellori seems to believe that he did, but the example he cites, the still-life in the *Lute Player*, is not a separate picture. Nevertheless, Caravaggio's statement as quoted by Giustiniani, that to do a good flower piece meant just as much work for him as to paint human figures, is a strong indication that he had done such pictures. For its time, such a dictum was almost "subversive," anticipating the scale of values of Manet and Cézanne. That Caravaggio should have done independent still-lifes is in itself not surprising. There had been fruit and flower pieces, especially in the North, long before Caravaggio's time, and they became something of an international fashion at the turn of the century, so that we find them in Spain, France and the Netherlands. In Rome, Baglione praises his friend, Mao Salini as "the first to paint flowers in vases" in Caravaggio's time (see text p. 80 and Longhi, *Paragone*, I, p. 36, who interprets Baglione's statement to mean that Mao was the first to do so after Caravaggio). Furthermore, Bellori's claim that the fruit and flower pieces of Caravaggio started a fashion of such still-lifes that continued to flourish long after the master's death, must have had some basis in fact. Thus it is the more astonishing that no isolated still-life from Caravaggio's hand has come down to us, except the Ambrosiana *Fruit Basket*; and it is not beyond question whether even this was an independent picture from the start. The cream-colored background overlaps the contours of the leaves in several places, indicating perhaps that it was added after the completion of the basket and its contents. This suggests the possibility that the *Fruit Basket* was painted as a kind of trial piece without background (a recent X-ray examination of the painting has revealed nothing of significance beneath the present surface). It cannot be connected directly with the *Supper at Emmaus*, because the basket is placed on the eye-level of the beholder, rather than seen from above. One might imagine that the present background was added at the request of Cardinal del Monte so that the panel could serve as a present for Federico Borromeo. Perhaps the narrow, dark strip on which the basket is placed was also added later; here again, as in the *Supper at Emmaus* (although less strongly) the basket overhangs the edge of the surface on which it rests, with the protruding portion casting a well-defined, curved shadow. On the other hand, this strip might have been there from the start, in which case it was probably wider than at present. That the panel was cut down to its present dimensions from a larger size, is an alternative not to be disregarded; we must note in this connection that the long twig on the right does not originate in the basket, but seems to reach into the picture from outside the frame so that it hangs in mid-air.

Caravaggio depicts the grapes, apples, figs, etc. in their full sensuous splendor, with gleaming surfaces and solid corporeality. Every fruit is accompanied by twigs and leaves of its own species, and, as a special display of dexterity, Caravaggio has added tiny droplets of water here and there. Yet his conception of nature rejects any thought of immaculate beauty and ideal completeness, so that he retains—one could also say he emphasizes—its imperfections, such as the wormholes in the apple and the diseased, curled-up vine leaf on the right.

EARLY PAINTINGS: ABOUT 1590 TO 1595

2. BOY PEELING FRUIT

SOURCES

Mancini, 59: mentions (after the *Boy Bitten by a Lizard*) "a boy who peels a pear with a knife."

COPIES   PAINTINGS

A. *Boy Peeling Fruit*. Hampton Court, 61.6 x 48.7 cm. Cat. no. 398.   PLATE 2
   Copy from a lost original. James II Catal. (538), "by Michael Angelo." Windsor, 1776, as "by Caravaggio"?

B. *Boy Peeling Fruit*. Roberto Longhi Collection, Florence, 68 x 62.5 cm. Mostra No. 52.
   A second copy, very faded, but in the opinion of Longhi (*Prop.*, p. 10), reflecting the original Caravaggio better than the Hampton Court version. Both versions illustrated by Longhi, *op. cit.*, pls. 8 and 9.

C. A third copy is in the collection of a London art dealer. The original must have been one of the earliest half-figures made by Caravaggio in Rome.

It is probable that all of these copies are derived from an original by Caravaggio. In none of them does the boy peel a pear, as Mancini indicates, but another fruit, perhaps a nectarine; the same fruit lies on the table before the boy. There is a remarkable resemblance between the facial types of these copies and those of the angel in the Hartford *St. Francis* and the boy on the left in the *Musica* at the Metropolitan Museum.

3. BOY WITH A BASKET OF FRUIT

SOURCES

Not mentioned specifically in the sources, but is associated with Caravaggio's juvenile works.

PAINTING

Boy with a Basket of Fruit. Rome, Borghese, No. 136. 70 x 67 cm. Mostra No. 2.   PLATE 3
   From the collection of Cavaliere d'Arpino, which was confiscated in 1607 by the administrators of Paul V and given to his nephew, Cardinal Scipione Borghese. In the 1706 inventory of the Borghese Collection, the painting is attributed to Caravaggio, together with the so-called *Bacchino Malato* of the same provenance. (See de Rinaldis in *Boll. d'Arte*, XXIX, 1935/1936, p. 577 ff.) It was accepted as an authentic Caravaggio by Voss (1925) and Longhi (1927). Marangoni (1921/1922) and Schudt (1942) called it an old and good copy.

   The basket of fruit was probably painted by Caravaggio while he was still in the studio of Arpino. However, in my opinion, the rather sugary, Murillesque head could easily be from the hand of another painter, perhaps someone in the shop of Arpino. There is a remarkable similarity of facial type between the boy in this painting and the central figure in the *Concert of Youths* at the Metropolitan Museum. See text, Chapter IV.

4. BACCHUS

SOURCES

Baglione, 136: After spending some months in the house of Giuseppe d'Arpino, "Caravaggio tried to get along on his own and made some other small pictures which were drawn from his own reflection in a mirror (alcuni quadretti da lui nello specchio ritratti). The first was a Bacchus with bunches of various kinds of grapes executed with great care, but a little dry."

PAINTINGS

PLATE 4

A. *Boy with Fruit (Bacchino Malato)*. Rome: Borghese. 0.66 x 0.52 m. Mostra No. 3.

Caravaggio probably painted several versions of this subject, and a number of paintings of Bacchus (or youths with bunches of grapes) have been attributed to him (see Schudt, p. 43 and Zahn, p. 34). Of these, the closest to the early style of Caravaggio is the so-called *Bacchino Malato* in the Borghese, which, like the *Boy with a Basket of Fruit*, found its way into the collection of Cardinal Scipione Borghese through the confiscation of Arpino's painting collection by papal authority in 1607. In the list of objects confiscated from Arpino, this painting is described as a "youth with a wreath of ivy around his head and a bunch of grapes in his hand" (see de Rinaldis *Boll. d'Arte*, 29, 1935/1936, p. 597). It was registered in the Borghese Collection in 1760 as a "satiro" by Caravaggio, but in later inventories of the gallery it was called alternately Lodovico Carracci, Tiarini and Bonzi. Longhi has proposed the theory that the boy in the painting is one of the self-portraits made from a mirror by Caravaggio when he was suffering from malaria (see Longhi, *Vita Artistica*, 1927, p. 28 f. and *Prop.* 1, p. 8). It has been suggested that Baglione had the Borghese painting in mind, instead of the Uffizi *Bacchus*, because of the two bunches of different kinds of grapes (alcuni grapoli d'uve diversi); see Mahon (*Burl. Mag.*, 1953, p. 215) who also says that a marginal note in Mancini's manuscript should be read as "a bacco by Caravaggio in the possession of the Cardinal Borghese." (It should be noted, however, that Baglione places the *Bacchus* after Caravaggio's departure from the shop of Arpino). Schudt (p. 53) considers the Borghese painting a doubtful work.

Provided that the *Bacchino Malato* (he is not as clearly a Bacchus as is the boy in the Uffizi painting, since he has no vine leaves in his hair or glass in his hand) is really a self-portrait, it must be dated extremely early—about 1589, according to the age of the boy represented. In spite of the documentary evidence, which seems to favor the attribution of this painting to Caravaggio, it is somewhat difficult to reconcile its style with that of such works as the Uffizi *Bacchus* and the *Flight to Egypt*.

B. *Bacchus*. Florence, Uffizi, 95 x 85 cm., no. 5312. Mostra No. 1.

PLATE 7

Since its discovery in 1917, this painting has generally been accepted as the *Bacchus* mentioned by Baglione. It corresponds to his description in that it shows different kinds of grapes and in the head of the boy, which could very easily be a kind of self-portrait made with the use of a mirror. Moreover, it is painted with careful attention to detail (con diligenza) and in a somewhat dry manner without deep shadows. However, it is curious that Baglione did not make a specific reference to the splendid fruit-basket, if this was the work he really had in mind.

The painting was found in a somewhat damaged condition in the storeroom of the Uffizi. It was restored and exhibited for the first time in the Mostra del Barocco in 1922. It was first published by Marangoni (*Riv. d'Arte*, x, 1917/1918, p. 12 f. and *Boll. d'Arte*, 1922, p. 224); see also: Longhi (*Prop.*, i, p. 8, note 5) and Mahon (*Burl. Mag.*, Jan. 1952, p. 19). For a discussion of this painting, see text, Chapter IV.

5. CONCERT OF YOUTHS (MUSICA)

SOURCES

Baglione, 136: "Caravaggio painted for the Cardinal del Monte a concert of youths."

Bellori, 204: "Caravaggio made for the Cardinal del Monte a concert of youths in half-figures."

PAINTING

Concert of Youths. New York, Metropolitan Museum. 92 x 118.5 cm.   PLATE 5

The inscription in the lower left corner is probably from the eighteenth century. The first two letters of the name are missing, which would indicate that the painting was cut on the left side; maybe it was cut on the right side as well.

This painting is known to have been in an English private collection at least since the 1920's (see letter to *Burl. Mag.*, April 1952, p. 119), and has recently been purchased by the Metropolitan Museum; it is published by Denis Mahon (*Burl. Mag.*, Jan. 1952, p. 3 ff. and *Metropolitan Museum Bulletin*, Oct. 1953, vol. XII, No. 2, p. 33 ff.).

It shows four seated youths with musical instruments and scores. The central figure, touching the strings of a lute with his right hand and tuning the instrument with his left, has his mouth open as though he were singing. A semi-nude figure on the right, seen from the back, looks at a score which he holds on his lap, and his violin, with the bow attached, lies beside him. Between this and the central figure are the head and shoulders of another boy who holds a long wind instrument; his mouth, like that of the central figure, is open as though he were singing. A fourth figure on the left leans over and breaks the stem of a bunch of grapes. It would seem that the last figure originally had wings which, according to the restorer, were overpainted by Caravaggio himself (*ibid.* note, 15). Each of the figures has a parallel in another known work by, attributed to or copied after Caravaggio: the boy on the left is comparable to the *Boy Peeling Fruit* (known only in copies); the face of the central figure, with its sensuous expression, is similar to the *Boy with a Basket of Fruit* in the Borghese Collection (see above) and the general conception of this figure also recalls the *Lute Player* in the Hermitage. The boy who holds the wind instrument is somewhat similar to the so-called *Bacchino Malato*, and the curl on his forehead is almost identical with that of the *Boy with a Basket of Fruit*. The seated figure seen from the rear recalls that in the *Cardsharps* and could also be related to the angel in the *Flight to Egypt*. Some details of the painting, for example the leaves and grapes and the knotted sashes worn by the boys, are similar to corresponding details in the *Bacchino Malato*, the Uffizi *Bacchus* and the *Saint Francis*. Mahon dates the *Musica* between 1594 and 1595, placing it later than all of the single figures which Caravaggio had painted previously; if this dating is correct, the painting would have to be considered a kind of anthology of the earlier juvenile works. On the other hand, if it were dated earlier, it could be supposed that the single figure paintings (including some slightly doubtful works such as the *Bacchino Malato* and the *Boy with a Basket of Fruit*) are derived from it.

The painting corresponds to what we would expect Caravaggio's lost *Musica* for Cardinal del Monte to have been like, both in its composition and in the phase of Caravaggio's stylistic development to which it belongs. Like the other juvenile works painted for del Monte, such as the *Cardsharps* and the *Fortune Teller*, it is composed of only a few half-figures, is light in tone, and clearly modeled. The painting is in bad condition; in some places the original surface has all but disappeared (it has recently been cleaned: for the details of its state of preservation, see Mahon, *ibid.*). Under the circumstances, it is understandable that a number of connoisseurs (who are not Caravaggio specialists) have refused to acknowledge this *Musica*, contrasting it with the smooth, clean beauty of the *Bacchus* or—even more conspicuously— the *Flight to Egypt*. There has also been speculation as to whether the picture might not be a kind of pasticcio or a collaborative work by several young artists in the workshop of Arpino, combining various heads and single figures done previously by Caravaggio or others. Nevertheless, the painting is attractive in its erotic lyricism, which has its origin in North Italian painting. I am inclined to consider it an authentic work of the very young Caravaggio.

The content of the painting is somewhat problematic. At first glance it seems to be simply a representation of young boys playing musical instruments and singing. However, the figure on the left, who breaks the stem of a bunch of grapes, does not participate in the music making. If the wings of this figure were a part of the original composition, the scene might be interpreted as an allegory of love and music, with a Bacchic reference in the bunch of grapes.

6. SAINT FRANCIS

SOURCES

In his testament of 1597, the Reverend Ruggero Tritonio da Udine, abbot of Pinerolo, bequeaths to his nephew Ruggero Tritonio "a painting of *St. Francis* (divi Francisci signum) painted with great diligence by the famous painter (celeberrimo pittore) Caravaggio," which had been given to him by the noble Octavius Costa of Genoa, as a token of mutual friendship. The testator declares that the painting shall stay in the family and not be alienated. His testament was published in Udine in 1612, after Tritonio's death (see Joppi, *R. Deputazione Veneta di Storia Patria . . . Contributo quarto . . . alla storia del Arte nel Friuli*, Venezia, 1894). The name Costa is known to us as a purchaser of two other paintings by Caravaggio— the *Walk to Emmaus*, made in the Sabine Mountains, and *Judith and Holofernes*.

PAINTINGS

There are two paintings of the same composition which have been related to the testament.

PLATE 6

A. *St. Francis in Ecstasy*. Wadsworth Athenaeum, Hartford, Connecticut. 91.5 x 128.4 cm. Mostra No. 17.

This picture was exhibited in 1938 in the Mostra della Pittura Napoletana. At that time it belonged to the Grioni Collection in Trieste, to which it had allegedly come from Malta (see Marangoni, *Internat. Studio*, 94, 1929, pp. 35/36).

B. *St. Francis*. Udine, Museo Civico. 93 x 129 cm.   PLATE 60

Had been in the possession of the Fistulario family and was given in 1852 by Conte Francesco to the church of S. Giacomo di Fagagna (cf. Joppi, *op. cit.*), and is now on loan to the museum.

Joppi regards the Udine painting as that mentioned in the testament. Most modern critics, however, consider it to be a copy, and the Hartford version is accepted by Longhi and others as the original. But, having seen only one of the versions, it is impossible for me to say with certainty which is actually from the hand of Caravaggio, or, if perhaps both are derived from a lost original. I have recently seen another copy of the scene in the possession of a New York dealer (93.98 x 130.18 cm.) which shows the prominent silhouette of a town in the left background.

Assuming that the composition is Caravaggio's, it is difficult to give a precise date. Oertel (*Pantheon*, 1938, p. 236) places it rather early, around the Doria *Flight to Egypt*. It is true that there are some resemblances in the rudimentary landscape, and we do not find landscapes in Caravaggio's later works. On the other hand, the composition and the execution show, in comparison with the *Flight*, a development which would point to a somewhat later period. If we accept the thesis that this composition goes back to the reference in the testament, the date of 1597 would be the terminus post quem non, but the style of the work would indicate a much earlier date.

The composition represents the moment just after St. Francis had received the stigmata; the wound of Longinus may be seen on the saint's breast. But the apparition of the crucified Savior in the air, which generally accompanies the scene, is not shown. Instead of the apparition, there is a shimmer of golden light on the horizon. This conception of Divinity as a magic light is characteristic of Caravaggio's way of thought, discussed in the chapter on the *Conversion of St. Paul*. The inclusion of this element in the composition strengthens the claim of Caravaggio's authorship.

Still another *Stigmatization of St. Francis* has been published as a Caravaggio by the owner, de Benedetti (*Emporium*, July 1949), Mostra No. 50. The attribution is supported by the facts that the painting was at one time in the Borghese Collection, and that there exists an engraving of it under the name of Caravaggio by F. Basan. To supplement these arguments, there is a signature and date on the page of the slightly open book. Unfortunately, however, the painting does not bear out these arguments. Longhi (*Enc. Ital., s.v.*, Baglione) once attributed this picture to Baglione, and at least it shows some resemblance to the Berlin *Amor Divino* by that master, which was also attributed to Caravaggio at one time.

7. REST ON THE FLIGHT TO EGYPT

Mancini, 59v: names the *Flight to Egypt* together with three other paintings by Caravaggio: the *Fortune Teller*, a *Saint John the Evangelist* (?), and the *Magdalene*, all made in a room of the house of Monsignor Fantin Petrignano.

Bellori, 203: mentions a rather large painting of the *Flight to Egypt*, together with other early paintings (*Fortune Teller* and *Magdalene*) in the palace of Prince Pamphili.

PAINTING   PLATE 8

Rest on the Flight to Egypt. Rome, Doria-Pamphili, No. 384. 133 x 162 cm., Cat. (Sestieri) No. 241. Mostra No. 6.

This painting has been attributed to Saraceni by various catalogues of the gallery since the late nineteenth century; also in the second edition of Burckhardt (*Cicerone*, ed. Otto Mündler, Leipzig, 1869, p. 1050), by Biancale, *Boll. d'Arte*, 1920, p. 8, and by Benkhard, *Caravaggio-studien*, p. 152.

The painting mentioned by Mancini as by Caravaggio must be the one still in the Doria, since he lists it together with three paintings which have been, and still are, in the possession of the Pamphili. This indicates that the *Flight* was known as a Caravaggio as early as about 1620. Also, the clear manifestations of its Lombard, particularly Lottesque, origin verifies the authenticity of the work. (Pevsner, *Zeitschr. f. Bild. Kunst*, 1927/1928, p. 278 f., Longhi, *Pin.*, 1929, VII, p. 283.)

The relation of this picture to Lotto, and that of its upper part with the ass and tree to Bassano, has been discussed in the text (see Chapter II, p. 45ff.). This painting contains one of the very few landscapes that Caravaggio ever painted. It is an intimate view into a

FIG. 85
Tintoretto, *Susanna* (detail).
Vienna, Kunsthistorisches
Museum.

setting of water, reeds, small bushes and trees, and has little in common with idyllic Giorgionesque landscape. The closest parallels are the two landscape dioramas in the background of Tintoretto's *Susanna* in Vienna and, for the foreground vegetation, Leonardo's *Madonna of the Rocks*. It is also comparable to Lotto's *Holy Family with St. Catherine* in Vienna (fig. 31), in which there is a similar framing of the view and silhouetting of the light-green leaves against darker foliage. Equally fine is the wicker flask and canvas sack at the left. The angel stands with his back to the spectator and plays the violin from the notes in the score held up for him by Joseph. He still retains the S-curve of Lombard manneristic figure types with which the young Caravaggio was familiar from the angels in the vault frescoes at the *Certosa di Garegnano* by Peterzano. Caravaggio's angel has been compared (Voss, *Malerei d. Barock*, p. 492; Panofsky, *Hercules am Scheidewege*, p. 126, note 1) to the figure of Voluptas, which is similarly seen from the back, in Annibale Carracci's painting of *Hercules at the Crossroads* (1595, Naples). Carracci's figure itself, however, is a variation of his earlier figure of *Virtus* in the Palazzo Sampieri in Bologna. Common to all these figures is the swirling drapery which covers the curved hips.

The lyrical sentiment of this painting, which is to be seen in the Lottesque composition as well as in the sharp, lucid, and gay coloring, is still very much in the Giorgionesque Lom-

FIG. 86
Peterzano, *Angel*. Certosa di
Garegnano (Milan).

FIG. 87
Annibale Carracci, *Hercules at the
Crossroads* (detail). Naples,
Galleria Nazionale.

bard tradition—an influence which never recurs to such a pervasive extent in Caravaggio's work. It can therefore be assumed that this was one of the early works painted in Rome.

There are certain obvious weaknesses in the execution—the stiffness in the hands and faces, and an almost mechanical enumeration of the long parallel feathers in the wings. Nevertheless, if the painting was really made by a very young artist, the force with which the natural objects are painted, without lapsing into trivial details, is astonishing. The picture has a delicate charm and a beauty of color, however, which Caravaggio in later years would have abhorred as being too beautiful.

8. FORTUNE TELLER

SOURCES

Mancini, 59v: mentions among the paintings which Caravaggio made in the house of Monsignor Petrignani "particularly a gypsy telling the fortune of a young man."

———— 145r: criticizes the technique of the naturalist painters as incompatible with the more explicit qualities of imagination, grace and expression (gratia et affetto); "one of the few works of this school in which one sees grace and expression is the *Fortune Teller* by Caravaggio, representing a gypsy girl telling the fortune of a young man, which is in the possession of Signor Alessandro Vittrice, a gentleman of Rome." A marginal note is added on the same page: "the gypsy demonstrates her roguishness by faking a smile as she removes a ring from the finger of the young man, while he in his simplicity and libidinosity looks at the pretty gypsy as she tells his fortune and lifts his ring."

———— 166r: Caravaggio sold the *Gypsy* (Zingara) for eight scudi.

Baglione, 136: mentions, in the same paragraph with some of Caravaggio's early works painted for the Cardinal del Monte, a picture "with beautiful color" depicting a gypsy telling the fortune of a youth.

Bellori, 203: tells how Caravaggio, in order to confirm his preference for natural rather than antique models, took a gypsy girl from the street and painted her predicting a young man's fortune: the "youth places his gloved hand on his sword and extends the other hand, bare, to the girl, who holds it, and he looks at her. . . ." He mentions that this picture could be seen in the palace of Prince Pamphilio (together with the *Flight to Egypt* and the *Magdalene*).

Scanelli, 199: mentions among the half-figure paintings by Caravaggio the "picture of the gypsy in the Vigna Pamfilia outside the Porta Pancratio."

PAINTINGS

A. *Fortune Teller*. Louvre, 99 x 131 cm., cat. 1926, no. 1122. Mostra No. 8.   PLATE 10

Chantelou tells of the arrival of the *Fortune Teller* in 1665 as a gift from Don Camillo Pamphili to Louis XIV (*Journal du voyage du Cavalier Bernin en France*, 1885, pp. 185/190). The painting is therefore confirmed as the one mentioned by Bellori and Scanelli in the Pamphili Collection. It is not known whether this is the painting which was in the possession of Cardinal del Monte or of Alessandro Vittrice or if there were two different paintings. It corresponds exactly to Bellori's meticulous description, even to the detail of the youth's one gloved hand. The painting was dampened by humidity during its transport from Italy and was not well received by Chantelou, who remarks in his journal that it is a poor picture: "la Cingara du Caravaggio (est) un pauvre tableau, sans esprit ni invention." The youth bears a marked resemblance to the *Lute Player* in Leningrad and to the *Bacchus* in the Uffizi, having the typical face of Caravaggio's early works. The smooth flat color is also characteristic of the early period (see Chapter II).

B. *Fortune Teller.* Capitoline, Rome. 115 x 150 cm. Mostra No. 9.   PLATE 11

Mentioned as an original Caravaggio in the inventory of the sale (1750) of the collection of Pio di Savoia (see Mostra Catalogue). A variation of the Louvre painting, it does not conform to Bellori's description, as the left hand is not gloved. Possibly it is the painting mentioned by Mancini (can the gypsy's gesture be interpreted as stealing a ring?). It is not necessarily an original, whereas the Louvre painting undoubtedly is. The features of the faces are blurred and the figures lack the square-shouldered firmness of the Louvre painting. In older literature it is always considered a free copy, often attributed to Saraceni. Recent critics have suggested that it is a late version of the Louvre painting by Caravaggio himself (Longhi, *Prop.*, p. 9, Schudt, p. 45, and Mahon, *Burl. Mag.*, July 1951, p. 112, note 112). See text p. 83.

DIVINE LOVE

See LOST PAINTINGS, Cat. No. 45.

9. THE CARDSHARPS (I BARI)

SOURCES

Bellori, 203-204: mentions a praiseworthy painting in the possession of Cardinal Antonio Barberini. ". . . it represents three half-figures of men playing cards. Here Michele represented a simple youth holding cards and dressed in a dark suit, whose head is well drawn from life. Opposite him in profile, a fraudulent youth, who leans with one hand on the gaming table and with the other held behind him, takes a false card from his belt. A third figure near the boy looks at the marks on the cards and with three fingers reveals them to his companion. The companion leans on the table exposing his shoulder to the light; he wears a yellow jacket striped with bands. There is nothing false in the coloring of this work. These are the first strokes from Michele's brush in the clear manner of Giorgione, with tempered shadows. . . . The *Card Game* was bought by Cardinal del Monte. . . ."

Scanelli 199: "In the collection of Cardinal Antonio Barberini is a painting by Caravaggio of card players, a subject (inventione) so well suited to Caravaggio's genius that the work is of rare beauty."

PAINTINGS   PLATE 12

A painting corresponding to Bellori's description was in the Sciarra Gallery in Rome until 1899. It probably came there from the Barberini Collection where it had been from at least the mid-seventeenth century. That it was still in the house of the Barberini in 1772 is shown by the engraving of the painting by Volpato of that date, inscribed "aedibus Barberini." It was sold in the sale of the Sciarra Collection in 1899 and thereafter disappeared.

There are several pictures which have recently been claimed as the Sciarra painting. One, in a private German collection (99 x 137 cm.) has been published by Fritz Baumgart (*Das Werk des Kunstlers*, I, 1939/40, pp. 482-524), who attempts to prove on the basis of a seal on the back of the picture that it came from the Sciarra Gallery. Longhi (*Prop.*, p. 99) calls it a "pessima copia." Another painting, in the possession of a New York dealer, is not entirely in good condition; the left half is much restored, whereas the young cheat on the right is very well executed and corresponds (after cleaning) to the photograph made by Braun of the picture in the Sciarra Collection.

Venturi (*Commentari*, I, 1950, p. 41) accepts the New York painting and places it immediately before the *First St. Matthew*, around 1592. Mahon (*Burl. Mag.*, January 1952, p. 19) dates the composition around 1593/94. Copies of the composition were made at an early date; see, for example, Bertolotti, II, p. 76 f., who records that a painting by Caravaggio representing "three playing persons," belonging to Marchese Sannesio, was stolen when the Marchese lent it in 1621 to Antonio Orsini to be copied. The original was valued at 200 scudi.

Marangoni, p. 51, doubts the authenticity of the Sciarra painting altogether, saying that the loose and insignificant composition, and especially the wooden quality of the middle figure speaks against Caravaggio's authorship. Schudt (no. 13) accepts the picture in the German collection. See also Zahn, p. 36.

The composition must be a fairly early one, since it was bought by Cardinal del Monte. However, it cannot be too early because of the resemblance of the young man on the right to the so-called Spada in the *Calling of Saint Matthew* (cf. Cat. Rais. No. 22, *Contarelli Chapel*, and text, p. 109).

10. BOY BITTEN BY A LIZARD

SOURCES

Baglione, 136: "A boy (fanciullo) bitten by a lizard (lucerta) that comes out of some flowers and fruits. It is a work of such diligence that the boy really appears to shriek."

Mancini, 59/59v: Shortly after Caravaggio came to Rome, during his stay with Pandolfo Pucci da Recanati, he painted for sale a child (putto) who cries from being bitten by a "racano," which he holds in his hand (che tiene in mano).

——— 166: says that Caravaggio sold it (il putto morso del racano) for "quindici giuli."

Manilli, Villa Borghese, 1650, p. 71: mentions in the Stanze di Dafne of the Villa Borghese a small painting of a child (putto) bitten by a crab (granchio) by Caravaggio.

PAINTINGS

Two paintings correspond to the description of Baglione, but not exactly to that of Mancini:

PLATE 9

A. *Boy Bitten by a Lizard*. Florence, Roberto Longhi Collection, 65.8 x 50 cm. Mostra No. 4.

Published by Longhi, *Pin.*, 1928, I, p. 21; (cf. also *Proporz.*, p. 8, note 1). There is no indication of the provenance of this painting.

B. *Boy Bitten by a Lizard*. London, Vincent Korda Collection. Formerly at Nuneham Park in the collection of the Viscount Harcourt. Enlarged to 70 x 56.75 cm.; original measurements: 65 x 48.7 cm. The work came from the collection of Sir Paul Methuen as a Murillo. Published by Borenius, *Apollo*, July 1925; Longhi (*op. cit.*, p. 21), calls it a "copia antica" or a "replica più fievole." Voss (*Kunst Chronik*, July 1951, p. 167) calls this the better version. Lionello Venturi (*Commentari* III, 1952, p. 197 ff.) published the Korda painting as the original, rejecting the version in the possession of Roberto Longhi. Quite to the contrary, Denis Mahon (*Art Bull.* June 1953, p. 214 note 13) rejects the Korda painting, suggesting that it is an early copy from about 1620; he accepts the Longhi painting. Since I have not seen the Korda painting after the recent cleaning, I am obliged to reserve my judgment. Unfortunately, I am unable to reproduce this painting here because the owner has refused permission.

The subject of the *Boy Bitten by a Lizard* is based, as Longhi has convincingly demonstrated (*Pin.*, 1929, VIII, p. 301), on a drawing by Sophonisba Anguisciola (fig. 42), the pupil of Bernardo Campi in Cremona. This drawing (wrongly attributed to Santo di Tito by Voss, *Zeichnungen d. Spaetrenaissance*, Munich, 1928, pl. 15) represents a boy weeping from the pinch of a crab that comes out of a basket held by an older girl who tries to comfort him; it was extremely popular in the sixteenth century.

Perhaps the painting of a putto bitten by a crab mentioned by Manilli, which is no longer in the Borghese, was wrongly ascribed to Caravaggio and was really a copy after Sophonisba's drawing. There is such a painting in Dijon which is labeled with the name of Sophonisba herself.

It seems impossible that Caravaggio made this painting just after his arrival in Rome as Mancini indicates. In my opinion, the strong foreshortening of the work goes beyond the rather flat and dry manner of Caravaggio's first Roman production. It seems not impossible to me that the painting of which Mancini speaks (a putto crying because he is bitten by a racano which he holds in his hand) was a still earlier work by Caravaggio with a subject that was somewhat different from the composition known to us (see text Chapter IV).

11. LUTE PLAYER

SOURCES

Baglione, 136: gives a detailed and loving account of a painting, belonging to Cardinal del Monte, of a youth (un giovane) playing the lute. "And this, said he, was the most beautiful piece he ever made." (Cf. Cat. Rais., *Still-life.*)

Bellori, 204: says that Caravaggio made for Cardinal del Monte a woman (una donna) playing the lute with the notes in front of her.

PAINTING

Lute Player. Leningrad, Hermitage, no. 217, 94 x 119 cm., Cat. 1933.   PLATE 13

The figure of the *Lute Player* is sitting behind a table on which are open part-books of music, a violin, fruits, and a radiant bouquet in a vase filled with water, in which there is a reflection of light (cf. *Boy Bitten by a Lizard*).

This is the only example of this subject which fully agrees with Baglione's description. Moreover, it came from the Giustiniani Gallery and was sold in Paris under the name of Caravaggio; it was acquired by the Hermitage in 1808. It is undoubtedly the same painting which belonged to Cardinal del Monte, and can thus be considered one of the juvenile half-figure works connected with this early Maecenas.

Only one problem presents itself: Baglione called the Lute Player "un giovane," and Bellori, who was evidently also speaking of del Monte's painting (although he describes the floral piece as a separate entity) says "una donna." Perhaps this discrepancy was caused by Caravaggio's using a boy model disguised as a girl, surely the same model who posed for the *Bacchus* and the *Boy Bitten by a Lizard*. This ambiguity of sex was noted as early as the sale catalogue of the Giustiniani Collection in Paris. It describes the *Lute Player* as an allegory of Man under the domination of love, showing how he has become effeminate and has lost his strength of character. The Catalogue of the Hermitage of 1838 interprets the picture as an "allégorie de l'amour" forming with two other works in the Giustiniani Collection (the *Amor Victorious* and Baglione's *Divine Love*) a "poème pittoresque de l'amour."

12. MAGDALENE

SOURCES

Mancini, 59v: refers to a "repentant Magdalene" (Magdalena convertita) among the early works made in the house of Petrignani.

Scanelli, 199: mentions among Caravaggio's works in the "Vigna Pamfilia" a full-sized figure "al naturale" of the Magdalene.

—— 277: Compares Caravaggio's figure with the Magdalene in Correggio's *Pietà* in Parma; Caravaggio's naturalism "is purely superficial, the figure deprived of grace, spirit and proper expression; she seems lifeless in every respect" (per ogni parte morta).

Bellori, 203: gives an extensive description of the *Magdalene* by Caravaggio in the palace of the Prince "Pamphilio" in order to demonstrate Caravaggio's naturalistic manner and his ability to "imitate the hues of nature with few colors. . . . The young girl is pictured seated on a chair with her hands in her lap in the act of drying her hair. He painted her in a room and placed on the floor an unguent-jar, necklaces and jewels and disguised her as a Magdalene. The face is turned slightly to the side, and the cheek, throat and chest are rendered in pure, light and natural hues. All this is accompanied by the simplicity of the whole figure in the white-sleeved blouse and yellow tunic pulled up to her knees revealing the white skirt of flowered damask."

PAINTING   PLATE 15

Magdalene. Rome, Doria-Pamphili, no. 380, 106 x 97 cm., Cat. Sestieri no. 375. Mostra No. 7.

This painting corresponds in every detail to Bellori's description. It was already known to Scanelli in 1657 under the name of Caravaggio. For the wrong attribution to Saraceni, cf. Cat. Rais., *Flight to Egypt*. It belongs obviously to Caravaggio's early period, though judging from its style, it would seem to be a little later than the *Flight to Egypt*. The painting is not well preserved (see Arslan, *Aut. Aut*, no. 5, 1951). The Magdalene, seated on a low stool, is seen from above in a way comparable to Flemish representations of the subject; cf. for example, Roger van der Weyden. (See text p. 95).

13. HEAD OF MEDUSA

Baglione, 136: "Among the works for the Cardinal del Monte, Caravaggio painted on a round shield (sopra una rotella rapportata), a frightful head of a Medusa with snakes for hair, which the Cardinal sent as a gift to Ferdinand, Grand Duke of Tuscany."

Bellori, 205: The head of the Medusa, given by Cardinal del Monte to the Grand Duke of Tuscany, was especially praised by Cavaliere Marino, first in glory among men of letters, whose portrait Caravaggio had painted.

Marino, Galeria, 1620, p. 28: "*La Testa di Medusa* in una rotella di Michelangnolo da Caravaggio nella Galeria del Gran Duca di Toscana."

Gaspare Murtola, Rime, Venezia 1604, p. 226: wrote a madrigal on the Medusa beginning, "E questa di Medusa / la chioma avvenelate / di mille serpe armata . . . etc." Quoted as referring to Caravaggio's *Medusa* by Corrado Ricci, "La Medusa degli Uffizi," *Vita d'Arte*, 1908, p. 1ff., although the poem makes no direct reference to the picture.

PAINTING   PLATE 14

Head of Medusa. Florence, Uffizi, tondo on wood, diam. 55.5 cm., Cat. 1926, p. 94, Mostra No. 5.

The head of the *Medusa* is painted upon an old tournament shield of the sixteenth century with a border of gold ornaments on a dark background; pieces of leather and velvet are still visible.

The wedding of Cosimo, to which Cardinal del Monte was invited, took place in 1608, and the *Medusa* was undoubtedly given in celebration of this event.

Ricci, *op. cit.*, p. 1ff., dates it early; Schudt, no. 14, dates it prior to the Contarelli Chapel. The painting is connected with the juvenile period, but certainly comes at the end of it. (For a fuller discussion, see Chapter II.)

14. SAINT CATHERINE

Bellori, 204: Caravaggio painted for Cardinal del Monte "a kneeling Saint Catherine, leaning against her wheel." This work and the "donna in camicia" (the *Lute Player*) were in Bellori's time in the rooms of Cardinal Antonio Barberini. "Both paintings were more intense in color, since Michele was already beginning to strengthen his shadows."

PAINTING

St. Catherine. Lugano, Thyssen Collection. 173 x 133 cm. Mostra No. 20.   PLATE 18

Recently bought from the Barberini Collection in Rome. Antonio Barberini (brother of the Pope and elected Cardinal in 1624) probably acquired this painting, together with the

Cardsharps and the *Lute Player* from the estate of Cardinal del Monte, who died shortly after 1625.

The painting has quite often been called a "school piece" or a copy (cf. Catalogue of the Mostra in the Pitti, 1922). Schudt claims that it has not the quality of the genuine works and at most it can be only a copy, but other art critics regard the painting as an original and on the whole praise it very highly: Voss, 1923, p. 80; Marangoni (hesitantly), *Arte Barocca*, 1927, p. 154; Zahn, p. 38; Pevsner, Barockmalerei, p. 132. Now, Longhi also accepts it (*Prop.*, n. 15), having recanted his former opinion that it was by Orazio Gentileschi (*L'Arte*, 1916).

The painting certainly possesses many characteristics of Caravaggio's art. The still-life of the broken wheel, placed in oblique foreshortening, is very much in Caravaggio's vein, as is also the playful crossing of the long and elegant sword at a right angle to the palm of martyrdom. The rich black dress of the seated princess billows gently out as in the Doria *Magdalene* and the damasked cushion also shows a similar pattern. The fine hands and the modeling of the features recall the *Lute Player* in the Hermitage, which, according to Bellori, was also painted for Cardinal del Monte at about the same time as this work.

The painting can be dated approximately 1595.

An old copy of the Barberini painting is in S. Jeronimo al Real, Madrid. (Cf. J. Ainaud, *Anales*, p. 387, no. 21, ill., p. 372.)

15. JUDITH AND HOLOFERNES

SOURCES

Baglione, 138: Caravaggio "painted a *Judith* cutting off the head of Holofernes for the Signori Costi." (The name Costa appears in connection with several of Caravaggio's works: cf. Cat. Rais., *Walk to Emmaus* and *St. Francis*.)

PAINTING   PLATE 19

Judith and Holofernes. Rome, Signor Vincenzo Coppi, 144 x 195 cm. Formerly in the possession of Marchese del Grillo.

In the early seventeenth century there are three references to a painting of Judith and Holofernes by Caravaggio: Baglione mentions a painting of the subject made for the Signori Costi (see above); Pourbus, in a letter of September 15, 1607, speaks of an easel painting of medium size with half-figures which was made by Caravaggio in Naples and which was for sale there (DOC. 70 and Cat. Rais. No. 29, *Madonna of the Rosary*) and in his testament of September 19, 1617, Finsonius bequeathed his share of a *Judith and Holofernes* by Caravaggio (along with the *Madonna of the Rosary*) to Abraham Vinck.

The painting of *Judith and Holofernes* from the Casa Coppi, which came to Milan during the last days of the Mostra del Caravaggio (published by Longhi, *Par.*, 19, p. 10 ff.) shows Judith severing the head of Holofernes who is lying on a bed before her with the upper part of his naked body terribly contorted. Judith is accompanied by a wrinkled old nurse who appears in profile at the right. The style of the painting seems later than the very early works which Caravaggio made in Rome, such as the Uffizi *Bacchus*, the *Flight to Egypt* and the *Fortune Teller*. It is possible that it was painted at about the same time as the Doria *Magdalene*, and it may not be only coincidence that the Judith wears the same long pearl earrings with a black ribbon which are seen lying beside the saint in the Doria painting. Still closer in style is the *St. Catherine* in Lugano. The *St. Francis*, of which there is a version in the Hartford Museum, also belonged to the Costi (see Cat. Rais. No. 5, *St. Francis*), and the style of this painting is not too dissimilar from that of the Casa Coppi painting. Although the work fits stylistically into Caravaggio's early maturity, it is not impossible that it is the same painting which Pourbus mentions as having been for sale in Naples around 1607. That the painting of which Pourbus speaks was made at Naples (as he states) is questionable (see Cat. Rais. No. 29, *Madonna of the Rosary*) and it is thus not necessarily a different painting from that mentioned by Baglione (an early work by Caravaggio might well have found its way into the Neapolitan market). In fact, all three of the references mentioned above may easily pertain to the same painting.

There are a number of disturbing weaknesses in the painting which are not usually seen in Caravaggio's work. For example, the surfaces are extremely hard and the long curving sweep of Judith's drapery is awkward and illogical. Still less like Caravaggio's usual manner is the lack of force in Judith's action as she cuts Holofernes' head from his shoulders (cf. the *Sacrifice of Isaac*).

There was a *Judith and Holofernes* attributed to Caravaggio in the Palazzo Zambeccari in Bologna. The President de Brosse describes the painting as follows: "*Judith coupant la tête à Holoferne*, par Michel-Ange de Caravage. Composition et expressions uniques. Remarquez l'horreur et la frayeur de Judith, les affreux débattements de Holofernes, le sang-froid et la méchanceté de la servante." (De Brosse, C., *Lettres Familières sur l'Italie*, Paris, 1931, p. 278. Written around 1740). A similar description is found in Lalande's *Voyages en Italie*, Geneva, 1790, vol. II, p. 94.

EARLY MATURITY

SMALLER RELIGIOUS PAINTINGS: CA. 1595 TO 1600

16. SACRIFICE OF ISAAC

SOURCES

Bellori, 208: "For the Cardinal Maffeo Barberini, who later became Pope Urban VIII, Caravaggio painted, besides a portrait, the *Sacrifice of Abraham* which represents Abraham holding his weapon near the throat of his fallen and screaming son."

PAINTING

Sacrifice of Isaac. Florence, Uffizi, No. 4659. 104 x 135 cm. Cat. 1926.　　　　PLATE 20

Given to the Uffizi in 1917 (communication from the Uffizi Gallery) by Fairfax Murray. Allegedly from the Sciarra Collection. It has sometimes been considered a copy (cf. Marangoni, *Arte Barocca*, 1927, p. 143 ff.).

The painting is composed of both Caravaggesque and un-Caravaggesque elements. The two main figures, Abraham and Isaac, correspond perfectly to Bellori's description of them and reflect the genuine power and passion of Caravaggio's invention. The venerable Abraham with his full, grey beard and grim expression, suggests the same model that served for the *Second Saint Matthew*. Isaac bears an unmistakable resemblance to Caravaggio's "automorphic" images like the so-called *St. John* in the Doria or the *Medusa* in the Uffizi (whose likeness to Isaac is even more striking because of the open mouth and anguished face). However, the face of the angel at the left is quite unlike that of the angel in the *Second Saint Matthew*; its metallic features are quattrocentesque, and the gesture of the hand is taken almost directly from Leonardo's *Madonna of the Rocks* in the Louvre. The ram at the right with its flattened horns is far too sheepish to claim any kinship with the vigorous crumple-horned animal in the Doria *St. John*. No less alien to Caravaggio is the landscape, which is lyrical in a Giorgionesque sense, but very unlike the only landscape in Caravaggio's undisputed oeuvre, the Tintorettesque background in the *Flight to Egypt*. Furthermore, a light sky seems inconsistent with the mature phase of Caravaggio's development to which the general compositional type of the *Sacrifice of Isaac* belongs. All of these incongruities seem to me to suggest the possibility that the Uffizi painting is not a copy, but a pasticcio.

Judging from the Caravaggesque elements, the composition dates from the mid-1590's, along with other similar half-length figures, in which case it would have been made while Maffeo Barberini was still protonotario and not, as Bellori indicates, when he was Cardinal (appointed in 1605).

Other compositions of the same subject attributed to Caravaggio are much less close in character to his art (e.g. the *Sacrifice of Isaac* that was formerly in the famous gallery of the Duke of Orleans and engraved by Vasseur. Cf. also Ainaud, *Anales* p. 385 ff., who enumerates no less than five paintings of the *Sacrifice* which he considers copies after·Caravaggio).

17. INCREDULITY OF THOMAS

SOURCES

Baglione, 137: Caravaggio painted for Ciriaco Mattei (besides *St. John the Baptist* and the *Walk to Emmaus*) a scene of Thomas touching with his finger the wound in the side of the Lord. (cf. Gaspare Celio, *Memoria*, Orbaan, p. 225, n. 3, who saw three paintings by Caravaggio in the Palazzo Mattei—an *Emmaus*, a *Pastor Friso*, and the *Taking of Christ*—does not mention the *Incredulity of Thomas*.)

Bellori, 207: Caravaggio, commissioned by Vincenzo Giustiniani, made a picture of "Saint Thomas thrusting his finger into the wound in the side of the Savior, who guides his hand, removing the shroud to reveal his chest."

Scanelli, 199: mentions in the gallery of the Ludovisi a painting of St. Thomas placing his finger in the side of Christ (in half-figures).

Sandrart, 189: relates that during the time Caravaggio was forced to hide in the palace of the Giustiniani (because of the Tomassoni incident), he painted Christ among his apostles, placing the finger of Saint Thomas into the Holy Wound at His side. "By good painting and modeling, Caravaggio succeeded in showing on the faces of all those present such an expression of astonishment and such naturalness of skin and flesh that in comparison all other pictures seemed to be of colored paper."

Malvasia, II, 305: mentions a "San Tommaso, originale del Caravaggio," which had come into the possession of the Lambertini family of Bologna. This must have been the same painting which had aroused the curiosity of Lodovico Carracci (*ibid.*, p. 10) because of Caravaggio's spectacular renown, but which had disappointed him; he said that he could not find in this painting anything but "a great contrast of light and shadow; it was too obedient to nature, lacked decorum, was of little grace and intelligence, and was clearly ruinous to good design." The harshness of Lodovico's comments are somewhat tempered by Malvasia's citing other instances where the painting had more positive effect. Alessandro Tiarini (*ibid.*, p. 208) for instance, was surprised at his own enthusiasm for Caravaggio's purity, sincerity, and force of color though he did not overlook his lack of majesty, decorum, and erudition. Tiarini went so far as to say that the languidness of the color in his earlier works had disappeared after he had had the opportunity to study carefully in his studio a copy of Caravaggio's *Saint Thomas* lent to him by the Legnani. Another Bolognese painter, Lionello Spada (p. 205) was apparently even more enthusiastic, for, not content with merely copying Caravaggio, he desired to make the personal acquaintance of the master.

PAINTINGS PLATE 22

A. *Doubting Thomas*. Potsdam, Neues Palast, 107 x 146 cm. (Before World War II, probably lost).

Bought by the royal family of Prussia from the Galleria Giustiniani in 1816 (sale cat., no. 86, *L'Incrédulité de Saint Thomas*). First published by Voss (*Jahrb. d. Pr. K.*, 44, 1923), the picture is regarded by most experts as an original (Zahn, p. 42; Schudt, p. 49).

B. Maragoni (*Arte Barocca*, pp. 142-143; *Dedalo*, 1922) discusses a copy in the Uffizi which he considers superior to the German painting.

Baglione's assertion that the painting was made for Ciriaco Mattei is not confirmed by Celio, who refers to a *Taking of Christ* rather than a *St. Thomas* in the collection of Mattei. Bellori and Sandrart state that the picture was commissioned by Vincenzo Giustiniani.

Caravaggio's composition of the *Incredulity of Thomas* must have been very impressive and influential, as is indicated by Malvasia's report on the Bolognese response to it (above). There are many copies (cf. Ainaud, *Anales*, p. 319). It is interesting to remark that a copy in Genoa was mentioned as early as 1606 by Bizoni (Relazione del Viaggio di Vincenzo Giustiniani, pubd. by A. Banti, *Europa Milleseicentosei*, Rome, 1942).

Another version in very bad condition is mentioned by Longhi (*Pin.*, 1928, p. 3 and *Proporz.*, p. 15) in the Museum at Messina (no. 25). This picture has always been attributed to the Messinese painter Alonso Rodrigues, an imitator of Caravaggio (cf. Mauceri, *Boll. d'Arte*, 1924/1925, p. 559 ff.). Longhi believes that it is by Caravaggio himself, made in Rome in the second half of the nineties and later transported to Sicily "chissà quando."

The date of the Potsdam picture must, for stylistic reasons, be in the late nineties, at about the same time as the two lateral paintings in the Contarelli Chapel. The influence of the neoclassical style which Annibale Carracci introduced into Rome at this time may be discernible in this painting as it is in the *Supper at Emmaus*.

The incident of the *Incredulity of Thomas* is given only in John 20: 24 ff. Thomas was not present with the other apostles when He appeared to them for the first time after the Resurrection. Thomas refused to believe the apostles when they told him that they had seen the Lord: "Except I shall see in his hands the print of the nails, and . . . thrust my hand into his side, I will not believe." And after eight days He again appeared in the midst of the disciples and said to Thomas: "Reach hither thy finger and behold my hands; and reach hither thy hand and thrust it into my side; and be not faithless, but believing."

In early representations of the scene, for example in Signorelli's painting at Loreto Cathedral, Thomas is usually shown beardless and much younger than the other apostles. But in some Northern examples (e.g. the Cologne Altar of the Bartholomew Master; Dürer in the *Small Passion*) he is shown bearded. The same is true of certain Venetian examples (Cima de Conegliano, Venice Academy; Lorenzo Lotto, Treviso, S. Niccolo). The realistic motif of Christ himself guiding the hand of Thomas as he feels the wound is based on a very old tradition. But we find parallels to Caravaggio's emphasis on the finger thrust into the wound only in Northern representations, especially in Dürer. Caravaggio is, as far as we know, the first painter to show the scene in half-figures. He used these pictorial devices ingeniously to concentrate the intensity of the scene and to convince the spectator of the reality of the event.

FIG. 88

Signorelli, *Doubting Thomas*. Loreto, Cathedral.

FIG. 89

Dürer, *Small Passion, Incredulity of Thomas*.

18. SUPPER AT EMMAUS

SOURCES

Bellori, Nota, 1664, 431: mentions the "very beautiful" work in the palace of the Marchese Patrizi, of the "Savior's supper at Emmaus with two Disciples by Michelangelo da Caravaggio."

Bellori, 208: mentions two versions of the *Supper at Emmaus* by Caravaggio. One for the Marchese Patrizi in which "Christ, in the center, is blessing the bread. One seated apostle, recognizing him, opens his arms. Another clutches the table staring in wonder. Behind stands the host with a cap on his head and an old woman carrying food." The other *Supper at Emmaus* was for Scipione Borghese and was, according to Bellori, "somewhat different" from the Patrizi version, the first being more saturated in color (più tinta). "Both imitate natural color very well while failing in decorum. Caravaggio often degenerates into low and vulgar forms."

————, p. 213. "In the *Supper at Emmaus,* besides the rustic character of the two apostles and of the Lord who is shown young and without a beard, Caravaggio shows the inn-keeper who serves with a cap on his head, and on the table there is a plate of grapes, figs and pomegranates out of season."

Scanelli, pp. 198/199: mentions especially, among the paintings of "tremenda naturalezza" in Roman galleries, the rather large picture in the Palazzo Borghese, representing Christ having supper with two pilgrims.

PAINTINGS

PLATE 24

A. *Supper at Emmaus.* London, National Gallery, 139 x 195 cm., Cat. no. 172.

Mentioned in Manilli, p. 88. Was in the Villa Borghese until about 1798. Then in the collection of Lord Vernon whence to the National Gallery in 1839.

Representations of the Supper at Emmaus were often used as decorations in the foresteria, or guest rooms, of convents. Scipione Borghese, however, included the picture by Caravaggio in his growing painting collection at the Villa Borghese where Manilli saw it as early as 1650.

The scene represents the moment when the two apostles Cleophas and Peter Simon, who had invited the unknown pilgrim to share their supper, recognize Christ by His blessing and breaking of the bread. (Luke 24: 30, 31.) Traditionally, either the blessing or the breaking of the bread could be chosen as the sign by which Christ reveals his identity. Among cinquecento examples Signorelli, as well as the two Lombard compatriots of Caravaggio, Romanino and Moretto, show Christ in the act of breaking the bread with both hands, while in Venice, Bellini, Catena, Titian, and Veronese show Him blessing the bread. In this respect Caravaggio has followed the example of the Venetians. Moreover, the composition as a whole also follows the Venetian type. It is very close to Titian's *Christ at Emmaus* at the Louvre, where the host similarly stands at Christ's right with his sleeves rolled up and his hands grasping his belt. Further, the dramatic gestures of the apostle at the right reflect those of the corresponding figure in Veronese's representation of the subject which Caravaggio certainly saw, since it was in Rome until 1624/1625 (now in Dresden).

However, Caravaggio did not entirely forsake his own Lombard background. His use of a

FIG. 90
Romanino, *Supper at Emmaus*. Brescia, Pinacoteca.

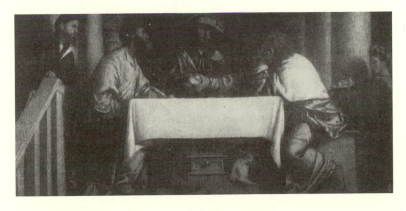

FIG. 91
Moretto, *Supper at Emmaus*. Brescia, Pinacoteca.

small table and the placement of the figures close to the picture surface, which bring the scene into a more intimate relationship with the spectator, were anticipated in the compositions of Moretto and Romanino; of course, Caravaggio goes much farther in this humanizing direction. The table seen slightly from above, and the strongly foreshortened arms of the apostles serve to project the scene towards the spectator. The realism of the objects on the table—the bread, the wine vessels, the chicken and the basket of fruit—heighten the actuality. It is

FIG. 92
Titian, *Supper at Emmaus*. Paris, Louvre.

probably not without significance that the fruit and leaves do not have the freshness and perfection of Caravaggio's early still-lifes, for example, that in the Uffizi *Bacchus*, but show marks of decay. Bellori's pedantic remark that the fruit is out of season (considering that the Supper at Emmaus would have occurred some time after Easter) shows a typically academic point of view, and one which smacks of the French Academy. The placement of the fruit basket in the precarious position on the edge of the table is also remarkable. It is difficult though to decide whether this, like the projection of the stool in the *Second Saint Matthew*, is simply an artistic device or if it has some deeper symbolic meaning.

The face of Christ is beardless, rather Leonardesque, but quite empty and almost effeminate, and is very different from the strong and bearded faces of Christ in Caravaggio's other paintings.

The diagonal lighting and the rather tight modeling of the figures relate the picture to the period of the *Martyrdom of Saint Matthew*; it can therefore be dated in the late nineties (see Longhi, *Pin.*, p. 32, note). At the time when the painting was presumably made, Scipione Cafarelli-Borghese was only about twenty years old and had not yet been made cardinal (he was born in 1576). The painting probably did not come into his possession until some years later.

COPIES

A drawing by Fragonard after the National Gallery picture, made in Rome while the painting was at the Palazzo Borghese, was engraved by Saint-Non in 1771. An engraving

FIG. 93

Fragonard, *Sketch after Caravaggio's Supper at Emmaus*
(engraved by Saint-Non).

FIG. 94

Fatoure, *Supper at Emmaus* (engraving
after Caravaggio).

of the composition by Pierre Fatoure (died Malta, 1629) shows Christ with a small beard (cf. R. Dumesnil, vol. VI); the same is true of a painting (London, dealer) which, in all other respects, conforms exactly to the National Gallery version.

B. *Supper at Emmaus*. Brera, Milan, 145 x 195 cm. Mostra No. 35.   PLATE 45

Until 1939 in the Patrizi Palace in Rome. Agrees exactly with Bellori's description of the Patrizi version.

In this picture a fifth figure of an old woman is added. Apart from the deeper shadows it is much more restrained than the London painting. The composition is restricted to a relatively shallow space behind the picture surface, and the gestures of the three main figures are far less dramatic. The old woman is similar to Saint Anne in the *Madonna del Serpe*, but introduces an element of genre which is not present in the London *Emmaus*. One can hardly doubt the authenticity of the picture, since its provenance is so clear; it is mentioned as early as 1624 in an inventory of the Casa Patrizi and valued at 300 scudi. It must be dated considerably later than the London version (i.e. after 1600), but it cannot be identified with the *Emmaus* that Caravaggio made in Zagarola in 1606, because this, according to Mancini, is a *Walk to Emmaus*. Marangoni (*Boll. d'Arte*, 1922/1923, p. 218) once doubted the authorship of the Brera painting (cf. Schudt, no. 40).

19. WALK TO EMMAUS

SOURCES

Baglione, 137: "Sign. Ciriaco Mattei also believed the rumor of Caravaggio's superiority," and ordered paintings from him, one of which was our Lord going to Emmaus.

Gaspare Celio (Memoria . . . see Orbaan, p. 225) mentions among the paintings by Caravaggio in the Palazzo Mattei, the one of Emmaus ("quella di Emmaus") together with the half-figure painting of the *Taking of Christ* and the *Pastor Friso*.

COPIES   PAINTING   PLATE 23

Walk to Emmaus. Hampton Court, No. 285, 52 x 64 inches, ca., 1929, p. 20. (Copy).

Acquired by Charles I in 1637; listed in van der Doort's catalogue, ca. 1639, as being in Whitehall under the title "Three Disciples," and ascribed to an imitator of Caravaggio; in another catalogue (ca. 1640) it is definitely given to Caravaggio. It was sold in 1651, but was back in Whitehall in 1665. Other copies mentioned at Chatsworth and elsewhere.

The interpretation of the content has been varied. It was early called the "Three Disciples," and in 1651, it was listed as "Three Fishermen." Longhi (*Prop.* fig. 15) suggests the Calling of Sts. Peter and Andrew. The subject, however, is certainly the Walk to Emmaus. Caravaggio chooses the exact moment when Christ, shown in the lead and as yet unrecognized by His companions, Peter Simon (with the fish) and Cleophas, responds to their bewilderment over the alleged resurrection: "Oh fools and slow of heart to believe all that the prophets have spoken. . . . And beginning at Moses and all the prophets, he expounded unto them in all the scriptures and things concerning himself." (Luke: 24, 25-27). These words are made very explicit by the gesture of Christ's hands; a similar gesture is to be found in Lelio Orsi's picture of the same subject (London National Gallery), which is otherwise very different, but indicates that it is a traditional motif for the scene (cf. also the *Walk to Emmaus* by Melone of 1527, now in the National Gallery in London, which came from Cremona where Caravaggio certainly saw it in his youth, and the predella by Signorelli, now in New York, *Klassiker der Kunst: Signorelli*, p. 71).

The composition would fit very well within the relatively smooth and elegant phase of the last years of the 1590's (cf. the *Doubting Thomas*), and can therefore be identified as a copy of the picture made for Ciriaco Mattei—the earlier of the two versions mentioned in the sources. The Hampton Court painting is in very bad condition; it is usually considered to be an old copy.

FIG. 95

Lelio Orsi, *Walk to Emmaus*. London, National Gallery.

20. SAINT JOHN THE BAPTIST

SOURCES

Baglione, 137: mentions, along with a *Walk to Emmaus* and a *Doubting Thomas*, "S. Giov. Battista, made for Signor Ciriaco Mattei, who had also fallen victim to the fashion for Caravaggio."

Celio ("*Memoria fatta . . .*" see Orbaan, p. 225) mentions in the Palazzo Mattei: a *Taking of Christ* in half-figure, an *Emmaus* and a *Pastor Friso* by Caravaggio.

Bellori, 204: "Caravaggio painted a *San Giov. nel Deserto*, a naked youth, seated, turning his face forward and embracing a lamb (agnello); it is to be seen in the palace of Cardinal Pio."

Scanelli, 199: A nude S. Giov. Battista in the Palazzo de'Borghese.

199: A nude S. Giov. Battista in the gallery of the Cardinal Pio.

Bertolotti II, p. 26: cites a "S. G. B. nel deserto di Michelangiolo da Caravaggio" mentioned in the will of Martino Longhi the younger who died in 1657.

PLATE 25

A. *St. John with a Ram*. Rome, Doria-Pamphili, 132 x 98 cm., Cat. Sestieri no. 394.

The provenance of the so-called *St. John the Baptist* in the Doria-Pamphili is not certain. Possibly it is the same picture which, according to Baglione, was made for Ciriaco Mattei, in whose home Gaspare Celio probably saw it in about 1622, together with two other paintings by Caravaggio. Celio calls it a *Pastor Friso*. This identification as a shepherd boy is easily under-stood because the naked boy sitting in the desert and embracing a large ram is without any attributes to make his identity clear. Mancini's reference to a "San Giov. Evangelista" (p. 150), made in the house of Petrignani, is probably an error; since all the other paintings (the *Fortune Teller*, the *Flight to Egypt* and the *Magdalene*), which he mentions in connection with the *St. John*, are, or have been, in the possession of the Doria, he could very well have had in mind the *San Giov. Battista*, which is now also in the Doria. The picture does not belong to the juvenile period; its stylistic relationship to the other persiflage on Michelangelo, the *Amor Victorious*, is very strong. It was probably painted around 1600. (See Chapter V, p. 89ff.)

PLATE 26

B. *St. John with a Ram*. Rome, Capitoline, Palazzo Senatorio. Canvas, 132 x 97 cm.

Denis Mahon (*Burl. Mag.*, June 1953, p. 213, note 7) has proved conclusively that this is the painting mentioned by Bellori as being in the possession of Cardinal Pio; it is also men-tioned by Scanelli. Mr. Mahon points out that a "S. Gio. Battista fanciullo, che scherza con l'Agnellino di Michel'Angelo da Caravaggio" was cited in 1697 in the "Palazzo Orsino in Campo di Fiore . . . presentemente abitato da Signori Pij" (*Descrizione di Roma Moderna*, Rome, 1697, p. 275) and that in 1765, the painting was listed among the pictures of the Capitoline Gallery (Roisecco, *Roma Antica e Moderna*, Rome, 1765, 1, p. 360). That the painting was in the Capitoline Gallery from the time of its foundation is indicated by the fact that the collection of Cardinal Pio was one of the original collections of the museum. The Capitoline canvas is almost identical with that in the Doria; the former is in much better condition, so that it is very difficult to judge the relative quality of the two paintings. How-ever, both are so close to Caravaggio that, as Mr. Mahon has suggested, there is no reason for excluding the possibility that the artist repeated the composition.

COPIES

Several copies of the composition are known: Marseilles; Pommersfelden; Herdringen, Coll. of Count Fuerstenberg (the last is published and discussed by Baumgart, *Das Werk des Kunstlers*, 1939/1940, p. 488 ff.).

PLATE 61

C. *St. John with a Ram*. Rome, Galleria Borghese. No. 267, 150 x 122 cm. Mostra No. 31.

This is probably the first painting mentioned by Scanelli. It is cited as early as 1613 as being by Caravaggio in Francucci's description of the Borghese Gallery (published in 1644). On this basis, Lionello Venturi (*Arte* XII, 1909, p. 40) accepts the painting as a Caravaggio, as does Longhi (*Precisioni* p. 201, and *Prop.* p. 100). Schudt (no. 75) places it among the doubtful works.

It is difficult to make a definite judgment about the authenticity of the work because of its condition. If it is really by Caravaggio, it would be related stylistically to the later Roman works, for example the *David* in the same collection, though it does not have the refinement of the *David*.

There is a charming painting of a youth holding some flowers in his right hand and a lamb climbing into his lap in the museum at Basel (102.5 x 83 cm. Mostra No. 45) which is certainly not by Caravaggio, but which is generally ascribed to his circle.

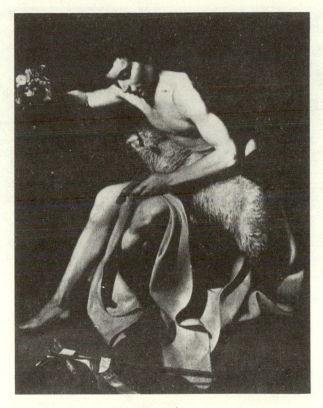

FIG. 96
St. John. Basel, Museum.

PLATE 44

D. *St. John the Baptist*. Kansas City, Nelson Gallery (formerly in the collection of Lord Astor) 172.5 x 134.5 cm. Mostra No. 23.

Of the various paintings of Saint John attributed to Caravaggio, one of the most remarkable is the seated youth with a staff in his right hand, which was recently found in England and is now in Kansas City. It is ascribed to Caravaggio by Longhi (*Prop.* 1943, p. 15). A copy of the same composition is in the museum at Naples and is there given to Manfredi. Less closely related to Caravaggio is a seated *Saint John* in the Galleria Nazionale in Rome (99 x 134 cm., Mostra No. 22), which Longhi (*Prop.* 1934, p. 14) also accepts as an original. All of these compositions seem fairly closely related, and it is quite possible that they are derived from a painting by Caravaggio. If the painting in Kansas City is an original (it is certainly the closest to Caravaggio in the whole group), it would represent a fairly advanced phase of his development; Longhi (*ibid.*) dates it around the time of the *Second Saint Matthew.*

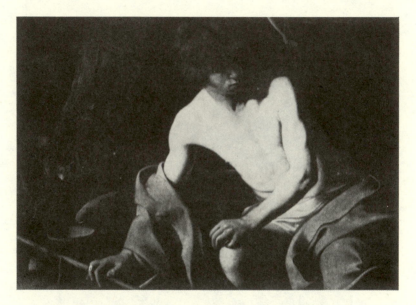

FIG. 97
St. John. Naples, Galleria Nazionale.

In a letter from the office of the Viceroy of Naples, dated August 19, 1610, a "quadro de San Juan Bautista" is mentioned among the belongings of Caravaggio which were confiscated after his death (DOC. 34). It is not impossible that the Kansas City painting or a related work had remained in the artist's possession.

21. TAKING OF CHRIST

SOURCES

Gaspare Celio, Memorie, pp. 134-135 (cf. Orbaan, p. 225, no. 1): mentions a *Taking of Christ* in half-figures (*quella della presa di Christo messe figure*) as one of the paintings by Caravaggio in the Palazzo Vecchio for the Marchese Mattei.

Bellori, 207: describes a *Taking of Christ in the Garden,* made for the Marchese Asdrubale Mattei. "Judas has his hand on the shoulder of the Master after the kiss; a soldier in full armor . . . extends his iron-clad hand toward the chest of Our Lord, who stands there patiently and humbly with his hands crossed. Behind, Saint John is running away, his arms flung out. He [Caravaggio] imitated the rust on the armor of that soldier, whose head and face are covered by the helmet, his profile slightly visible. Behind, a lantern is raised, beyond which appear two more heads of armed men."

Nota, 43: Bellori mentions the *Seizure in the Garden* by M. d. Caravaggio as belonging to the Duke Girolamo Mattei.

COPY   PAINTING   PLATE 27

The original is lost, but Longhi has published a copy (*Prop.*, p. 13f., fig. 16, Coll. L. Sannini, Florence, Mostra No. 54), which corresponds exactly to Bellori's careful description. This enables us to appreciate the general structure at least of one of Caravaggio's most monumental and dramatic compositions.

In accordance with Mark (14:51-52), the youth who runs away at the left, his mouth open in a cry and his arms raised in fright, is not St. John as Bellori says, but a young follower of Christ, perhaps the gardener, whose linen cloth is torn from his naked body by the soldiers as he is trying to escape. In the *Large Passion*, Dürer rendered this incident with two small

FIG. 98
Dürer, *Large Passion: Taking of Christ.*

figures running through the fields in the background. In a copy after Correggio in the Parma Gallery, this incident is made the central action of the scene. Caravaggio made this terror-stricken figure intimately connected with the main event by curving an end of his linen cloth, grasped by a soldier in back at the right, like an antique velum so that it ties together the two impressive heads of Christ and Judas. The moment represented is immediately after the treacherous kiss, in contrast to representations by Giotto, Dürer, and others. The genre scene of Peter cutting off the ear of Malchus, generally shown in connection with the Judas kiss, is here omitted. The shifting accent of light on the faces, hands and armor are caused by the lantern raised by the bearded man in armor at the right (in the copy not easily distinguishable). This is one of the rare specific night-scenes by Caravaggio.

The date of the original must have been the second half of the nineties, as Longhi also believes, around the time of the *Doubting Thomas*, and not far distant from the *Martyrdom of St. Matthew*, in which there is an equally terrified boy, rushing sidelong out of the picture.

An interesting painting of this subject—and one which Caravaggio possibly, but not certainly knew—was made by his antagonist, Arpino and is now in the Borghese. It is mentioned in a

FIG. 99
Arpino, *Taking of Christ*. Rome, Borghese.

marginal note to Baglione's *Vite* (p. 370) by Bellori, who calls it the most beautiful of Arpino's works. The exact date of the painting is not known, but it was confiscated in 1606 along with the other paintings in Arpino's studio and thus found its way into the collection of Scipione Borghese. Here the subject is treated in a much more complicated way and includes the incident of St. Peter cutting off the ear of Malchus. The scene is illuminated by a soft, artificial light in the foreground, and a moon shines in the upper right. Caravaggio's interpretation is more concentrated and dramatic, being painted in half figures, but he might have been impressed by the nude figure running off to the left in Arpino's painting and by his curious night light.

THE CROWNING WITH THORNS

See LOST PAINTINGS, Cat. No. 46.

ECCE HOMO

See LOST PAINTINGS, Cat. No. 47.

22. THE CONTARELLI CHAPEL, SAN LUIGI DEI FRANCESI, ROME

GENERAL SOURCES

Inscription in the pavement of the chapel: 1590 (DOC. 39).

Mancini, 59v: mentions "Li quadri di S. Luigi," but makes no further comment.

Baglione, 136-137: "With the help of his Cardinal, he obtained the commission for the chapel of the Contarelli in San Luigi dei Francesi. Over the altar he made St. Matthew with an angel; at the right is the calling of the Apostle by the Savior; at the left the Saint is struck down on the altar by the executioner, with other figures."

Bellori, 20: According to Bellori, Marino, in his great enthusiasm for the work of Caravaggio, introduced the painter to the Monsignori Crescenzi (Melchiore and Virgilio). Virgilio, as heir of the Cardinal Contarelli, chose Caravaggio, in cooperation with Giuseppe d'Arpino, to do the paintings for the chapel in S. Luigi, assigning, on the advice of Marino, to Giuseppe, an expert in fresco, the overhead figures, and to Caravaggio the oil paintings.

Scanelli, p. 197: mentions among the works of Caravaggio in Rome as easily the best those in San Luigi, the French National church. He praises especially the story of St. Matthew called by Christ to the Apostolate, as one of his richest (pastose), most plastic and natural compositions, which shows the high capacity of paintings for imitating the true reality. Scanelli complains that the chapel is almost without light, and that to the disgrace of the virtuosi and the author himself the paintings can be seen only imperfectly.

HISTORY OF THE CHAPEL

Matteo Contarelli (made Cardinal under Gregory XIII) acquired the chapel which bears his name in 1565 and in this year he commissioned Girolamo Muziano to do the decorations. The original program, as set down in the contract (DOC. 37) is as follows: the *Calling* and *Martyrdom of St. Matthew* were to be painted on the lateral walls, the *Saint with his Angel* above the altar, and on the vault three scenes of the *Saint* (of which the center one was to have been the baptism of the king and queen of Ethiopia). In addition to these scenes, there were to be four prophets in the corners of the vaults. All of these paintings were to be made in fresco, except for the altarpiece which was to be painted in oil. Muziano, it seems, never began the work (he did paint a similar program in the Mattei Chapel at Sta. Maria Aracoeli) and little or nothing was done toward the execution of the program until after the death of Contarelli in 1585. The official heir of the Contarelli estate was Virgilio Crescenzi, who was thus in charge of the large amount of money with which the chapel had been endowed. The inscription on the floor of the chapel, dated 1590, bears Virgilio Crescenzi's name. He died in December of 1592, but he had retired before this, leaving the administration of the chapel in the hands of his son, Abbot Giacomo Crescenzi.

In 1587, a contract was made between "the Contarelli heirs" and the Flemish sculptor, Cornelisz Cobaert, called Coppe Fiamingo, for a statue of St. Matthew and the Angel to be placed on the altar of the chapel instead of the oil-painting originally planned. The contract allowed four years for the completion of the statue, but Coppe, an extremely eccentric man (see Baglione, *Vite*), never finished it; the figure of the angel was added later by Francucci, and the work was given to the church of Sta. Trinità dei Pellegrini by Francesco Contarelli, a nephew of the cardinal, where it is today. On May 27, 1591, another contract (not preserved, but mentioned in a later document, DOC. 41) was made with an unnamed artist for paintings in the chapel to be completed within two years. This unnamed artist was surely Giuseppe d'Arpino, whose frescoes decorate the vault of the chapel today: the Sibyls, Prophets and stories from the life of St. Matthew (recently restored; see I. Faldi, "Gli affreschi della cappella Contarelli e l'opera giovanile del Cavalier d'Arpino," *Boll. d'Arte* XXXVIII, ser. IV, 1953, p. 47ff.). Van Mander (1604, fol. 190v.) says that Arpino returned from Naples soon after the fall of 1589, called back by the death of his father, and began "hereafter" his work at San Luigi, which "for some reason" was never finished.

The chapel remained in an unfinished state for a number of years, with the result that the clergy of San Luigi began to make petitions to the Pope against the Crescenzi (as early as December 1594; DOC. 40). The clergy claimed that nothing had been done in the chapel and accused the Abbate Giacomo Crescenzi of having neglected its completion with fraudulent intentions, so that in 1596, eleven years after the death of the cardinal, it remained boarded up and could not be used for masses (see Hess, *Burl. Mag.*, June 1951, p. 191, note 41). The Pope was asked to order an investigation by "visita apostolica," which investigation was made in May 1597. An avviso of July 1597 (see *Roma*, 1934, p. 30 and Hess, *loc. cit.*, note 46) states that the allowance for the chapel from the estate of Cardinal Contarelli was placed under the authority of the Fabbrica di San Pietro in order to put an end to the dispute. As we know from a promissory note (DOC. 43) Arpino was given a last opportunity to complete his long-interrupted work in the chapel; this promissory note was valid for only one year. Doubtlessly the work which Arpino was now to do was the decoration of the lateral walls, which, as is indicated by a statement of the Crescenzi of July 8, 1597 (DOC. 41), had not been touched, and they were still not painted in March 1598.

In the documents concerning the Contarelli Chapel, Caravaggio's name is mentioned only once: in 1601, he is named as a witness in the prosecution of a certain François Bonnet, who was expelled from the governing body of San Luigi in June of this year. Moreover, there are no contracts or records of payment for the paintings which Caravaggio executed in the chapel. At least until November 1597 there was still a chance of Arpino's completing the work, and consequently Caravaggio cannot have received an official commission before this date. This, however, does not rule out the possibility that he had begun the lateral paintings unofficially before this time.

FIG. 100
Arpino, *Vault decoration of the Contarelli Chapel.*
Rome, San Luigi dei Francesi.

On May 1, 1599, a meeting of the governing body of the church was held in which it was resolved that the chapel should be opened, and two chaplains, Claudio Vincy and Andrea Berger, were appointed for the celebration of masses (DOC. 44). One would think that at this time the decorations for the chapel were more or less finished. However, Caravaggio may still have made changes in the lateral paintings, especially the *Martyrdom* (for which he made a number of preliminary projects) even after the chapel was opened for services. That the latter was the case is indicated by a number of recently discovered documents touching upon the carpenter's work in the chapel. From these it is known that the lateral paintings were not affixed to the walls until December of 1600 (DOCS. 44A, 44B, 44C, 44D). Judging from its style, the final altarpiece for the chapel, the *Second Saint Matthew*, seems to be considerably later than either the *Calling* or the *Martyrdom*. Again, this is confirmed by the carpenter's record which shows that the frame for the final altarpiece was made in October of 1602.

The most difficult problem in studying the chronology of Caravaggio's paintings for the Contarelli Chapel, is the dating of the *First Saint Matthew*. Since there are no documents referring specifically to it, the exact date of the decision to replace Cobaert's statue with a painting (see Baglione, *Vita*) is purely a matter of conjecture. The earliest date for this decision would be November 1591, when Cobaert's contract with the Crescenzi was to have ended; the latest date would be that on which Caravaggio received the commission to do the lateral paintings, which, as has been indicated, is itself not known exactly.

A. FIRST SAINT MATTHEW

SOURCES

Baglione, 137: "A certain *Saint Matthew*, which was originally made for the altar of San Luigi dei Francesi, and which no one had liked, was taken by Giustiniani only because it was by Caravaggio."

Bellori, 20: "Something happened which made Caravaggio almost despair for his reputation: the priests removed the *Saint Matthew*, his first public work, from the altar, saying that the figure had no decorum, did not look like a saint, sitting with crossed legs and with his feet crudely exposed to the people. Marchese Vincenzo Giustiniani intervened in behalf of Caravaggio, arranging with the priests to take the painting for himself and to have a second one made which is now there. Giustiniani took Caravaggio's first *Saint Matthew* into his house, placing it together with three other Evangelists by the most celebrated painters of the time, Guido, Domenichino and Albani."

Sandrart, 189: "He painted the Evangelist St. Matthew, before whom an angel in a white garment holds the book on which he writes."

PAINTING   PLATE 28

Saint Matthew and the Angel, Berlin, Kaiser Friedrich Museum, No. 365, 2.23 x 1.83 m. Allegedly destroyed by fire in 1944. It came to Berlin from the Giustiniani Collection in 1815 (sale catalogue, Paris, no. 86).

There are no documents referring specifically to the *First Saint Matthew*. The painting was certainly made for the Contarelli Chapel and Baglione is probably right in saying that it was to be used on the altar instead of the statue which Cobaert had been commissioned to do. The work was taken by Vincenzo Giustiniani for his own collection and was eventually replaced by the *Second Saint Matthew*, which is now on the altar of the chapel. As was said above, the dating of the *First Saint Matthew* is extremely problematic. (For a stylistic and iconographical discussion of the painting, see text, pp. 96-100.)

B. CALLING OF SAINT MATTHEW

SOURCES

Baglione, 137: related that in his presence Federico Zuccari once looked at Caravaggio's paintings in San Luigi and said: "What is all the noise about? I cannot see anything but the thought (pensiero) of Giorgione in the painting of the saint called to the Apostolate. Grinning and shaking his head about such a to-do, he shrugged his shoulders and went away with God." (For a discussion of the translation of this passage, see: Longhi, *Paragone*, 17 May, 1951, p. 9; and the reply by Denis Mahon, *Burl. Mag.*, Sept. 1951.)

Bellori, 20: "On the right side of the altar is Christ calling Saint Matthew to the Apostolate, in which several heads are portrayed in a natural manner, among them the saint, who, interrupting his counting of money, turns to the Lord, his hand on his breast. Nearby an old man puts his spectacles on his nose and looks at the youth at the corner of the table who draws all the money to himself."

Sandrart, 189: recognizes the subject matter but gives an incorrect description of the painting. "Caravaggio represents Christ entering a dark room with two of his disciples, where he finds the tax collector Matthew drinking and playing cards and dicing with a group of rogues. Matthew fearfully hides the cards in one hand and lays the other to his breast, revealing in his face the shock and shame caused by the realization that he is unworthy to be called by Christ to the apostolate. One of the rogues with one hand sweeps his money from the table into his other hand and slinks shamefully away, all of which is true to life and nature itself."

P A I N T I N G   PLATE 29

Calling of St. Matthew. West wall, Contarelli Chapel, oil on canvas. 3.38 x 3.48. Mostra No. 14.

This is the earliest of the two lateral paintings which Caravaggio made for the chapel.

PLATE 29F

The X-ray (Venturi, see below) indicates that the changes in this painting were not nearly so extensive as in the *Martyrdom*. The left side is unchanged except for the contour of the face of the young boy who sits beside St. Matthew and the right leg of the seated figure seen from the rear. In the right side of the painting, Caravaggio seems originally to have intended to show Christ entering the room alone, and he occupied more or less the same position of his companion (the so-called St. Peter) in the final version. Also, his outstretched hand was turned farther down than in the final version.

C. MARTYRDOM OF SAINT MATTHEW

SOURCES

Bellori, 206: "On the other side is the Martyrdom of the Saint; he is in priestly robes, stretched out on a bench. The almost nude executioner opposite brandishes his sword to strike. The other persons draw back in horror. The composition and movements, however, are not adequate for the story, even though he remade it twice (*rifacesse due volte*). The darkness and the color hide these two pictures from sight."

Sandrart, 189: has obviously seen the painting very superficially, for he calls it an Expulsion from the Temple.

P A I N T I N G   PLATE 30

Martyrdom of St. Matthew. East wall, Contarelli Chapel, oil on canvas, ca. 328 x 348 cm. Mostra No. 15.

The story of the slaying of St. Matthew on the order of King Hirtacus of Ethiopia is recounted in the *Acta Sanctorum* (T. vi September). Schudt's observation of another composition beneath the present surface of the painting, in which the main group of figures was considerably lower, has recently been confirmed by X-ray studies. These X-rays also confirm Bellori's remark that Caravaggio remade the composition two times. They are rather complicated and therefore more difficult to read than the X-rays of the *Calling*. The most significant thing which they show is Caravaggio's way of experimenting with the poses and positions of various figures directly on the canvas before arriving at final compositional solutions. The individual stages in the evolution of the composition of the *Martyrdom* are not altogether clearly distinguishable, but they seem to be roughly as follows. Originally the saint stood before the altar with his hands raised as though to ward off the blow of the first executioner, who stands to the left with a dagger(?) upraised in his right hand. The winged angel on the right, holding the gospel of the saint and pointing to heaven with his right hand, seems a counterpart to the relatively small executioner who runs in from the left side of the painting. This second executioner, seen in profile and holding a sword in his right hand, attacks the saint, who is now indicated only by two roughly sketched heads in a position (perhaps kneeling) inter-mediate between that of the standing saint and the fallen saint of the final version. Just above the line of the neck and shoulder of this second executioner is a head which is said to be a portrait of the artist himself, corresponding to the portrait higher on the canvas in the final composition. The role of the helmeted soldier seen from the rear in the foreground of the X-ray study (standing astride the child on the ground with outstretched and suppliant arm) is somewhat difficult to specify. He probably represents another member of the armed band charged with the execution of the saint; compositionally he seems to be simply a repoussoir figure which Caravaggio painted perhaps to have a spatial reference point behind which he could work. The terrified figure of a woman on the far left of the X-ray study (with her right arm outstretched and her left hand to her face) can possibly be identified as Iphigenia, the daughter of the former king of Ethiopia, whom King Hirtacus wished to marry (the head of this figure is, incidentally, extremely beautiful and very characteristic of Caravaggio). All of the figures in the X-ray studies are considerably lower on the canvas than are the figures in the final composition, and the upper portion of the picture was to have been filled by a large, simple architectural piece, with plain cornices, Ionic pilasters and a niche for the altar before which the saint is slain (for an analysis of the composition see pp. 110ff.).

D. SECOND SAINT MATTHEW

SOURCES

Bellori, 20: "Caravaggio made every effort to succeed with the second picture: He made the Saint, who is writing the Gospel, look quite natural with one knee bent and resting on the stool. His hands are on the small table and he dips his pen into the inkwell on the book. At the same time he turns his face to the left toward the angel who, suspended in air . . . , speaks to him, signalling to him by touching the left hand with the right index finger. The color makes the angel seem distant . . . his nude arms and breast and fluttering white veil are set against the darkness of the background."

PAINTING

PLATE 31

Second St. Matthew. North wall, Contarelli Chapel, San Luigi, Rome, 2.95 x 1.95 m. Mostra No. 16.

In Caravaggio's second version *Saint Matthew* is presented in a much more conventional way than in the first. The combination of the angel approaching from the sky with the apostle who sits writing the Gospel depends on an old and venerable tradition.

In the San Luigi picture it appears that Matthew has just begun to write. With his knee on the stool he is seen in a transitory position as if in his excitement to record the words of the angel he could not wait until he had fully settled himself at the table. This momentary effect is emphasized by the stool which dangles precariously, with one of its legs over the edge of the platform. Matthew dips his pen into the inkwell, which he holds in his left hand. (In older representations it is often the angel who holds the inkwell for the evangelist.) The head, in contrast to the *First St. Matthew*, is of the normal patriarchal type, with a long grey beard and partly bald head. He turns his head and looks up so intensely at the angel that the lines on his forehead stand out. Matthew has a small, thin halo, whereas in the first version he has none. The angel has dark wings, half-hidden but similar to those of the *Amor Victorious*, and is enveloped in great flowing drapery. He is suspended in the air, foreshortened to such a degree that only the upper part of his body is visible. His face, very different from that of the angel in the *First Saint Matthew*, is that of a gamin and resembles the mischievous physiognomy of the *Amor Victorious*, only with a more serious expression in uttering the divinely inspired words; even the dark, curling locks are similar.

The *Second Saint Matthew*, which was substituted for the withdrawn version, is not only utterly different in spirit, but stylistically as well it belongs to a quite different period. It is no longer painted in the voluminous relief style which drives the picture space forward toward the spectator, but it is carefully arranged to keep the whole composition behind the surface, separated from the spectator. (Compare, for example, the left leg of St. Matthew in the two pictures; in the one case it extends forward and crosses the boundary between picture space and real space, while in the other case it is placed parallel to the picture plane.)

This picture is stylistically the most advanced of the three paintings in the chapel, and has therefore been placed at the very end of the years in which the Contarelli Chapel was decorated. We have already noted its similarity to the *Amor Victorious* of about 1603, and the facial type of St. Matthew is also strikingly similar to the St. Peter in the Cerasi Chapel. As was mentioned above, the frame for the final altarpiece was made in October of 1602; the painting would therefore seem to have been made in that year.

LITERATURE

The most important modern literature dealing with the problems of the Contarelli Chapel is the following: H. Chéramy, *Rass. d'Arte,* IX, 1922, pp. 170/174; W. Voss, *Jahrb. der preuss. Knstslgn.,* 44, 1923, pp. 90ff.; and *Die Malerei des Barock in Rom,* 1925; N. Pevsner, *Z.f.b.K.,* 61, 1928/1929, p. 388; R. Longhi, *Pinacoteca,* I, 1928, p. 22; L. Schudt, *Caravaggio,* 1942, pp. 46/47; *Mostra del Caravaggio,* Milan, 1951; J. Hess, *Burl. Mag.,* June 1951, pp. 186ff.; D. Mahon, *Burl. Mag.,* July 1951, pp. 223ff., Sept. 1951, pp. 286ff., and Jan. 1952, pp. 3ff.; L. Venturi and G. Urbani, *Studi radiografici sul Caravaggio,* 1953, Jacques Bousquet, "Documents inédits sur Caravage," *La Revue des Arts,* 1953, p. 103ff.

THE MONUMENTAL ROMAN STYLE: 1600-1606

23. AMOR VICTORIOUS

SOURCES

Baglione, 137: Caravaggio made for the Marchese Vincenzo Giustiniani a "seated Cupid" (Cupido a sedere). The wonderful color of this painting was the cause of the intemperate love of Giustiniani for the works of Caravaggio (si che egli dell' opere del Caravaggio fuor' de termini invaghissi).

Bellori, 207: Along with the half-figures (by Caravaggio) belonging to Marchese Vincenzo Giustiniani (the *Crowning with Thorns* and the *Doubting Thomas*), Caravaggio painted a *Victorious Amor* with his arrows raised in his right hand, and arms, books, and other objects as trophies lying at his feet.

Scanelli, 199: Like the *Saint John in the Desert* in the collection of Cardinal Pio which has such fine realistic flesh tones, the *Amoretto* in the possession of Prince Giustiniani was one of the most highly esteemed works of Caravaggio in a private collection.

Sandrart, 190: "Caravaggio made for the Marchese Giustiniani a lifesized Cupid modeled after a boy of about twelve years, seated on a celestial globe, and raising his bow in his right hand. On his left are sundry art instruments, a book for studies, and a laurel wreath (or branch). The Cupid has big brown eagle wings. Everything is correctly and neatly designed, in strong color and relief—almost as in nature. The picture hung in a gallery of 120 paintings. On the advice of Sandrart, it was covered with a green silk curtain, and shown only after the rest of the paintings had been seen, so as to avoid overshadowing the other works. Because of this picture it came about that Caravaggio was again permitted to walk in the streets as a free man" ("he used this liberty," says Sandrart, "to enjoy the company of young ruffians, mostly painters and fighters, whose motto was, nec spe, nec metu, 'no hope, no fear!' ").

(*Bertolotti,* II, p. 62, see DOC. 12): In the trial of Baglione versus Orazio Gentileschi, Caravaggio, etc., Orazio Gentileschi speaks, in his testimony of September 14, 1603, of an "amor terreno" by Caravaggio. Orazio testifies that in concurrence with this work Baglione made an "amor divino" dedicated to the Cardinal Giustiniani, the brother of Vincenzo, but that this work received less praise than Caravaggio's. (Baglione's painting came with the Giustiniani Collection to the Berlin Museum under the name of Caravaggio. Voss reestablished the name of its rightful author (*J. d. K.,* 44, 1923, pp. 95ff. A second version by Baglione came to the Italian embassy in Berlin).

PAINTING   PLATE 32

Amor Victorious. Berlin, Kaiser Friedrich Museum, 154 x 110 cm. No. 369. Cat. 1909/209. Mostra No. 21.

The picture came to the Berlin Museum in 1815 from the Giustiniani Collection. This painting can in no case be dated later than 1603, when it was mentioned by Orazio Gentileschi. That it was painted shortly before this trial is suggested by two facts: Gentileschi mentions in his testimony that Caravaggio had borrowed and returned to him in the course of the previous six or eight months a pair of wings, which we may assume were used for the *Amor Victorious* (DOC. 12); Sandrart relates that this painting received such acclaim that it earned Caravaggio his freedom to be with his friends again. This story must be related to the trial mentioned above, especially since it is confirmed by a legal act of September 25, 1603 (see Bertolotti, II, p. 64). This act states that the governor of Rome, on the intercession of the French ambassador, who had put up security (probably because of the work in San Luigi dei Francesi), granted freedom to Caravaggio on condition that he present himself in court in a month, promise not to offend the plaintiff (Baglione), and remain in his house, or at least not leave it without written permission from the governor himself. A comparison between the fattura of the Cupid and the Christ Child in the *Madonna del Serpe* seems to confirm the rather late dating, as does a comparison between the head of the Cupid and that of the angel in the *Second Saint Matthew*. (For the relation to the *Victory* of Michelangelo and for the iconography, see text, p. 91.) It is usually dated rather early (Longhi, 1592/1594).

24. CERASI CHAPEL

SOURCES

Contract: Tiberio Cerasi, general treasurer in the time of Clement VIII, acquired in July 1600, not long before his death (May 3, 1601), a chapel on the left of the high altar of Sta. Maria del Popolo. There is preserved a contract between the Cerasi and Caravaggio for the decoration of the chapel, published by Denis Mahon (*Burl. Mag.*, June 1951, p. 227). The contract is dated 24 September, 1600, and contains the statement that "Dominus Michael Angelus Merisius de Caravaggio . . . egregius in Urbe Pictor" promised to make for Tiberio Cerasi two paintings on cypress wood, 10 palmi long by 8 palmi wide (duo quadro cupressus longitudinis palmor decem et latitudinis octo). The paintings were to represent the mystery of the conversion of St. Paul and the martyrdom of St. Peter and were to be finished within eight months from the date of the contract. Furthermore, Caravaggio promised to submit projects and drawings for the paintings before their execution. The fee of the work was fixed at 400 scudi, of which Caravaggio received 50 scudi in advance. He received the residual and final payment for the work on November 10, 1601 (DOC. 42).

Inscription: There is an inscription on the left wall of the Cappella dell'Assunta which states that Tiberio Cerasi is buried in the chapel which he had constructed and decorated before his death in May 1601 (In Hoc Sacello Ab Ipso Ante Obitum Constructo Atque Exornato).

Mancini, Cod. Marciana 59v: in his enumeration of Caravaggio's works mentions the Cerasi chapel "al popolo."

Mancini, Cod. Pal., pp. 115ff.: mentions in the possession of the Cardinal Sannesio paintings which are copied and retouched (copiati e ritoccati) from those which are in the church of the Madonna del Popolo in the Cerasi Chapel (see DOC. 45 and *Paragone*, May 1951, p. 47). This passage is not in the Marciana manuscript of Mancini, but it is added in the Palatine variant, which is probably later.

Baglione, 137: "In Sta. Maria del Popolo at the right of the main altar on the side walls of the chapel of the Signori Cerasi are Caravaggio's *Crucifixion of Saint Peter* and, facing it, the *Conversion of Saint Paul*. The two subjects were first painted in another way, but because they did not please the patron they were taken by Cardinal Sannesio. Caravaggio then painted the two versions one sees now (in oil because he used no other medium); luck plus fame carried him through."

Bellori, 207: "In the church of the Madonna del Popolo in the chapel of the Assumption painted by Annibale Carracci, Caravaggio painted the two lateral paintings, the *Crucifixion of Saint Peter* and the *Conversion of Saint Paul*, which lacks any action."

Scanelli, p. 198: mentions two paintings on the sides of a chapel in the church of the Madonna del Popolo, one of the *Crucifixion of Saint Peter*, the other of the *Conversion of Saint Paul*; between them is a painting by Annibale Carracci.

FIRST VERSIONS   P A I N T I N G S

If we accept Baglione's statement, rather than the somewhat confusing information of Mancini in the Florentine manuscript (see above), there can be no doubt that Caravaggio painted two versions of both the *St. Paul* and the *St. Peter*, the first versions being different from the second ones (in un altra maniera). Since the contract of September 1600 (see above) precisely stipulates the use of cypress wood for the paintings and since the works now in Sta. Maria del Popolo are on canvas, the latter do not meet the requirements of the contract.

Whether or not the first versions of the Cerasi paintings were completed within the eight months stipulated in the contract, by May 1601, is not known. Moreover, it cannot be said when it was decided to replace the first versions with the second ones. We do know, however, that Caravaggio received final payment for his work in the chapel on November 10, 1601, and it must be assumed that all of the paintings had been finished by this date.

PLATE 62

A. *Conversion of St. Paul*. Rome, Coll. Odescalchi-Balbi. 237 x 189 cm. Mostra No. 13 (on cypress wood).

The painting is on cypress wood as stipulated in the contract of September 1600. In the position of the St. Paul and of the Christ, and in the movement of the horse into the depth of the picture, this work is still related to the tradition of Michelangelo's fresco in the Paolina Chapel. There are decidedly Caravaggesque elements in the work, such as the face of the angel supporting Christ, which greatly resembles that of the *Amor Victorious* (Berlin), or of the Isaac in the *Sacrifice of Isaac* (Uffizi). However, the whole composition is crowded and composed in crossing diagonals, somewhat in the manner of Central Italian painters such as Federico Barocci (*S. Vitale* at the Brera, 1583). In this way it would show a development of the compositional ideas of the *Martyrdom of St. Matthew*. Published as an original first version of the *Conversion of Saint Paul* by Antonio Morassi (*Emporium*, March 1947, pp. 95ff. and in the catalogue, Mostra della pittura del Seicento in Liguria, p. 99). Longhi once called it a "cosa fiamminga c. il 1620" (*Prop.*, p. 101) but he now accepts the work as a Caravaggio and places it very early in his career (Catalogue of the Mostra del Caravaggio, 1951, p. 19).

I cannot agree with Longhi's dating of the work, nor do I recognize a close relationship with Antonio Campi's composition of the *Conversion* in San Paolo in Milan. Denis Mahon is doubtful of the authenticity of the painting (see discussion of the work by Mahon and Morassi, *Burl. Mag.*, April 1952, pp. 118-119). Whether or not this is really the first version by Caravaggio for the chapel is extremely difficult to decide.

B. *Crucifixion of Saint Peter.* Leningrad, Hermitage, No. 2182. 232 x 201 cm.   PLATE 63

Acquired by the Hermitage in 1808 as a genuine Caravaggio, through the negotiations of Vivant Denon, from Mme. Levi Montmorency, who had acquired it from the Giustiniani Collection. Possibly a copy of the first version of the *Crucifixion of Saint Peter* mentioned by Baglione.

The painting certainly cannot be from the same hand as the Balbi-Odescalchi *Conversion*; it is on canvas (not cypress wood) and it is of inferior quality. Nevertheless, considering the provenance and the general character of the work, it is quite conceivable that it at least reflects Caravaggio's first version of the *Martyrdom of Saint Peter*. Longhi (*Prop.*, 59, N. 83) may be correct in ascribing it to the Genovese painter, Saltarello, under whose name a painting of the *Crucifixion of Saint Peter* was reported to be in the possession of the Giustiniani. This, however, does not exclude the possibility that the work is a copy after Caravaggio, since Soprani (*Vite de Pittori Genovese*, 1674, p. 83) relates that while Saltarello was in Rome he exclusively made copies of the most considered works and so overburdened himself with this that he took sick ("dal gran travaglia oppressa la natura s'infermò") and eventually died. Thus the painting in Leningrad may be a copy or a version made by Saltarello for the Principe Giustiniani. The painting mentioned by Longhi as having been exhibited in Rome in 1870 cannot be the same as the Leningrad painting, since the latter was acquired by the Hermitage in 1808. Waagen (*Gemaeldesammlung der Kaiserlichen Hermitage* in St. Petersburg, 1870, p. 82) accepts the work as an original Caravaggio and suggests that it inspired Rubens' painting of the same subject in the church of St. Peter in Cologne. (See W. Friedlaender, *Warburg Journal*, vol. 8, 1945.)

FINAL VERSIONS

Rome, Sta. Maria del Popolo, Cerasi Chapel. Both 230 x 175 cm. Mostra Nos. 26-27.

The final versions are definitely in "un altra maniera," as Baglione states. They are, as is often the case with second versions, much more concentrated and simplified, in contrast to the cluttered compositions of the presumed first versions. The dramatic impact caused by this concentration and compression of the forms and of the composition explains the great impression which these works made on contemporary and later generations.

C. *Conversion of Saint Paul*   PLATE 33

For stylistic and iconographical discussion see Chapter I.

D. *Crucifixion of Saint Peter*   PLATE 34

For stylistic and iconographical discussion see Chapter I.

The many copies after the *Crucifixion of Saint Peter*, especially in Spain (see J. Ainaud, *Anales*, vol. v, 1947, p. 382, nos. 7-10) are ample proof of the influence of the paintings. It is interesting to remark that Gerard Honthorst executed a drawing (Oslo) after the painting as early as 1616.

FIG. 101
Rubens, *Crucifixion of St. Peter*.
Cologne, St. Peter's.

FIG. 101A
Honthorst, drawing after Caravaggio's
Crucifixion of St. Peter. Stockholm.

25. DEPOSITION OF CHRIST

SOURCES

Mancini, 59v: "The *Cristo Deposto* is in the Chiesa Nuova."

Baglione, 137: "In the Chiesa Nuova, in the second chapel to the right, is the *Cristo Morto* about to be buried and some other figures, all done in oil; they say that it is his best work."

Bellori, 207: "The *Deposition of Christ* in the Chiesa Nuova of the Fathers of the Oratorio is among the best works ever made by Michele and is therefore justly held in highest esteem. The figures are assembled on a stone in the opening of the sepulchre. The Holy Body is in the center and is supported by Nicodemus, who embraces Christ's legs under the knees; and in the lowering of the hips the legs (from the knees down) are extended. On the other side Saint John puts one arm under the shoulder of the Redeemer, whose head is thrown back, his breast deathly pale, and his arm falling down with the shroud. The nude is drawn with the force of the most exact imitation. Behind are the three Maries, one with her arms upraised, one with a veil to her eyes, and the third looking at the Lord."

Scanelli, 199: "Of extraordinary excellence is the dead Christ being carried to burial, in the Chiesa Nuova."

PAINTING

PLATE 35

Deposition of Christ. Rome, Vatican Gallery, No. 386, 300 x 203 cm., *Guida della Pinacoteca,* 1933, p. 32; painted for Sta. Maria in Vallicella (Chiesa Nuova); taken to Paris in 1797 for the Musée Napoleon; returned to Rome and installed in the Vatican ca. 1815. An outline

FIG. 102

Guattani, *Deposition* (after Caravaggio).

engraving by Guattani of 1784 shows clearly the entrance to the rock-hewn sepulchre in which Joseph of Arimathea laid the Savior's body (Matthew 27: 57-60, etc.). In the original painting, this cave entrance is discernible, but it is not easily visible in most of the reproductions.

In 1571 Pietro Vittrice, the old and faithful friend of San Filippo Neri, acquired a chapel in Sta. Maria in Vallicella, the new church of the Filippini. This chapel was one of a series dedicated to the mysteries of the Holy Virgin and contained a painting of the *Pietà.* Around 1601 Vittrice decided to replace the old altarpiece and Caravaggio was commissioned to paint the new one. On the basis of the documentary evidence from the *Libro dei Decreti* of the Chiesa Nuova furnished by Lucia Lopresti (*L'Arte,* xxv, 1922, p. 116) it would seem that the painting was begun in 1602, although it is not impossible that Caravaggio received the commission for the work during the last months of 1601. In September 1604 (*ibid.*) the nephew of Pietro Vittrice (who also owned *The Fortune Teller*) asked that the old altarpiece of the *Pieta*, including its frame, be given to him. On the basis of this Lopresti and Schudt (no. 31) date the picture 1602/1604. However, the date 1604 is not conclusive for Caravaggio's painting since it is quite possible that it was finished much earlier. I would therefore date the painting around 1602/1603.

A recent interpretation of the picture shows that it is not simply an Entombment in the ordinary sense of the word, since the stone upon which the figures are placed alludes to the stone of unction, which is intimately associated with the Pieta. The arrangement of the figures conveys the event of the Entombment, but the stone of unction also implies the Pieta (corresponding to the dedication of Vittrice's chapel) and the combination thus produces a kind of *Andachtsbild*. (See Mary Ann Graeve, M.A. Thesis, New York University, Institute of Fine Arts, 1950.) The oblique position of the stone also has a symbolic meaning; about the probable connection with the "cornerstone" of the Church see Chapter VI on *Character and Religion*, p. 17. The style of the work directly continues the composition and formal concentration found in the final paintings of the Cerasi Chapel.

FIG. 103
Rubens, *Deposition*. Collection of Prince Liechtenstein.

FIG. 104
Fragonard, Sketch after Caravaggio's *Deposition* (engraved by Saint-Non).

COPIES

A free copy by Rubens (sometimes doubted) is in the Liechtenstein Gallery, Vienna; among other changes, it eliminates the Mary with the upraised hands. The suggestion by Argan (*Parallelo*, 1943, no. 2) that this figure was not in the original is unfounded; cf. Longhi, *Proporz.*, p. 100, for a strong refutation. There is an engraving by Saint-Non after a drawing which Fragonard made of the painting. An investigation of the condition of the picture reveals that it suffered a repainting, probably while in Paris. For a Northern interpretation of this composition see Theodoor van Baburen (von Schneider, pl. 18A).

26. MADONNA DI LORETO

SOURCES

Mancini, 59v: mentions the *Madonna di Loreto* after the *Madonna della Scala* (*Death of the Virgin*) and before the *Madonna del Serpe*.

Baglione, 137: "In the second chapel on the left of S. Agostino, Caravaggio painted in a natural manner a *Madonna di Loreto*. There are two pilgrims, a man with muddy feet, a woman with a messy and dirty bonnet. The populace made a great clamour over the disparaging treatment of certain elements which should have been handled with more respect in such an important work."

Bellori, 206-207: "Subsequently (after the Contarelli chapel), Caravaggio made another painting in the chapel of Signor Cavalletti in S. Agostino. The Madonna stands with the Child, who is in the act of blessing, in her arms. Two pilgrims with their hands together kneel before her; the first is a poor man with bare feet and leather breeches, with his pilgrim's staff leaning against his shoulder; beside him is an old woman with a bonnet on her head."

Scanelli, p. 198: mentions in Sant'Agostino a painting by Caravaggio of "the Virgin standing with the Christ Child, and to the left a pilgrim and an old woman kneeling before her in devotion. Whoever looks at this painting must confess that the spirit of the pilgrims is well rendered, and shows their firm faith as they pray to the image in the pure simplicity of their hearts. On the other hand, it is evident that the painting lacks proper decorum, grace and devotion; this, in fact, has already been observed by the best intellects and greatest masters. . . ."

Passeri, Vite, ed. Hess, p. 347, Life of Guercino (not in the 1772 ed.); cf. Hess, *Boll. d'Arte*, XXVI, 1932/1933, p. 43: "In the first chapel to the left of the entrance in S. Agostino Caravaggio painted the Holy Virgin with the Child in Her arms and two pilgrims adoring Her. At the time he lived in the Casa agl'otto cantoni, in one of the little streets behind the Mausoleum of Augustus. The model for the Virgin was a young girl of poor but honorable family who lived nearby with her widowed mother and was wooed by a notary of whom the mother did not approve on the grounds that all notaries are doomed to damnation. The notary protested angrily with foul accusations to the mother when he discovered she was allowing her daughter to go in the house of a villainous and cursed painter. Caravaggio was so infuriated by this slander that he attacked the notary on the Piazza Navona, hitting him over the head with a hatchet. He then fled to San Luigi dei Francesi and took refuge for a long time. The notary recovered slowly, and only after some time did they settle their feud."

Madonna di Loreto. Rome, S. Agostino, Cavalletti chapel, first on the left of the entrance. 260 x 150 cm. Mostra No. 29.

Corresponds to the descriptions in the sources. The picture is also called the *Madonna dei Pellegrini* because of the two pilgrims who kneel before the Virgin as she appears over the threshold of a doorway or niche flanked by a fluted pilaster possibly representing part of the Santa Casa in Loreto. Hanging to the right of the doorway, there appears to be the skin from the head of a small lamb. This may be the Paschal Lamb symbolizing the sacrifice of Christ. The Madonna seems to float over the threshold, Her feet barely touching the top of the entrance stone; she holds the child who gives the sign of benediction to the pilgrims. Perhaps the slightly archaic character of the Virgin's pose is a deliberate allusion to the ancient statue of the miraculous Madonna which stood over the main altarpiece in the interior of the Santa Casa in Loreto, acting as intercessor for the pleas of the pilgrims. A free copy of the picture is in the Munich Museum, with two cherubs in the upper right, and two pilgrims' hats at the lower left. Another copy is in the Cathedral at Langres, brought there in 1605 by Richard Tassel.

According to documents published by Lucia Lopresti (DOC. 50) Ermes Cavalletti made a testament in 1603 leaving a certain sum for his heirs to build and decorate the first chapel on the left of S. Agostino. The decoration and the altar picture of the chapel, therefore, cannot have been ordered before 1603. The touching story of Passeri about the poor and innocent girl who served Caravaggio as a model for the *Madonna di Loreto,* and of the assault on the notary in the Piazza Navona, has the ring of a romantic fabrication. Anyway, Passeri gives no date. His story is probably based on the fact that Caravaggio really did attack a notary in the Piazza Navona, and that a woman of uncertain domicile (*Lena che sta in piedi à Piazza Navona*) was involved. Here we have an exact date in the court proceedings of the notary against Caravaggio—July 29, 1605 (DOC. 21). However, no definite conclusions can be drawn as to the date, as Hess (*loc.cit.*) and following him Schudt (nos. 32-33) attempted to do by combining the two stories.

Nevertheless, because of the style and because of the date of Cavalletti's testament, a date of about 1604 must be approximately right. Longhi formerly (*Pin.*, p. 32) dated it considerably earlier, around 1597, because he believed that Baglione was speaking chronologically in mentioning the picture shortly after the Contarelli Chapel; secondly, because of the archaic and statuesque style of the Virgin; and thirdly, because of the stylistic connection with the *Amor Victorious* (which, however, probably dates later; see Cat. Rais. No. 23, *Amor Victorious*), but he has recently accepted the evidence of the documents (see Cat. of the Mostra and Chapter VI).

27. MADONNA AND CHILD WITH SAINT ANNE
(MADONNA DEL SERPE)

SOURCES

Mancini, 59v: includes the Palafrenieri altar at St. Peter's in his enumeration of Caravaggio's works.

Baglione, 137-138: "For S. Pietro Vaticano Caravaggio made a Saint Anne and the Madonna, who holds the child between her legs, crushing the head of the serpent with the foot. This work was executed for the Palafrenieri of the Palace, but was taken from the building on the order of the Cardinals and then presented by the Palafrenieri to Cardinal Scipione Borghese."

Bellori, 213: the painting of "St. Anne was taken from one of the minor altars of the Vatican basilica because it so vilely represented the Virgin with Christ, a naked boy, as one can see in the Villa Borghese."

PAINTING

PLATE 37

Madonna del Serpe. Rome, Borghese Gallery, no. 110, 292 x 211 cm. Mostra No. 30.

Manilli, pp. 60-61, "Il quadro di S. Anna con la Vergine che calca il capo di serpente con un bambino in piede è del Caravaggio."

The history of the painting is rather obscure and complicated. We know from the literary sources only that it was made for the Society of the Palafrenieri, the "Horseguards" of the Vatican, and that it was given by this society to Scipione Borghese, the nephew of Paul V, who became cardinal in 1605. Bellori relates that the painting was removed from the altar in St. Peter's because of its impropriety (the reason he usually gives), but Baglione, always more cautious and reliable, says merely that it was taken from the building on order of the Cardinals.

The Society of the Palafrenieri, founded in the mid-fourteenth century, had their own chapel or altar near the entrance of Old St. Peter's, dedicated to their patroness St. Anne. They had hung over the old icon of St. Anthony Abbot, to whom the chapel had originally been dedicated, their own image of St. Anne. When the altars in this part of the church were desecrated (October 1605) to make room for the construction of the new nave, the Palafrenieri could not obtain a place in the new church, as they had hoped, but were removed to the *Sacristia Vecchia.* One of the altars in the inner octagon of the *Sacristia Vecchia* was then dedicated to their patroness, St. Anne, on the order of the pope. To this altar belonged a painting of St. Anne standing behind the Virgin and Child with two saints on either side; Chattard and other writers on the Vatican, in an understandable error, have called this a work of Caravaggio (later ascribed to *il Fattorino Penni*). Caravaggio's painting, as we see it now in the Borghese, could not have been destined for this small altar: the height of the chapel, according to Chattard (p. 234), of 14½ palmi, or about 3.12 m., could hardly have accommodated the huge dimensions of Caravaggio's altarpiece, which is almost three meters high. Probably for this reason, the Palafrenieri were permitted to place their image of St. Anne, "manu di Michelangelo da Caravaggio," in the much larger chapel of St. John Chrysostom. This must have been a provisional arrangement until a permanent location could be found for the painting. Finding a new place, however, seems to have been more difficult than had been expected (even though the nearby church of Sta. Anna dei Palafrenieri had recently been completed); and consequently the young and greedy art lover, Scipione Borghese, lost no time in using his influence as nephew of the Pope to persuade the Palafrenieri to turn the work over to him for his growing collection. (See: Tiberius Alpharanus, *De Basilicae anti-quissima et nova structura*, written about 1580, published by Cerrati, Rome, 1914, pp. 51, 67; and Fr. Cancellieri, *De Secretaris Basilicae Vaticanae Veteris et Novae*, Rome, 1786, Tome III, pl. 1272; Chattard, *Nova Descrizione del Vaticano*, Rome, 1762, I, pp. 234/244; Vasi, *Itinerario di Roma*, 1794, p. 694.)

A noticeable difference in style exists between the Madonna and Child on the one hand, and St. Anne on the other. The rendering of the Virgin is smooth, like that of the *Madonna di Loreto*, her skin soft and clear. The brushwork of the St. Anne, however, is vigorous and loose, rather than polished, and it recalls that of the *David* in the Borghese, although the St. Anne is of a more impressive stature. The Madonna's dress, daring in its deep decolletage, is designed to stress her grace and youthful energy; the body of the Boy is also sturdy and expressive of His power. St. Anne, on the other hand, is clad in a heavy garment, wrapped around her columnar figure; she wears a turban headdress so that she looks like one of the aged matrons of antique Roman sculpture. The dress of the Virgin is coral-colored, contrasting with the dark-green skirt, while St. Anne is immersed in a rich and subtle variety of ochres, ranging from a dark shadowy brown to a gray with greenish and bluish tints.

This striking discrepancy might be explained by a deliberate effort of the artist to distinguish between the ages of the persons represented. But the feeling of distinctness between the two halves of the picture finds a puzzling confirmation when we realize that the left half of Caravaggio's picture follows an earlier painting by Ambrogio Figino so closely, both in content and in form, that it can be called an iconographical copy, though reversed, perhaps after an engraving (see Longhi, *Pin.*, 1928/1929, p. 314). Figino's painting is now in the church of S. Antonio Abate, Milan, where it was transferred from San Fedele in Milan (see Lomazzo, *Trattato*, 1584, II, p. 383, who mentions it as being in San Fedele; and Torre, *Ritratto di Milano*, Milan, 1674, p. 44, who refers to it as being in S. Antonio Abate).

Figino's composition was probably chosen as a model because his group of the Madonna and Child illustrated the solution of a theological controversy. In one manuscript of the Vulgate, the text reads *ipse*, in another *ipsa*; thus in the first it is Christ who treads upon the serpent of sin and heresy, while in the second this task is performed by the Virgin (the Protestants naturally insisted that the first was correct). Figino shows the Mother and Son carrying out the action together: the small foot of the Christ Child rests on that of the Madonna and in this way they both crush the serpent. This ingenious compromise had recently been made canonical in a bull of Pius V (E. Mâle, *L'Art religieux après le Concile de Trente*, 1932, p. 37f.). As far as I know, Figino was the first artist to visualize this interpretation. It is therefore understandable that Caravaggio's patrons should have wanted to conform to the papal bull and asked Caravaggio to follow Figino's iconography.

Still it remains to be explained why the Palafrenieri wanted a representation of the *Madonna del Serpe* at all. St. Anne is usually shown within an intimate family gathering, her role being purely domestic and grandmotherly. Rarely does she reach the grand stature given her by Leonardo in his *Virgin and St. Anne.* The Palafrenieri already had a painting of this more humble type (see above); they wanted, quite naturally, something more provocative and modern. St. Anne's presence in a scene of quasi-political activity, the crushing of heresy, which normally does not concern her, can be logically justified by her religious character.

FIG. 105
Madonna and Saints, ascribed to "Il Fattorino Penni." Rome, Vatican.

FIG. 106
Figino, *Madonna and Child crushing the Serpent.*
Milan, S. Antonio Abate.

St. Anne is the venerable receptacle for the conceptio immaculata; Mary entered her womb through miraculous and immaculate means at the moment of her meeting with Joachim at the Golden Gate. The *Madonna del Serpe* is a variation on the theme of the *Immaculata* in that the Virgin is shown as a victor over sin. As the "bearer" of the Virgin's purity, St. Anne is therefore appropriately present, even though the Virgin does not sit upon her lap, which was the older and more direct way of symbolizing their relationship. Caravaggio demonstrated the meaning with sublime grandeur; St. Anne's superhuman quality suggests a Michelangelo Sibyl, and her tense expression may reflect a Leonardesque prototype.

Although Caravaggio's meaning can be explained in this way, it remains iconographically unique; I have been unable to find another example of a combination of St. Anne with the *Madonna del Serpe,* before or after Caravaggio's time. There must have been some connection between the Palafrenieri and the Milanese tradition around 1600 which made this curious iconography possible, but we have no precise information about a connecting link. It may be significant that Carlo Borromeo had dedicated an Oratorio to the Immaculate Virgin in the church of S. Antonio Abate in Milan. This church had come into the possession of the Theatine order at the time, and Figino's picture may already have been transferred there by the time Caravaggio used it as his model. It is rather tempting to see some connection between the fact that the first chapel of the Palafrenieri near the entrance of Old St. Peter's had originally been dedicated to S. Antonio Abate, who was also the patron saint of the Milanese church which received Figino's painting.

Despite its discrepancies, the painting as a whole hangs together well, not only iconographically, but also formally and psychologically. The separate parts of the composition are ingeniously drawn together; the curve of the Virgin's body and neck line, adopted from Figino, are emphatically set off against the dark background and she leans toward the towering figure of St. Anne in such a way that the two seem intimately related. The attention of all three figures, the Madonna, the resolute Child and the contemplative St. Anne, is concentrated on the smiting of the evil monster, and all three faces express the various emotions called forth by this act: devoted duty, revulsion and anguish.

The snake, although not as a symbol of vice, occurs also in ancient cults of Dionysus, and this may have had some influence on Christian art. The nude Christ Child in Caravaggio's composition is close to the boy on the Dionysus and Ariadne sarcophagus in the Walters Art Gallery, Baltimore (cf. Olsen-K. Lehmann-Hartleben, *Dionysiac Sarcophagi in Balti-*

FIG. 107
Dionysius and Ariadne Sarcophagus
(detail). Baltimore, Walters
Art Gallery.

more, fig. 9). Here, the boy looks down at a large snake which emerges from a basket, on which a tall and stately goddess places her foot; a smaller Silenus-like figure bends over the boy. The grouping of the three figures strongly recalls Caravaggio's composition. Figino himself may have known an antique prototype of this kind, but it is Caravaggio, whether through direct knowledge of such a source or not, who gives a truly classic monumentality to the group.

28. DEATH OF THE VIRGIN

SOURCES

Mancini, 59v, 152r-v, 160v: In the enumeration of Caravaggio's works Mancini lists the *Death of the Virgin* directly after the paintings in San Luigi; he relates that it had been rejected by the fathers of Sta. Maria della Scala and was then taken by the Duke of Mantua. The reason for the removal of the painting from the church was that the Virgin "resembled a courtesan." He continues, "One can see how much wrong the moderns do: if they decide to depict the Virgin, Our Lady, they portray her like some filthy whore from the slums" (meretirice sossa delli Ortacci). He refers to a critique of Pliny that certain painters of ancient Rome made their figures look lascivious because they used their concubines as models (la sua bagascia). "And in our own times . . . for a similar lascivity, the good fathers of the Scala felt obliged to remove Caravaggio's beautiful painting. . . . Perhaps this is why that poor fellow suffered so much trouble in his lifetime."

Baglione, 138: "For the Madonna della Scala in Trastevere, Caravaggio painted the *Death of the Madonna*. But because he so disrespectfully (con poco decoro) made the Madonna swollen-up and with bare legs, it was removed, and bought by the Duke of Mantua to be placed in his splendid gallery."

Bellori, 213: "The same fate (of being refused) met the *Death of the Virgin* in the church of the Scala, removed because the Virgin had been made to look too much like the swollen corpse of an ordinary dead woman."

PAINTING

Death of the Virgin. Louvre, Paris, 369 x 245 cm.   PLATE 38

Painted in 1605/1606 for the chapel of Laertio Cherubini in the church of Sta. Maria della Scala, which was built in the 1590's and was given later by Pope Clement XII to the Spanish order of the Carmelitani Scalzi da Santa Teresa. The fathers rejected the work for reasons of decorum, as the sources explain. They replaced it with a *Death of the Virgin* by Carlo (Saraceni) Veneziano, who belonged to the circle of Caravaggio's followers. The altar was decorated by a close friend of Caravaggio, Onorio Longhi (cf. Titi, *Studio di pittura*, Roma, 1647, p. 45).

As in the case of the *First Saint Matthew*, and probably also of the *Madonna del Serpe*, the painting was immediately coveted by an art collector; it became secularized. Peter Paul Rubens, who was deeply impressed by Caravaggio's work during his stay in Italy, recommended the *Death of the Virgin* to his patron, the Duke of Mantua. At that time, February 1607, the painting was certainly no longer in the hands of Caravaggio who, banished from Rome, still awaited an act of grace from Paul V. The agent of the Duke, Giovanni Magno, in his correspondence with the court of Mantua, informs us of the transactions concerning the painting. He had to deal with an owner whose name is not revealed, either a delegate of the church or the man who had originally donated the painting to the church (presumably Cherubini, who had replaced the Caravaggio with the Saraceni). The price was relatively high, 300 scudi, and in one of his letters Giovanni Magno wonders if its value had not depreciated through the absence of the artist and because it was a rejected piece. He says that he cannot trust his own judgment because he is not sufficiently initiated into the occult science of the art experts, but he knows that Caravaggio is one of the most famous of the young moderns and the *Death of the Virgin* supposedly one of his finest works. The high standing of Caravaggio was confirmed in Magno's eyes by the testimony of experts, especially Rubens, and still more by the express wish of the Università of painters (many of whom were famous), to be allowed to see and study the painting (a courtesy which Caravaggio had evidently not permitted). Magno, rather flattered, consented graciously to exhibit the work for a week before it went to Mantua; Rubens meanwhile busily constructed a box, specially made to ship the uncommonly large work. (Correspondence of Giovanni Magno in Rome with Annibale Chieppo in Mantua, February to April, 1607. The original letters are in the Archivio Gonzaga. Cf. Ruelens, *Correspondance de Rubens* . . . , Antwerp, I, 1887, 362ff.).

In 1627 upon the dissolution of the Gonzaga Gallery, the *Death of the Virgin* was bought by Charles I of England. In the inventory of the sale of 1627 it was priced at 600 pounds, equal to Giulio Romano's *Nativity with Longinus*, now in the Louvre. At the sale of the collection of Charles I in 1649, the painting was purchased by Jabach, who in 1671 sold it to Louis XIV. (A. Luzio, *La galeria dei Gonzaga venduto all'Inghilterra nel 1627/1628*, Milan, 1913, p. 106, no. 239.)

In the Italian tradition for representations of the Death of the Virgin, the bier on which the Virgin lies is placed parallel to the picture plane, with two apostles standing upright, one at her feet, the other at her head, and the other apostles grouped more or less symmetrically behind the bier. This type, very formal and hieratic, derives ultimately from the Byzantine form and is, in essence, a devotional rather than a narrative scene. (See, for example, the *Dormition* of Giotto, Berlin, K. F. Mus.) Caravaggio deviates from this tradition by placing the bier at a slightly oblique angle. He dramatizes the scene by giving the apostles attitudes which express the whole range of emotions, from quiet contemplation to deep and agonized mourning. Further, he shockingly exposes the feet of the Virgin and dresses her in extremely humble clothes (recalling Savonarola's wish to have the Virgin portrayed not as the *Regina Coeli* but as a poor and humble woman; cf. Schnitzler, *Savonarola*, Munich, 1923).

The mourning female seated in front of the bier with her head bent low (probably the Magdalene) bears a striking resemblance to the corresponding figure in the famous *Dormition* tympanum at Strasbourg (early thirteenth century) which is found in Italian examples through the fourteenth century, but then disappeared until it was revived by Caravaggio. The figure of the Virgin, with her foreshortened face and outstretched arm, is somewhat similar to Annibale Carracci's Virgin in the *Lamentation* in Parma (see Voss, *Malerei des Barock in Rom*, p. 150).

FIG. 108
Giotto, *Dormition of the Virgin*. Berlin, Kaiser Friedrich Museum.

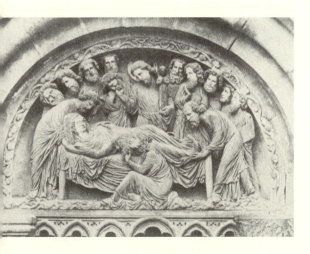

FIG. 109
Dormition of the Virgin (tympanum). Strasbourg, Cathedral.

FIG. 110
Dürer, *Death of the Virgin*.

The great flowing curtain at the top is an impressive decorative element coming from Venetian art. At the same time, it serves to remind us that the chamber is a bedroom and thereby that the Virgin's death is a deeply human event, although the genre-like intimacy of the Northern tradition, as in the engraving of Duerer, is avoided.

By these means, Caravaggio was able to loosen the rigidity of the Italian scheme without destroying its formal quality, and to humanize the event without giving up the hieratic impressiveness of the traditional representations.

29. MADONNA OF THE ROSARY

SOURCES

Bellori, 214: mentions at the end of the biography the paintings by Caravaggio which were outside Italy. One of these is the painting of the "*Rosario*, preserved in the Dominican church at Antwerp, a work which has brought his brush great fame."

PAINTING

Madonna of the Rosary. Vienna Museum, 364 x 249 cm., cat. 1938, no. 496.   PLATE 39

The painting came to Vienna from the church of the Dominicans in Antwerp who presented, or sold, it to Emperor Joseph II during his sojourn in Antwerp in 1786. It was replaced by a very good copy (cf. C. Haas, *K. K. Bilder Galerie im Belvedere in Wien*, 1821).

According to a document of 1651 in the archives of the Dominicans, the painting was donated to them in Antwerp by a group of painters and art lovers (doer diverse liefhebbers): Breughel, Rubens, Van Balen, Cooymans (who collected works by Manfredi, cf. Sandrart, 190), and several others. "They considered this painting by Michelangelo da Caravaggio to be an extraordinarily great work of art and not too expensive (nist hoogh van prys). Therefore, in affection for the chapel and because they wanted to keep such a rare piece in Antwerp, they bought it for 1800 guldens." Cf. A. Goevaerts, "Notice historique sur un tableau de Michel Angelo Caravaggio," *Journal des Beaux-Arts*, xv, Bruxelles, 1895). The document does not mention when or from whom the painting was bought. There is, however, a strong indication that it came from the estate of the painter, Abraham Vinck, who died in Amsterdam around 1620, shortly after he had been bequeathed sole ownership of the painting in the will of the former co-owner, the painter Louis Finson (Ludovicus Finsonius or Louis Vinçon), who died in 1617. Finson is said to have brought the *Madonna of the Rosary* from Naples to the Netherlands. (Cf. A von Schneider, *Caravaggio und die Niederländer*, 1933, p. 87; Wurzbach, *Niederlandisches Künstler Lexicon*, I, 1906; Thieme-Becker, K. L.: Finsonius, Vincks.)

How the painting fits into Caravaggio's career, when it was commissioned, for what town and church, and where it was made, are questions which have not been answered with any certainty. The style indicates the later years of Caravaggio's activity, and the work has generally been placed in the time of Caravaggio's sojourn in Naples. This large painting was surely intended as a main altarpiece in a Dominican church, as is indicated by the subject matter, the miracle of the Rosary; the Madonna and Child, St. Dominic, who holds the rosaries before the faithful, and Saint Peter Martyr, with two other Dominican monks.

The first mention of the painting is in a letter from Pourbus, court painter at Mantua, written from Naples in September of 1607, saying that he had seen some good things (qualche cosa di buono) by Michel Angelo da Caravaggio which were being offered for sale. The more important of the two works mentioned by Pourbus is a "rosary" made as a large altar-piece (ancona), about 18 palmi high and rather expensive—"they want no less than 400 ducati." He claims that this "rosary" (as well as the other painting, a *Judith*) was made in Naples (fatto qui). (Cf. Luzio, *La Galleria dei Gonzaga*, Milan, 1913, p. 278.) However, no indication is given of how Pourbus had come to hear of this work or through what channels it was being sold; no story of a rejection, no rumor of a dissatisfied patron.

In my opinion the *Madonna of the Rosary* can be connected with a painting which, as we know from documentary evidence, was ordered from Caravaggio as early as 1605 by the Duke of Modena for a chapel in a Modenese church. (The church is not named, leaving open the possibility of San Domenico.) The official unveiling was scheduled for the day of the Nativity of the Virgin (September 18), but, as recounted in the letters of the Duke's agent, Fabio Masetti, written between August 1605, and August 1607 (DOCS. 58-69), this was an ill-fated commission due to Caravaggio's persistent failure to deliver the work. In 1605, according to Masetti, Caravaggio was for a short time a fugitive in Genoa as the result of a brawl with a notary. When he returned to Rome not even the intervention of his old patron, Cardinal del Monte, could induce the capricious artist, this "cervello stravagantisso," to deliver the altarpiece to the hands of Masetti. It must have been well in progress, for in October and November of 1605 Caravaggio successfully prevailed on Masetti for an advance payment of 32 scudi, promising to deliver the painting within a week. But this promise was not kept and a half year later (end of May, 1606) occurred the tragic incident of Caravaggio's killing Ranuccio da Terni in an insipid quarrel in which he was himself badly wounded. Despite these misfortunes, Masetti doggedly pursued Caravaggio for the altarpiece and in the following July wrote the painter (whose whereabouts at this point, whether still in Rome or in flight, are not clear) that if he did not deliver the painting within the next week, he need not bother to labor further on it (altrimente non occorre, che più si affatica). When he wrote his next letter, September 1606, Massetti had heard that Caravaggio was taking refuge in Pagliano in the Sabine Mountains. He expected him to be paroled, but having finally and quite naturally lost all patience, he wished for the painter's return only for the sake of recovering the wasted 32 scudi. As we know, the parole was not granted at this time and Caravaggio never returned to Rome.

The altarpiece for Modena, still unfinished, was probably taken to Naples by Caravaggio and there transferred to other hands for completion and for the market. One can conclude from Pourbus' letter of September 1607, that he was not in contact with the artist, but that new owners—art dealers or art-dealing painters—were offering the paintings "di mano di Caravaggio" at an unusually high price. Caravaggio was evidently already on his way to Malta by this time. A date as early as July 1607, has been suggested for his arrival in Malta (cf. *Burl. Mag.*, 1935, p. 173), and although this proposal is without substantial documentation, Caravaggio's departure from Naples must have taken place around this time, viz., between

July and September 1607. He was still in the Sabine Mountains in September 1606. The length of his stay in Naples cannot have amounted to much more than ten or eleven months, in which time he executed, apart from a few smaller pieces, the two important works, the *Seven Acts of Mercy* for the Misericordia, with many scenes and figures, and the *Flagellation* for San Domenico. There was hardly enough time for the execution of a third big altarpiece as large as the *Madonna of the Rosary*. Besides, Caravaggio would never have begun such a work without a commission, and if it had been commissioned in Naples, then there is no reason why it should not still be there, in S. Domenico Maggiore. The work must have been made before Caravaggio went to Naples, and, since the months of refuge in the Sabines produced only easel paintings, it must have been made in the time prior to the tragic incident of May 1606, specifically in the period from 1605 to 1606, when he is known to have worked on the commission for Modena.

The completion of the *Madonna of the Rosary* in Naples by other hands would explain the unevenness of its quality. The composition as a whole is undoubtedly Caravaggio's own invention and was probably far advanced when he quit work on it. The triangular structure in the lower tier of the figure quintet, with their beseeching hands, is in color scheme, plastic strength and expressive motion, one of the great manifestations of Caravaggio's art. Equally expressive are the hands and the lean spiritual faces of Saint Dominic on the left and Peter Martyr on the right. The Madonna must have been sketched in and underpainted by Caravaggio, but the face lacks the decisive character of the *Madonna di Loreto* or the *Madonna del Serpe*. The Christ Child with the light curly hair, which is not dissimilar to the Christ Child in the *Madonna del Serpe*, seems to be by Caravaggio's own hand. Decidedly un-Caravaggesque, however, is the red curtain, which is weak and mechanical compared to the rich, monumental curtain in the *Death of the Virgin*. Nor is the portrait of the donor at the left by Caravaggio, who would never have permitted such a "capitalistic" intruder into his devout and sober composition, though it must be by someone well versed in the technique of Caravaggio. The hooded monk in the background behind Peter Martyr may also be a portrait, perhaps of a Dominican prior.

We do not know who executed these un-Caravaggesque portions of the surface, but certainly a great interest in the art of Caravaggio existed at this time among the Flemish painters, witness Rubens and Pourbus, who coveted the few available works. Third-rate artists like Vinck and Finsonius who were in Naples some time between 1607 and 1612, probably took whatever opportunity they could to acquire works of Caravaggio for business as well as for artistic purposes, especially in Naples where the paintings may have been available at bargain prices because of the circumstances into which the artist had been forced. In Finsonius' testament of September 19, 1617, Abraham Vinck is named co-owner of the two paintings by "Michel Angel Crawats," the *Rosary* and a *Judith and Holofernes* (see *Oud Holland*, 36, 1918, p. 197). The sometimes outspokenly Caravaggesque manner of Finsonius' own rather weak style is manifested in the *Magdalene* at Marseilles (cf. Cat. Rais., *Magdalene*), which is signed Finson, Naples, 1612, and which the most experienced connoisseur of Caravaggio, Longhi, has briefly considered as a genuine work of the master bearing a false signature (cf. *Prop.*, p. 16, no. 27). A document of 1630 (cf. *Oud Holland*, 1886, p. 7 ff.) specifies a painting of the "distribution of the paternoster by the Predicants," which came from the estate of Finsonius and was sold at a very low price, 600 gulden, because it was considered a mere copy of an original Caravaggio by Finsonius. Whether the painting mentioned was the one which went to the Dominicans at Antwerp, or whether it was a copy, is difficult to tell: we have no date of purchase of the *Rosary* by Rubens and his friends for the Antwerp church. Because Finsonius was so much involved in the painting's history and because he was such a fervent Caravaggist, it is tempting to think that he had a hand in the finishing of the painting, but there is no real proof of this.

In an engraving by L. Vorsterman, the portrait of the donor shows a quite different person

FIG. 111
Vorsterman, *Madonna of the Rosary*
(engraved after Caravaggio).

from the man in the Vienna painting. All the parts which interested Caravaggio most, especially the group of ardent supplicants for the divine grace symbolized by the rosary, are by him. But the remainder, including most of the upper part of the work, was, in my opinion, finished by another hand, even though it may have been outlined and thinly underpainted by Caravaggio. In any event, the painters and art lovers who bought the painting overlooked the discrepancies and presented it to the Dominican church in Antwerp as a Caravaggio. It is, however, significant that suspicion continued until it went to Vienna, for the guide books and descriptions of the church relate that the portrait at the left was of a Flemish merchant and gave to the portraitist the noblest name they could find, that of Anthony Van Dyck.

According to tradition, the worship of the Rosary originated in about 1208, when the Virgin appeared to Saint Dominic while he was at prayer one night in the chapel of Notre Dame at Prouille. She held a Rosary in her hand and, after teaching him how to say it, she commanded him to preach it to the world. By the time of the Counter-Reformation, the worship of the Rosary had attained tremendous popularity and, especially after the Battle of Lepanto (1572) against the Turks, the victory of which was attributed to the Rosary, it was repeatedly confirmed by papal bulls (in Caravaggio's time by Clement VIII, 1593). The popularity of the cult is witnessed by the numerous representations, found most often, of course, in Dominican churches, of the Virgin's appearance to St. Dominic. The special attraction of the cult was its all-inclusive and democratic spirit, a quality of which Caravaggio had taken advantage by giving great emphasis to poor and common worshipers. Unusual also in the Vienna picture is the fact that the Virgin does not directly give the Rosary to St. Dominic, but rather with a regal gesture bids Her submissive servant to distribute the Rosaries among the eagerly waiting people. (Concerning the expressive significance of the raised arms, and the possible relation to Lotto's late painting of the same subject, see text, p. 48.)

30. DAVID WITH THE HEAD OF GOLIATH

SOURCES

Bellori, 208: Caravaggio painted for Cardinal Scipione Borghese "a half-figure of David. The head of Goliath, which David holds by the hair, is a self-portrait. He represents David as a bareheaded youth, one shoulder out of his shirt, grasping his sword by the hilt. The color is of the boldest depths and shadows in order to give the figures and composition the force Caravaggio always required."

Bellori, 214: mentions among the paintings outside of Italy another half-figure of David, owned by the Conte di Villa Madiana.

PAINTINGS

PLATE 40

A. *David with the Head of Goliath*. Rome, Borghese Gallery, No. 455, 125 x 101 cm. Mostra No. 32.

Mentioned by Manilli in his inventory of the Villa Borghese in 1650. This is undoubtedly the painting described by Bellori, whose claim that the head of Goliath is a self-portrait is probably correct. Manilli, in his description of the Villa Borghese (Rome, 1650, p. 67) states that Caravaggio wanted to portray himself (volle ritrarre se stesso) in the head of Goliath and that in the David he painted "il suo Caravaggino." The facial type corresponds to Gigli's description of Caravaggio's pallid face, his mass of curly hair and his deep-set eyes (*La pittura trionfante,* 1615), on which Bellori's unflattering characterization is probably based (p. 214). There is a close resemblance between Goliath and the bearded man in the background of the *Martyrdom of Saint Matthew* (King Hirtacus) who has also been considered a self-portrait (cf. Marangoni, *Dedalo,* II, p. 794; Schudt, no. 25). Goliath represents the facial type generally identified with Caravaggio as he is best known from the engraved portrait on the frontispiece of Bellori's biography and from the drawing by Leoni in the Uffizi. The identification of himself with Goliath, the victim of a superior and innocent power, may easily have been in Caravaggio's mind with all its psychological implications. David is painted with uncommon tenderness; his soft gentle face and sad expression are in sharp contrast to the Medusa-like head of Goliath with its open mouth and blood trickling down the throat. The date falls in the late Roman years, 1605/1606 (cf. Pevsner, p. 387; Longhi, *Pin.,* p. 27).

COPY

B. The *David* by Caravaggio, which in 1617 was brought from Naples to Spain by the Count of Villa Mediana, is not known. Venturi (1910, p. 269) tries to identify it as the *David* in the Vienna Museum (no. 485, 95 x 165 cm., Mostra No. 38) but gives no proof. Schudt (no. 42) accepts the Vienna painting as an original by Caravaggio. Marangoni (p. 44) says it is by a follower of the master. In my opinion it is an inferior work, definitely not by Caravaggio. The same is true of the *David* in the Prado Museum (published by Venturi, *Studi dal Vero,* p. 369; cf. J. Ainaud, *Anales,* p. 385, no. 14, ill.).

31. SAINT JEROME

SOURCES

Bellori, 208: For Cardinal Scipione Borghese, Caravaggio painted a *"Saint Jerome* writing with concentration; he extends his hand and the pen toward the inkwell."

PAINTING   PLATE 41

A. *St. Jerome Writing.* Rome, Borghese Gallery, no. 56, 112 x 157 cm. Mostra No. 33.

In 1659 mentioned by Manilli, *Villa Borghese,* pl. 85: "Stanza del Moro, il San Girolamo, che sta scrivendo, è del Caravaggio."

Later attributed to Gius. Ribera (cf. A. Venturi, *Museo e Gall. Borghese,* 1893, p. 62, no. 56). Reassigned to Caravaggio by Modigliani (see L. Venturi, *Arte,* XII, 1909, p. 39). Marangoni (*Caravaggio,* p. 38) calls it a copy; Pevsner (*Z. f. P. K.,* 1927/1928, p. 387) and Schudt (p. 54, no. 77) reject it on stylistic grounds. Longhi (*Precis. Coll. Borgh.,* p. 181) emphatically reaffirms the authenticity of the work.

I agree fully with Longhi. The Borghese *Saint Jerome* is a characteristic work of Caravaggio's later Roman years. It was made for Scipione Borghese about the same time as the beautiful *David,* to which the *Saint Jerome* is stylistically close in the fluid treatment of light, in retaining the bodies within a slightly receding closed space, and in the evident, but very subtle movement toward the spectator. The bearded old man, his bald head slanting a bit forward, is a further development of similar types in Caravaggio's earlier work (the man with the eyeglasses in the *Calling of Saint Matthew*, Saint Peter in the *Crucifixion*, and the attendant in the *Conversion*), and is closest to the head of the long-bearded Apostle who stands almost in the center of the *Death of the Virgin* of 1605.

B. *St. Jerome in Meditation*. Spain, Montserrat. 110 x 81, Mostra No. 34.   PLATE 42

   The painting of *St. Jerome in Meditation* at the convent of Montserrat in Spain came there from a Roman collection in 1911. It shows the saint almost in full-length, and the facial type is the same as that in the Borghese painting. Longhi (*Prop.*, 1, 1943, p. 16) accepts it as an original by Caravaggio. (See also Ainaud, *Annales*, 1947, p. 395.) In my opinion this canvas lacks the distinction of that in the Borghese and may well be a very clever imitation.

32. FAINTING MAGDALENE

SOURCES

Mancini, 60: While Caravaggio remained in hiding in Zagarola (near Palestrina) he painted a *Magdalene* which was bought by Costa in Rome.

Baglione, 138: After Caravaggio had fled from Rome and was in Palestrina he painted a "Santa Maria Maddalena."

Bellori, 208: Under the protection of the Duke Marzio Colonna in Zagarola Caravaggio painted the *Magdalene* in half-figure.

COPIES   PAINTINGS   PLATES 46, 47

The *Magdalene* painted by Caravaggio during his refuge in the Sabine Mountains is known only from copies. The *Repentant Magdalene* in the Museum of Marseilles (1.26 x 1.00 m.), signed by the Flemish painter, Finson and, dated 1612, is not an original composition by Finsonius but, as Longhi says (Prop. 1943, p. 16), a copy after Caravaggio. Another copy which is somewhat different in dimension (0.87 x 1.10 cm.) is in the collection of Don Santiago Alorda in Barcelona (Mostra No. 80); it was painted by another Netherlander, Wybrand der Geest from Laenwerden. Here Caravaggio is given full credit for the composition: "Imitando Michaelem Angelum Carrava . . . Mediolan., Wibrandus de Geest, Friesius, Ao. 1620." In this copy one can see more clearly than in the Finsonius copy the skull under the left arm and opposite, in the dark background, the unguent jar decorated with small angel heads. The foreshortening of the Magdalene's face recalls the head of the Madonna in the *Death of the Virgin* in the Louvre (see Ainaud, *Anales*, p. 393, ill. p. 388 and Longhi, *Prop.*, p. 16, fig. 24, both of whom cite more copies).

WALK TO EMMAUS

See LOST PAINTINGS, Cat. No. 48.

33. FLAGELLATION OF CHRIST

SOURCES

Bellori, 209: "For the church of San Domenico Maggiore Caravaggio was commissioned (gli fu data a fare) to paint a *Flagellation of Christ at the Column* in the chapel of the Signori di Franco."

PAINTING   PLATE 48

Flagellation of Christ. Naples, San Domenico Maggiore, 286 x 213 cm. Mostra No. 37.

This is one of the main paintings made during Caravaggio's sojourn in Naples. It was commissioned by the Signori di Franco for their chapel in San Domenico Maggiore. The painting is somewhat damaged and was restored recently. Published by de Rinaldis, *Boll. d'Arte*, N.S., VIII 1928/1929, pp. 49-54.

The movement and anatomical construction of the figure of Christ is derived from the executioner in the *Martyrdom of St. Matthew*. However, Christ's body is more simplified and broader and deeper shadows are used to bring out the plastic form. The loincloths of the two figures are also very similar, although that of Christ is more simply constructed.

The face of Christ belongs to the same type as that in the *Calling of St. Matthew*. The long line of the neck and shoulder had been a favorite motif of Caravaggio since it was first used for the Madonna in the *Flight to Egypt*; the neck line is emphasized here even more than

FIG. 112
Sebastiano del Piombo, *Flagellation*.
Rome, S. Pietro in Montorio.

in the famous *Flagellation* by Sebastiano del Piombo in S. Pietro in Montorio, which certainly influenced Caravaggio's general conception. Caravaggio uses this powerful horizontal of the neck and shoulder to oppose the broken vertical of Christ's body, thereby heightening the impression of utter exhaustion and submission—very different from the High Renaissance conception of Sebastiano, where everything is of a sober and idealized beauty. It is also interesting to compare Caravaggio's conception with the decidedly baroque representation of the scene by Lodovico Carracci, made about ten years earlier.

In the faces of Christ's tormentors, Caravaggio recalls the almost caricatured countenance of the man who helps to raise the cross in the *Crucifixion of St. Peter*. The kneeling youth on the left, whose head is almost hidden in a deep brown shadow, is in the act of binding a bunch of twigs into a flay. The strange twist in the feet and legs of Christ recalls somewhat the position of the Virgin's legs in the *Madonna di Loreto*.

COPIES

A contemporary copy of Caravaggio's painting is in the same chapel at San Domenico Maggiore. Another *Flagellation* in the Macerata Pinacoteca (Mostra No. 58) is, according to Longhi (*Prop.*, 1943, p. 18), a copy after Caravaggio, from his late period.

FIG. 113
Lodovico Carracci, *Flagellation*.
Bologna, Pinacoteca.

34. SEVEN ACTS OF MERCY

SOURCES

Bellori, 209: ". . . Caravaggio painted the Seven Works of Mercy for the Chiesa della Miseri-cordia, a painting about 10 palmi long; the head of an old man is seen sticking out of the bars of a prison, sucking the milk of a woman who bends over him with her breast bared. Among the other figures appear the feet and legs of a dead person being carried to the sepulchre; and from the light of the torch carried by the one who supports the body, the rays spread over the priest in a white surplice, and the color is luminous, enlivening the composition."

———— 213. ". . . in Naples, among the Seven Works of Mercy, there is a man who, raising his flask, drinks with open mouth, disgustingly letting the wine run into it."

Scaramuccia, *Le Finezze de Pennelli Italiani*, Pavia, 1674, p. 75: "In the Templo della Misericordia in Naples, over the main altar, are represented the Seven Works of Mercy in a picturesque and, as a whole, bizarre manner."

P A I N T I N G

PLATE 49

Seven Acts of Mercy. Naples, Chiesa del Monte della Misericordia. 390 x 260 cm. Mostra No. 36.

This painting was made in 1607 during Caravaggio's sojourn in Naples. It is the main altarpiece for the church of the Misericordia which had only recently been built (1601, see Sarnelli, *Guida de' Forestiere*, Napoli, ed. 1708, p. 77). The Confraternity of the Monte della Misericordia was dedicated to such pious works as helping the poor, assisting the sick, redeeming Christian slaves from the hands of the infidels, and giving shelter to pilgrims, etc. . . .

The subject of the *Seven Acts of Mercy* derives from the words given in Matthew 23:35, 36, ". . . For I was hungered, and ye gave me meat; I was thirsty, and ye gave me drink; I was a stranger, and ye took me in; naked, and ye clothed me; I was sick, and ye visited me; I was in prison, and ye came unto me." The burial of the dead, which is not mentioned in Matthew, only came to be included as the seventh among the Acts of Mercy in the thirteenth century.

For the most part, previous representations of the Seven Acts of Mercy were arranged so that each act was given separately, either in a separate panel or in a clearly defined area. However, there are some rare instances before Caravaggio in which all the acts were included in one frame, e.g. the painting attributed to Martin de Voss (Rotterdam, Boymans Museum, no. 332), and the triptych of Bernard van Orley in the Antwerp Museum of 1525 (in which, however, the acts are divided into three and four on either wing). Beyond the fact that these are both northern examples, they are of little interest in relation to Caravaggio, for he is certainly the first painter to attempt a juxtaposition of all the acts in a unified, monumental composition. As usual, he has not changed the iconography fundamentally, but has added new implications. At least four of the Acts are represented in terms of personalities: Giving drink to the thirsty is exemplified by Samson, in the left background, who drinks the water which God has caused to come from the jaw bone of an ass (Judges, 15:19; similar to the famous *Samson* by Guido Reni); in the foreground St. Martin is cutting his cloak in half for the benefit of the poor man lying at his feet, to illustrate the clothing of the naked. Behind Saint Martin is a pilgrim who is being received by a host who points the way to shelter. The pilgrim, with his bearded, dignified face is probably meant to be Christ the Pilgrim, since it is not unusual for Christ to be shown inconspicuously among the recipients of the acts of mercy. Most interesting is the scene at the right, illustrating the story of Cimon and Pero, the

{208}

Caritas Romana; Caravaggio has used it here to exemplify two acts in one: the feeding of the hungry and the visiting of the prisoner, which is a combination specifically indicated by Valerius Maximus (Book 5, Chapter 4, 7). The unusual motif of the *Caritas Romana* (cf. Pierino del Vaga, Palazzo Doria, Genoa, and the engraving by Reverdinus, Bartsch, vol. 15, p. 4872, of 1542) was included in the Seven Acts of Mercy by Mattias Bolzetta, the engraver of a series of prints of about 1650 (published by Mather, *Gaz. d B.-A.*, Dec. 1942); these seem to go

FIG. 114
Pierino del Vaga, *Caritas Romana.*
Genoa, Palazzo Doria.

back to some Venetian source which may very possibly have been the common prototype for both Bolzetta and Caravaggio.

The other two acts do not seem to have been cast into such concrete form. Very faintly seen in the shadows at the extreme lower left is a curly-haired youth with hands clasped in prayer, who may represent either the sick man awaiting his visitors or a Christian slave hoping for liberation from the infidels. In the background is the burial of the dead, with a man holding the feet of the corpse and a cleric carrying the torch.

An unusual innovation is the Madonna and Child carried by two angels in the upper part of the painting. This motif is related to the Madonna della Misericordia, and it is probable that Caravaggio introduced it at the request of the Confraternity.

Some of the figures are portraits, probably of superiors of the Confraternity, especially the host who receives the pilgrim, and the cleric holding the torch. In contrast to Caravaggio's Roman pictures, the facial types are, on the whole, much more individualized and strongly modeled. The scene is illuminated by a strong raking light coming from the left; the torch marks the center of the canvas, and thus has considerable importance in forming a compositional focus, but its effect as a source of light is confined to the figure of the cleric (who would otherwise be plunged into darkness). The apparition at the top is surprising in its powerful dramatic impact, which contrasts with the lack of movement in the lower figures. To produce this effect, Caravaggio again returned to the figure from Michelangelo's *Last Judgment*, which he had already used in the *Martyrdom of St. Matthew*.

DENIAL OF ST. PETER

See LOST PAINTINGS, Cat. No. 49.

RESURRECTION

See LOST PAINTINGS, Cat. No. 50.

ST. FRANCIS

See LOST PAINTINGS, Cat. No. 51.

35. CRUCIFIXION OF SAINT ANDREW

SOURCES

Bellori, 214: in the enumeration of Caravaggio's works exported from Italy mentions a painting of the *Crucifixion of Saint Andrew* which the Viceroy of Naples, Conte de Benavente, had taken to Spain.

COPIES   PAINTING   PLATE 64

A *Crucifixion of Saint Andrew* was brought in 1610 from Naples to Spain by Conte di Benavente (Viceroy in Naples, 1603-1610) who placed it in his palace at Valladolid; it is described in the inventory of 1653 of paintings belonging to the Benavente family as a very big work by "Micael Angel Carabacho," showing "Saint Andrew nude, about to be fixed on the cross, with three executioners and one woman" (con tres sayones y una muger). (Cf. J. Ainaud, *Anales y Boletin de los Museos de Arte de Barcelona*, vol. II, 1947, p. 380.) It is not impossible that the painting was made during Caravaggio's second sojourn in Naples.

A painting of the same subject from the estate of the Flemish painter, Louis Finsonius, was in the sale of Abraham Vinck in 1619; it was expertized by Pieter Lastman and other painters as an original Caravaggio (cf. *Oud Holland*, 1886, p. 7). However, it cannot have been genuine (as Longhi considers possible), since the inventory of 1653 verifies that the original was in Valladolid; probably it was a copy after Caravaggio's work made by Finsonius when he was in Naples.

We can form an idea of Caravaggio's composition from what may be a copy in the Museo Provinciale in Toledo (published by Longhi, *Prop.*, pp. 8, 17, fig. 26). So far as one can distinguish from the bad reproduction of this painting, the composition is not quite in accord with the description in the inventory; it contains one executioner on a ladder, and one old woman below at the left, a man in armor and several vague figures in the background at the right.

36. BEHEADING OF ST. JOHN THE BAPTIST

SOURCES

Bellori, 209: "Caravaggio was commissioned to paint the *Beheading of St. John* for the church of San Giovanni. The Saint has fallen to the ground while the executioner is taking his knife from the sheath at his side, as if he had not quite killed him at once with his sword; he grasps the Saint by the hair to cut his head from his body. Salome watches intently and an old woman with her is horror-stricken at the spectacle, while the warden of the prison, in Turkish garb, points to the atrocious massacre. In this work Caravaggio used every power of his brush, having worked at it so feverishly that he left the canvas to show through in the half-tones."

PAINTING

Beheading of St. John the Baptist. Malta, La Valletta, Cathedral, 361 x 520 cm.   PLATE 51

The picture was painted toward the end of 1608 in Malta. It is very large and very poorly preserved. In a general way this work reflects Caravaggio's reminiscences of his youth, when he saw Antonio Campi's representation of the same subject in San Paolo, Milan. More striking is the resemblance of the architectural setting to the same Campi's *Visit of the Empress to St. Catherine* in S. Angelo, Milan (FIG. 26), which has a similar grated window at the right and a large arched opening to the left. Caravaggio's picture, however, differs from that of Campi in the elimination of the artificial light, and in the clear and sober delineation of the architecture. Also in contrast to Campi is the severe geometrical composition with the semicircle of the figures repeated in the arch of the entrance above—showing Caravaggio at his most classical.

The scene takes place in a kind of courtyard before a prison. St. John lies on the ground and the executioner bends over him grasping him by the hair with one hand and with the other clasping the knife at his hip. The prison-keeper stands behind pointing to the platter which Salome holds ready to receive the head of the Saint. An old woman also stands in the rear clasping her head in horror. Two prisoners are seen behind the bars of the window at the right.

37. SAINT JEROME

SOURCES

Bellori, 210: For the church of San Giovanni, La Valletta, Malta, in the chapel of the Italian Nation, he painted a half-figure of *Saint Jerome* over the door (as a pendant to a Magdalene).

PAINTING

St. Jerome Writing. Malta, La Valletta, Church of San Giovanni.   PLATE 52

This painting seems to be the same half-figure of St. Jerome which is described by Bellori as one of the "sopraportas" of this church. Cf. Caravaggio's earlier and slightly different representation of the saint (Cat. Rais. No. 31).

38. SLEEPING AMOR

SOURCES

Baldinucci, Notizie, IV, p. 201 ff.: In his description of the façade of the Palazzo dell'Antella, painted in 1619, Baldinucci refers to the figure of a *Cupid* sleeping near a swan, made by Giovanni da San Giovanni, who copied it from a painting by the hand of Caravaggio in the palace of the Grand Duke. He adds that although one work was done in fresco and the other in oil, one was as good as the other.

PAINTINGS

A. *Sleeping Cupid*. Florence, Pitti, 071 x 105 cm., no. 13. Mostra No. 40. PLATE 53

An inscription on the back of the painting reads: "Opera di Michelangelo Marese Da Caravaggio i[n] Malta 1608." The painting must have come to Florence at an early date, since its composition was used by Giovanni da San Giovanni in a fresco of *Cupid with a Swan* of about 1620 on the façade of the Palazzo dell'Antella, Piazza Santa Croce, Florence, as Baldinucci relates (now destroyed).

Marangoni (*Arte Barocca*, pp. 156/157) subscribes to the attribution of the Pitti painting to Caravaggio on the basis of Baldinucci's remarks, as well as for stylistic reasons. He relates the style of the Cupid to that of the *San Giovanni nel Deserto* in the Borghese (see also Giglioli, *Rivista d'Arte*, 1909, p. 151).

B. *Sleeping Cupid*. Indianapolis, U.S.A. Private Collection, 25¾" x 41½". PLATE 54

When this painting was recently discovered in the possession of a New York art dealer, it was thinly but completely overpainted with the figure of a Christ-Child sleeping, his head upon a crown of thorns. Thorough cleaning revealed a sleeping Cupid under this Christ-Child, and the Cupid corresponds in almost every detail to the painting in the Pitti. With the removal of the overpainting two wings appeared, one in the background with a curved light streak, the other spread out before the figure; also the bow with its loose string, and arrows in the boy's hand, as well as the quiver with arrows under his head, in the place of the crown of thorns. Only the wooden board on which Cupid lies, which was later changed into the stem of the Cross, cannot be discovered in the Pitti painting.

The X-rays of the picture showed, apart from numerous pentimenti, traces of a face in the upper left corner, foreshortened, and similar to the head of St. Lucy in the *Martyrdom of St. Lucy*, painted at about the same time in Syracuse. All these factors seem to indicate that the painting in Indianapolis is not a copy after the Pitti painting. Although there are no definite examples of Caravaggio's repeating himself literally, it is not impossible that this *Cupid*, his first mythological figure since the *Amor Victorious* in Berlin, was painted on the commission of one of the knights of Malta and that because of the appealing theme, a duplicate was ordered from Caravaggio to be sent to the Grand Duke of Tuscany.

The motif of the Sleeping Cupid is well known from the frequent antique examples (see Reinach, *Statuaire*, I, pp. 442-443).

MARY MAGDALENE

See LOST PAINTINGS, Cat. No. 52.

SAINT JEROME

See LOST PAINTINGS, Cat. No. 53.

39. BURIAL OF SAINT LUCY

SOURCES

Bellori, 210: "In Syracuse Caravaggio painted the picture for the church of St. Lucy, which stands by the sea outside the city; he painted the dead Saint Lucy with a bishop who is blessing her and two men digging her grave."

PAINTING   PLATE 55

Martyrdom of St. Lucy. Syracuse, Church of St. Lucy, 408 x 300 cm. Mostra No. 41.

The painting is in very bad condition, often repainted (recently restored by the Istituto del Restauro in Rome), and only some traces of Caravaggio's hand can be seen in the figures of the Saint and the Deacon standing above her. It was probably painted toward the end of 1608, immediately upon Caravaggio's arrival from Malta. He received the commission to paint the burial of the famous Syracusian saint for the Church of St. Lucy from the magistrate of the town.

Caravaggio, or his patrons, have chosen an unusual moment from the legend of the Saint; she is often represented holding her eyes on a platter, but the moment of her burial is rarely depicted. Here she is lying on the ground and the traditional sword wound is visible in her neck. The two gigantic grave-diggers provide repoussoirs between which the saint's pathetic body and the half-circle of very realistically rendered mourners are seen. The female kneeling with her head between her hands makes a gesture similar to that of the standing woman in the *Decapitation* in Malta. Above is the vast, empty space of a wall, the device which Caravaggio had been developing since the *Calling of Saint Matthew*, providing here an effective foil for the quiet drama of the action below. To the left, in the rear, is a great arched opening, according to legend, the entrance to the Syracusian catacombs.

Schudt, no. 63 (unrestored), no. 64 (restored); Mauceri, *Boll. d'Arte*, N.S. IV, 1924/1925, p. 559; Bottari, *L'Arte*, 38, 1935, p. 41.

40. RESURRECTION OF LAZARUS

SOURCES

Bellori, 210: "In the chapel of the Signori Lazzari of the Chiesa de' Ministri de' gli Infermi, Caravaggio painted the Resurrection of Lazarus. Lazarus is shown supported outside the sepulcher; he opens his arms at the voice of Christ who calls him and extends His hand toward him. Martha weeps and the Magdalene is stunned, and there is one man who puts his hand to his nose to protect himself from the stench of the corpse. The painting is large, and the figures have a cave for a background. The greatest light is on the nude figure of Lazarus and those who support him. The painting is most highly esteemed for its realistic power."

Resurrection of Lazarus. Messina, Museo Nazionale, 380 x 275 cm., no. 404. Mostra No. 43.

The Genoese merchant Lazzari, who lived in Messina, built the main chapel in the Chiesa dei Crociferi in Messina, in 1608. On June 10, 1609, he gave to the church a painting of the *Resurrection of Lazarus* by "Michelangelo Caravaggio Gerosolemitanus"; this picture must have been made in Messina in the first months of 1609. (Bottari, *L'Arte*, 1935, p. 39; Sacca, *Arch. Stor. Mes.*, VII, 1907, pp. 66-69.) Mauceri (*Boll. d'Arte*, IV, 1924/1925, p. 52) believes that the painting was possibly executed by someone else after a sketch by Caravaggio. Pevsner (*Z. f. b. K.*, 61, 1927/1928, p. 387) thinks it is probably a copy. There have been frequent restorations. See also Schudt, 1942, and Longhi (Prop. I, 1943, p. 16).

FIG. 115
Sebastiano del Piombo, *Resurrection of Lazarus.*
London, National Gallery.

The grand conception of the painting leaves little doubt that the composition is by Caravaggio, although it is difficult to say how much remains from his hand. The picture differs from the description of Bellori in that the figure holding his nose is absent, or hidden, as is the grotto in the background. The composition is again divided into two halves, with only the lower part filled with figures; the upper part is, in its present state, quite empty, but probably originally had some background element, as in the *St. Lucy*, perhaps the cave mentioned by Bellori.

The Resurrection of Lazarus (John 13) has been represented in Christian art from the time of the catacombs. Representations are frequent in the North in the fifteenth century, but in Italy during the Renaissance the subject is illustrated only sporadically. Of the important examples the nearest in time to Caravaggio is that of Sebastiano del Piombo (National Gallery, London). The difference in Caravaggio's conception of the miracle from all previous examples, including that of Sebastiano, consists mainly in the position of Lazarus; the corpse is shown in an oblique position, stiff, with its arms outstretched; the only signs of life are the spread fingers of Lazarus' right hand, startlingly visible in the center of the painting above the heads of the group.

The group of Lazarus and those around him bears a striking resemblance to the arrangement of the *Pietà* in Northern examples beginning with Roger van der Weyden (see Chapter VI, fig. 84 and below). The diagonal body of Lazarus with one arm hanging down, his head thrown back and his legs crossed, is like that of Christ; and the sister who embraces Lazarus corresponds to the Mater Dolorosa of the Pietà. It is possible that Caravaggio saw some painting reflecting Roger's composition, perhaps even in Sicily.

FIG. 116
Roger van der Weyden, *Pietà*. Earl of Powys Collection.

In keeping with this iconography transferred from the Pieta, Caravaggio has given to the whole composition a sombre and mysteriously luminous atmosphere. The depth of religious emotion removes the whole composition from the narrative and relates it to the devotional character of the Pietà and the Deposition.

41. NATIVITY

SOURCES

Bellori, 210: "In the church of the Capuchins at Messina Caravaggio made a painting of the *Nativity* picturing the Virgin with the Child before a decayed barn, with its boards and rafters bared; St. Joseph leans on his staff, and there are several shepherds in adoration."

Placido Sampieri, *Iconologia della gloriosa Virgine Maria*, Messina, 1644: "on the main altar of the Capuchin church is an artful picture of the Madonna del Parto, a work of the excellent painter Michelangelo da Caravaggio, considered by the connoisseurs as something singular, because of its artistry."

PAINTING

Nativity. Messina, Museo Nazionale, no. 403. 314 x 211 cm. Mostra No. 42.   PLATE 56

This is the painting described by Bellori which was executed for the Capuccini on order of the Senate of Messina, for which Caravaggio was allegedly paid 1000(?) scudi. The picture, which was painted in 1609, is in rather bad condition.

See E. Mauceri, Il Caravaggismo in Sicilia ecc., *Boll. d'Arte*, N.S., IV, 1925, pp. 559 ff.; V. Sacca, Mich. da C., *Archiv. Stor. Mes.*, VIII, 1906, p. 41 ff.

The Messina painting has been sharply criticized because of the "ignoble" position of the Virgin seated on the ground (see the reference given in Sacca, *op. cit.*, p. 44), and from a social point of view this criticism is understandable, if not justifiable. Caravaggio has chosen the poorest and most desolate place for the birth of the Lord, going farther in his social realism even than modern "poor folk" painters like Courbet and Millet. The scene is set in a naked and dilapidated barn, in the rear of which is a large opening through which one sees a burning strip of sunset shining in the dense tenebrosity. To the right in a diagonal row is a group of haggard, bearded men (among them St. Joseph) who watch and stare animal-like at the miracle before their eyes. The stark and moving figure of the Madonna is set against the silhouettes of the ox and the ass who hover above her. She is the "Madonna del Parto," reposing upon a miserable heap of straw with one arm against the manger and pressing the tiny child to her breast and mouth—a perfect expression of the Virgin's humility. (See text, Chapter VI, p. 127.)

42. ADORATION WITH ST. FRANCIS AND ST. LAWRENCE

SOURCES

Bellori, 211: "In Palermo, after leaving Messina, Caravaggio made another Nativity for the Oratorio della Campagnia di San Lorenzo; the Virgin contemplates the new-born child, with SS. Francis and Lawrence. St. Joseph is seated, and there is an angel above; the lights are diffused among the shadows of the night."

Adoration with St. Francis and St. Lawrence. Palermo, Oratorio di San Lorenzo. 268 x 197 cm. Mostra No. 44.

Painted in Palermo in 1609. Fairly well preserved. Mauceri, *Boll. d'Arte*, N.S. IV, 1924/1925, p. 560 f.; F. Meli, *Dedalo*, VI, 1925/1926, pp. 229-234.

In contrast to the Messina *Nativity*, the Palermo painting is much more traditional in placing the Child alone on the ground with the other persons grouped around Him in worship. The attendant worshipers present a more civilized aspect than the wild shepherds of the Messina painting; the conventional atmosphere of the Palermo picture is also reinforced by the sudden appearance of an angel at the top of the composition, going back to the motif of the *Second St. Matthew*. The tall figure on the left with his head bowed and his arms crossed has some resemblance to the St. John in Rosso's *Crucifixion* at Volterra.

43. SALOME WITH THE HEAD OF ST. JOHN

SOURCES

Bellori, 211: "On Caravaggio's second journey to Naples he painted for the Grand Master a half-figure of Herodiade with the head of St. John in a basin."

PAINTING

Salome. Escorial. Casita del Pricipe. 116 x 140 cm. Mostra No. 44 bis. PLATE 59

This probably is the painting which, according to Bellori, Caravaggio made in Naples for the Grand Master of Malta with the intention of placating his anger. Longhi accepts the painting as an original by Caravaggio (see *Par.*, 15 March, 1951). Ainaud reserves his judgment, but places the painting close to Caravaggio (*Anales*, p. 392). The painting has allegedly suffered great damage from fire in the seventeenth century and has recently been restored. If it is really the painting cited by Bellori, it would be the last work which we know of by Caravaggio, and stylistically it would belong to his last period. It is of extremely high quality. The grave and moving figure of Salome is of especially great beauty. The head of the old nurse is comparable to the St. Anne in the *Madonna dei Palafrenieri*, and the executioner is somewhat similar to the half-naked shepherd in the Messina *Nativity*.

44. PORTRAITS

SOURCES

Mancini, 59v: mentions among the early works of Caravaggio a portrait of an innkeeper painted while Caravaggio was recovering from an illness.

———— 60r. (marginal note). Caravaggio painted portraits for Barberini (fece ritratti p[er] Barberini).

Bertolotti II, 26: In the testament of Martino Longhi, the younger, are mentioned portraits of his mother and father, Onorio Longhi and Caterina Campani, by Caravaggio. Martino died in 1657.

Baglione, 138: Caravaggio "went to Malta and was invited to pay his respects to the Grand Master whose portrait he painted. As a sign of his satisfaction this exalted personage presented him with the mantle of St. John and made him Cavaliere di Gratia."

Bellori, 201: says that the young Caravaggio made portraits during the five years he spent in Milan.

———— 205: "Caravaggio painted the portrait of Cavaliere Marino, the most glorious among men of letters."

———— 205: "He painted the portrait of Msgr. Melchiorre Crescenzi, clerico di camera, to whom he had been introduced by Marino; he also made portraits of Virgilio Crescenzi, the heir of Cardinal Contarelli."

———— 208: "For Cardinal Maffeo Barberini, who was later the Sovereign Pontiff, Urban VIII, he painted, in addition to his portrait, a *Sacrifice of Abraham.* . . ."

———— 208: "Cardinal Scipione Borghese, pleased with these and other works that Caravaggio did for him, introduced him to Pope Paul V, of whom he made a seated portrait for which he was well rewarded."

———— 209: "Caravaggio wished very much to receive the Cross of Malta which was usually given per grazia to notable persons for merit and virtue. He therefore went to Malta and when he arrived he was introduced to the Grand Master, Vignacourt, a French nobleman. Caravaggio portrayed him standing dressed in armor and seated without armor, wearing the robe of a Grand Master; the first of these portraits is in the Armory of Malta. As a reward for this the Grand Master presented him with the Cross of Malta."

———— 214: mentions among the works owned by the Count of Villa Mediana a *Portrait of a Youth with an Orange Blossom in his Hand* by Caravaggio.

PAINTINGS

Bellori's reference to portraits painted in Milan can be dismissed as pure invention. Nor do we know anything about the early *Innkeeper* which, according to Mancini, Caravaggio painted while recovering from an illness, probably after he had left the Ospedale della Consolazione. Whether or not Caravaggio ever painted a portrait of the Cavaliere Marino is also uncertain; in any event, it could not have been as early as Bellori assumes (at the beginning of the time when the artist worked for San Luigi dei Francesi), since Marino came to Rome only about 1600. Of the alleged portraits of the two Crescenzi nothing remains.

Thus, only four portraits mentioned in the sources are pertinent to our study: the portraits of the so-called *Caterina Campani, Paul V, Maffeo Barberini* and *Alof de Vignacourt.*

PRESERVED PORTRAITS   PLATE 16

A. *Portrait of a Young Woman.* Berlin, Kaiser Friedrich Museum. 66 x 53 cm. no. 356.

The painting came from the Galleria Giustiniani; a sales catalogue of the Giustiniani collection refers to it as a representation of the "Courtesan Phyllis."

If, as Voss has suggested (*J.d.K.*, 44, 1923, p. 81), this is the portrait of Caterina Campani mentioned in the will of Martino Longhi the younger, it would seem to date from the nineties. The prominence of the bouquet of orange blossoms which the lady holds to her breast indicates that the portrait was made on the occasion of her marriage. Onorio Longhi (an architect, and son of Martino Longhi the elder) was a very close friend of Caravaggio and it would have been quite natural for the artist to paint portraits of him and his young wife. The exact date of Onorio's marriage to Caterina is not known, but since he was about four years older than Caravaggio (he was born around 1569), one could suppose that it took place some time in the early nineties. The style of the painting would also indicate a fairly early date. It is comparable to the *Magdalene* in the Doria and the *Judith and Holofernes*. In both of these there are pear-shaped earrings similar to those worn by the lady in the Berlin portrait, and the costumes are similar in all three works.

There is no trace of the companion portrait of Onorio mentioned in the will of Martino the younger. However, one could imagine that the painting of a young man with orange blossoms referred to by Bellori as being in the collection of the Count of Villa Mediana might have represented Onorio as a bridegroom.

PLATE 17

B. *Portrait of Maffeo Barberini*. Florence, Collection of Principe Corsini. 121 x 95 cm. Mostra No. 10.

The painting was exhibited in the Palazzo Barberini until it was inherited recently by the Corsini. It shows the future Urban VIII (born, 1568; Cardinal, 1606) standing before a table, his right hand resting on a book. The portrait was called a Pulzone until Venturi (1912) attributed it to Caravaggio. Longhi now believes it to be by a follower of Pulzone. Denis Mahon (*Burl. Mag.*, Jan. 1952, p. 19) dates it 1594-95. In spite of certain weaknesses in the painting, its closeness to Caravaggio's early works seems to me to indicate that the attribution is correct.

C. *Portrait of Paul V*. Rome, formerly in the Palazzo Borghese. 203 x 119 cm.   PLATE 40

The picture was published by Venturi (*Arte*, XIII, 1910, p. 276 ff.). It must have been painted after May 1605, the year in which Paul V was elected to the papacy. It seems to have been uninterruptedly in the possession of the Borghese.

Stylistically it is comparable to the Borghese *David*, especially in the treatment of the light which models the narrow pleats of the drapery; however, the attribution to Caravaggio seems somewhat controversial. Voss (*Barockmalerei*, p. 446) and Schudt (no. 45) accept it as a Caravaggio. Longhi (*Prec.*, Borghese, p. 183) declares that the attribution to Caravaggio is "senza fundamento"; he reaffirmed this judgment in 1943 (*Prop.*, p. 38) with convincing reasons.

Another painting of *Paul V* in the Villa Borghese (no. 73) was attributed to Caravaggio as early as 1650 by Manilli, but according to Longhi (*ibid.*), it is a copy of part of the portrait in the Palazzo Borghese. Martinez (*Discursos*, ed. 1866, p. 123) mentions a portrait of *Paul V* by Caravaggio, but his description does not correspond to the painting in the Borghese.

PLATE 50

D. *Portrait of Alof de Vignacourt*. Paris, Louvre, no. 1124. 195 x 134 cm. Mostra No. 39.

The early history of this painting is rather obscure. We know only that the portrait of the Grand Master of the Order, Alof de Vignacourt, standing in full armor, as described by

Bellori, was bought from a certain Monsieur Hoursel, secretary of Monsieur de la Vrillière, by the king. An entry in the *Comptes des Batiments du Roi* for February 1, 1670, records "une somme de 14.300 livres pour payer aux sieurs Vinot et Hoursel" for paintings including "un portrait d'un Grand Maître de Malte, faict par Michel Lange . . ." (Bonaffée, *Dictionnaire des Amateurs*, p. 240). We do not know, however, how the painting found its way into the possession of Monsieur Hoursel, and still less how it left the armory of Malta.

There is another portrait of the Grand Master still preserved in the armory of Malta. However, according to Maindron (see below), it is much inferior in quality to the Louvre painting and shows no sign of Caravaggio's brush. One might conclude, therefore, that Bellori, who was probably never in Malta, had heard of this painting and assumed that it was by Caravaggio. Further, it would be quite understandable if, after the trial in which the fugitive Caravaggio was infamously ousted from the order, Vignacourt did not want to have a portrait of himself by this artist hanging in an official place. In this way, perhaps, the painting was sent to France after the Grand Master's death.

There is not a trace of the seated portrait, which Bellori mentions without giving a location for it.

Longhi (*Prop.*, p. 39) makes some unfavorable comments about the quality of the Louvre painting ("the four legs in single-file on the same plane, with a turbid but undramatic

FIG. 117
Titian, *Allocution of General Vasto*. Madrid, Prado.

atmosphere . . . etc.") and doubts "fieramente" its authenticity. He finds no parallel in Caravaggio's other works, and especially not in the portrait of the donor in the *Madonna of the Rosary* (painted shortly before he went to Naples). However, in my opinion, the portrait in the *Madonna of the Rosary* is not by Caravaggio anyway (see *Madonna of the Rosary,* Cat. Rais. No. 29).

In spite of the rather bad condition of the painting, the composition of the Grand Master in armor with the elegant little page at his side is very impressive; it is comparable to the group of General Vasto and his page in Titian's *Allocution of General Vasto* in the Prado. The pose of the page and the attitude of the General in armor holding his baton make it seem very likely that Titian's picture served as an inspiration to Caravaggio. In any event, it is impossible that a mediocre painter like Lionello Spada could have produced such a powerful composition, as has been suggested. The age of the man represented in the Louvre painting corresponds to that of Vignacourt, who was 59 years old in 1608.

Maindron (*Revue de l'Art*, XXIV, 1908, pp. 241/254) states that the armor of the Louvre painting is from a period around 1550 (Titian's *Allocution* is from ca. 1541) and that it is still preserved in the armory of Malta, along with other armor which belonged to Vignacourt. The portrait which is still in the armory shows the Grand Master in armor of his own time.

PAINTINGS MENTIONED IN THE SOURCES
FOR WHICH NEITHER ORIGINAL CANVASES
NOR INDISPUTABLE COPIES ARE KNOWN

45. DIVINE LOVE

SOURCES

Baglione, 136: "Caravaggio made (for Cardinal del Monte) an Amore Divino, who overcomes the Profane."

PAINTING

Baglione's statement surely cannot refer to the painting of *Divine Love* now in the Berlin Museum, which Voss (*J.d.K.*, 44, 1923, pp. 95ff.) gave back to its rightful author, Baglione himself, after it had for a long time been attributed to Caravaggio.

The *Amore Divino* which Caravaggio made for the Cardinal, now lost, must have been painted considerably earlier than his *Amor Victorious* and Baglione's *Amore Divino*, since the latter were made for the Giustiniani. Caravaggio's picture would have been the only religious, or semi-religious, painting among all the works done for Cardinal del Monte and it would be of great interest to know how the young Caravaggio treated such a serious subject.

46. CROWNING WITH THORNS

SOURCES

Bellori, 207: "For the Marchese Vincenzo Giustiniani, who ordered from Caravaggio, among other paintings, a *Crowning with Thorns*."

PAINTING   PLATE 65

No painting of this subject which, according to Bellori, was made for the Marchese Giustiniani, is mentioned in the Paris sale catalogue of the Giustiniani collection. Longhi (*Prop.*, p. 18) considers that the *Crowning with Thorns* in the Vienna Museum (127 x 165 cm.), Mostra No. 59, which he had formerly attributed to Caracciolo, could be an old and good copy after an original by Caravaggio (not after the Giustiniani painting, but one made in Naples, 1606/1607). Certainly the painting reflects Caravaggio's style, especially in the forcefully integrated composition which recalls the earlier-mentioned *Taking of Christ* (see Cat. Rais. No. 21) as does the armor of the soldier on the left. Also the thick chest and the long, tense line of the neck and right shoulder of Christ recalls the figure of Christ in the Naples *Flagellation*. I am inclined to agree with Longhi's attribution of the work to Caracciolo, or to another Neapolitan artist working under the strong influence of Caravaggio's late style.

47. ECCE HOMO

SOURCES

Bellori, 208: "Caravaggio painted for the Signori Massimi an *Ecce Homo*, which was taken to Spain."

No trace remains in Spain of the *Ecce Homo*, made for the Massimi, which was allegedly taken there (cf. J. Ainaud, *Anales*, p. 382). Sacca (*Archivio Storico Messinense*, VII, 1906, p. 73) mentions an *Ecce Homo* which Caravaggio made for a certain Nicolao di Giacomo in Messina. In the Museo Nazionale in Messina there is an *Ecce Homo* with Pilate and executioners, attributed to Caravaggio (194 x 112). Mauceri (*Boll. d'Arte* 1921/22, p. 581 ff.) takes it for the work of a Sicilian follower of Caravaggio. Longhi (*Prop.*, p. 37) calls it a crude copy (cf. also Mostra no. 61). As this book goes to press, a painting which is said to be an original *Ecce Homo* by Caravaggio has just been found in Genoa and published by Longhi (Paragone, no. 51).

48. WALK TO EMMAUS

SOURCES

Mancini, 60: "in Zagarola Caravaggio made a *Christ going to Emmaus* (and a *Magdalene*) which was bought by Sign. Costa."

Bellori, 208: While taking refuge in Zagarola, under the protection of Duke D. Martio Colonna, Caravaggio painted a *Christ in Emmaus* between two apostles and another half figure of the Magdalene.

No trace remains of the picture which Caravaggio painted in 1606 in the Sabine Mountains after his flight from Rome, and which was allegedly in the possession of the Signori Costi. It has been suggested (Mahon, *Burl. Mag.*, 1952, p. 19) that the painting made in Zagarola was not a *Walk to Emmaus*, but rather a *Supper at Emmaus*, and therefore possibly the second "Supper" now in the Brera (see: Cat. Rais. No. 18). However, in my opinion, Mancini's words, "Cristo che va in Emmaus" refers specifically to a *Walk to Emmaus,* and Bellori can very well have had this subject in mind when he wrote, "Cristo in Emmaus tra due apostoli." (Cf. no. 19, *Walk to Emmaus*.)

49. DENIAL OF ST. PETER

SOURCES

Bellori, 209: "The *Denial of St. Peter* in the Sacristy of S. Martino is held to be one of Caravaggio's best paintings in Naples. The maidservant points to St. Peter, who faces her and, with his hands apart, denies Christ. It is in a nocturnal light and there are other figures warming themselves at the fire."

PAINTING

The painting of the *Denial of St. Peter*, which is now in the Sacristy of San Martino, is not by Caravaggio, nor does it seem to be a copy after Caravaggio's lost picture. It does not follow Bellori's description in that the other figures are not warming themselves at a fire, but are seated around a table, engaged in a game of dice. This painting seems to me to belong to the group around Saraceni, as does the picture of the same subject in the Vatican.

50. RESURRECTION

SOURCES

Bellori, 209: mentions among the paintings of Caravaggio made in Naples a Resurrection for the church of Santa Anna dei Lombardi.

Mancini, Addition to Vat. Barb. Lat. 4315, Fol. 145v: "In S. Anna, the church of the Lombards, in the street of Montoliveto, there is a very beautiful picture of the *Resurrection*" (quoted from Longhi, *Prop.* p. 36/37).

Scaramuccia, 1674, pp. 75-76: "One of the works made in Naples was an altarpiece in the church of S. Anna dei Lombardi: the *Resurrection of Christ*. Christ is represented not as usual, agile, and triumphant in the air, but is shown in Caravaggio's audacious manner of coloring, with one foot in and the other outside the sepulcher on the ground, so that one is somewhat apprehensive at such extravagances. Although the painter has pleased many by the novelty of his inventions, he should be blamed for having relinquished that decorum which is proper to the person of Christ. He has treated a great subject, but not as an ideal, for he could paint nothing without the model before him."

PAINTING

The painting for Santa Anna dei Lombardi has disappeared.

It is interesting that Scaramuccia was displeased with Caravaggio's showing Christ with one foot inside, the other outside the sepulcher on the ground. Examples of the *Resurrection* of the sixteenth and early seventeenth centuries usually do show Christ risen above the sepulcher, but there are many earlier examples with Christ in a position similar to that described by Scaramuccia (e.g., the Mantegna School, *Resurrection*, Bergamo).

51. ST. FRANCIS

SOURCES

Mancini, Addition to Vat. Barb. Lat. 4315, fol. 145v: "In the same church and chapel (Sta. Anna dei Lombardi, Naples) is a St. Francis in the act of receiving the stigmata" (quoted from Longhi, *Prop.* 36/37).

PAINTING

The painting mentioned by Mancini is not known, but another representation of St. Francis, which may be a copy of a fairly late work by Caravaggio, has been published by Longhi (*Prop.* 1, 1943, p. 17). This painting, now in the Cremona Museum (Mostra No. 60), shows the saint in contemplation before a skull, crucifix and book rather than in the act of receiving the stigmata.

52. MARY MAGDALENE

SOURCES

Bellori, 210: In Malta Caravaggio painted in San Giovanni two sopra-porte in half-figure. one a *Magdalene*.

The painting which, according to Bellori, Caravaggio painted for the church of S. Giovanni in Malta is not known.

53. SAINT JEROME

SOURCES

Bellori, 210: "In Messina, for the Capuchin Monks, he painted a *Saint Jerome* writing on the book (Bible)."

PAINTING

No trace remains of this painting of Saint Jerome which Caravaggio made in Messina.

54A. SAINT SEBASTIAN

Bellori, 214: "One of his best works, a figure of *St. Sebastian* with two executioners . . . was taken to Paris."

PAINTING

No trace of this painting remains.

MISTAKEN ATTRIBUTIONS IN THE LITERARY SOURCES

54. SAINT SEBASTIAN

SOURCES

Scanelli, 199: "In the gallery of the Duke of Modena, a half-figure of a nude *St. Sebastian* (companion-piece to a *St. Agostino*)."

PAINTINGS

No trace of the painting remains.

Obviously Scanelli refers to no. 292 in the gallery of Modena, recently attributed to Lionello Spada. A companion piece to no. 481 of the gallery.

55. SAINT AUGUSTINE

SOURCES

Scanelli, 199: "In the gallery of the Duke of Modena, a half-figure of S. Agostino with a pen in his hand, in a moment of inspiration."

PAINTING

This painting is obviously no. 481 in the gallery of Modena, recently ascribed to Serodine.

56. JOVE, NEPTUNE AND PLUTO

SOURCES

Bellori, 214: "It is said that in Rome there is a painting by the hand of Caravaggio of *Jove, Neptune, and Pluto*, in the Ludovisi garden in the Casino at the Porta Pinciana, which belonged to Cardinal del Monte."

PAINTING

No trace remains of this work, and such a painting by Caravaggio probably never existed. As far as we know Caravaggio never made decorative paintings. Cardinal del Monte (see letter of Fabio Masetti, August 24, 1605) remarked that Caravaggio refused to paint a loggia for the Principe Doria.

57. DENTIST

SOURCES

Scanelli, 199: mentions in the possession of the Grand Duke of Tuscany, "a painting of half-figures, in the usual naturalistic manner, of a Charlatan drilling the tooth of a peasant. This painting would have been one of Caravaggio's best performances if it were better preserved."

PAINTING

Such a subject would have been very unusual for Caravaggio, and it may be supposed that Scanelli took a work of a late Caravaggist (perhaps Honthorst) to be a work of Caravaggio himself.

PART III

BIOGRAPHIES AND DOCUMENTS

LIST OF BIOGRAPHIES AND DOCUMENTS

INTRODUCTION

THE most important accounts of Caravaggio's life and work are found in the writings of two seventeenth-century biographers: Giovanni Baglione (1571-1644) and Giovanni Pietro Bellori (1615-1696). A third and less well known source on the artist is the *Trattato* of Giulio Mancini (1558-1630) which as yet has never been completely published. Baglione's *Vite de Pittori Scultori ed Architetti* was not published until 1642, but it is quite possible that some of his biographies and particularly the one on Caravaggio had been written much earlier. Since Baglione was a painter working in Rome at the same time as Caravaggio (like Caravaggio, Baglione worked for members of the Giustiniani family) he was in a position to have complete, firsthand information about the Roman artistic community to which Caravaggio belonged. In spite of his antagonism toward Caravaggio (he brought a libel suit against Caravaggio and his circle in 1603) his account of Caravaggio's activities and of his works is sober, factual, and in most cases more reliable than that given by Bellori. However, Baglione concerned himself only with artists who worked in Rome and his information about Caravaggio's last years outside of Rome is incomplete. Bellori's *Vite* were published in 1672 and his approach to Caravaggio is colored by his own classicistic point of view (he was a great admirer of Nicolas Poussin). Moreover, as a littérateur he was inclined to make misleading conclusions about Caravaggio's works and the events of his life. Although Bellori was not as directly informed about Caravaggio as was Baglione, he managed to gather some extremely valuable information about the artist, especially concerning his post-Roman years. Mancini's *Trattato* was written around 1620, about ten years after the death of Caravaggio. As a dilettante in matters of art (professionally he was a physician), Mancini was much less systematic than either Baglione or Bellori. Nevertheless, his references to Caravaggio are quite helpful even though, as he says himself, much of his information is based on hearsay and is rather anecdotal.

In addition to these Italian biographies there are two very interesting accounts of Caravaggio written by the Northerners, Karel van Mander (1548-1606) and Joachim von Sandrart (1606-1688). In the *Schilderboeck*, published in 1604, van Mander gave the earliest published notice on Caravaggio. Although his information was based on reports from an acquaintance in Rome (one Floris van Dijck) who was there around 1600, his account does not add very much to our factual knowledge of Caravaggio. The importance of his notice lies rather in the fact that it affords us an indication of Caravaggio's personality and of his reputation at the very beginning of the seventeenth century. The *Teutsche Academie*, which contains a full biography of Caravaggio, was published by Sandrart in 1675. He had been in Rome as a young man, between 1629 and 1635, and had lived in the palace of the Marchese Giustiniani, Caravaggio's old patron, where he surely had the opportunity to acquire much information about the artist. However, his biography was written from memory many years after his return to Germany and it is extremely confused and inexact, even though it is amusing and valuable as a literary document. Some other seventeenth-century references to Caravaggio in the *Vite* of Giovanni Battista Passeri and in the treatises of Francesco Scanelli and Luigi

Scaramuccia are included in this section or in the Catalogue Raisonné, in connection with the events or paintings to which they refer.

The documents which follow the biographies are divided into two general categories, those which refer to Caravaggio's life and those which refer to his paintings. The first category includes two epitaphs (DOC. 35) written after Caravaggio's death by his friend Milesi, a Roman notary; these epitaphs are of special importance because they give Caravaggio's age at the time of his death, thus stabilizing his birth date. Of still greater importance is the contract (DOC. 1) which Caravaggio's brother concluded with the Milanese painter, Peterzano, for the apprenticeship of the young artist. The numerous police records concerning Caravaggio's various offenses, and in particular his quarrel with Baglione and the circumstances of his murder of Ranuccio Tomassoni, are of interest not only from the point of view of his psychology but also from that of general cultural history. These documents are complemented by the avvisi, the public news announcements of the time, which give brief reports of the Tomassoni affair, of an assault made on Caravaggio in Naples, and of his death in Port'Ercole. The Maltese documents recounting his reception into the Order of St. John and his ignominious expulsion from the order a short time later are printed here in extenso from a transcription generously placed at my disposal by Mr. Kenneth Donahue. In the category of documents referring to Caravaggio's works are the usual contracts, inscriptions and testaments; of these the documents on the paintings at San Luigi dei Francesi and Sta. Maria del Popolo which were recently published by Mr. Denis Mahon are especially important. Also included in this category are the letters from the agents of the Dukes of Mantua and Modena, first published by Lionello Venturi. Although the main importance of these letters is the information which they give about the *Death of the Virgin* and the *Madonna of the Rosary*, they also contain many interesting sidelights on the events of Caravaggio's life. For the most part, the texts assembled here are printed exactly as they appeared when they were first published. However, in cases where the original documents were available, whole or partial revisions of the texts have been made.

In preparing the texts and English translations of the biographies and documents which follow, I have had the generous assistance of numerous colleagues and students. The translations of the police records from Bertolotti are the result of considerable effort and care on the part of Dr. Marco Treves. The other Italian texts have been studied and worked over by Miss Mirella d'Ancona, Miss Giustina Scaglia and Mr. Dario Covi. Dr. H. W. Janson has been generous with his time and advice throughout the work. Dr. William Heckscher was helpful in preparing some of the Latin documents and in correcting the text and translation of van Mander's biography of Caravaggio. Drs. Wolfgang Stechow and Jan G. van Gelder also worked on the van Mander. Dr. Richard Salomon was able to decipher the rather difficult text of the contract for the paintings in the Cerasi Chapel. I owe a special debt of gratitude to Dr. Erwin Panofsky who corrected many of the texts and translations, enriching them with numerous excellent suggestions. Dr. Panofsky also made the final revision of the entire section.

1. BIOGRAPHIES

GIOVANNI BAGLIONE

La Vita di Michelagnolo da Caravaggio, Pittore

NACQUE in Caravaggio di Lombardia Michelagnolo, e fu figliuolo d'un Maestro, che
murava edificii, assai da bene, di casa Amerigi. Diedesi ad imparare la dipintura, e
non havendo in Caravaggio, chi a suo modo gl'insegnasse, andò egli a Milano, ed
alcun tempo dimorovvi. Dapoi se ne venne à Roma con animo di apprender con diligenza
questo virtuoso essercitio. E da principio si accomodò con un pittore Siciliano, che di opere
grossolane tenea bottega.

Poi andò a stare in casa del Cavalier Gioseppe Cesari d'Arpino per alcuni mesi. Indi provò
a stare da se stesso, e fece alcuni quadretti da lui nello specchio ritratti. Et il primo fu un
Bacco con alcuni grappoli d'uve diverse, con gran diligenza fatte; ma di maniera un poco
secca. Fece anche un fanciullo, che da una lucerta, la quale usciva da fiori, e da frutti, era
morso; e parea quella testa veramente stridere, ed il tutto con diligenza era lavorato. Pur non
trovava a farne esito, e darli via, ed a mal termine si ridusse senza danari, e pessimamente
vestito sì, che alcuni galant'huomini della professione, per carità, l'andavano sollevando, infin
che Maestro Valentino a s. Luigi de'Francesi rivenditore di quadri glie ne fece dar via alcuni;
e con questa occasione fu conosciuto dal Cardinal del Monte, il quale per dilettarsi assai della
pittura, se lo prese in casa, ed havendo parte, e provisione pigliò animo, e credito, e dipinse
per il Cardinale una musica di alcuni giovani ritratti dal naturale, assai bene; ed anche
un giovane, che sonava il Lauto, che vivo, e vero il tutto parea con una caraffa de fiori
piena d'acqua, che dentro il reflesso d'una finestra eccellentemente si scorgeva con altri
ripercotimenti di quella camera dentro l'acqua, e sopra quei fiori eravi una viva rugiada
con ogni esquisita diligenza finta. E questo (disse) che fu il più bel pezzo che facesse mai.[1]

Effigiò una Zinghera, che dava la ventura ad un giovane con bel colorito. Fece un'Amore
divino, che sommetteva il profano. E parimente una testa di Medusa con capelli di vipere,
assai spaventosa sopra una rotella rapportata, che dal Cardinale fu mandata in dono a Ferdinando gran Duca di Toscana.

Per opera del suo Cardinale hebbe in s. Luigi de'Francesi la cappella de'Contarelli, ove
sopra l'altare fece il s. Mattheo con un'Angelo. A man diritta, quando l'Apostolo è chiamato
dal Redentore, ed a man manca, quando sù l'altare è ferito dal carnefice con altre figure. La
volta però della cappella è assai ben dipinta dal Cavalier Gioseppe Cesari d'Arpino.

Quest'opera, per havere alcune pitture del naturale, e per essere in compagnia d'altre fatte
dal Cavalier Gioseppe, che con la sua virtù si haveva presso i professori qualche invidia
acquistata, fece gioco alla fama del Caravaggio, ed era da'maligni sommamente lodata. Pur
venendovi a vederla Federico Zucchero, mentre io era presente, disse, Che rumore è questo?
e guardando il tutto diligentemente, soggiunse, Io non ci vedo altro, che il pensiero di Giorgione

Giovanni Baglione, *Le Vite de' Pittori, Scultori, et Architetti*, Rome, 1642, pp. 136 ff.

nella tavola del Santo, quando Christo il chiamò all'Apostolato; e sogghignando, e maravigliandosi di tanto rumore, voltò le spalle, ed andossene con Dio. Per il Marchese Vincenzo Giustiniani fece un Cupido a sedere dal naturale ritratto, ben colorito sì, che egli dell'opere del Caravaggio fuor de'termini invaghissi; ed il quadro d'un certo s. Matteo, che prima havea fatto per quell'altare di s. Luigi, e non era a veruno piacciuto, egli per esser'opera di Michelagnolo, se'l prese; ed in questa opinione entrò il Marchese per li gran schiamazzi, che del Caravaggio, da pertutto, faceva Prosperino delle grottesche, turcimanno di Michelagnolo, e mal'affetto co'l Cavalier Gioseppe. Anzi fe cadere al rumore anche il Signor Ciriaco Matthei, a cui il Caravaggio havea dipinto un s. Gio. Battista, e quando N. Signore andò in Emaus, ed all'hora che s. Thomasso toccò co'l dito il costato del Salvadore; ed intaccò quel Signore di molte centinaia di scudi.

Nella prima cappella della chiesa di s. Agostino alla man manca fece una Madonna di Loreto ritratta dal naturale con due pellegrini, uno co'piedi fangosi, e l'altra con una cuffia sdrucita, e sudicia; e per queste leggierezze in riguardo delle parti, che una gran pittura haver dee, da popolani ne fu fatto estremo schiamazzo.

Nella Madonna del Popolo a man diritta dell'altar maggiore dentro la cappella de'Signori Cerasi sù i lati del muro sono di sua mano la Crocifissione di s. Pietro; e di rincontro ha la Conversione di s. Paolo, Questi quadri prima furono lavorati da lui in un'altra maniera, ma perche non piacquero al Padrone, se li prese il Cardinale Sannesio; e lo stesso Caravaggio vi fece questi, che hora si vedono, a olio dipinti, poiche egli non operava in altra maniera; e (per dir cosi) la Fortuna con la Fama il portava.[2]

Nella Chiesa nuova alla man diritta v'è del suo nella seconda cappella il Christo morto, che lo vogliono sepellire con alcune figure, a olio lavorato; e questa dicono, che sia la migliore opera di lui.

Fece anch'egli in s. Pietro Vaticano una s. Anna con la Madonna, che ha il putto fra le sue gambe, che con il piede schiaccia la testa ad un serpe; opera da lui condotta per li Palafrenieri di palazzo; ma fu levata d'ordine de'Signori Cardinali della fabrica, e poi da'Palafrenieri donata al Cardinale Scipione Borghese.

Per la Madonna della Scala in Trastevere dipinse il transito di N. Donna, ma perche havea fatto con poco decoro la Madonna gonfia, e con gambe scoperte, fu levata via; e la comperò il Duca di Mantova, e la mise in Mantova nella sua nobilissima Galleria.

Colori una Giuditta, che taglia la testa ad Oloferne per li Signori Costi, e diversi quadri per altri, che per non stare in luoghi publici, io trapasso, e qualche cosa de'suoi costumi dispiego.

Michelagnolo Amerigi fu huomo Satirico, ed altiero; ed usciva tal'hora a dir male di tutti li pittori passati, e presenti per insigni, che si fussero; poiche a lui parea d'haver solo con le sue opere avanzati tutti gli altri della sua professione. Anzi presso alcuni si stima, haver'esso rovinata la pittura; poiche molti giovani ad essempio di lui si danno ad imitare una testa del naturale, e non studiando ne'fondamenti del disegno, e della profondità dell'arte, solamente del colorito appaganzi; onde non sanno mettere due figure insieme, nè tessere historia veruna, per non comprendere la bontà di sì nobil'arte.

Fu Michelagnolo, per soverchio ardimento di spiriti, un poco discolo, e tal'hora cercava occasione di fiaccarsi il collo, o di mettere a sbaraglio l'altrui vita. Pratticavano spesso in sua compagnia huomini anch'essi per natura brigosi: ed ultimamente affrontatosi con Ranuccio Tomassoni giovane di molto garbo, per certa differenza di gioco di palla a corda, sfidaronsi, e venuti all'armi, caduto a terra Ranuccio, Michelagnolo gli tirò d'una punta, e nel pesce della coscia feritolo il diede a morte. Fuggirono tutti da Roma, e Michelagnolo andossene a Pellestrina, ove dipinse una s. Maria Maddalena. E d'indi giunse a Napoli, e quivi operò molte cose.

Poscia andossene a Malta, ed introdotto a far riverenza al gran Maestro, fecegli il ritratto; onde quel Principe in segno di merito, dell'habito di s. Giovanni il regalò, e creollo Cavaliere ·di gratia. E quivi havendo non so che disparere con un Cavaliere di Giustitia, Michelagnolo gli fece non so che affronto, e però ne fu posto prigione, ma di notte tempo scalò le carceri, e se ne fuggi, ed arrivato all'isola di Sicilia operò alcune cose in Palermo; ma per esser perseguitato dal suo nemico, convennegli tornare alla Città di Napoli; e quivi ultimamente essendo da colui giunto, fu nel viso cosi fattamente ferito, che per li colpi quasi più non si riconosceva, e disperatosi della vendetta, con tutto che'egli vi si provasse, misesi in una felluca con alcune poche robe, per venirsene a Roma, tornando sotto la parola del Cardinale Gonzaga, che co'l Pontefice Paolo V. la sua rimissione trattava. Arrivato ch'egli fu nella spiaggia, fu in cambio fatto prigione, e posto dentro le carceri, ove per due giorni ritenuto, e poi rilassato, più la felluca non ritrovava si, che postosi in furia, come disperato andava per quella spiaggia sotto la sferza del Sol Leone a veder, se poteva in mare ravvisare il vascello, che le sue robe portava. Ultimamente arrivato in un luogo della spiaggia misesi in letto con febre maligna; e senza aiuto humano tra pochi giorni mori malamente, come appunto male havea vivuto.[3]

Se Michelagnolo Amerigi non fusse morto sì presto, haveria fatto gran profitto nell'arte per la buona maniera, che presa havea nel colorire del naturale; benche egli nel rappresentar le cose non havesse molto giudicio di scieglere il buono, e lasciare il cattivo. Nondimeno acquistò gran credito, e più si pagavano le sue teste, che l'altrui historie, tanto importa l'aura populare, che non giudica con gli occhi, ma guarda con l'orecchie. E nell'Accademia il suo ritratto è posto.

[1] Marginal note by Bellori in a copy of Baglione in the Vatican Library, first page:
Macinava li colori in Milano, et apprese a colorire et per haver occiso un suo compagno fuggì dal paese in bottega di mess. Lorenzo siciliano ricoverò in Roma dove, essendo estremamente bisognoso et ignudo, faceva le (teste) per un grosso l'una et né faceva tre il giorno, poi lavorò in casa di Anteveduto Gramatica mezze figure manco strapazzate. (canceled)
Michelangelo ritraeva tutte le sue figure da un lume medio et le faceva tutte ad un solo piano senza digradarle.
[2] Marginal note, second page:
Baglione
Bestia
Federico Zuchero era Pittore di . . . (canceled) è degno di gran lode il Caravaggio

che solo si mise ad imitare la natura contro l'uso di tutti gli altri che imitavano gli altri artefici. fu di statura piccola e brutto di volto.

[3] Marginal note, fourth page:

Morì l'anno 1609.

MICHELANGELO was born in Caravaggio in Lombardy and was the son of a fairly well-to-do master-builder named Amerigi. When he began to study painting he had to go to Milan because there was no one in Caravaggio who could give him proper training. He remained in Milan for some time and afterward went to Rome with the earnest intention of learning this praiseworthy profession. At first he was associated with a Sicilian painter who had a shop which turned out crude works of art.

Next he stayed for some months in the house of the Cavaliere Giuseppe d'Arpino. After this he tried to get along on his own and made some other small pictures which were drawn from his own reflection in a mirror. The first was a *Bacchus* with bunches of various kinds of grapes executed with great care but a little dry. He also painted a *Boy Bitten by a Lizard* which emerges from some flowers and fruits. The boy actually seems to cry out and the whole is carefully executed. However, he was unable to find a market for these works and finally found himself in a deplorable condition without money and practically in rags. Some gentlemen of the profession took pity on him and came to his aid and finally Maestro Valentino, an art dealer of San Luigi, arranged to take some of these works off his hands. On this occasion he made the acquaintance of the Cardinal del Monte, an enthusiastic lover of painting, who took Caravaggio into his house, and now, having a place to live and receiving an allowance, he regained his courage and reputation and painted for the Cardinal a *Concert of Youths* which was quite well drawn from nature. He also made a painting of a youth playing a lute which is lively and realistic; in it is a carafe of flowers filled with water in which one can easily distinguish the reflections of a window and other objects in the room. On the flowers is fresh dew which is rendered with exquisite accuracy. And this, he said, was the most beautiful painting he ever made.

He made a beautifully colored painting of a gypsy telling the fortune of a young man and a painting of *Divine Love Conquering Profane Love*. He also painted a rather terrifying *Head of the Medusa* with vipers for hair which was put on a round shield and presented by the Cardinal del Monte to the Grand Duke Ferdinand of Tuscany.

With the help of his Cardinal, he obtained the commission for the chapel of the Contarelli at San Luigi dei Francesi. Over the altar he made a *St. Matthew* with an angel; on the right is the *Calling of the Apostle* by the Saviour, and on the left the Saint is struck down on the altar by the executioner, with other figures. The vault of the chapel, however, is very well painted by Cavaliere Giuseppe d'Arpino.

Because of the naturalness of certain of Caravaggio's works at San Luigi his fame increased, the more so since these paintings were in the company of those by d'Arpino, whose talent was enviously acknowledged by his colleagues. Thus Caravaggio received the most exaggerated praise from the most spiteful people. But when Federico Zuccari came to look at them he said in my presence, "What is all the fuss about?" and as he carefully examined the entire work, he added, "I don't see anything here but the thought (pensiero) of Giorgione in the picture of the saint called to the Apostolate by Christ." Smiling and marveling at all this excitement, he shrugged his shoulders and then turned his back and left. Caravaggio made a seated *Cupid* done from life for the Marchese Vincenzo Giustiniani in which the color was so very good that thereafter Giustiniani had an unlimited enthusiasm for his works. Giustiniani also took for himself the picture of a certain *St. Matthew* which had been destined for the altar of San Luigi, but which no one had liked, simply because it was the work of Caravaggio. The Marchese was brought to this opinion by the great clamor which had been started by Prosperino, a painter of grotesques, who was one of Caravaggio's great advocates and at the same time was on bad terms with Cavaliere Giuseppe. Ciriaco Mattei was likewise seduced by the clamor; for him Caravaggio had painted a *St. John the Baptist*, *Our Lord going to Emmaus* and then a *St. Thomas* touching the wound in the Savior's side. Thus Caravaggio relieved this gentleman of many hundreds of scudi.

In the first chapel on the left in the church of S. Agostino he did a *Madonna of Loreto*, portrayed from life, with two pilgrims, one with muddy feet and the other wearing a soiled and torn cap. Because of the banality of his approach to the fundamental aspects of great painting, the populace made a great to-do about the picture.

In [Sta.] Maria del Popolo on the right side of the main altar, on the side walls of the chapel of the Signori Cerasi are Caravaggio's *Crucifixion of St. Peter* and, opposite it, the *Conversion of St. Paul*. These pictures were worked in another manner; but because they did not please the patron, they were taken by Cardinal Sannesio, and Caravaggio then painted the two pictures which one now sees there—in oil, because he used no other medium. Luck and Fame, so to speak, carried him through.

In the Chiesa Nuova, in the second chapel on the right is the *Dead Christ* about to be buried and some other figures, all done in oil, and this is said to be his best work.

For St. Peter's in the Vatican, Caravaggio made a *St. Anne and the Madonna*; the Virgin holds the Child between her legs, who, with the foot, crushes the head of the serpent. This work was executed for the Palafrenieri of the palace, but it was removed from the building by order of the Cardinals in charge of the edifice and then given by the Palafrenieri to the Cardinal Scipione Borghese.

For the Madonna della Scala in Trastevere Caravaggio painted the *Death of the Madonna*. However, because he had indecorously depicted her swollen and with bare legs, it was removed and bought by the Duke of Mantua to be placed in his splendid gallery.

For the Signori Costi, he painted a *Judith* cutting off the head of Holofernes and for others various pictures which I shall omit because they are not in public places; instead I will say something of his habits.

Michelangelo Amerigi was a satirical and haughty man; he would often speak badly of all painters of the past and present, no matter how distinguished they were, because he thought that he alone with his works had surpassed all the other men of his profession. However, some people consider him to have been the very ruination of painting, because many young artists, following his example, simply copy heads from life without studying the fundamentals of drawing and the profundity of art and are satisfied with color values alone. Thus they are incapable of putting two figures together or of composing a story because they do not understand the high value of the noble art of painting.

Because of the excessive ardor of his spirit, Michelangelo was a little dissolute and sometimes he seemed to look for the occasion to break his neck or even to risk the lives of others. He spent much time in the company of people who, like himself, were by nature quarrelsome and in the end he got into a fight with Ranuccio Tomassoni, a very likable young man. Because of certain differences over a game of ball they challenged one another to a duel and came to arms. Michelangelo gave Ranuccio a thrust which sent him to the ground with a wounded thigh and then killed him. Everyone involved in the affair fled from Rome and Michelangelo went to Palestrina where he painted a *Mary Magdalene*. From there he went to Naples and executed many paintings.

Afterwards he went to Malta and was invited to pay his respects to the Grand Master whose portrait he painted. As a sign of his satisfaction this exalted personage presented him with the mantle of St. John and made him Cavaliere di Gratia. In Malta Michelangelo had a dispute with a Cavaliere di Giustitia and somehow insulted him. For this he was thrown into prison, but escaped at night by means of a rope ladder and fled to the island of Sicily. In Palermo he executed several works, but because he was still being pursued by his enemy he had to return to Naples. There his enemy finally caught up with him and he was so severely slashed in the face that he was almost unrecognizable. Having given up the hope of avenging himself, although he had attempted to do so, he got together his few belongings and, boarding a felucca, he set out for Rome. He was returning to Rome on the word of Cardinal Gonzaga who was arranging for his pardon from Paul V. When Caravaggio went ashore he was mistakenly arrested. He was held for two days in prison and when he was released, the felucca was no longer to be found. This made him furious and in his desperation he started out along the beach in the cruel July sun, trying to catch sight of the vessel which was carrying his belongings. Finally he reached a village on the shore and was put to bed with a malignant fever. He was completely abandoned and within a few days he died miserably—indeed, just as he had lived.

If Michelangelo Amerigi had not died so soon he would have done a great deal for art through his great ability to paint from nature, even though he lacked judgment in choosing the good and omitting the bad in the things which he represented. Nevertheless, he acquired a great reputation and people paid more for his paintings of heads than for the figure compositions of others. Thus popularity is so important that people look at works of art not with their eyes, but with their ears. His portrait was placed in the Academy.

MICHELANG.º
MERIGI
DA
CARAVAGGIO

PIETRO BELLORI

Michelangelo da Caravaggio

DICESI che Demetrio antico Statuario fù tanto studioso della rassomiglianza che dilettossi più dell'imitatione che della bellezza delle cose; lo stesso habbiamo veduto in Michelangelo Merigi, il quale non riconobbe altro maestro che il modello, e senza elettione delle megliori forme naturali, quello che à dire è stupendo, pare che senz'arte emulasse l'arte. Dupplicò egli con la sua nascita la fama di Caravaggio nobile castello di Lombardia, patria insieme di Polidoro celebre pittore; l'uno, e l'altro di loro si esercitò da

Pietro Bellori, *Vite de' Pittori, Scultori et Architetti*, Rome, 1672, pp. 201 ff.

giovine nell'arte di murare, e portò lo schifo della calce neile fabbriche; poiche impiegandosi
Michele in Milano col padre, che era muratore, s'incontrò à far le colle ad alcuni Pittori, che
dipingevano à fresco, e tirato dalla voglia di usare i colori, accompagnossi con loro, ap-
plicandosi tutto alla pittura. Si avanzò per quattro, ò cinque anni, facendo ritratti, e dopo,
essendo egli d'ingegno torbido, e contentioso, per alcune discordie, fuggitosene da Milano,
giunse in Venetia, ove si compiacque tanto del colorito di Giorgione, che se lo propose per
iscorta nell'imitatione. Per questo veggonsi l'opere sue prime dolci, schiette, e senza quelle
ombre, ch'egli usò poi; e come di tutti li pittori Venetiani eccellenti nel colorito, fu Giorgione
il più puro, e'l più semplice nel rappresentare con poche tinte le forme naturali, nel modo
stesso portossi Michele, quando prima si fissò intento a riguardare la natura. Condottosi à
Roma vi dimorò senza ricapito, e senza provedimento, riuscendogli troppo dispendioso il
modello, senza il quale non sapeva dipingere, nè guadagnando tanto che potesse avanzarsi
le spese, siche Michele dalla necessità costretto andò à servire il Cavalier Giuseppe d'Arpino,
da cui fù applicato à dipinger fiori, e frutti si bene contrafatti, che da lui vennero à frequentarsi
à quella maggior vaghezza, che tanto hoggi diletta. Dipinse una caraffa di fiori con le tra-
sparenze dell'acqua, e del vetro, e co' i riflessi della fenestra d'una camera, sparsi li fiori di
freschissime rugiade, e altri quadri eccellentemente fece di simile imitatione. Ma esercitandosi
egli di mala voglia in queste cose, e sentendo gran rammarico di vedersi tolto alle figure,
incontrò l'occasione di Prospero Pittore di grottesche, ed uscì di casa di Giuseppe, per con-
trastargli la gloria del pennello. Datosi perciò egli à colorire, secondo il suo proprio genio,
non riguardando punto, anzi spregiando gli eccellentissimi marmi de gli Antichi, e le
pitture tanto celebri di Rafaelle, si propose la sola natura per oggetto del suo pennello.
Laonde essendogli mostrate le statue più famose di Fidia, e di Glicone; accioche vi accom-
modasse lo studio, non diede altra risposta, se non che distese la mano verso una moltitudine
di huomini, accennando che la natura l'haveva à sufficienza proveduto di maestri. E per
dare autorità alle sue parole, chiamò una Zingana, che passava à caso per istrada, e condottala
all'albergo, la ritrasse in atto di predire l'avventure, come sogliono queste donne di razza
Egittiana: Fecevi un giovine, il quale posa la mano col guanto sù la spada, e porge l'altra
scoperta à costei, che la tiene, e la riguarda; ed in queste due mezze figure tradusse Michele
si puramente il vero che venne à confermare i suoi detti. Quasi un simil fatto si legge di
Eupompo antico pittore; se bene hora non è tempo di considerare insino à quanto sia lodevole
tale insegnamento. E perche egli aspirava all'unica lode del colore, siche paresse vera l'incarnatione, la pelle, e'l sangue, e la superficie naturale, à questo solo volgeva intento l'occhio,
e l'industria, lasciando da parte gli altri pensieri dell'arte. Onde nel trovare, e disporre le
figure, quando incontravasi à vederne per la Città alcuna, che gli fosse piaciuta, egli si fermava
à quella inventione di natura, senza altrimente esercitare l'ingegno. Dipinse una fanciulla à
sedere sopra una seggiola con le mani in seno, in atto di asciugarsi li capelli, la ritrasse in
una camera, e aggiungendovi in terra un vasello d'unguenti, con monili, e gemme, la finse
per Madalena. Posa alquanto da un lato la faccia e s'imprime la guancia, il collo, e'l petto,
in una tinta pura, facile, e vera, accompagnata dalla semplicità di tutta la figura, con le
braccia in camicia, e la vesta gialla ritirata alle ginocchia dalla sottana bianca, di damasco

fiorato. Questa figura habbiamo descritta particolarmente per indicare li suoi modi naturali, e l'imitatione in poche tinte sino all verità del colore. Dipinse in un maggior quadro la Madonna, che si riposa dalla fuga in Egitto: Evvi un'Angelo in piedi, che suona il violino, San Giuseppe sedente gli tiene avanti il libro delle note, e l'Angelo è bellissimo; poiche volgendo la testa dolcemente in profilo, và discoprendo le spalle alate, e'l resto dell'ignudo interrotto da un pannolino. Dall'altro lato siede la Madonna, e piegando il capo, sembra dormire col bambino in seno. Veggonsi questi quadri nel palazzo del Principe Pamphilio, ed un altro degno dell'istessa lode nelle camere del Cardinale Antonio Barberini, disposto in trè mezze figure ad un giuoco di carte. Finsevi un giovinetto semplice con le carte in mano, ed è una testa ben ritratta dal vivo in habito oscuro, e di rincontro à lui si volge in profilo un giovine fraudolente, appoggiato con una mano sù la tavola del giuoco, è con l'altra dietro, si cava una carta falsa dalla cinta, mentre il terzo vicino al giovinetto guarda li punti delle carte, e con tre dita della mano li palesa al compagno, il quale nel piegarsi sù'l tavolino, espone la spalla al lume in giubbone giallo listato di fascie nere, nè finto è il colore nell'imitatione. Sono questi li primi tratti del pennello di Michele in quella schietta maniera di Giorgione, con oscuri temperati; e Prospero acclamando il nuovo stile di Michele accresceva la stima delle sue opere con util proprio, fra le prime persone della Corte. Il giuoco fù comprato dal Cardinale del Monte, che per dilettarsi molto della pittura, ridusse in buono stato Michele, e lo sollevò, dandogli luogo honorato in casa fra suoi gentilhuomini. Dipinse per questo Signore una musica di giovani ritratti dal naturale in mezze figure, una Donna in camicia, che suona il liuto con le note avanti, e Santa Caterina ginocchione appoggiata alla rota; li due ultimi sono ancora nelle medesime camere, ma riescono d'un colorito più tinto, cominciando già Michele ad ingagliardire gli oscuri. Dipinse San Giovanni nel deserto, che è un giovinetto ignudo à sedere, il quale sporgendo la testa avanti, abbraccia un agnello; e questo si vede nel palazzo del Signor Cardinal Pio. Ma il Caravaggio, che così egli già veniva da tutti, col nome della patria chiamato, facevasi ogni giorno più noto per lo colorito, ch'egli andava introducendo, non come prima dolce, e con poche tinte, ma tutto risentito di oscuri gagliardi, servendosi assai del nero per dar rilievo alli corpi. E s'inoltrò egli tanto in questo suo modo di operare, che non faceva mai uscire all'aperto del Sole alcuna delle sue figure, ma trovò una maniera di campirle entro l'aria bruna d'una camera rinchiusa, pigliando un lume alto, che scendeva a piombo sopra la parte principale del corpo, e lasciando il rimanente in ombra à fine di recar forza con vehemenza di chiaro, e di oscuro. Tanto che li pittori all'hora erano in Roma presi dalla novità, e particolarmente li giovini concorrevano à lui, e celebravano lui solo, come unico imitatore della natura, e come miracoli mirando l'opere sue, lo seguitavano à gara, spogliando modelli, ed alzando lumi; e senza più attendere à studio, ed insegnamenti, ciascuno trovava facilmente in piazza, e per via il maestro e gli esempi nel copiare il naturale. La qual facilità tirando gli altri, solo i vecchi pittori assuefatti alla pratica, rimanevano sbigottiti per questo novello studio di natura; nè cessavano di sgridare il Caravaggio, e la sua maniera, divolgando ch'egli non sapeva uscir fuori dalle cantine, e che povero d'inventione, e di disegno, senza decoro, e senz'arte, coloriva tutte le sue figure ad un lume, e sopra un piano, senza degradarle: Le quali accuse però non rallentavano il volo alla sua fama. Haveva il Caravaggio fatto il ritratto del Cavalier Marino, con premio di gloria trà gli huomini di lettere, venendo nell'Accademie cantato il nome del poeta, e del pittore; si come dal Marino stesso fù celebrata particolarmente la testa di Medusa di sua mano, che il Cardinale del Monte donò al Gran Duca di Toscana. Tantoche il Marino per una grandissima benevolenza, e compiacimento dell'operare del Caravaggio l'introdusse seco in casa di Monsignor Melchiorre Crescentij Chierico di Camera: colorì Michele il ritratto di questo dottissimo Prelato, e l'altro del Signor Virgilio Crescentij, il quale restato herede del Cardinale Contarelli, lo elesse à concorrenza di Giuseppino alle pitture della cappella in San Luigi de' Francesi. Così il Marino, che era amico di questi due pittori, consigliò, che a Giuseppe pratichissimo del fresco, si distribuissero le figure di sopra nel muro, ed a Michele li quadri ad olio. Quì avvenne cosa, che pose in grandissimo disturbo, e quasi fece disperare il Caravaggio, in riguardo della sua riputatione; poiche havendo egli terminato il quadro di mezzo di San Matteo, e postolo sù l'altare, fù tolto via da i Preti, con dire che quella figura non haveva decoro, nè aspetto di Santo, stando à sedere con le gambe incavalcate, e co'piedi rozzamente esposti al popolo. Si disperava il Caravaggio per tale affronto nella prima opera da esso pubblicata in Chiesa, quando il Marchese Vincenzo Giustiniani si mosse à favorirlo, e liberollo da questa pena; poiche interpostosi con quei Sacerdoti, si prese per se il quadro, e glie ne fece fare un altro diverso, che è quello si vede hora sù l'altare; e per honorare maggiormente il primo portatolo à casa, l'accompagnò poi con gli altri trè Vangelisti di mano di Guido, di Domenichino, e dell'Albano, trè li più celebri pittori, che in quel tempo havessero fama. Usò il Caravaggio ogni sforzo, per riuscire in questo secondo quadro: e nell'accommodare al naturale la figura del Santo, che scrive il Vangelo, egli la dispose con un ginocchio piegato sopra lo scabello, e con le mani al tavolino, intingendo la penna nel calamaio sopra il libro. In questo atto volge la faccia dal lato sinistro verso l'Angelo, il quale sospeso sù l'ali in aria, gli parla, e gli accenna, toccando con la destra l'indice della mano sinistra. Sembra l'Angelo lontano da color finto, e stà sospeso sù l'ali verso il Santo, ignude le braccia, e'l petto, con lo svolazzo d'un velo bianco, che lo cinge nell'oscurità del campo. Dal lato destro l'altare vi è Christo, che chiama San Matteo all'Apostolato, ritrattevi alcune teste al naturale, trà le quali il Santo lasciando di contar le monete, con una mano al petto, si volge al Signore; ed appresso un vecchio si pone gli occhiali al naso, riguardando un giovine che tira à se quelle monete assiso nell'angolo della tavola. Dall'altro lato vi è il martirio del Santo istesso in habito sacerdotale disteso sopra una banca: e'l manigoldo incontro brandisce la spada per ferirlo, figura ignuda, ed altre si ritirano con horrore. Il componimento, e li moti però non sono sufficienti all'historia; ancorche egli la rifacesse due volte; e l'oscurità della cappella, e del colore tolgono questi due quadri alla vista. Seguitò à dipingere nella Chiesa di Santo Agostino l'altro quadro della Cappella de' Signori Cavalletti, la Madonna in piedi col fanciullo fra le braccia in atto di benedire: s'inginocchiano avanti due Pellegrini con le mani giunte; e'l primo di loro è un povero scalzo li piedi, e le gambe, con la mozzetta di cuoio, e'l bordone appoggiato alla spalla, ed è accompagnato da una vecchia con la cuffia in capo. Ben tra le megliori opere, che uscissero dal pennello di Michele si tiene meritamente in istima la Depositione di Christo nella Chiesa Nuova de' Padri dell'Oratorio; situate le figure sopra una pietra nell'apertura del sepolcro.

Vedesi in mezzo il sacro corpo, lo regge Nicodemo da piedi, abbracciandolo sotto le ginocchia, e nell'abbassarsi le coscie, escono in fuori le gambe. Di là San Giovani sottopone un braccio alla spalla del Redentore, e resta supina la faccia, e'l petto pallido à morte, pendendo il braccio col lenzuolo; e tutto l'ignudo è ritratto con forza della più esatta imitatione. Dietro Nicodemo si veggono alquanto le Marie dolenti, l'una con le braccia sollevate, l'altra col velo à gli occhi, e la terza riguarda il Signore. Nella Chiesa della Madonna del Popolo entro la Cappella del'Assunta dipinta da Annibale Carracci, sono di mano del Caravaggio li due quadri laterali, la Crocifissione di San Pietro, e la Conversione di San Paolo, la quale historia è affatto senza attione. Seguitava egli nel favore del Marchese Vincenzo Giustiniani, che l'impiegò in alcuni quadri, l'Incoronatione di spine, e San Tomaso, che pone il dito nella piaga del costato del Signore, il quale gli accosta la mano, e si svela il petto da un lenzuolo, discostandolo dalla poppa. Appresso le quali mezze figure, colorì un Amore vincitore, che con la destra solleva lo strale, ed à suoi piedi giacciono in terra armi, libri, ed altri stromenti per trofeo. Concorsero al diletto del suo pennello altri Signori Romani, è tra questi il Marchese Asdrubale Mattei gli fece dipingere la presa de Christo all'horto, parimente in mezza figure. Tiene Giuda la mano alla spalla del maestro, dopo il bacio; intanto un Soldato tutto armato stende il braccio, e la mano di ferro al petto del Signore, il quale si arresta patiente, ed humile con le mani incrocicchiate avanti, fuggendo dietro San Giovanni, con le braccia aperte. Imitò l'armatura rugginosa di quel soldato coperto il capo, e'l volto dall'elmo, uscendo alquanto fuori il profilo; e dietro s'inalza una lanterna, seguitando due altre teste d'armati. Alli Signori Massimi colorì un Ecce Homo che fù portato in Ispagna, ed al Marchese Patritij la Cena in Emaus, nella quale vi è Christo in mezzo che benedice il pane, ed uno de gli Apostoli à sedere nel riconoscerlo, apre le braccia e l'altro fermo le mani sù la mensa, e lo riguarda con maraviglia: evvi dietro l'hoste con la cuffia in capo, ed una vecchia, che porta le vivande. Un'altra di queste inventioni dipinse per lo Cardinale Scipione Borghese alquanto differente; la prima più tinta, e l'una, e l'altra alla lode dell'imitatione del colore naturale; se bene mancano nella parte del decoro degenerando spesso Michele nelle forme humili, e vulgari. Per lo medesimo Cardinale dipinse San Girolamo, che scrivendo attentamente, distende la mano, e la penna al calamaio, e l'altra mezza figura di Davide, il quale tiene per li capelli la testa de Golia che è il suo proprio ritratto, impugnando la spada, lo figurò da un Giovine discoperto con una spalla fuori della camicia, colorito con fondi ed ombre fierissime, delle quali soleva valersi per dar forza alle sue figure, e componimenti. Si compiacque il Cardinale di queste, e di altre opere, che gli fece il Caravaggio, e l'introdusse avanti il Pontefice Paolo V. il quale da lui fù ritratto à sedere, e da quel Signore nè fù ben rimunerato. Al Cardinale Maffeo Barberini, che fù poi Urbano VIII. Sommo Pontefice, oltre il ritratto, fece il sacrificio di Abramo, il quale tiene il ferro presso la gola del figliuolo che grida, e cade.

Non però il Caravaggio con le occupationi della pittura, rimetteva punto le sue inquiete inclinationi; e dopo ch'egli haveva dipinto alcune hore del giorno, compariva per la Città con la spada al fianco, e faceva professione d'armi, mostrando di attendere ad ogn'altra cosa fuori che alla pittura. Venuto però à rissa nel giuoco di palla a corda con un giovine suo amico, battutisi con le racchette, e prese l'armi, uccise il giovine, restando anch'egli ferito.

Fuggitosene di Roma, senza denari, e perseguitato ricoverò in Zagarolo nella benevolenza del Duca D. Martio Colonna, dove colorì il quadro di Christo in Emaus frà li due Apostoli, ed un altra mezza figura di Madalena. Prese dopo il camino per Napoli; nella qual Città trovò subito impiego, essendovi già conosciuta la maniera, e'l suo nome. Per la Chiesa di San Domenico maggiore gli fù data à fare nella cappella de'Signori di Franco la flagellatione di Christo alla colonna, ed in Santa Anna de' Lombardi la Risurrettione. Si tiene in Napoli frà suoi quadri megliori la negatione di San Pietro nella Sagrestia di San Martino, figuratovi l'Ancella, che addita Pietro, el quale volgesi con le mani aperte, in atto di negar Christo; ed è colorito à lume notturno, con altre figure, che si scaldano al fuoco. Nella medesima Città, per la Chiesa della Misericordia dipinse le sette Opere in un quadro lungo circa dieci palmi: vedesi la testa di un vecchio, che sporge fuori dalla ferrata della prigione suggendo il latte d'una Donna, che à lui si piega con la mammella ignuda. Fra l'altre figure vi appariscono li piedi, e le gambe di un morto portato alla sepoltura; e dal lume della torcia di uno, che sostenta il cadavero, si spargono i raggi sopra il Sacerdote con la cotta bianca, e s'illumina il colore, dando spirito al componimento. Era il Caravaggio desideroso di ricevere la Croce di Malta solita darsi per gratia ad huomini riguardevoli per merito e per virtù, fece però risolutione di trasferirsi in quell'Isola, dove giunto fù introdotto avanti il Gran Maestro Vignacourt Signore Francese. Lo ritrasse in piedi armato, ed à sedere disarmato nell'habito di Gran Maestro, conservandosi il primo ritratto nell'Armerìa di Malta. Laonde questo Signore gli donò in premio la Croce; e per la Chiesa di San Giovanni gli fece dipingere la decollatione del Santo caduto à terra; mentre il Carnefice, quasi non l'habbia colpito alla prima con la spada, prende il coltello del fianco, afferrandolo ne'capelli per distaccargli la testa dal busto. Riguarda intenta Herodiade ed una vecchia seco inhorridisce allo spettacolo, mentre il Guardiano della prigione in habito turco, addita l'atroce scempio. In quest'opere il Caravaggio usò ogni potere del suo pennello, havendovi lavorato con tanta fierezza, che lasciò in mezze tinte l'imprimitura della tela: Si che, oltre l'honore della Croce, il Gran Maestro gli pose al collo una ricca collana d'oro, e gli fece dono di due schiavi, con altre dimostrationi della stima, e compiacimento dell'operar suo. Per la Chiesa medesima di San Giovanni, entro la Cappella della natione Italiana dipinse due mezze figure sopra due porte, la Madalena, e San Girolamo, che scrive; e fece un'altro San Girolamo con un teschio nella meditatione della morte, il quale tuttavia resta nel palazzo. Il Caravaggio riputavasi felicissimo con l'honore della Croce, e nelle lodi della pittura, vivendo in Malta con decoro della sua persona, ed abbondante di ogni bene. Ma in un subito il suo torbido ingegno lo fece cadere da quel prospero stato, e dalla benevolenza del Gran Maestro; poiche venuto egli importunamente à contesa con un Cavaliere nobilissimo, fù ristretto in carcere, e ridotto à mal termine di strapazzo, e di timore. Onde per liberarsi, si espose à gravissimo pericolo, ed iscavalcata di notte la prigione, fuggì sconosciuto in Sicilia, così presto che non potè essere raggiunto. Pervenuto in Siracusa, fece il quadro per la Chiesa di Santa Lucia, che stà fuori alla Marina: dipinse la Santa morta col Vescovo, che la benedice; e vi sono due che scavano la terra con la pala per sepelirla. Passando egli dopo à Messina, colorì à Cappuccini il quadro della Natività, figuratavi la Vergine col Bambino fuori la capanna rotta e disfatta d'assi, e di travi; e vi è San Giuseppe appoggiato al bastone con alcuni pastori in adoratione. Per le medesimi Padri dipinse San Girolamo, che stà scrivendo sopra il libro, e nella Chiesa de' Ministri de gl'infermi, nella Cappella de' Signori Lazzari, la Risurrettione di Lazzaro, il quale sostentato fuori del sepolcro, apre le braccia alla voce di Christo, che lo chiama, e stende verso di lui la mano. Piange Marta, e si maraviglia Madalena, e vi è uno, che si pone la mano al naso per ripararsi dal fetore del cadavero. Il quadro è grande, e le figure hanno il campo d'una grotta; col maggior lume sopra l'ignudo di Lazzaro, e di quelli che lo reggono, ed è sommamente in istima per la forza dell'imitatione. Ma la disgratia di Michele non l'abbandonava, e'l timore lo scacciava di luogo in luogo; tantoche scorrendo egli la Sicilia, di Messina si trasferì à Palermo, dove per l'Oratorio della Compagnia di San Lorenzo fece un'altra Natività; la Vergine che contempla il nato Bambino, con San Francesco, e San Lorenzo, vi è San Giuseppe à sedere, ed un Angelo in aria, diffondendosi nella notte i lumi fra l'ombre. Dopo quest'opera non si assicurando di fermarsi più lungamente in Sicilia, uscì fuori dell'Isola, e navigò di nuovo à Napoli, dov'egli pensava trattenersi, sin tanto che havesse ricevuto la nuova della gratia della sua remissione, per poter tornare à Roma; e cercando insieme di placare il Gran Maestro, gli mandò in dono una mezza figura di Herodiade con la testa di San Giovanni nel bacino. Non gli giovarono queste sue diligenze; perche fermatosi egli un giorno, sù la porta dell'hosteria del Ciriglio, preso in mezzo da alcuni con l'armi, fù da essi mal trattato, e ferito nel viso. Ond'egli quanto prima gli fù possibile montato sopra una feluca, pieno d'acerbissimo dolore s'inviò à Roma, havendo già con l'intercessione del Card. Gonzaga, ottenuto dal Papa la sua liberatione. Pervenuto alla spiaggia, la guardia Spagnuola che attendeva un altro Cavaliere, l'arrestò in cambio, e lo ritenne prigione. E se bene fù egli tosto rilasciato in libertà, non però rividde più la sua feluca che con le robbe lo conduceva. Onde agitato miseramente da affanno, e da cordoglio, scorrendo il lido al più caldo del Sole estivo, giunto a Porto Hercole, si abbandonò, e sorpreso da febbre maligna, morì in pochi giorni, circa gli anni quaranta di sua vita, nel 1609, anno funesto, per la pittura, havendoci tolto insieme Annibale Carracci, e Federico Zuccheri. Così il Caravaggio si ridusse à chiuder la vita, e l'ossa in una spiaggia deserta, ed all'hora che in Roma attendevasi il suo ritorno, giunse la novella inaspettata della sua morte, che dispiacque universalmente; e'l Cavalier Marino suo amicissimo se ne dolse ed adornò il mortorio con li seguenti versi.

> Fecer crudel congiura
> Michele à danni tuoi Morte, e Natura;
> Questa restar temea
> Da la tua mano in ogni imagin vinta,
> Ch'era da te creata, e non dipinta;
> Quella di sdegno ardea,
> Perche con larga usura,
> Quante la falce sua genti struggea,
> Tante il pennello tuo ne rifecea.

Giovò senza dubbio il Caravaggio alla pittura venuto in tempo che non essendo molto in uso il naturale, si fingevano le figure di pratica, e di maniera, e sodisfacevasi più al senso della vaghezza che della verità. Laonde costui togliendo ogni belletto, e vanità al colore, rinvigorì le tinte, e restituì ad esse il sangue, e l'incarnatione, ricordando à pittori l'imitatione. Non si trova però che egli usasse cinabri, nè azzurri nelle sue figure; e se pure talvolta li havesse adoperati, li ammorzava, dicendo ch'erano il veleno delle tinte; non dirò dell'aria turchina, e chiara, che egli non colorì mai nell'historie, anzi usò sempre il campo, e'l fondo nero; e'l nero nelle carni, restringendo in poche parti la forza del lume. Professavasi egli inoltre tanto ubbidiente al modello, che non si faceva propria ne meno una pennellata, la quale diceva non essere sua, ma della natura; e sdegnando ogn'altro precetto, riputava sommo artificio il non essere obligato all'arte. Con la quale novità hebbe tanto applauso, che à seguitarlo sforzò alcuni ingegni più elevati, e nutriti nelle megliori scuole, come fece Guido Reni che all hora si piegò alquanto alla maniera di esso, e si mostrò naturalista, riconoscendosi nella Crocifissione di San Pietro alle Trè Fontane, e così dopò Gio: Francesco da Cento. Per le quali lodi il Caravaggio non apprezzava altri che se stesso, chiamandosi egli fido, unico imitatore della natura; contuttociò molte, e le megliori parti gli mancavano, perche non erano in lui, nè inventione, nè decoro, nè disegno, nè scienza alcuna della pittura, mentre tolto da gli occhi suoi il modello restavano vacui la mano, e l'ingegno. Molti nondimeno invaghiti della sua maniera, l'abbracciavano volentieri, poiche senz'altro studio, e fatica si facilitavano la via al copiare il naturale, seguitando li corpi vulgari, e senza bellezza. Così sottoposta dal Caravaggio la maestà dell'arte, ciascuno si prese licenza, e nè seguì il dispregio delle cose belle, tolta ogni autorità all'antico, ed à Rafaelle, dove per la commodità de' modelli, e di condurre una testa dal naturale, lasciando costoro l'uso dell'historie, che sono proprie de' pittori, si diedero alle mezze figure, che avanti erano poco in uso. All'hora cominciò l'imitatione delle cose vili, ricercandosi le sozzure, e le deformità, come sogliono fare alcuni ansiosamente; se essi hanno à dipingere un armatura, eleggono la più rugginosa, se un vaso, non lo fanno intiero, ma sboccato, e rotto. Sono gli habiti loro calze, brache, e berrettoni, e così nell'imitare li corpi, si fermano con tutto lo studio sopra le rughe, e i difetti della pelle e dintorni, formano le dita nodose, le membra alterate da morbi. Per li quali modi il Caravaggio incontrò dispiaceri, essendogli tolti li quadri da gli altari, come in San Luigi habbiamo raccontato. La medesima sorte hebbe il Transito della Madonna nella Chiesa della Scala, rimosso per havervi troppo imitato una Donna morta gonfia. L'altro quadro di Santa Anna fù tolto ancora da uno de minori altari della Basilica Vaticana, ritratti in esso vilmente la Vergine con Giesù fanciullo ignudo, come si vede nella Villa Borghese. In Santo Agostino si offeriscono le sozzure de' piedi del Pellegrino: ed in Napoli frà le sette opere della Misericordia, vi è uno, che alsando il fiasco, beve con la bocca aperta, lasciandovi cadere sconciamente il vino. Nella cena in Emaus, oltre le forme rustiche delli due Apostoli, e del Signore figurato giovine senza barba, vi assiste l'hoste con la cuffia in capo, e nella mensa vi è un piatto d'uve, fichi, melagrane, fuori di stagione. Si come dunque alcune herbe producono medicamenti salutiferi, e veleni perniciosissimi, così il Caravaggio, se bene giovò in parte, fù nondimeno molto dannoso e mise sottosopra ogni ornamento, e buon costume della pittura. E veramente li pittori sviati dalla naturale imitatione, havevano bisogno di uno, che li rimettesse nel buon sentiero; ma come facilmente, per fuggire uno estremo, s'incorre nell'altro, così nell'allontanarsi dalla maniera, per seguitar troppo il naturale, si scostarono affatto dall'arte, restando ne gli errori, e nelle tenebre; finche Annibale Carracci venne ad illuminare le menti ed à restituire la bellezza all'imitatione. Tali modi del Caravaggio acconsentivano alla sua fisonomia, ed aspetto: era egli di color fosco, ed haveva foschi gli occhi, nere le ciglia, ed i capelli; e tale riuscì ancora naturalmente nel suo dipingere. La prima maniera dolce, e pura di colorire fù la migliore, essendosi avanzato in essa al supremo merito, e mostratosi con gran lodo ottimo coloritore lombardo: Ma egli trascorse poi nell'altra oscura, tiratovi dal proprio temperamento, come nè costumi ancora era torbido, e contentioso; gli convenne però lasciar prima Milano, e la patria, dopo fù costretto fuggir di Roma, e di Malta, ascondersi per la Sicilia, pericolare in Napoli, e morire disgratiatamente in una spiaggia. Non lascieremo di annotare li modi stessi del portamento è vestir suo, usando egli drappi e velluti nobili per adornarsi; ma quando poi si era messo un'habito, mai lo tralasciava, finche non gli cadeva in cenci. Era negligentissimo nel pulirsi; mangiò molti anni sopra la tela di un ritratto, servendosene per tovaglio mattina, e sera. Sono pregiati li suoi colori dovunque è in conto la pittura; fù portata in Parigi la figura di San Sebastiano con due ministri, che gli legano le mani di dietro: opera delle sue megliori. Il Conte di Benavente, che fù Vice-Re di Napoli, portò ancora in Ispagna la Crocifissione di Santo Andrea e'l Conte di Villa Mediana hebbe la mezza figura di Davide, e'l ritratto di un giovine con un fiore di melarancio in mano. Si conserva in Anversa, nella Chiesa de' Domenicani il quadro del Rosario, ed è opera che apporta gran fama al suo pennello. Tiensi ancora in Roma essere di sua mano Giove, Nettunno e Plutone nel Giardino Ludovisi à Porta Pinciana, nel Casino, che fù del Cardinale del Monte, il quale essendo studioso di medicamenti chimici, vi adornò il Camerino della sua distilleria, appropiando questi Dei a gl'elementi col globo del mondo nel mezzo di loro. Dicesi che il Caravaggio sentendosi biasimare di non intendere nè piani, nè prospettiva, tanto si aiutò collocando li corpi in veduta dal sotto in sù che volle contrastare gli scorti più difficili. E ben vero che Questi Dei non ritengono le loro proprie forme, e sono coloriti ad olio nella volta, non havendo Michele mai toccato pennello à fresco, come li suoi seguaci insieme ricorrono sempre alla commodità del colore ad olio, per ritrarre il modello. Molti furono quelli, che imitarono la sua maniera nel colorire dal naturale, chiamati perciò Naturalisti. . . .

DEMETRIUS, the ancient sculptor, is said to have been so eager to render the likeness of things that he cared more for imitating them than for their beauty. We have seen that the same is true of Michelangelo Merisi: he recognized no other master than the model and did not select the best forms of nature but emulated art—astonishingly enough—without art. The fame of the noble citadel, Caravaggio, in Lombardy was doubled by his birth since it was already the birthplace of Polidoro; both of them began as masons, carrying hods of mortar for constructions. When Michele was working in Milan with his father, who was a mason, he happened to prepare the sizing for some painters who were executing frescoes. Driven by his wish to handle colors himself, he kept company with them and dedicated himself entirely to painting. He went ahead for the next four or five years, painting portraits, but then, because of his turbulent and contentious nature, he got into trouble and had to leave Milan. He went to Venice where he was so pleased with Giorgione's color that he chose him as his guide in art. As a result of this, his first works are sweet, clean and without those shadows which he later used. Since of all the Venetian painters who excelled as colorists, Giorgione was the purest and simplest in representing natural forms with a few tones, Michele proceeded in the same manner when he first set himself to look at nature intently.

In Rome, he lived without a fixed lodging and without resources. Models were too expensive for him and without one he did not know how to paint, nor did he earn enough to take care of his expenses in advance, so he was forced to enter the services of Cavaliere Giuseppe d'Arpino. He was employed by him to paint flowers and fruits, which he imitated so well that from here on they began to attain the high degree of beauty so fully appreciated today. He painted a carafe of flowers in which he showed the transparency of the glass and of the water and in which one can see the reflection of a window in the room; the flowers are sprinkled with the freshest dew drops. He also made other excellent paintings of this kind, but he worked on such subjects with reluctance, feeling great regret at seeing himself kept away from figure painting. Thus he took an opportunity offered him by Prospero, a painter of grotesques, and left the house of Giuseppe to compete with him for artistic fame. Now he began to paint according to his own genius. He not only ignored the most excellent marbles of the ancients and the famous paintings of Raphael, but he despised them, and nature alone became the object of his brush. Thus when the most famous statues of Phidias and Glycon were pointed out to him as models for his painting, he gave no other reply than to extend his hand toward a crowd of men, indicating that nature had provided him sufficiently with teachers. To prove his words he called a gypsy who happened to be passing in the street and, taking her to his lodgings, he drew her in the act of fortune-telling as is the custom of these women of the Egyptian race. In this painting he also showed a youth with his gloved hand on his sword and the other hand bare, extended to the woman who holds and examines it. With these two half-figures Michele captured reality so well that he indeed confirmed what he had said. Almost the same is told about the ancient painter Eupompos, but this is not the time to discuss the laudability of such doctrines. Since Caravaggio aspired only to the glory of color, so that the complexion, the skin and blood and the natural surfaces might appear real, he directed the attention of his eyes and the energy of his mind exclusively to this end, leaving aside all other concepts of art. Therefore in finding and arranging his figures, whenever it happened that he came upon someone in the town who pleased him, he was fully satisfied with this invention of nature and made no effort to exercise his brain further. He painted a young girl seated on a chair with her hands in her lap in the act of drying her hair; he portrayed her in a room with a small ointment vessel, jewels and gems placed on the floor; thus he would have us believe that she is the *Magdalene.* She holds her face a little to one side, and her cheek, neck and breast are rendered in pure, facile, and true tones, which are enhanced by the simplicity of the whole composition. She wears a blouse, and her yellow dress is drawn up to her knees over the white underskirt of flowered damask. We have described this figure in particular in order to characterize his naturalistic method and the way in which he imitates real color using only a few tints. On a large canvas he painted the *Rest on the Flight into Egypt*; here there is a standing angel playing a violin, while the seated St. Joseph holds the music book for him; the very beautiful angel turns his head sweetly in profile, displaying his winged shoulders and the rest of his nude body except for the part covered by a linen cloth. On the other side sits the Madonna and, bowing her head, she seems to sleep with the baby at her breast. These paintings are in the palace of Prince Pamphili. Another painting which is worthy of the same praise is in the apartment of Cardinal Antonio Barberini, and it represents three half-figures of men playing cards. Here Michele represented a simple youth holding cards and dressed in a dark suit, his head well drawn from life. Opposite him in profile, a fraudulent youth who leans with one hand on the gaming table and with the other, held behind him, takes a false card from his belt. A third figure near the boy looks at the marks on the cards and with three fingers reveals them to his companion. The companion leans on the table exposing his shoulder to the light; he wears a yellow jacket striped with black bands. There is nothing false in the coloring of this work. These are the first strokes from Michele's brush in the clear manner of Giorgione, with tempered shadows. By acclaiming Michele's new style, Prospero augmented the renown of his works among the leading persons of the court—to his own advantage as well as to that of Caravaggio. *The Card Game* was bought by Cardinal del Monte, who was such an enthusiastic lover of paintings that he helped Caravaggio out of his difficulties by giving him an honored place in his household. For this prelate Michele painted a *Concert of Youths* in half-figures, drawn from life; a woman in a blouse playing a lute with the music before her and a *St. Catherine* on her knees leaning against her wheel. The last two paintings, which are still in the same room, show a more saturated coloring, since Michele was already beginning to strengthen his shadows. He painted *St. John in the Desert* as a seated, nude youth who thrusts his head forward and embraces a lamb; this painting is in the palace of Cardinal Pio. Caravaggio (for he was now generally called by the name of his native town) was making himself more and more notable for the color scheme which he was introducing, not soft and sparingly tinted as before, but reinforced throughout with bold shadows and a great deal of black to give relief to the forms. He went so far in this manner of working that he never brought his figures out into the daylight, but placed them in the dark brown atmosphere of a closed room, using a high light that descended vertically over the principal parts of the bodies while leaving the remainder in shadow in order to give force through a strong contrast of light and dark. The painters then in Rome were greatly impressed by his novelty and the younger ones especially gathered around him and praised him as the only true imitator of nature. Looking upon his works as miracles, they outdid each other in following his method, undressing their models and placing their lights high; without paying attention to study and teachings, each found easily in the piazza or in the street his teacher or his model for copying nature. This facile manner attracted many, and only the old painters who were accustomed to the old ways were shocked at the new concern for nature, and they did not cease to decry Caravaggio and his manner. They spread it about that he did not know how to come out of the cellar and that, poor in invention and design, lacking in decorum and art, he painted all his figures in one light and on one plane without any gradations. These accusations, however, did not retard the growth of his fame. Caravaggio painted the portrait of Cavaliere Marino, the most famous among men of letters, and the names of the poet and the painter were thus celebrated together in the academies. The *Head of Medusa* by Caravaggio, which Cardinal del Monte gave to the Grand Duke of Tuscany, was particularly praised by Marino. Thus it happened that Marino, because of his good will toward Caravaggio and the pleasure which he took in his works, introduced him into the house of Monsignor Melchiorre Crescenzi, the clerk of the papal court. Michele painted the portrait of this most learned prelate and another one of Virgilio Crescenzi, who, as the heir of Cardinal Contarelli, chose him together with Giuseppino to execute the paintings in the chapel of S. Luigi dei Francesi. Marino, who was a friend of both painters, suggested that the figures high up on the wall be assigned to Giuseppe, an expert in fresco, and the paintings in oil to Michele. Then something happened which greatly disturbed Caravaggio and almost made him despair of his reputation. After the central picture of *St. Matthew* had been finished and placed on the altar, it was taken away by the priests, who said that the figure with his legs crossed and his feet crudely exposed to the public had neither decorum nor the appearance of a saint. Caravaggio was in despair because of this affront to the first of his works in a church; however, the Marchese Vincenzo Giustiniani acted in his favor and freed him from this grief. He intervened with the priests, took the painting for himself, and had Caravaggio do another in a different way, which is the one now seen above the altar. To show how much he honored the first painting he took it in his house, and later placed beside it paintings of the other three Evangelists: by Guido, Domenichino, and Albani, the three most celebrated painters of the time. Caravaggio exerted every effort to succeed in his second picture; he tried to give a natural pose to the saint writing the gospel by showing him with one knee bent on the stool and with his hands on the small table in the act of dipping his pen in the inkwell placed on the book. He turns his face to the left toward the winged angel who, suspended in air, speaks to him and makes a sign to him by touching the index finger of his left hand with that of his right hand. The color makes the angel seem far away as he floats, suspended on his wings, in the direction of the saint; his arm and breast are nude and a fluttering white veil surrounds him in the darkness of the background. On the right side of the altar is a *Christ Calling St. Matthew to the Apostolate*. Here several heads are drawn from life, among which is the saint, who interrupts his counting of money and with one hand on his breast, turns toward the Lord. Close to the saint is an old man placing his spectacles on his nose and looking at a young man seated at one corner of the table, drawing the coins to himself. On the other side is the *Martyrdom* of the saint who, dressed in priestly robes, is stretched out on a bench. Above him is the nude figure of the executioner brandishing his sword to strike him, while other figures draw back in horror. The composition and the movements however, are not adequate for the story, even though Caravaggio repeated it twice. The darkness of the chapel and of the color makes it difficult to see these two pictures.

After this in the chapel of the Signori Cavalletti in the church of Sto. Agostino, he executed a standing *Madonna* holding the Child in her arms and in the act of giving benediction. Kneeling before her are two pilgrims with folded hands; one is a poor man with bare legs and feet, a leather pilgrim's cape, and his staff leaning on his shoulder; he is accompanied by an old woman with a cap on her head. One of the best works by Caravaggio is the *Deposition of Christ* in the Chiesa Nuova of the Oratorians which has received well-deserved praise. The figures in the painting are placed on a stone in the opening of the sepulcher. In the center Nicodemus supports the Sacred Body under the knees, embracing it, and as the hips are lowered, the legs jut out. On the other side St. John places one arm under the shoulder of the Redeemer whose face is upturned and his breast deathly pale; one arm hangs down with the sheet and all the nude parts are drawn forcefully and faithfully from nature. Behind Nicodemus are seen the mourning Marys, one with her arms upraised, another with her veil raised to her eyes, and the third looking at the Lord.

In the church of the Madonna del Popolo in the chapel of the Assumption, painted by Annibale Carracci, are the two side pictures by Caravaggio, the *Crucifixion of St. Peter* and the *Conversion of St. Paul*, which story is entirely without action.

Caravaggio continued to be favored by the Marchese Vincenzo Giustiniani, who commissioned him to make some pictures, the *Crowning with Thorns* and *St. Thomas* placing his finger in the wound of the Lord's side; the Lord draws St. Thomas' hand closer to him and pulls the shroud away from His breast. Besides these half-figures he painted a *Victorious Amor* raising his arrow in his right hand; arms, books, and other instruments are lying at his feet as trophies. Other Roman gentlemen were also pleased with his works and vied with one another to obtain them. Among them was the Marchese Asdrubale Mattei, who had him paint the *Taking of Christ in the Garden*, which is also in half-figures. Judas lays his hand on the shoulder of the Lord after the kiss, and a soldier in full armor extends his arm and his ironclad hand to the chest of the Lord who stands patiently and humbly with his arms crossed before him; behind, St. John is seen fleeing with outstretched arms. Caravaggio imitated even the rust on the armor of the soldier whose head is covered by a helmet so that only his profile can be seen; behind him a lantern is raised and one can distinguish two more heads of armed men. For Massimi he painted an *Ecce Homo* which was taken to Spain, and for the Marchese Patrizi he did the *Supper at Emmaus*. Here Christ is blessing the bread and one of the apostles seated at the table recognizes Him and stretches out his arms while the other apostle rests his hands on the table and stares at Him in wonderment. Behind the table are the host with a cap on his head and an old woman who brings food. For Cardinal Scipione Borghese he painted a somewhat different version of the subject; the first is in deeper tones but both are praiseworthy for their imitation of natural color even though they lack decorum. For Michele's work often degenerated into low and vulgar forms.

For the same Cardinal he painted *St. Jerome*, who writes attentively, extending his hand to dip his pen in an inkwell; for him he also painted a half-length *David* holding by its hair the head of Goliath—Caravaggio's own portrait. David, who is shown grasping the hilt of his sword, is represented as a bareheaded youth with one shoulder out of his shirt. The picture has the bold shadows which Caravaggio liked to use to give force to his figures and compositions.

The Cardinal, pleased with these and other works that Caravaggio did for him, introduced him to Pope Paul V, of whom he made a seated portrait for which he was well rewarded.

For Cardinal Maffeo Barberini, who was later the Sovereign Pontiff, Urban VIII, he painted, in addition to his portrait, a *Sacrifice of Abraham*, in which Abraham holds the knife near the throat of his son who screams and falls.

Caravaggio's preoccupation with his painting did not calm the restlessness of his spirit. Having spent some hours of the day in his studio, he would appear in various parts of the city with his sword at his side as though he were a professional swordsman, giving the impression that he attended to everything but painting. In a ball game, he had an argument with one of his young friends and they began to beat each other with the rackets. Finally, they resorted to arms, and Caravaggio killed the youth and was also wounded himself. Having fled from Rome, penniless and pursued, he found refuge in Zagarolo under the protection of the Duke, Marzio Colonna. There, he painted the picture of *Christ at Emmaus* between two apostles as well as a half-length figure of the *Magdalene*. Afterward he went to Naples where he immediately found commissions because his manner and name were already known there. In the chapel of the Signori di Franco in the church of S. Domenico Maggiore he was commissioned to do the *Flagellation of Christ* at the column and at Santa Anna de' Lombardi the *Resurrection*. In Naples his *Denial of St. Peter* in the sacristy of S. Martino is considered to be among his best works. Here the servant-girl points to St. Peter who, turning around, opens his hands in the act of denying Christ; the painting is a night scene in which one sees various figures warming their hands at a fire. For the church of the Misericordia in the same city, he painted the *Seven Acts of Mercy*, a painting about ten palmi long. Here, one sees an old man who sticks his head out between the bars of a prison and sucks milk from the bared breast of a woman who bends down to him. Elsewhere in the painting appear the feet and legs of a dead man who is being carried to the sepulcher; the light from a torch carried by the man who supports the corpse shines on the white surplice of the priest, illuminating and giving life to the composition.

Caravaggio wished very much to receive the Cross of Malta which was usually given "per grazia" to notable persons for merit and virtue. He therefore went to Malta and, when he arrived, he was introduced to the Grand Master, Wignacourt, a French nobleman. Caravaggio portrayed him standing dressed in armor and seated without armor, wearing the robe of a Grand Master; the first of these portraits is in the Armory of Malta. As a reward for this the Grand Master presented him with the Cross of Malta. For the Church of S. Giovanni he had him paint the *Beheading of St. John* who has fallen to the ground while the executioner, as though he had not quite killed him with the blow of his sword, takes his knife from his side and grasps the saint by the hair in order to cut off his head. Salome looks on with fascination, while an old woman with her is horror-stricken at the spectacle, and the warden of the prison, who is dressed in Turkish garb, points to the atrocious massacre. Caravaggio worked on his painting with such fervor that the priming shows through the half-tones. In addition to honoring Caravaggio with the Cross of Malta, our Grand Master gave him a precious chain of gold and two slaves along with other signs of his esteem and satisfaction with his work. Also for S. Giovanni, in the Italian Chapel, he painted two half-figures over the doors: the *Magdalene* and *St. Jerome* writing. He painted another *St. Jerome*, meditating upon death with a skull before him, which is still in the Palace. Caravaggio was overjoyed that he had been honored with the Cross and that his painting was so much praised. He was also happy to be able to live with dignity and an abundance of good things.

But all of a sudden his turbulent nature brought this prosperity to an end and caused him to lose the favor of the Grand Master; because of a very inopportune quarrel with a most noble Cavaliere he was thrown into prison and was subjected to misery, fear, and maltreatment. With great personal danger, he managed to escape from prison in the night and fled unrecognized to Sicily with such great speed that he could not be overtaken. Having arrived in Syracuse, he made a picture for the church of Santa Lucia which is outside the city on the seashore. Here, he painted the dead *St. Lucy* blessed by the Bishop and showed two men who are digging her grave with shovels. Next, he went to Messina where he painted a *Nativity* for the church of the Capuchins; the Virgin and Child are placed before the dilapidated shed, with its boards and rafters falling apart, and St. Joseph leans on his staff while shepherds adore the Child. For the same fathers he painted a *St. Jerome* writing in a book and in the chapel of the Signori Lazzari of the Chiesa de'Ministri degli Infermi he made the *Resurrection of Lazarus*. Lazarus is shown supported outside the sepulcher; he opens his arms at the voice of Christ who calls him and extends his hand toward him. Martha weeps, the Magdalene marvels, and there is a man who puts his hand to his nose to protect himself from the stench of the corpse. The painting is large, and the figures are placed on the ground of a cave with the strongest light on the nude figures of Lazarus and those who support him. The painting is most highly esteemed for its realistic power. But Caravaggio's misfortune did not abandon him and fear drove him from place to place. He hurried across Sicily from Messina to Palermo and there for the Oratorio di San Lorenzo he painted another *Nativity*, representing the Virgin contemplating the newborn Babe with St. Francis, St. Lawrence, St. Joseph seated, and an angel above. The lights are diffused among the shadows of the night.

When this work was finished he felt that it was no longer safe to remain in Sicily and so he left the island and sailed back to Naples, intending to remain there until he received news of his pardon so that he could return to Rome. At the same time seeking to regain the favor of the Grand Master of Malta, he sent him as a gift a half-length figure of *Salome* with the head of St. John the Baptist in a basin. These attentions availed him nothing, for stopping one day in the doorway of the Osteria del Ciriglio he found himself surrounded by several armed men who manhandled him and gashed his face. Thus as soon as it was possible he boarded a felucca, and, suffering the bitterest pain, he started out for Rome. Through the intercession of Cardinal Gonzaga he had already obtained his liberation from the Pope. When he went ashore the Spanish guard arrested him by mistake, taking him for another Cavaliere, and held him prisoner. Although he was soon released, the felucca which was carrying him and his possessions was no longer to be found. Thus in a state of anxiety and desperation he ran along the beach in the full heat of the summer sun, and when he reached Porto Ercole he collapsed and was seized by a malignant fever. He died within a few days at about forty years of age in 1609, a lamentable year for painting since it also took Annibale Carracci and Federico Zuccari.

Thus Caravaggio finished his life and was buried on a deserted shore. Just when his return was awaited in Rome, came the unexpected news of his death, which was universally regretted, and the Cavaliere Marino, his very close friend, mourned his death and honored his memory with the following verses:

> Death and Nature, Michele, made a cruel plot against you;
> Nature feared being surpassed by your hand in every image that you
>   created, rather than painted;
> Death burned with indignation because your brush returned to life, with
>   large interest, as many men as his scythe could cut down.

There is no question that Caravaggio advanced the art of painting because he came upon the scene at a time when realism was not much in fashion and when figures were made according to convention and manner and satisfied more the taste for gracefulness than for truth. Thus by avoiding all prettiness and vanity in his color, Caravaggio strengthened his tones and gave them blood and flesh. In this way he induced his fellow painters to work from nature. Nowhere did Caravaggio use cinnabar reds and azure blues in his figures and even when he sometimes had to use them, he toned them down, saying that they were the poison of colors. He never introduced clear blue atmosphere into his pictures; on the contrary he always used black for the ground and the depths and also for the flesh tones, limiting the force of the light to a few places. Moreover, he followed his model so slavishly that he did not take credit for even one brush stroke, but said that it was the work of nature. He repudiated every other precept and considered it the highest achievement in art not to be bound to the rules of art. Because of these innovations he received so much acclaim that some artists of great talent and instructed in the best schools were impelled to follow him. For example, Guido Reni adapted himself for a time to the manner of Caravaggio, showing himself to be a realist, as one can see by looking at the *Crucifixion of St. Peter* in the church of the Tre Fontane. And so, later on, did Giovanni Francesco Guercino.

Such praise caused Caravaggio to appreciate no one but himself and he claimed to be the one faithful imitator of nature. With all this, many of the best elements of art were not in him; he possessed neither invention, nor decorum, nor design, nor any knowledge of the science of painting. The moment the model was taken away from his eyes his hand and his imagination remained empty. Nevertheless, many artists were infatuated by his manner and accepted it willingly, since without study or effort it enabled them to make facile copies after nature and to imitate forms which were vulgar and lacking in beauty. With the majesty of art thus suppressed by Caravaggio, everyone did as he pleased, and soon the value of the beautiful was discounted. The antique lost all authority, as did Raphael, and because it was so easy to obtain models and paint heads from nature, these painters abandoned the use of histories which are proper to painters and redirected themselves to half-length figures which were previously very little used. Now began the representation of vile things; some artists began to look enthusiastically for filth and deformity. If they have to paint armor they choose the rustiest; if a vase, they do not make it complete but broken and without a spout. The costumes they paint are stockings, breeches and big caps and when they paint figures they give all of their attention to the wrinkles, the defects of the skin and the contours, depicting knotted fingers and limbs disfigured by disease.

Because of this Caravaggio encountered much displeasure and some of his pictures were taken down from their altars, as we have said to be the case at San Luigi. The same thing has happened to his *Death of the Virgin* in the Church of the Scala because it imitated too closely the corpse of a woman. Another of his paintings, the *Virgin and St. Anne,* was taken down from one of the minor altars of the Vatican Basilica because the Virgin and the nude Christ Child were too indecently portrayed (as one can see in the Villa Borghese). In Sant' Agostino, one is presented with the dirt on the Pilgrim's feet and in Naples among the *Seven Works of Mercy,* there is a man who raises his flask to drink and lets the wine run into his open mouth in a coarse way. In the *Supper at Emmaus,* besides the rustic character of the two apostles and of the Lord who is shown young and without a beard, Caravaggio shows the innkeeper who serves with a cap on his head and on the table there is a plate of grapes, figs, and pomegranates out of season.

Like herbs which produce salutary medicaments as well as the most pernicious poisons, Caravaggio, though he did some good, nevertheless caused a great amount of damage and played havoc with every embellishment and good usage of painting. Indeed, painters who strayed too far from nature needed someone to set them in the right path again, but how easy it is to fall into one extreme while fleeing from another. By withdrawing from mannerism and following nature too closely they separated themselves from art altogether and remained in error and darkness until finally Annibale Carracci came to enlighten their minds and to restore beauty to the representation of nature.

Caravaggio's way of working corresponded to his physiognomy and appearance. He had a dark complexion and dark eyes, black hair and eyebrows and this, of course, was reflected in his paintings. His first manner, with its sweet and pure color, was his best; in it he made the greatest achievements and proved himself to be the most excellent Lombard colorist. But later, driven by his peculiar temperament, he gave himself up to the dark manner, and to the expression of his turbulent and contentious nature. Because of his temperament, Caravaggio was forced to leave Milan and his homeland and then to flee from Rome and from Malta, to go into hiding in Sicily, to live in danger in Naples and to die in misery on a deserted beach. Something should also be said of his dress and of his behavior. He adorned himself with velvet and other fine materials but when he had put on one costume, he never changed it until it had fallen into rags. He was very negligent of personal cleanliness and for many years morning and evening he used the canvas of a portrait as a tablecloth.

Caravaggio's colors are prized wherever painting is esteemed. One of his best works, a figure of *St. Sebastian* with two executioners tying his hands behind his back, was taken to Paris. The count of Benevento, who was Viceroy of Naples, took his *Crucifixion of St. Andrew* to Spain and the Count of Villa Mediana owned the half-length figure of *David* and the *Portrait of a Youth* with an orange blossom in his hand. The church of the Dominicans in Antwerp preserves his painting of the *Rosario*, a work which has made him very famous. In Rome, in the Ludovisi Garden at Porta Pinciana, in the Casino which belonged to Cardinal del Monte, there is also a *Jupiter, Neptune, and Pluto* which is thought to be by Caravaggio; the Cardinal, who was interested in chemical medicine, properly adorned his laboratory with these gods to signify the elements with the globe of the world in the midst of them. It is said that when Caravaggio heard himself blamed for not understanding either planes or perspective, he challenged such criticism by arranging his figures to be seen from below (al di sotto in sù) so as to compete with the most difficult foreshortenings. However, these gods do not retain their proper forms and they are all painted in oil on the vault, since Michele had never painted in fresco, just as his followers always take the easy way of using oil color to portray the model. Many were those who imitated his manner of painting from nature and for that reason they were called "naturalists."

GIULIO MANCINI

Trattato . . . .

Deve molto questa nostra età *[questo nostro secolo]* a Michelangelo da Caravaggio, per il suo *[nuovo]* modo di colorire che ha introdotto seguito adesso assai comunemente. *[che ha introdotto che adesso da molti è seguitato et abbracciato].* Questo nacque in Caravaggio di assai honorati cittadini (marginal note: poichè il Padre fu maestro di Casa et Architetto del Marchese di Caravaggio) *[equali a qual'si voglia di questa terra].* Studiò da fanciulezza per 4 (o 5) *[tre o quattro]* anni in Milano con diligenza, ancorche di quando in quando facesse *[volesse mostrare d'essere sciocco facendo di quando in quando]* qualche stravaganza causata da quel calor e spirito così grande. *[nata e fatta dal calor' di quel ingegno così grande.]* Doppo se ne passò a Roma d'età in circa 20 anni dove essendo poco provisto di denari stette con Pandolfo Pucci da Recanati benefiziato di S. Pietro dove le conveniva andar per la parte, et altri servitij non convenienti all'esser suo *[servitù non convenienti al suo natale, e virtù]*, e quel ch'è peggio, se la passava la sera con un insalata, quale li serviva per antipasto, pasto e pospasto, e come dice il Caporale per companatico e per stecco d'onde dopo alcuni mesi partitosi con poca sodisfattione chiamò poi questo benefizíato suo padrone, Monsignor Insalata. In questo tempo *[Nel tempo che vi stette]* fece per esso alcune copie di devotione, che sono in Recanati, e per *[sè da]* vendere un putto che piange per esser stato morso da un Racano, che tiene in mano, *[che fu causa che vendutolo, e preso animo da poter vivere da sè, si partì da questo suo così scarso maestro o Padrone,]* e doppo pur un putto, che mondava una pera *[mela]* con il cortello, et il ritratto d'un hoste dove si ricoverava. Fra tanto fu assalito da una *[grave]* malatia, che trovandolo senza denari fu necessitato andarsene allo Spedal della Consolatione, dove *[e]* nella convalescenza *[, e dopo,]* fece molti quadri per il Priore che se li portò in Cicilia *[Siviglia]* sua patria. Doppo mi vien detto che stesse in casa del Cav.ʳ Giuseppe, e di Mons.ʳ Fantin Petrignani, che li dava commodità d'una stanza nel qual tempo fece molti quadri, et in particolare una Zingara, che dà la Bonaventura ad un giovanetto. La Madonna che và in Egitto, la Madalena convertita, s. Gio. Evangelista *[, et altro,]* e dopo il Christo deposto nella Chiesa nova, li quadri di S. Luigi, la morte della Mad.ⁿᵃ. della Scala, che l'ha adesso il Ser.ᵐᵒ di Mantova fatta levar di detta Chiesa da quei padri, perchè in persona della Madonna haveva ritratto una Cortigiana, *[da lui amata, e così scrupolosa, e senza devozione et in particolare appresso que' buoni Padri;]* la Mad.ⁿᵃ. di Loreto in S. Agostino, e quella dell'Altar de Palafrenieri in S. Pietro, molti quadri che possiede l'Ill.ᵐᵒ Borghese, al Popolo la Cappella del Cerasi, molti quadri privati, in casa Mattei, Giustiniano, e Sennesio *[che possiede adesso l'Ill.ᵐᵒ. Borghese con molti quadri privati che si vedono per quei studij privati, et imparticolare in casa Mattei, Giustiniani e Card.ˡᵉ. Senesio, che sono copiati, e ritoccati da quelli che sono nella Madonna del Popolo nella Cappella del (Cerasi)].* In ultimo per alcuni eventi, che corse pericolo di vita, che per salvarsi aiutato do Onorio Longo amazzò l'inimico *[d'essere ammazzato che per salvarsi ammazzò*

Giulio Mancini. *Trattato* . . . Mss. It. 5571, Bibl. Marciana, Venice, pp. 59-61 and variant readings from Cod. Pal. 597, Bibl. Nat., Florence, pp. 115 ff. in italics. See *Paragone* 17, 1951, p. 47.

l'inimico (aiutato ancora a riparargli la superchieria dal Sig. Honorio Longo che a questi giorni se n'è passato all'altra vita)] fu necessitato fuggirsi da Roma e di primo salto fu in Zagarola, ivi, trattenuto secretamente da quel Prencipe *[che molto bene lo conosceva]* dove fece una Madalena e Christo che va in Emaus, che lo comprò in Roma il Costa, *[che lo mandò a vendere a Roma,]* e con questi denari se ne passò a Napoli, dove operò alcune cose, e di lì se ne passò a Malta, dove condusse alcune opere con gusto del Gran Maestro, che in segno di honore, come dicono, gli dette l'habito di sua religione, donde partitosi con speranza di rimettersi viene à Civita Vecchia (marginal note: Portercole), dove soprapreso da febre maligna, in colmo di sua gloria, che era d'età di 35 in 40 anni, morse, *[forse]* di stento, e senza cura, et in luogo ivi vicino *[dove era ritirato]* fu sepellito, *[e così fu quasi una morte violenta con quella di Pulidoro suo paesano assassinato in Campagna, e questo derelitto d'aiuto che era cosa degna di considerazione il vedere il fine così simile in due paesani et Artefici di medesima professione morir quasi d'una medesima o almen simile morte, seguita dell'uno e dell'altro con grandissimo danno della professione; perchè]* non si puo negare che per una figura sola, per le teste e colorito, non sia arrivato ad un gran segno, e che la profession di questo secolo non li sia molto obligata. Ma *[si deve avvertire]* che questo suo gran saper d'arte, l'haveva accompagnato con una *[gran]* stravaganza di costumi, perche *[Che per fare intendere, e dimostrare questa verità, è da sapere, che]* haveva un unico fratello sacerdote, huomo di lettere, e bon costumi qual sentendo i gridi *[valor]* del fratello, gli venne voglia di vederlo, e mosso da fraterno amore, *[per tale effetto]* se ne viene a Roma, e sapendo che era trattenuto in casa dell' Illmo. Card^{le} del Monte e il stravagante modo del fratello, pensò esser bene di far prima motto all' Illmo Card.^{le} et esporli il tutto, come fece. *[et appreso il stravagante modo di procedere, avanti che si scoprisse al fratello, pensò esser bene di far reverenza prima al Cardinale, e esplicarli il tutto.]* Hebbe bonissime parole che tornasse frà tre giorni. *[et il buon sacerdote se n'andò via con avvertenza che fra tre giorni si lasciasse rivedere.]* Obbedisce. Fratanto il Card^{le} chiama Michelangelo, gli dimanda se ha parenti, gli risponde che nò, ne potendo creder che quel sacerdote gli dicesse bugia in cosa, che si poteva ritrovare, e che non gli risultava utile, perciò fra tanto fà cercare frà paesani *[e che lo scrivesse quant'ai parenti come lo vedeva. Restò stupefatto il Card^{le} che o questo negasse, o quello asserisse una cosa tanto chiara, e facil ad essere ritrovata, nè poteva credere che quel sacerdote d'aspetto d'huomo da bene gli havesse a dir bugia, e con pericolo in cosa che non gli poteva risultare in ben' nessuno; ma però per venire in cognizione del vero indubitato, fa intendere per un suo Gentilhuomo ad alcuni Paesani]* se Michelangelo havesse fratelli, e chi, e trovò che la bestialità *[la verità e carità era dalla parte del Prete, e la bugia e bestialità]* era dalla parte di Michelangelo. Torna il Prete doppo i tre giorni, *[secondo il comandamento fattogli,]* e trattenuto dal Card^{le} fa chiamar Michelangelo e mostrandoli il fratello disse che non lo conosceva, ne essergli fratello. *[Prete gli disse, se lo conosceva, e se gli fusse fratello; negò l'un e l'altro]* Onde il povero Prete intenerito alla presenza del Card^{le} gli disse: Fratello io son venuto tanto da lontano, sol per vedervi, et havendovi visto, ho ottenuto quello che desideravo, essendo io in stato per grazia di Dio, come sapete, che non ho bisogno di voi, ne per me, ne per i miei figli, mà sì ben per i vostri, se Dio m'havesse concesso gratia di farvi accompagnare, e vedervi successione. Dio vi dia da far bene, come io ne miei Sacrificij *[ne prego]*, e pregarò S. D. M.^{tà}. et il medesimo so che farà vostra sorella nelle sue pudiche e verginali orationi. Nè si movendo Michelangelo à queste parole di ardente e scentillante amore, si partì il buon sacerdote senza haver dal fratello un'buon viaggio a Dio. Onde non si puo negare, che non fusse stravagantissimo e con queste sue stravaganze, non si sia tolto qualche decina d'anni di vita, e minutasi *[oscurato]* in parte la gloria acquistata con la professione, *[che con l'arte s'è acquistato,]* e col vivere si sarebbe agumentato con grand utile de studiosi di simil professione.

Our age owes much to Michelangelo da Caravaggio for the manner of coloring which he introduced and which is now quite generally followed. He was born in Caravaggio of quite worthy parents, since his father was a major-domo and architect of the Marchese da Caravaggio. When he was still a boy, he studied diligently for four (or five) years in Milan, although from time to time he committed some extravagances caused by his hot temperament and high spirits. Afterwards, at about the age of twenty, he went to Rome, where, poorly provided with money, he stayed with Pandolfo Pucci da Recanati, who was a beneficiary of St. Peter's, where he had to work for his keep and perform services which did not befit him, and, what was worse, in the evening he was given salad as appetizer, entrée and dessert. . . . He was greatly dissatisfied and left within a few months and afterward he called this patron Monsignor Insalata. During this period he made for him some copies of devotional images which are to be found in Recanati; for the market he made a boy who cries because he is bitten by a lizard which he is holding in his hand, and afterward one who is peeling a pear with a knife, and the portrait of an innkeeper who gave him a place to live. At this time he fell ill and being without money he was forced to go to the Hospital of the Consolation, where during his convalescence he made many pictures for the Prior, who afterward took them with him to Sicily.* I am told that he later stayed in the house of Cavaliere Giuseppe and Monsignor Fantin Petrignani who gave him the use of a room. During this time he made many pictures, and in particular a gypsy telling a young man's fortune, the *Flight into Egypt*, the penitent *Magdalene, St. John the Evangelist*, and then the *Deposition of Christ* in the Chiesa Nuova, the pictures at San Luigi, the *Death of the Virgin* for Sta. Maria della Scala which is now in the possession of the Duke of Mantua and which the fathers had removed from the church because Caravaggio had used a courtesan as the model for the person of the Madonna, the *Madonna di Loreto* in S. Agostino, the *Palafrenieri Altar* in St. Peter's, many pictures which are in the possession of the Most Illustrious Borghese, the Cerasi Chapel in the Church of Sta. Maria del Popolo, and many privately owned paintings in the houses of the Mattei, Giustiniani and Sannesio. Ultimately, because of certain events, his life became endangered, and in self-defense, seconded by Onorio Longhi, he killed his adversary and had to flee from Rome; he stopped first at Zagarola where he was hidden by the Prince [of Palestrina]. There he painted a *Magdalene*, and *Christ going to Emmaus*, which was bought by Costa in Rome. With the money which he earned from this he went to Naples where he executed different works, and from there to Malta. In Malta he did some

* Note variant in Palatine manuscript: Seville.

paintings which pleased the Grand Master, who, it is said, as a sign of his esteem gave him the habit of the order. He left there with the hope of being pardoned and went to Civita Vecchia [Port'Ercole] where, stricken with a malignant fever, he died miserably and without care, at the height of his glory, being about thirty-five or forty years of age. He was buried nearby. It is undeniable that he made great progress in painting single figures and heads and in the use of color and that our profession in this century is greatly indebted to him. However, his great knowledge of art was accompanied by an extravagance in his habits. He had only one brother, who was a priest and a reputable man of letters, and when he heard of Michele's fame, he desired to see him and, moved by fraternal love, went to Rome. He knew that Michele was staying in the house of Cardinal del Monte and, being aware of his brother's eccentricities, he thought it best to speak first with the Cardinal and explain everything to him, which he did. The Cardinal kindly asked him to return in three days and he agreed to this. Meanwhile the Cardinal called Michelangelo and asked him if he had any relatives; his answer was no. Because the Cardinal could not believe that the priest would lie about a matter which could be investigated and from which nothing could be gained, he had inquiries made among Michele's countrymen to find out if Michele had brothers and if so who they were, and he found that the infamy was on the side of Michele. The priest returned after three days and was received by the Cardinal, who sent for Michele and confronted him with his brother, but Michele said that he did not know him and that he was not his brother. To this the poor priest said with tenderness in the presence of the Cardinal, "Brother, I have come a long way just to see you, and having seen you, I have fulfilled my desire. As you know, in my position, thank God, I do not need you for myself or for any children of mine, but rather for your own children if God would allow me to arrange a marriage for you and see you with children. God help you to do good and in my services, I will pray to the Divine Majesty for you and I know our sister will do the same in her chaste and virginal prayers." But Michele was not moved by these words of heartfelt affection and the good priest left without so much as a goodby from his brother. It cannot be denied that Caravaggio was very extravagant, and that these extravagances shortened his life by at least ten years and diminished somewhat the glory which he had won through his profession; and had he lived longer, he would have grown and that would have been of benefit to the students of the same profession.

KAREL VAN MANDER

Het Leven der Moderne
oft dees-tijtsche doorluchtighe Italiaensche Schilders . . . Het tweedde Boeck
van het Leven der Schilders. Tot Alkmaer, 1603

T'LEVEN VAN NOCH ANDER ITALIAENSCHE SCHILDERRS
DIE TEGHENWOORDIGH TE ROOM ZIJN

[Part III of: *Het Schilder-Boeck* . . . , Haarlem, 1604] fol. 191 *recto*.

D ER is oock eenen *Michael Agnolo* van *Caravaggio*, die te Room wonderlijcke dinghen doet: hy is oock ghelijck den *Ioseph* voor verhaelt / uyt der armoede op gheclommen door vlijt / cloeck en stoutlijck alles aenvattende / en aennemende / ghelijck eenighe doen / die niet en willen door blooheyt oft cleenherticheyt t'onder blijven: maer vrymoedigh / en onbeschroemt hun selven voort doen / en hun voordeel over al stoutlijck versoecken / t'welck doch alst eerlijck / op taemlijcke wijse / met beleeftheyt toegaet / niet te mispreijsen is: want t' gheluck wilt hem selven van t'self ons dickwils so niet aenbieden / het moet somtijts van ons ghetenteert / aengheport / en versocht wesen. Desen *Michael Agnolo* dan heeft alree met zijn wercken groot gherucht / eere / en naem gecreghen. Hy heeft ghedaen een Historie tot *S. Laurens in Damas*, neffens die van *Iosepino*, daer in zijn leven van verhaelt is: hier in heeft hy gemaect een Naenken / oft Reusken / dat nae *Iosephs* Historie toe siende de tongh uyt steeckt / schijnende of hy aldus *Iosephs* werck wilde bespotten: want hy is een die van geen Meesters dinghen veel houdt: doch sy selven niet openlijck prijsende. Dan zijn segghen is / dat alle dinghen niet dan *Bagatelli*, kinderwerck / oft bueselinghen zijn / t'zy wat / oft van wien gheschildert / soo sy niet nae t'leven ghedaen / en gheschildert en zijn / en datter niet goet / oft beter en can wesen / dan de Natuere te volghen. Alsoo dat hy niet eenen enckelen treck en doet / oft hy en sittet vlack nae t'leven en copieert / end' en schildert. Dit en is doch geené quaden wegh / om tot goeden eyndt te comen: want nae Teyckeninge (of sy schoon nae t' leven comt) te schilderen / is so ghewis niet / als t'leven voor hebben / en de Natuere met al haer verscheyden verwen te volghen: doch behoefde men eerst so verre gecomen te wesen in verstandt / dat men t'schoonste leven uyt t'schoon onderscheydé en uyt te kiesen wist. Nu isser neffens dit Cooren weder dit Kaf / dat hy niet stadigh hem ter studie en begheeft / maer hebbende een veerthien daghen ghewrocht / gaet hy der twee / oft een maendt teghen wandelen / met t' Rapier op't sijde / met een knecht achter hem / van d'een Kaetsbaen in d'ander / seer ghenegen tot vechten en krackeelen wesende / soo dat het seldtsaem met hem om te gaen is. Welcke dingen onse Const heel niet en ghelijcké: Want *Mars* en *Minerva* zijn doch noyt de beste vrienden gheweest: dan soo veel zijn handelinghe belangt / die is sulcx / datse bevallijck seer is / in een wonder fraey maniere / om de Schilder-jeught nae te volgen.

Appendix, oft aenhangh van het Schilder-boeck: . . .

['t] is my qualijck bericht / dat *Michael Agnolo Caravaggio* door zijn gheschildert Reusken de dinghen van *Ioseppijn* bespot.

THERE is also a certain Michael Angelo of Caravaggio who is doing remarkable things in Rome. Just like the Joseph (Giuseppe) discussed above, he also has risen from poverty through his industry and by tackling and accepting everything with farsightedness and courage, as some people do who refuse to be held down through timidity or through lack of courage but who advance themselves candidly and fearlessly and who boldly pursue their gain—a procedure which if it is taken in honesty, in a proper manner, and with discretion, deserves no censure. For Fortuna will offer herself by no means frequently of her own accord; at times we must try her, prod her, and urge her.

Already this Michael Angelo has achieved with his works great repute, honor and a name. He did a story at S. Lorenzo in Damaso, next to that of Josepino (Giuseppe) of which an account is given in his (Giuseppe's) Life.* In it he has painted a dwarf or little fellow who, looking at Joseph's picture sticks out his tongue, as if he wished to ridicule Joseph's work. For he is one who cares little for the work of other masters, yet will not praise his own openly. He holds that all works are nothing but bagatelles, child's work, or trifles, whatever their subject and by whomever painted, unless they be done and painted after life and that nothing could be good and nothing better than to follow Nature. Whence it is that he will not do a single brushstroke without close study from life which he copies and paints. Surely this is no wrong way to achieve a good end. For to paint after drawings, even though they be done after life, is in no wise as reliable as facing life and to follow Nature with all her different colors. Yet one should first have reached a degree of insight that would enable one to select and distinguish from the beauty of life that which is most beautiful. But again there is beside the grain the chaff, to wit that he does not pursue his studies steadfastly so that after a fortnight's work he will swagger about for a month or two with his sword at his side and with a servant following him, from one ball-court to the next, ever ready to engage in a fight or argument, with the result that it is most awkward to get along with him. All of which is wholly incompatible with our Art. For certainly Mars and Minerva have never been the best of friends. Yet as regards his way of painting, it is such that it is very pleasing in an exceedingly handsome manner, an example for our young artists to follow.

Appendix attached to the Schilder-boeck. . . . On fol. 191, line 14 from the top: I have been ill-informed that Michael Angelo Caravaggio mocked at the work of Josephino with the little fellow whom he painted.

* See fol. 189 *recto*.

JOACHIM VON SANDRART

Michael Angelo Marigi von Caravaggio, Mahler

Michael Angelo, gebürtig von Caravaggio, einen Ort in Longobardia unweit Mailand gelegen, ware zwar von guten Eltern des Adelichen Geschlechts Amarigi, aber durch grosse Begierde zu der edlen Mahlkunst merklich aufgestiegen, wie er dann zu Rome viele bewunderungswürdige Werke gefärtiget. Es ware dieser Caravaggio unter allen Italienern der erste, welcher seine Studien von denen angewöhnten alten Manieren ab und auf die einfältige Ausbildung der Natur, nach dem Leben zoge. Dannenhero beflisse er sich, keinen Strich anderst als nach dem Leben zu thun und stellte sich zu dem Ende dasjenige, so er abbilden wolte, in seinem Zimmer so lang in der Natur vor, biss er solcher nach Genüge in seiner Arbeit nachgefolget. Damit er aber auch die vollkommene Rondirung und natürliche Erhebung desto bässer herfür bringen möchte, bediente er sich fleissig dunkler Gewölber oder anderer finsterer Zimmer, die von oben her ein einiges kleines Liecht hatten, damit die Finsterniss dem auf das model fallenden Liecht durch starke Schatten seine Macht lassen und darmit eine hocherhobene Rundierung verursachen möchte.

So verachtete er nun alles, was nicht nach dem Leben gemacht war, nannte es Bagatell, Kinder- und Bossen-Werk, weil nichts bässers seyn könte, als was der Natur am ähnlichsten. Und zwar ist auch solches kein übel Weg, zur Vollkommenheit zu gelangen, weilen nach den Zeichnungen und Gemälde niemals so gut als die Natur selbst seyn können, sie seyen auch so schön, als sie immer wollen. Dannenhero folgten seiner Manier fast durchgehends alle Italienische Mahler nach, bereiteten sich auch Mahlzimmer nach seiner Art, und ist hernach diese Manier auch in Hoch- und Nieder-Teutschland nachgeahmet worden.

Obwol er nun wegen seiner grossen Kunst hohen Ruhms würdig geachtet, auch von männiglich gelobet wurde, so ware doch sehr übel mit ihm umzugehen, weil er nicht allein von keines einigen Meisters Arbeit sehr viel hielte (wiewol er seine eigne auch nicht öffentlich rühmte) sondern darbey auch sehr zänkisch und seltsam ware und gern Raufhändel suchte. Von dieser seiner bösen Gewonheit angetrieben, kam er auch mit dem damals florirenden Mahler Josepho d'Arpin in Händel, welcher sonst wegen seiner Kunst, Höflichkeit und grossen Reichtum hochgehalten wurde. Diesen griffe unser Künstler nicht allein mit spitzfindigen Stichelreden an, sondern mahlte ihm auch zu trutz und Spott eine Historie zu S. Lorenzo in Damas, neben die, so gemeldter Joseph dahin gemacht: In selbige bildete er einen nackenden Riesen, der über Josephs Werk die Zunge ausstreckte, als ob er das selbe verspotten wolte. Im Anfang mahlte er auf scharfe truckene Manier, bildete viel Angesichter und halbe Bildere, deren eins ein Kindlein mit einem Kretzen voll blumen und Obst gehalten, woraus ein Eydex das Kind in die Hand gebissen, desswegen solches bitterlich scheinte zu weinen, dass es vortreflich zu sehen, wormit sein Lob durch Rom merklich gewachsen. Und weil Arpino meistens grosse Werke in fresco gemacht, selbige aber vor sich selbst nimmermehr in Colorit noch Stärke oder eigentlichen Wahrheit den Oelfarben gleichen, hingegen Cara-

Joachim von Sandrart. *Teutsche Academie der Bau- Bild-, und Mahlerey-Künste*, Nürnberg, 1675, pp. 189 ff.

vaggio in diesen Stucken ganz verwunderlich ware, forderte er den Joseph und andere mehrere in einen Wettstreit heraus, wordurch endlich Händel entstanden und sie zu den Degen gegriffen, auch ein Jüngling, genannt Ranuccio Tomassino, darunter todt geblieben, wesshalben Caravaggio weichen und sich in den Palast unsers Marches Justinians, als Protectors aller Virtuosen, retiriren muste, der seine Arbeit hoch geachtet, auch von selbigen zum meisten gehabt, die doch sonst schwerlich zu bekommen waren.

In wärender Zeit nun, da er sich so verstecken muste, mahlte er in gedachten Palast, wie Christus des Thomas Finger in Gegenwart der andern Aposteln in seine heilige Wunden steckt. Da bildete er nun in aller Anwesenden Angesichtern durch gutes mahlen und rundiren eine solche Verwunderung und Natürlichkeit an Haut und Fleisch aus, dass meist alle andere Gemälde dabey nur als illuminirt Papier schienen. Ingleichen mahlte er den Evangelisten Matthaeus, welchem ein Engel in weissem Kleid das Buch vorhält, darein er schreibt, und noch andere Figuren sehr gross; dann seine meiste Profession ware Lebensgrosse, halb und ganze Bilder dem Leben gleich zu machen. Er mahlte auch für La Madonna Dal popolo, in einer Capelle, Die Creutzigung S. Peters, auch wie S. Paulus von dem Pferd fallend aufgehoben wird; das Pferd ist ein Scheck und scheint lebendig su Seyn.

Wiederum mahlte er zwey grosse Blätter zu S. Louvois di Francesci, bey Prinz Justinians Palast über. Das erste war, wie Christus, unser Seeligmacher, die Juden, Käuffer und Zöllner samt ihren Krämen und Kaufftischen über Hauffen wirft und sie aus dem Tempel treibet; noch verwunderlicher aber ist das ander Blat, worinnen vorgestellt, wie Christus in ein finster Zimmer mit zween der seinen eingetreten und den Zöllner Matthaeum bey einer Rott Spitzbuben mit Karten und Würflen spielend und trinkend sitzen findet. Matthaeus, als furchtsam, verbirgt die Karten in der einen Hand, die andre legt er auf seine Brust und • gibt in seinem Angesicht den Schrecken und die Schamhaftigkeit zu erkennen, die er darüber gefast, dass er als unwürdig von Christo zum Apostelamt beruffen wird; einer streicht mit der einen Hand sein Geld von Tisch in die andere und machet sich ganz schamhaft davon, welches alles dem Leben und der Natur selbst gleichet. Mehr ist von seiner Hand in Rom zu sehen, alla Chiesa Nova die Grablegung Christi, worvon ich eine gute Copia zeigen kan; Al Santo Augustino unser liebe Frau mit dem Kindlein Jesus, das von zweyen knienden Pilgramen angebetet wird. Zu Antorf ist in der Dominicaner-Kirch ein grosses Blat, wie S. Domenico den Andächtigen den Rosenkranz austheilet, und ferner ebendaselbst unser lieben Frauen Verscheidung in Beyseyn der meisten Aposteln, so gleichfalls ein sehr grosses Werk ist.

Nachmalen mahlte er für unsere Kunst Vatter Marches Justinian einen Cupido in Lebensgrösse nach Gestalt eines ohngefehr zwölffjährigen Jünglings, sitzend auf der Weltkugel und in der Rechten seinen Bogen über sich haltend, zur Linken allerley Kunstinstrumenta, auch Bücher zu Studien und ein Lorbeerkranz auf den Büchern; Cupido hatte nach seiner Gestalt grosse braune Adlersflügel, alles zusammen in Corectura gezeichnet, mit starker colorit, Sauberheit und solcher Rundirung, dass es dem Leben wenig nachgegeben. Dieses Stuck ware neben andern hundert und zwanzigen, von den fürtreflichsten Künstlern gemacht, in einem Zimmer und offentlich zu sehen, aber es wurde auf mein Einrahten mit einem dunkelgrün seidenen Vorhang bedeket und erst, wann alles andere zu Genüge gesehen worden, zulezt gezeigt, weil es sonsten alle andere Raritäten unansehentlich gemacht, so dass es mit guten Fug eine Verfinsterung aller Gemälden mag genennet werden. Dernthalben beliebte es auch einem fürnehmen Cavallier so wol, dass er in Beyseyn unserer vieler 1000 Pistoleten dafür offerirt. Aber unser Patron, welcher järlich in die 80 biss 90,000 Cronen mehr Einkommens gehabt als was er järlich (da doch an Kunstsachen grosse Summen aufgegangen) verzehrt hat, wie ich ihme dieses Erbieten, indeme er am Podagra krank gelegen, vorgetragen und eine Antwort begehrt, darüber gelächelt und gesprochen: Dite a questo Corteggio Cavallier, che se egli mi puol far acquistar un altro quadro di questa sostanza, gli ne pagerò il doppia cio è 2,000 Pistole. Blieb also der Kauf zurück und das Lob der verlangten Kunst-Vollkommenheit bey diesem so hoch berühmten Cupido des Marchesen Justinian. Er brachte auch durch dieses Werk zuwegen, dass ihme wieder erlaubt wurde, frey auf den Strassen zu handeln und zu wandeln, dessen er sich dann gleich mit seinen jungen Leuten, meist keker herzhafter Gesellen, Mahler und Fechter, die sich wol des Sprichtworts nec spe, nec metu, ohne Hoffnung und Furcht, bedient.

Bald darauf geschahe es, dass Joseph d'Arpin zu Pferd nach Hof geritten und ihme Michael Angelo da Caravaggio begegnet, der ihn dann alsobald anredte und zuschrie: Es wäre nun eben die rechte Zeit, ihren alten Streit mit dem Degen gegeneinander auszumachen, weil sie beede mit Gewehr versehen, er solte nur fein bald von Pferd heruntersteigen, und machte sich also zum rauffen färtig. Joseph aber antwortete, dass ihme, als vom Papst gemachten Cavalier, nicht gezieme, sich in Streit einzulassen gegen einem, der kein Cavalier seye, mit welchem höflichen Streich und Antwort er den Caravaggio mehrer verwundt als mit seinem Degen hätte geschehen mögen, indeme solche Rede Caravaggio also bestürzt und verirrt gemacht, dass er alsobald (weil er nicht auszusetzen gedacht) alles das Seinige den Juden um paar Geld verkaufft und sich nacher Malta zu dem Grossmeister begeben, mit dem Vornehmen, auch bald Ritter und Cavalier zu werden; massen er generos wider den Türken seine Caracannen vollbracht, auch allda die Enthauptung des H. Johannis Baptistae, die daselbst zu Malta in der Kirche steht, und sehr verwunderlich ist, weil selbige die wahre Natürlichkeit scheint, mit noch wenig andern Gemälden gemacht. Als er nun zum Ritter geschlagen worden, hat er gleich darauf nacher Rom stark zugeeilt, um vorhabenden seinen Rauffhandel mit dem von Arpin auszumachen. Diese Eile aber hat ihm ein hitziges Fieber verursacht, und ist er eben zu Arpin, wo sein Widersacher geboren, der sich auch deshalben von selbigem Ort schreibet, erkranket ankommen und gestorben. Sein End wurde von allen fürnehmen Häuptern in Rom beklaget, weil er noch viel Gutes in dieser Kunst hätte mögen an Tag bringen. . . .

Michael Angelo, a native of Caravaggio, a town in Lombardy, situated not far from Milan, was born of good parents, the noble family Amarigi, but rose considerably through great devotion to the lofty art of painting, in as much as he executed many admirable works in Rome. It was this Caravaggio who, first among all Italians, diverted his studies from the old, traditional manners and toward the candid representation of nature from life. Therefore he was determined never to make a stroke except from life, and toward that end he placed before himself in his room in real life whatever he wished to depict until he had imitated it in his work to his own satisfaction. But, as he also wished to effect a more perfect roundness and natural relief, he regularly made use of gloomy vaults or other dark rooms which had one small source of light from above; so that the darkness, by means of strong shadows, might leave power to the light falling upon the model, and thus produce an effect of high relief.

Thus he despised everything which was not modeled after life; such things he called bagatelles, child's play and puppet work, because nothing could be better than that which most resembled nature. And, indeed, this is not a bad way to arrive at perfection because drawings and paintings, however beautiful they may be, can never be as good as nature itself. Thereafter, practically all Italian painters followed his manner, arranging their studios as he did; and afterward this manner was imitated in Upper and Lower Germany.

Although he was held in high fame because of his great art, and each and everyone praised him, it was nevertheless very difficult to get along with him; for not only did he have little respect for the works of other painters (though he did not openly praise his own works either), but he was also quarrelsome and strange, and loved to look for a fight. Because of this evil habit, he had a falling out with the then prosperous painter, Giuseppe d'Arpino, who was generally held in high esteem because of his ability, courtesy and wealth. Our artist did not only attack him with pointed epithets in order to challenge him but also painted a picture in S. Lorenzo in Damaso next to the one which the aforesaid Joseph had painted. In this picture he represented a nude giant who sticks out his tongue at Giuseppe's work as if he wished to ridicule it.

In the beginning he painted many faces and half-length figures in a sharp, dry manner. One of these is that of a child with a basket of flowers and fruit, from which a lizard emerges, biting the hand of the child who begins to cry bitterly, so that it is marvellous to look at and it caused his reputation to increase notably throughout Rome. Because Arpino generally painted large works in fresco, which does not in itself have the same strength of color or the intrinsic truth of oil colors, and because Caravaggio was very excellent in the latter, he offered Joseph and many others a challenge which resulted in endless quarrels. This brought them to swords' points, and a youth, named Ranuccio Tomassoni, thereby lost his life. Because of this Caravaggio had to flee and retired to the palace of our Count Giustiniani, protector of all virtuosi, who valued his paintings very highly; he had the greatest number of them although usually they were difficult to acquire.

During this time in which he had to hide in this manner, he painted in the aforesaid palace, *Christ*, in whose holy wounds *Thomas*, in the presence of the other apostles, is putting his finger. By means of good painting and modeling he was able to show on the faces of all those present such an expression of astonishment and naturalness of skin and flesh that in comparison all other pictures seemed to be colored paper. In this same way he painted the *Evangelist Matthew* writing in a book held before him by a white-clothed angel, and many other paintings with very large figures, since most of his work was in life-size, full- and half-length, just as in real life. He also painted for the Madonna del Popolo, in a chapel, the *Crucifixion of St. Peter*, and *St. Paul* being picked up after he had fallen from his horse. The horse is a piebald and seems to be alive.

He also painted two large canvases in S. Luigi dei Francesi, opposite Prince Giustiniani's palace. The first shows Christ, our Savior, driving the Jews, merchants, and publicans, one and all from the temple, with their booths and counters in disorder. But even more marvellous is the other canvas where Christ is represented in a dark room, which He has entered with two of His followers and finds the tax collector *Matthew* in the company of a gang of rogues with whom he is playing cards and dice, and sitting about drinking. Matthew, as if afraid, conceals the cards in one hand and places the other on his breast; in his face he reveals that alarm and shame which is the result of his feeling that he is unworthy to be called to the Apostolate by Christ. One of the other men takes his money from the table by sweeping it with one hand into the other, and attempts to sneak away; all of which seems true to life and nature itself. More of his work can be seen in Rome at the Chiesa Nuova, the *Interment of Christ*, of which I can show a good copy; at Sant' Agostino, *Our Lady with the Child Jesus* who is being worshiped by two kneeling pilgrims. In the Dominican Church at Antwerp is a large canvas of *St. Dominic* distributing the rosary among the pious; and, further, in the same place the *Death of our Lady* in the presence of most of the Apostles which is likewise a very great work.

Furthermore, he painted for our art patron, Marchese Giustiniani, a life-size *Cupid*, modeled from a youth about twelve years old, sitting on the globe and holding his bow over his head with his right hand. At the left are all sorts of art instruments, as well as books for study and a laurel wreath lying on the books. The figure of Cupid has large, brown eagle's wings, all drawn with correctness, strong color, cleanness, and such plasticity that it yields very little to life itself. This piece was publicly exhibited in a room with another hundred and twenty made by the most prominent artists; however on my advice it was covered with a dark green silk curtain, and only when all the other paintings had been seen to satisfaction, was it finally uncovered, for otherwise it would have made the other curiosities insignificant; not without reason may this painting be called "the eclipse of all paintings." A Cavalier of high rank liked it so much that he offered one thousand pistoles (ducats) for it in the presence of all of us. But when I brought this offer to our patron, who had a yearly income of eighty to ninety thousands cronen over his annual disbursements (in spite of the large sums spent on art objects), and asked for an answer—he was sick with gout at the time—he smiled at it and said: "Tell that noble Cavalier that if he can get me another picture with the same qualities, I will pay him double, that is, two thousand pistoles." The sale, therefore, did not come off, and the glory of the artistic perfection required by the Marchese Giustiniani remained with his so famous Cupid. Through this work Caravaggio also succeeded in again obtaining permission to go about the streets and behave as a free man; he immediately availed himself of this permission in the company of his young pals, mostly swaggering, hearty fellows—painters and swordsmen—who lived by the proverb: *nec spe, nec metu* (without hope; without fear).

Soon thereafter, it happened that Giuseppe d'Arpino, riding to court on horseback, was met by Michael Angelo da Caravaggio. Immediately he addressed him and cried out to him that since both were armed now would be a good time to end their old quarrel by a duel. He told him to get off his horse at once and got ready for a fight. Joseph answered, however, that it was not fitting for a cavalier, named by the Pope, to duel with one who was not a cavalier. With this politely-cutting answer, he wounded Caravaggio more than he might have with his sword, for this talk so stunned and confused Caravaggio that he immediately (as he did not intend to defer the matter) sold all his belongings to the Jews for whatever he could get, and set out for Malta and the Grand Master with the purpose of soon becoming himself a knight and cavalier. He generously fitted out a carack (ship of burden) against the Turks, and painted there the *Beheading of St. John the Baptist*, the same one which is in the church at Malta, and which is very marvelous because it appears so genuinely natural, as well as a few other paintings. As soon as he was knighted, he hurried back to Rome with the intention of settling his quarrel with d'Arpino. This haste, however, resulted in a high fever and he arrived in Arpino (the very birthplace of his adversary, who signed himself as from that town) as a sick man and died. His end was mourned by all the distinguished leaders in Rome because he might still have done great things in his art.

2. DOCUMENTS CONCERNING CARAVAGGIO'S LIFE

APPRENTICESHIP

1. CONTRACT WITH PETERZANO

In nomine Domini anno a nativitate millesimo quingentesimo octuagesimo quarto indicione duodecima die veneris sesta mensis aprilis. Michael Angelus de Meritiis filius q. domini Firmi porte orientalis, parochie S. Georgi ad puteum album Mediolani, parte una et nobilis dominus Simon Petezanus filius domini Francisci predictarum porte et parochie, parte altera volutarie etc. omnibus modis etc. devenerunt ad infrascripta pacta et conventiones inviolabiliter attendenda in hunc modum ut infra videlicet.

In primis convenerunt, quod dictus Michaelangelus teneatur stare et habitare cum dicto domino Simone ad adiscendum artem pictoris et hoc annos quattuor proxime futuros die hodie inceptos et quod dictus Michael Angelus se exercebit in ipsa arte die noctuque secundum consuetudinem dicte artis bene et fideliter; et quod non committet dolum nec fraudem in bonis domini Simonis; et quod dictus dominus Simon teneatur et obligatus sit tenere dictum Michaelem Angelum in dicto eius domo et apotheca, et eum instruere in ipsa arte toto posse suo, et facere quod in fine dictorum annorum quattuor sit sufficiens et expertus in dicta arte et a se ipso laborare sciat; et dictus Michael Angelus teneatur dare et solvere dicto domino Simoni pro eius mercede scutos viginti auri et in auro valoris librarum sex im- perialium pro singulo scutto solvendo anticipate de sex menses in sex mensibus per dictum Michaelem Angelum dicto Domino Simoni et successive ecc. donet ecc.; ex quibus dictus dominus Simon ex nunc contentus fuit etc. recepisse etc. et ibidem presentialiter etc. a praedicto Michaele Angelo ibi presente etc. ac dante ibidem presentialiter ut supra scutta decem auri et in auro valoris prefati et hoc anticipate iuxta conventa ut supra proximorum mensium sex et reliqua scutta dictus Michael Angelus promisit obligando . . . pignori dicto domino Simoni presenti etc. ea dare et solvere domino Simoni aut ejus heredibus quam citius et ante quam eveniant dicti menses sex. Sub refectione damnorum. Pacto quod dictus Michael Angelus durantibus dictis annis quattuor non possit nec valeat se recedere a servitijs dicti domini Simonis nec ire ad servitia aliquorum aliorum de ipsa arte in presenti civitate nec alibi absque spetiali licenta dicti domini Simonis et haec omnia sub poena scuttorum quadraginta octo auri et in auro valoris prefati superius expressi pro toto eo tempore quo restabit obligatus cum dicto domino Simone applicandorum dicto domino Simoni in casu contraventionis. Et pro predictis omnibus et singulis per dictum Michaelem Angelum at- tendendis, eius precibus et instantia extiterunt fideiussores dominus Baptista filius quondam domini Firmi et Bartholomeus pater et filius de Baschis ambo porte et parochie Sebastiani Mediolani et uterque eorum in solidum etc. Ita quod in solidum teneantur etc. cum renuntiis debitis etc. et maxime renuntiatione promissi pacti alieni quia scientes pactum alienum promisisse tamen teneri volunt etc. faciens tamen prefatus dominus Bartholomeus predicta omnia et singula in presentia etc. principalis procuratori sui ibi presentis et eidem filio suo licentiam dantis ac jurantis etc. suo credere pro dicta etc. etc. in et ad utilitatem predicti eius fili et pro juribus . . . et pro predictis etiam omnibus et singulis in presenti instrumento contentis dicte partes sese vicissim cum renuntiis debitis etc. possint et valeant coram quibuscumque jus dicentibus et in forma regie ducalis camere Mediolani quorum jurisdictioni sese supposuerunt etc. et extendatur etc. eius in facultate supplicandi iuxta stillum mei notari etc. etc. Quare dictus Michaelangelus et dicti ejus fideiussores parte una et dictus dominus Simon parte altera et quilibet eorum respective cesserunt cum renuntiis debitis promisserunt obbligationum pignori sibi vicissim et ad invicem habere rathum et non contravenire sub refectione etc. et sub poena scutorum centum auri per partem non attendentem parti attendenti qua poena nihilominus etc. quae omnia etc. pacta executiva.

Insuper dicte partes et fideiussores et quilibet eorum juraverunt habere rathum et non contravenire et etiam sub refectione etc. et de predictis etc.

Actum in domo habitationis prefati domini Simonis Petezani sita ut supra presentibus dominis Gaspare de Porta Romana filio quondam Francisci Porte orientalis parochie S. Marie Passerelle Mediolani et domino Johanne Baptista de la Platea filio d. Jeromini P. Orientalis parochie S. Babile intus Mediolani protonotariis. Textes Magnificus Dominus Johannes Baptista de Monte f.q. magnifici domini Augustini P. Orientalis Parochie S. Babile intus Mediolani et Antoni da Zuffis f. domini Petri P. Orientalis parochie S. Pauli in compito Mediolani et domino Johanne Baptista de Thoscanis f. quondam d. Johannis Baptiste P. Orientalis parochie S. Georgi ad puteum omnes noti ac idonei.

From *Archivi d'Italia*, Serie II, Anno XVIII, 1951, pp. 140-142. First published in part by Pevsner, in *Zeit. f. B. K.*, 1927-28, vol. 61, pp. 390-391.

[ABRIDGED TRANSLATION] In the year of our Lord 1584, on the sixth of April, the party of the first part, Michelangelo Merisi, son of Master Firmo from the parish of S. Giorgio al Pozzo Bianco, and the party of the second part, the noble Master Simon Peterzano, son of Master Francesco, from the same place, arrived at the following agreements and covenants to be inviolably observed in the manner hereinafter set forth: first they have agreed that the said Michelangelo shall be required to dwell and reside with the said Master Simon in order to learn the art of a painter, and this for the next four years, beginning today. Michelangelo shall be required to practice this art day and night and faithfully and well, as is customary in this art. He shall not damage or misuse the property of Master Simon, and the aforesaid Master Simon shall be obliged to keep the said Michelangelo in his house and shop and to instruct him in the said art to the best of his ability and to see that at the end of the said four years he is skilled in the said art and is able to work on his own. And the said Michelangelo shall be required to give to said Master Simon twenty gold scudi . . . as his fee. And during the four years the said Michelangelo cannot and shall not leave the service of the said Master Simon and shall not go into the service of others of this profession in this city or elsewhere, without permission from the said Master Simon. And the penalty for this shall be the payment of forty-eight gold scudi. . . . Baptista, the son of the late Master Firmo and Bartolomeo de Baschis, father and son . . . have agreed to be the guarantors . . . etc. etc.

[The contract was concluded in the house of Peterzano.]

POLICE RECORDS CONCERNING CARAVAGGIO

2. Testimonio di Onorio Longo   *25 ottobre 1600*

"Una volta alla Scrofa parlando con amici dissi certe parole . . . che un pittore certo Marco Tullio passando prese per sè, mentre io non lo conosceva punto. Ci siamo dati dei pugni; fummo partiti. Era meco Michelangiolo Merisio pittore che ci partì.

"Michelangiolo era allora convalescente e si faceva portare la spada da un putto, ma non la cavò; fu Marco Tullio che prese il fodero e me lo scagliò. Michelangiolo poteva appena star in piedi così non poteva trarre la spada."

A. Bertolotti, *Artisti Lombardi a Roma nei secoli XV, XVI e XVII*, vol. ii, Milan, 1881. pp. 18, 49-76.

Testimony of Onorio Longo   *25 October 1600*

"Once, in Via della Scrofa, speaking with friends, I said certain words . . . which a painter, one Marco Tullio, who was passing, took as meant for himself, whereas I didn't know him at all. We exchanged fisticuffs. We were separated. Michelangelo Merisi, the painter, was with me. He separated us."

"Michelangelo was then convalescent, and had a boy carry his sword for him, but did not unsheath it. It was Marco Tullio who seized the scabbard and flung it at me. Michelangelo could hardly stand; so he could not draw the sword."

19 novembre 1600

3. [La prima querela trovata porta la data del 19 novembre 1600, ed era presentata al Governatore di Roma da certo Girolamo Spampa di Monte Poliziano, abitante in casa del R.ᵐᵒ De Bagnis alla Valle, contra Michelangiolo Merisi da Caravaggio, pittore in casa dell'Ill.° e R.° Cardinale De Monte.]

"Dovete sapere come venerdì a sera p. p. alle tre hore di notte venendo dall'Accademia da studiare, quando fui alla Scrofa e ci era meco il signor Orazio Bianchi, mentre bussava dal Candelottaro per aver candele venne il querelato e con un bastone e mi cominciò a dare delle bastonate e me ne dette parecchie. Io mi difesi come potevo gridando: Ah traditore a questo modo si fa! Vennero certi macellai con lumi ed allora Michelangiolo trasse la spada e mi tirò una stoccata che mi parai col ferraiolo, in cui fece uno squarcio come potete vedere e poi se ne fuggì. Allora lo conobbi mentre prima non aveva potuto conoscerlo."

[Orazio Bianchi da Lione in casa del Cardinale Bonaiuti confermò la deposizione.]

Bertolotti, *op. cit.*, p. 50.

19 November 1600

[The first known complaint bears the date 19 November 1600, and was filed with the Governor of Rome by one Girolamo Spampa of Montepulciano, who lived in the house of the Most Reverend De Bagnis near S. Andrea della Valle, against Michelangelo Merisi of Caravaggio, a painter living in the house of the Most Illustrious and Reverend Cardinal De Monte.]

"You should know that last Friday night, three hours after nightfall [8:00 p.m.], while returning from the Academy, where I had been studying, when I got to Via della Scrofa—

Mr. Orazio Bianchi was with me—and I was knocking at the candlemaker's door to get some candles, the defendant came up with a stick and began to beat me. He gave me a good many blows. I defended myself as best I could, shouting: 'Ah, traitor, is that a way to act!' Some butchers arrived with lights, and then Michelangelo drew his sword and made a thrust at me, which I parried with my cloak, in which he made a gash, as you can see, and then fled. Then I recognized him, whereas previously I had not been able to recognize him."

[Orazio Bianchi of Lyons (?), living in the house of Cardinal Bonaiuti, confirmed Spampa's deposition.]

Die Mercurii 7. Februarii 1601.

4. Pro Michelangelo Caravaggio requisito et processato pro vulnere ense illato in manu Flavio Canonico olim Sergenti militum Custodie Arcis S. Angeli in societate Honorii Longi, sine periculo, sed cum cicatrice remansura. Contra Curiam et Fiscum. Ill^{mus} et R^{mus} Dominus Gubernator stante consensu et pace a dicto Flavio offenso obtentis mandavit, processum relationem Barberij et omnia alia contra ipsum data de causa existentia cassari et aboleri, ipsumque premissorum occasione de cetero non molestari, omni meliori etc. Super quibus etc. presentibus sociis etc.

Archivio di Stato: Liber Actorum, vol. 121, fol. 72.

Wednesday, 7 February 1601

In favor of Michelangelo Caravaggio, summoned and prosecuted for a sword wound which he had inflicted on the hand of Flavio Canonico, a former sergeant of the guards of Castel Sant' Angelo, with the complicity of Onorio Longhi, without danger to life, but with a permanent scar. Against the court and the administration: the most Illustrious and Reverend Lord, the Governor [of Rome], in view of the accord and reconciliation obtained from the aforesaid Flavio who was the injured party, ordered that the lawsuit and the report of Barberio and all other documents existing against the aforesaid [Caravaggio] for the above mentioned cause shall be cancelled and annulled and that the same [Caravaggio] shall not be molested any further on the ground of the aforesaid incident. . . .

ROMA

5. Libello famoso in favore della curia e fisco

CONTRO

Onorio Longo romano
Michelangiolo Merisio da Caravaggio pittore
Orazio Gentilesco pittore
Filippo Trisegni pittore romano

Bertolotti, *op. cit.*, p. 51. A more complete transcription of the records of this law suit appeared in *Archivi*, serie II, anno XVIII, pp. 252 ff., 1951. Unfortunately I was unable to obtain this transcription in time to incorporate it in the present text but the variations are not very important ones.

ROME

Action for Libel on behalf of the Court and the State

AGAINST

Onorio Longo of Rome,   Orazio Gentileschi, a painter,
Michelangelo Merisi of Caravaggio, a painter,   Filippo Trisegni, a painter, of Rome.

6. Querela di Giovanni Baglione pittore: *28 Agosto 1603*

"Dovete sapere che io fo professione di pittore et essercito in Roma da parecchi anni; et adesso occorre che hauendo io fatto un depinto della resurrettione di N. S. al Padre Generale della Compagnia del Giesù, dopo essersi scoperto detto quadro che fu questa pasqua di resurretione p. p. li Onorio Longo, Michelangiolo Merisio, Orazio Gentileschi pretendeno farlo loro, cioè dico Michelangiolo, perciò questi per inuidia con suoi aderenti Onorio e Orazio suoi amici sono andati sparlando del fatto mio con dir male di me et biasimare le opere mie et in particulare hanno fatto alcuni uersi in mio disonore et uittoperio et datili et dispensatili a più et diuerse persone quali sono questi che io ui esibisco i quali l'ho hauuti da M.° Tomasso Solini pittore et per quanto mi ha detto l'ha hauuti da Filippo Trasegno pure pittore et che una parte di detti uersi detto Filippo li scrisse in sua presentia che sono questi che comincia *Gioan Bagaglia* et fenisce *et della pittura uittuperio* et gl'altri come questi in questo quarto foglio che comincia *Gioan Coglione* et fenisce *altrimenti ei saria un becco futtuto*. Però io do querela contro li sodetti et altri che c'hauessero tenuto mano o in qualsiuoglia modo ne fussero consapeuoli et si trouassero colpeuoli di questo fatto, dimandando che contro di loro si proceda, come importa la giustitia perchè li sudetti querelati sempre mi hanno perseguitato, sono stati miei emoli et me hanno havuto invidia, uedendo che le mie opere sono in consideratione più che le loro et per uerificatione di ciò potrete essaminare il detto Tomasso et poi domando sia astretto detto Filippo dal quale si saprà meglio il fatto d'ogni cosa et contro di lui ancora ne do querela pretendendo sia consapeuole assieme cogli altri di questi uersi infamatori fatti contro di me."

Gian bagaglia tu non sei un 'acca
Le tue pitture sono pituresse
Volo vedere con esse
Che non guadagnerei
Mai una potacca
Che di cotanto panno
Da farti un paro di bragesse
Che ad ognun mostrarai
Quel che fa la cacca.
Che li belli con quel suo cazzor
Da merlo piu non la fotte
Portela adunque
I tuoi disegni e cartoni

Che tu ai fatto a Andrea pizzicarolo
O veramente forbetene il culo
Alla moglie di Marturegli Caprotta,
Perdonami, dipintore, se io non ti adulo
Che della collana che tu porti indegno sei
Et della pittura vituperio.

Archivio di Stato di Roma anno 1603. vol. 28, fol. 383. (Omitted by Bertolotti.)

[Tralascio i brutti e scurrili versacci producendone soltanto ad esempio i seguenti]

Gian c . . . ion senza dubio dir si puole
A quel che biasimar si mette altrui
Che può cento anni esser mastro di lui
Nella pittura intendo la mia prole
Poichè pittor ti uor chiamar costui
Che non può star mai par con colui.

.   .   .   .   .   .

.   .   .   .   .   .

Se io mettermi volesse a ragionar
Delle braure fatte da questui
No bastarian interi un mese o dui.
Vieni un poco qua tu che uo biasimar
L'altrui pitture et sai pur che le tue
Si stano in casa tua a chiodi ancora
Vergognandoti tu mostrarle fuora
In fatti i vo'l'impresa abandonare
Che sento che mi abonda tal materia
Massime s'intrassi nella catena
Dono che al collo indegnamente porta
Che credo certo (meglio) se io non erro
A pie glie ne staria una di ferro.

.   .   .   .   .   .

[In seguito della querela unita al corpo del reato il governatore di Roma passò al procedimento.]
Bertolotti, *op. cit.*, pp. 51-53.

COMPLAINT OF GIOVANNI BAGLIONE, a painter: *28 August 1603*

"You should know that I am a painter by profession and have been practising in Rome for a good many years. Now, it happened that I had painted a picture of Our Lord's Resurrection for the Father General of the Society of Jesus. Since the unveiling of said picture on Easter Sunday of this year, Onorio Longo, Michelangelo Merisi, and Orazio Gentileschi, who had aspired to do it themselves—I mean Michelangelo—that is why, from envy, the latter and his friends and adherents, Onorio and Orazio, have been attacking my reputation by speaking evil of me and finding fault with my works. In particular, they have made some verses in my dishonor and vilification and have given and distributed them to several and sundry persons. I exhibit some of them to you, which I got from Master Tommaso Solini, the painter, who, from what he told me, got them from Filippo Trisegno, also a painter. He added that some of these verses had been written by Filippo in Tommaso's presence. They are these here beginning 'Gioan Bagaglia' and ending 'and the disgrace of painting,' and the others such as these in this quarto sheet of paper, beginning 'Gioan C———' and ending 'otherwise he would be a damned cuckold!' Therefore, I lodge a complaint against the above-named and anyone else who may have given them assistance or in any way may have been their accomplices, and will be found guilty of this act. I ask that they be prosecuted as the law requires, because the above-named defendants have always been persecuting me, have been jealous of me and bear me envy, seeing that my works are held in higher esteem than theirs. For a confirmation of my allegations you may examine the said Tommaso. And further, I ask that the said Filippo be summoned, from whom you will learn more accurately everything that took place. Against him, too, I lodge a complaint, claiming that he is guilty along with the others of these defamatory verses made against me."

[Bertolotti introduces an expurgated example of one of these poems]

> He doubtless deserves to be called Gian C———
>> Who undertakes to find fault with another
>> Who could be his master for a hundred years.
> With my words I am referring to painting,
>> Since this man (Baglione) claims to be called a painter,
>> Though he never could rank with that man (Caravaggio).
>
> . . . .
>
> Were I to undertake to discourse
>> About this man's exploits,
>> An entire month or two would not be enough.
> Come hither, please, you who presume to find fault
>> With other men's paintings, and yet know that your own
>> Are still nailed up in your house
>> Because you are ashamed to show them in public.
> Indeed I will abandon my undertaking
>> Because I feel that I have too great an abundance of subject-matter,
>> Especially if I were to enter upon the chain,
> The gift which he wears round his neck unworthily,
>> For I certainly think that—if I am not mistaken—
>> An iron one on his feet would be more fitting.

[Acting upon the complaint joined to the libelous papers the Governor of Rome passed to the proceedings.]

7. ESAME DI TOMMASO quondam Battista Solini romano abitante in via della Croce:

"Di quanto mi hauete dimandato ui deuo dire per la uerità che io conosco Filippo Trisegno pittore da doi anni in qua per esser ancor io pittore dal quale circa doi o tre mesi sono mi furno dati *in scriptis* alcuni versi infamatori contro la persona di Giouanni Baglioni pittore et me li diede con occatione che io un giorno andando insieme con detto Filippo a spasso et dimandandoli che cosa si diceua fra pittori del quadro che detto Gioanni (Baglione) haueua fatto nella chiesa del Giesù mi disse che Michelangelo da Caravaggio, Honorio Longo et Horatio Gentileschi tutti e tre pittori haueuano fatto certi uersi contro detto Gioanni et contro di me per esser suo compagno per il fatto di detto quadro sopra il fatto di detto quadro et così di lì ad alcuni giorni dopo con belle parole detto Filippo me diede una carta scritta di parecchi uersi contro detto Gioanni che era in quarto foglio et mi disse che l'haueua fatti detto Horatio assieme con Ottauio [Leoni] Padouano medesimamente pittore et che Ludouico Bresciano pur pittore l'andaua distribuendo a diuersi pittori et che in particolare li haueua dati a un certo Mario [Arconio] parimente pittore che sta nel Corso.

". . . Di li poi a non so quanti giorni . . . mi disse (Filippo) che l'haueuan fatto detti Michelangelo et Honorio et che lui l'haueua hauuto da una bardassa di essi Honorio et Michelangelo chiamato G. B. che habita dietro a banchi et di più mi disse che detto Michelangelo hauendo saputo che esso Filippo haueua hauuti in mano detti sonetti l'haueua auertito che stesse in ceruello che questi sonetti non capitassero in mano di detto Gioanni et in man mia, perchè ci sarebbe nato qualche rumore . . . dicendomi anche che un certo Bartolomeo servitore del detto Michelangelo andaua distribuendo a chi ne uoleua di questi sonetti ed altri ancora. . . .

. . . Ritengo che per invidia Michelangiolo ed Orazio abbiano fatti detti versi e Onorio perchè intrinsico loro e poi ebbe lite col Baglione."

Bertolotti, *op. cit.*, pp. 53-55.

EXAMINATION OF TOMMASO, son of the late Battista Salini, of Rome, living in Via della Croce:

Concerning what you have asked me, I must tell you, to be truthful, that I have known the painter, Filippo Trisegno for the last two years, because I am also a painter. Two or three months ago he gave me in writing some defamatory verses against the painter, Giovanni Baglione. He gave them to me on the occasion of a walk which I took one day with the said Filippo. Having asked him what the painters were saying about the picture painted by Giovanni (Baglione) for the Church of the Gesù, he told me that Michelangelo da Caravaggio, Onorio Longo, and Orazio Gentileschi, painters all three, had made certain verses about the said picture, against the said Giovanni and me, because I am Giovanni's companion. Some days later the said Filippo gave me a quarto sheet of paper with many verses against the said Giovanni written upon it and told me that they had been composed by the said Orazio together with Ottavio Padovano, likewise a painter, and that Ludovico Bresciano, also a painter, was distributing them to several painters and in particular had given a copy to one Mario, likewise a painter, who lives on the Corso.

". . . I forget how many days later, . . . the said Filippo told me that the verses were by

Michelangelo and Onorio, and that he had got them from a boy friend of the said Onorio and Michelangelo by the name of G. B. who lives behind the Banchi. [In the full version of Caravaggio's testimony, he claims to know nothing of this Giovanni Battista.] He added that the said Michelangelo, having heard that the said Filippo had had the said sonnets in his hands, had warned him to have his wits about him, and not to let these sonnets fall in the hands of the said Giovanni or into mine, lest some scandal should arise. . . . Filippo also told me that one Bartolomeo, a servant of the said Michelangelo was distributing these and other sonnets to any who asked for them. . . .

". . . I believe that Michelangelo and Orazio made the said verses out of envy, and Onorio, because he is their intimate friend and, moreover, had a dispute with Baglione."

8. Deposizione di Filippo figlio di Domenico Trisegno, romano pittore.   *11 settembre 1603*

". . . Thomasso (Mao Solini) voleua sapere chi me li haueua dati nominando per indovinare Michelangelo da Caravaggio, Bartolomeo suo servitore, Oratio Gentileschi, Lodovico Parmigianino, Francesco Scarpellino. Io dissi che quando mi aurebbe insegnato di fare una figura sbattimentata allhora glielo uoleuo dire; ma lui non me imparò mai et così non glie la disse. . . . Altra uolta il Rotolanti mi disse aver altra poesia che mi lasciò copiare presso uno speziale, cominciaua *Giouanni Baglione*. Gli addimandai chi l'haueua fatta et me rispose che l'haueua fatto un giouine che andaua alla logica et alla fisica. . . ."

Deposition of Filippo, son of Domenico Trisegno of Rome, a painter.   *11 September 1603*

". . . [Tommaso] (Mao Salini) wanted to know who had given me the verses and tried to guess, naming Michelangelo da Caravaggio, Bartolomeo his servant, Orazio Gentileschi, Lodovico Parmigianino, and Francesco Scarpellino. I told him that when he would teach me to paint a figure with cast shadows, then would I tell him. But he never taught me, and so I never told him. . . . On another occasion, Rotolanti told me that he had another poem which he let me copy in a druggist's shop. It began "Giovanni Baglione." I asked him who composed it. He answered that the poem was by a young student of logic and medicine.

9. Esame di Orazio quondam G. B. de Gentileschi, pisano pittore.   *12 settembre 1603*

". . . i sonetti sottoscritti Rinaldo ebbi da un certo Giovanni Maggi intagliatore et pittore che habita nel uicolo de Bergamaschi. . . ."

Bertolotti, *op. cit.*, p. 58.   *12 September 1603*

[Orazio, son of the late G. B. de Gentileschi, of Pisa, a painter, declares that he had the sonnets from one Giovanni Maggi, an etcher and painter. . . .]

13 settembre 1603

10. [Filippo Trisegno, romano, sostiene la sua deposizione in faccia al Tommaso Solino, il quale persiste nella sua.]

Bertolotti, *op. cit.*, p. 58.   *13 September 1603*

[Trisegno and Salini insist on their former depositions.]

11. Esame di Michelangiolo Merisio da Carauaggio: *13 settembre 1603*

"Fui preso l'altro giorno in Piazza Navona non so perchè sia."

"L'essercitio mio è di pittore."

"Io credo cognoscere quasi tutti li pittori di Roma et cominciando dalli valenthuomini io cognosco Gioseffe, il Caraccio, il Zucchero, il Pomarancio, il Gentileschi, Prospero, Gio. Andrea, Gio. Baglione, Gismondo e Giorgio Todesco, il Tempesta et altri."

"Quasi tutti li pittori che ho nominati di sopra sono miei amici, ma non sono tutti valentuomini."

"Quella parola valenthuomo appresso di me uuol dire che sappi far bene dell'arte sua, così un pittore valenthuomo che sappi depingere bene et imitar bene le cose naturali."

"De quelli che ho nominati di sopra non sono miei amici nè Gioseffe nè Gio. Baglione, nè il Gentileschi, nè Giorgio Todesco perchè non mi parlano, gli altri tutti mi parlano et conuersano con me."

"Delli pittori che ho nominati de sopra et per buoni pittori Gioseffe, il Zuccharo, il Pomarancio, et Annibale Caracci et gli altri non li tengo per ualenthuomini."

"Li valenthuomini sono quelli che si intendono della pittura et giudicaranno buoni pittori quelli che ho giudicati io buoni et cattivi; ma quelli che sono cattiui pittori et ignoranti giudicaranno per buoni pittori gl'ignoranti come sono loro."

"Io non so che nessun pittore lodi et habbi per buon pittore nessuno de quelli pittori che io non tengho per buoni pittori. Mi sono scordato de dirui che Antonio Tempesta ancora quello è ualentuomo."

"Io non so niente che ce sia nessun pittore che lodi per buon pittore Giovanni Baglione."

"L'opere di G. Baglione l'ho viste quasi tutte cioè alla Madonna dell'Orto la Cappella grande, a S. Gio. Laterano un quadro ed ultimamente al Gesù la resurettione di Xpo."

"Questa pittura a me non piace perchè è goffa e l'ho per la peggio che habbia fatta et detta pittura io non l'ho intesa lodare da nessun pittore e con quanti pittori io ho parlato a nessuno ha piaciuto se non fusse lodata da uno che ua sempre con lui che lo chiamano l'angelo custode che staua là quando la fu scoperta a lodarla che lo chiamano per Mao."

"Quando io la uidi c'era con me Prospero et Gio. Andrea et l'ho uista altre uolte con l'occasione d'andare al Giesù."

"Può essere che Mao se diletti et che impiastri anche lui; ma io non ho mai uisto opere nessune di esso Mao."

"Conosco Onorio Longo quale è molto mio amico, et conosco anco Ottavio [Leoni] Padouano, ma non gli ho mai parlato."

"Col primo non ho mai parlato per conto della Resuretione del Baglione; et il Gentileschi è più de tre anni che non mi ha parlato."

"Io cognosco un Lodovico Bresciano et Mario pittori. Questi staua una uolta con me, et e tre anni che se partì da me e non gli ho mai più parlato e a Ludovico non gli ho mai parlato."

"Bartolomeo fu già mio seruitore: andò due mesi sono alli castelli del Soderino."

"Signor no che io non me deletto de compor uersi nè uolgari nè latini."

"Non ho mai saputo che vi sieno rime o prose contro il Baglione."
Bertolotti, *op. cit.*, pp. 58-60.

EXAMINATION OF MICHELANGELO MERISI OF CARAVAGGIO   *13 September 1603*

[The questions are omitted; only the answers are given.]

"—I was seized the other day in Piazza Navona, I don't know why."

"—My profession is that of a painter."

"—I think I know nearly all the painters in Rome. Beginning with the good artists, I know Giuseppe [d'Arpino], [Annibale] Carracci, [Federico] Zuccari, [Cristoforo] Pomarancio, Gentileschi, Prospero [Orsi], Giovanni Andrea [Donducci], Giovanni Baglione, Gismondo [Lair] and George the German [Hoefnagel], [Antonio] Tempesta, and others."

"—Nearly all the painters mentioned above are my friends, but not all are *valentuomini* [good artists]."

"—This word *valentuomo*, in my use of it, means a man who knows how to practice his art well. Thus, a painter is a *valentuomo* if he knows how to paint well and to imitate well natural things."

"—Of those mentioned above, neither Giuseppe, nor Giovanni Baglione, nor Gentileschi, nor George the German are my friends, for they don't speak to me. All the others speak and converse with me."

"—Of the painters mentioned above, I regard as good painters Giuseppe, Zuccari, Pomarancio, and Annibale Carracci. The others I don't consider *valentuomini*."

"—*Valentuomini* are those who have a real understanding of painting. They will pronounce to be good painters those that I have pronounced to be good, and bad those I have pronounced bad. But bad and ignorant painters will pronounce good those who are ignorant like themselves."

"—I don't know of any painter who praises and regards as a good painter any of those whom I don't reckon as good. I forgot to say that Antonio Tempesta, too, is a good artist."

"—I know nothing about there being any painter who will praise Giovanni Baglione as a good painter."

"—I have seen nearly all of Giovanni Baglione's works; namely, the Great Chapel in the Madonna dell' Orto, a picture in St. John Lateran, and lately *Christ's Resurrection* in the Gesù."

"—I don't like this painting, because it is clumsy. I regard it as the worst he has ever done. I have never heard any painters praise the said painting. Of all the painters I have spoken to, none liked it, except perhaps one [Salini] who is always with Baglione and whom they call his guardian angel. When it was unveiled he was standing by, praising it. They call him Mao."

"—When I saw it, Prospero and Giovanni Andrea were with me, and I have seen it at other times, when I had occasion to go to the Gesù."

"—It may be that Mao, too, daubs a little, for a pastime. But I have never seen any works by Mao."

"—I know Onorio Longo, who is a great friend of mine, and I also know Ottavio Padovano, but I have never spoken to him."

"—With the former I have never spoken about Baglione's *Resurrection*. And Gentileschi has not been speaking to me for over three years."

"—I know a Lodovico Bresciano and a Mario, painters. The latter once stayed with me, but left me three years ago, and I have not spoken to him since. To Lodovico I have never spoken."

"—Bartolomeo was formerly my servant. Two months ago he went to Soderini's in the Castelli."

"—No sir, I don't amuse myself composing verses, either in Italian or Latin."

"—I have never heard of the existence of rhymes or prose works against Baglione."

12. Deposizione di Orazio Gentileschi: *14 Settembre.*

"Io cognosco tutti li pittori di Roma da un tempo in qua et la prima cosa tutti li principali.

"Questi sono Gioseffe, Anibal Caracci, Giouanni dal Borgo, il Pomarancio, Michelangelo da Carauaggio, Durante del Borgo, Giovanni Baglione et altri che non me ne ricordo, che sono della prima classe.

"Io sono amico de tutti questi pittori ma c'e bene una certa concorrenza fra noi come a dire che hauendo io messo un quadro di S. Michele Arcangelo a S. Gio. de' Fiorentini, Baglione se mostrò mio concorrente et ne mise uno altro all'incontro che era un amor deuino, che lui haueua fatto a concorrenza d'un amor terreno de Michelangelo da Carauaggio quale amor deuino lui l'haueua dedicato al Cardinale Giustiniano et se bene detto quadro non piacque quanto quello de Michelangelo non dimeno per quanto s'intese esso Cardinale gli donò una collana. Detto quadro haueua molte imperfettione che io gli disse che haueua fatto un huomo grande et armato che uoleua esser nudo et putto et cosi lui ne fece poi un altro quale era poi tutto ignudo.

"Non parlai più al Baglione dopo la cosa di quel S. Michele et anco prima perche nell'andar per Roma lui aspetta che io gli facci di beretta et io aspetto che facci beretta a me et anco il Caravaggio, se bene amico aspetta che io lo saluti sebbene amici, ma deue esser sei o otto mesi che io non ho parlato al Caravaggio sebbene ha mandato a casa mia per una veste da cappuccino che gliela imprestai et un par d'ale che mi rimandò deue essere 10 giorni."
Bertolotti, *op. cit.*, pp. 62-63.

Deposition of Orazio Gentileschi: *14 September*

"I have known all the painters of Rome for some time. In the first place, I know all the leading ones.

"These are Giuseppe, Annibale Carracci, Giovanni dal Borgo, Pomarancio, Michelangelo da Caravaggio, Durante dal Borgo, Giovanni Baglione, and others whom I don't recall. These belong to the first class.

"I am a friend of all these painters. There is, however, a certain rivalry among us. For instance, when I placed a picture of St. Michael the Archangel in St. John's of the Florentines, Baglione showed his rivalry by placing another picture opposite it. This was a Divine Love, which he had painted in order to rival an Earthly Love by Michelangelo da Caravaggio. This Divine Love he had dedicated to Cardinal Giustiniani, and although this picture was not liked so well as Michelangelo's, nonetheless, from what was reported, the Cardinal presented him with a [golden] chain. This picture had many imperfections, as I told him, for he had painted an armed full-grown man, whereas it should have been a nude child. So later he painted another, which was entirely nude.

"I never spoke to Baglione again after the incident of the St. Michael. And seldom even before, because when walking about Rome he waits for me to lift my cap to him and I wait for him to lift his cap to me. Caravaggio, too, though he is my friend, expects me to greet him first, though we are friends. However, it must be six or eight months since I spoke to Caravaggio last, though he sent to my house for a Capuchin's frock, which I lent him, and for a pair of wings, which he sent back to me about ten days ago."

Die 25 septembris 1603

13. Pro Michelangelo Merisio de Caravaggio None carcerato pro pretenso libello famoso, contra fiscum. Ill^mus dominus Gubernator etc. moderando aliud decretum factum, attento verbo dato ipsi Illmo domino Gubernatori, ut asserit, per Ill^mum dominum oratorem Regis Christianissimi de eum representando infra mensem proximum coram eodem Illmo eiusque Curia et interim de non offendendo sub poenis arbitrio etc., necnon iniuncto precepto de non discedendo e domo sue habitationis sine licentia in scriptis etc. sub poena triremium arbitrio etc. relaxari inter omnes etc. Super quibus etc. Presentibus sociis testibus etc.

Preceptum—Deinde fuit per me etc. intimatum praeceptum predictum Presentibus Johanne Bap[tis]te Constantis romano et Antonio de Porchia Cancellario testibus etc.

In favor of Michelangelo Merisi of Caravaggio, imprisoned in the Tor di Nona for an alleged libel; against the Administration. The Most Illustrious Lord, the Governor [of Rome], modifying another decree that he had issued, heeding the promise given to the same Illustrious Governor, as he says, by the Most Illustrious Lord, the Ambassador of the Most Christian King [i.e. the ambassador of France] that he would make the defendant reappear within the next month before the same Most Illustrious Lord and his Court, and that meanwhile he [the defendant] would not commit any offense under penalties at the discretion of the Governor etc. . . . and that he would not, in violation of the command issued to him, leave his residence without written permission etc. under the penalties of the galleys at the discretion etc.; to be released among all etc. upon which etc. in the presence of the witnesses etc.

Archivio di Stato: Liber Actorum, vol. 132, fol. 1b, 2a.

14. Querela contro Michelangiolo da Caravaggio, pittore   *24 aprile 1604*
[Pietro de Fosaccia dal Lago Maggiore, servo nell'albergo del Moro espone]

"Circa le 17 hore stando detto querelato assieme a doi altri a magnare dell'osteria del Moro alla Madelana doue io sto per garzone et hauendoli portato otto carcioffi cotti cioè quattro nel buturo et quattro col olio, detto querelato mi ha domandato quali erano quelli al buturo et quelli all'olio. Io li ho risposto: Che li odorasse, che facilmente hauerebbe conosciuto quali erano cotti nel buturo et quelli che erano all'olio. Lui alhora è montato in collera et senza dirmi altro ha preso un piatto di terra et me l'ha tirato alla uolta del mostaccio, che me ha colto in questa guancia manca doue son restato un poco ferito. Et poi si è dirizzato et ha dato di mano alla spada di un suo compagno che staua su la tauola con animo forse di darmi con ella, ma io me gli sono leuato dinanzi et son uenuto qua all'officio a darne querela. Si è trouato presente il signor Curtio Martiri, il signor Rotilio procuratore degli Orfanelli."

Bertolotti, *op. cit.*, pp. 67-68.

A COMPLAINT against Michelangelo de Caravaggio, the painter. 24 *April 1604*

[Pietro de Fosaccia of Lake Maggiore, a servant in the inn of the Blackamoor, states]

"About seventeen hours [12:30 p.m.] the above-named defendant with two other men was eating in the Tavern of the Blackamoor, near the Church of the Magdalene, where I am employed as a waiter. I had brought him eight cooked artichokes, to wit, four cooked in butter and four in oil, and the said defendant asked me which were done in butter and which in oil. I replied: 'Smell them, and you will easily know which are cooked in butter and which in oil.' Thereupon, he flew into a rage and without further words seized an earthen plate and flung it at my face. It hit me here in the left cheek, wounding me slightly. Then he got up and snatched the sword of one of his companions, which was lying on the table, perhaps with intent to strike me. But I got away from him and came here to the office to file a complaint. Sgr. Curzio Martiri and Sgr. Rotilio, director of the Orfanelli, were present."

15. PIETRO ANTONIO DE MADII piacentino, copista: 25 *aprile*

"Era a pranzo all'osteria del Moro oue da altra banda vi era Michelangiolo da Caravaggio pittore. Intesi domandare da lui se i carciofoli erano all'olio o al burro essendo tutti in un piatto. Il garzone disse: Non lo so et ne pigliò uno et se lo mise al naso. Il che hauendo hauto a male Michelangiolo si leuò in piedi in collera e gli disse: Se ben mi pare, becco fott . . . ti credi di seruire qualche barone. Et prese quel piatto con dentro i carciofoli e lo tirò al garzone nel uiso. Non vidi Michelangiolo cacciar mano alla spada contro lo stesso."

PIETRO ANTONIO DE MADII of Piacenza, a copyist, states: 25 *April*

"I was having dinner at the Tavern of the Blackamoor. On the other side of the room there was Michelangelo da Caravaggio, the painter. I heard him ask whether the artichokes were done in oil or butter, they being all in one plate. The waiter said: 'I don't know,' and picked one up and put it to his nose. Michelangelo took it amiss, sprang to his feet in rage, and said: 'If I am not mistaken, you damned cuckold, you think you are serving some bum.' And he seized the plate with the artichokes on it and threw it at the waiter's face. I did not see Michelangelo grasp the sword to threaten the waiter."

[A dì 20 ottobre 1604 era in carcere per altro.]

16. MICHELANGIOLO MERISIO DA CARAVAGGIO: 20 *ottobre 1604*

"Fui preso l'altra sera nella strada della Ternità che va al Popolo ed erano quattro ore di notte. E fu preso con me Spauenta Ottaviano ed altro. Fummo arrestati perchè fu tirato un sasso e si voleva che io dicessi chi l'aveva tirato mentre io non sapeva. Io dissi ai birri: andate a cercare chi gettò il sasso e non parole ingiuriose."

Bertolotti, *op. cit.*, p. 69.

[On October 20, 1604 he was in jail for another offense.]

MICHELANGELO MERISI DA CARAVAGGIO: *20 October 1604*

"I was seized the other night on the street leading from the Trinità dei Monti to Piazza del Popolo [Via del Babuino]. It was four hours after nightfall [9:30 p.m.]. Spaventa Ottaviano and another man were seized with me.

"We were arrested because a stone had been thrown and they wanted me to tell who had thrown it, whereas I didn't know. I told the constables: 'Go and look for the man who threw the stone, and no more abusive words.'"

1604, die 18 novembris

17. . . . Idem (*corporalis*) retulit che alle cinque hore de notte alla chiavica del Bufalo fu fermato dalli miei huomini Michelangelo da Caravaggio che portava spada et pugnale, et domandatoli se haveva licenza disse de sì et la mostrò, et così li fu resa, et dissi che lo lasciassero andare, et così io dissi: "bona notte Signore," et lui rispose forte: "ti ho in culo," et così io detti arresto et non volsi comportare questa cosa, et così lo feci pigliare et dapoi che fu ligato disse: "ho in culo te et quanti par tuoi si trovano," et così lo mandai prigione a Tor di Nona.

Patrizi, M. L., *Il Caravaggio e la nuova critica d'arte*, Recanati, Simvoli, 1921, p. 157.

18 November 1604

The same corporal reported that "at five hours after nightfall [10:30 p.m.] at the conduit of the Bufalo, Michelangelo da Caravaggio, who was carrying a sword and dagger, was halted by my men. When asked if he had a license, he answered, 'Yes,' and presented it, and so he was dismissed, and I told him he could leave, and said 'Good-night, Sir.' He replied loudly, 'Shove it. . . .' and so I arrested him, since I did not wish to bear such a thing. I ordered my men to take him, and when he was bound he said, 'You and as many as are with you can shove it. . . .' and so I put him in the jail of Tor di Nona."

[Eccolo a sua volta ricorrente alla giustizia.]

18. DEPOSIZIONE di Michelangiolo Merisi da Caravaggio, pittore: *16 febbraio 1605*

"Alli giorni passati mi venne a trovare Cosimo Coli foriere o sotto foriere di S. S. e me domandò un tappeto quale diceva haver dato ad Alessandro Ricci in mio nome io non sapendo niente mandai a vedere il libro della foreria ove si trovò segnato un tappeto del valore di 40 scudi consegnato nel modo suddetto. Avendo saputo che detto Alessandro si trova prigione fo instanza che non sia relassato se prima non hauerà restituito detto tappeto."

Bertolotti, *op. cit.*, pp. 69-70.

[Next it was Caravaggio's turn to appeal to the law:]

DEPOSITION of Michelangelo Merisi of Caravaggio, the painter: *16 February 1605*

"A few days ago Cosimo Coli, harbinger or under-harbinger of His Holiness came to see me and asked me for a rug which he said he had given to Alessandro Ricci for me. Knowing nothing about the matter, I sent to inspect the book in the harbinger's office where a rug worth 40 scudi delivered as aforesaid was found to be entered. Having heard that the said Alessandro is in jail, I petition that he shall not be released unless he has first returned the said rug."

28 maggio 1605.

19. [Ed ora nuovamente in carcere lo troviamo, soltanto invece di quelle del Governatore sta nelle Senatorie. A di 28 maggio 1605, il capitano Pirro bargello della Curia di Campidoglio riferiva:]

"Questa notte sulle 7 hore stando io assieme con miei sbirri a far l'aspettativa a Santo Ambrosio al Corso uenne uno chiama Micalangelo quale portaua spada et pugnale et fermato et adimandato se haueua licenza di portar dette arme mi ha detto di no; lo feci pigliar et menar prigione et ne do relatione conforme al mio debito acciò sia casticato conforme al giusto." (R. Relazione dei sbirri, 1604-1605, f. 145).

[Il bargello diedesi perfino la pena di disegnare la figura della spada e del pugnale a lato alla sua relazione. Ecco ora l'esame del carcerato Merisi:]

"Io sono stato preso nella strada del Corso de rincontro alla chiesa di Santo Ambrosio che poteua essere uicino alle otto hore che era giorno et son stato preso perchè haueua spada et pugnale.

"Io non ho licenza nessuna di portar spada e pugnale *in scrittis*, eccettuato a bocca il signor Gover.^re di Roma haueua ordinato al bargello e suo caporale che mi lasciasse portare; altra licenza non ho."

Riconosce l'arme levatagli dai birri.

Fu messo *ad largam* con tre giorni di tempo per far le sue difese.

[Trovasi in margine della relazione del bargello questa nota:]

Relaxatus gratis et fuerunt restituta arma.

Bertolotti, *op. cit.*, pp. 70-71.

28 May 1605

[Now we find him in jail again; but instead of being in the Governor's jail he is in the Senators'. On May 28, 1605 Captain Pirro, Captain of the police of the Court of the Capitol, reported:]

"Last night about seven hours after nightfall [3:00 a.m.] as I was on patrol with my constables at Sant' Ambrogio on the Corso, there came a man by the name of Michelangelo, wearing a sword and dagger. Stopped and asked whether he had a license to carry the said weapons, he said he had not. I had him arrested and brought to jail, and I now make my report, as is my duty, that he may be punished according to justice."

[The captain even took the trouble to draw a picture of the sword and dagger on the margin of his report. And here is the examination of the prisoner Merisi:]

"I was seized on the street of the Corso in front of the Church of Sant' Ambrogio. It may have been eight hours after nightfall, [4:00 a.m.] for it was light, and I was seized because I had a sword and dagger.

"I have no written license to carry a sword and dagger. However, the Governor of Rome had given oral orders to the captain and his corporal to let me carry them. I have no other license."

He recognized the weapons taken from him by the constables.

He was allowed to go at large, with three days' time to prepare his defense.

[On the margin of the captain's report this note is to be found:]

He was released without bail and the weapons were returned to him.

20 luglio 1605

20. [Altre brighe tosto seguirono, trovando che a dì 20 luglio 1605 Cherubino Alberto da Borgo S. Sepolcro pittore al Popolo, Girolamo Crocichia da Narni *sutor* ad Sforzam, Prospero Orsi pittore al Salvatore in Campo e Ottaviano Gabriello librario in piazza dell'Angone promettono che Michelangiol da Caravaggio, carcerato in torre di Nona, si ripresenterà avanti il Governatore e sua curia sotto pena di scudi 100 e che non offenderà, nè farà offendere Laura e sua figlia Isabella pelle quali vi fu processo sotto pena di scudi 100.

Bertolotti, *op. cit.*, p. 71.

20 July 1605

[He got into trouble again, for we find that on 20 July 1605, Cherubino Alberto of Borgo San Sepolcro, a painter, living in Piazza del Popolo, Girolamo Crocicchia of Narni, a shoemaker in Piazza Sforza, Prospero Orsi, a painter at San Salvatore in Campo, and Ottaviano Gabriello, a bookseller in Piazza dell'Angone, promise that Michelangelo da Caravaggio, jailed in Torre di Nona, will appear before the Governor and his Court subject to a 100 scudi penalty in case of non-appearance, and that he will not offend nor cause others to offend Laura and her daughter Isabella, by whom he had been sued, on pain of a 100 scudi fine.

29 luglio 1605

21. [Il notaio de' Malefizi, visitò Mariano Pasqualone de Accumulo notaio nell'Offizio di Paolo Spada che, con giuramento, depone:]

"Io sono qui all'Officio perchè sono stato assassinato da Michelangiolo da Caravaggio pittore nel modo che dirrò a V. S. Il signor Galeazzo e me, addesso che può essere un'hora di notte in circa, spasseggiando in Navona avanti il palazzo del signor Ambasciadore di Spagna mi sono sentito dare una botta in testa dalla banda di dietro, che io sono subbito cascato in terra et sono restato ferito in testa, che credo sia stato un colpo di spada, che come se uede io ho una ferita in testa dalla banna manca et poi se ne è fuggito via.

"Io non ho uisto chi sia stato quello che mi ha ferito, ma io non ho da fare con altri che con detto Michelangelo perchè a queste sere passate avessimo parole sul Corso lui et io per causa di una donna chiamata Lena che sta in piedi a piazza Nauona passato il palazzo overo il portone del Palazzo del signor Sertorio Teofilo, che è donna di Michelangelo. Di gratia V. S. mi spedischi presto acciò mi possi medicare."

[Accordatagli la domandata licenza si passò ad esaminare Galeazzo Roccasecca scrittore di lettere apostoliche che depone:]

"Vidi uno con un'arme sfoderata in mano che mi è parso una spada o pistolese, che subito si è reuoltato ha fatto tre salti.

". . . Portaua un ferraiolo negro in una spalla, solo udii che il ferito disse che non poteva esser altri che Michelangelo da Caravaggio."

Bertolotti, *op. cit.*, pp. 71-72.

29 July 1605

[The Clerk of the Criminal Court visited Mariano Pasqualone of Accumoli, a notary, in the office of Paolo Spada. Pasqualone on oath testified:]

"I am here in the office because I have been assaulted by Michelangelo da Caravaggio, the painter, as I am going to relate. As Mr. Galeazzo and I—it may have been about one hour after nightfall [8:30 p.m.]—were strolling in Piazza Navona in front of the palace of the Spanish Ambassador, I suddenly felt a blow on the back of my head. I fell to the ground at once and realized that I had been wounded in the head by what I believe to have been the stroke of a sword. As you can see, I have a wound on the left side of my head. Thereupon, the aggressor fled.

"I didn't see who wounded me, but I never had disputes with anybody but the said Michelangelo. A few nights ago he and I had words on the Corso on account of a girl called Lena who is to be found at the Piazza Navona, past the palace, or rather the main door of the palace of Mr. Sertorio Teofilo. She is Michelangelo's girl. Please, excuse me quickly, that I may dress my wounds."

[He was granted the permission he had asked for, and Galeazzo Roccasecca, Writer of Apostolic Letters, was examined next. He testified:]

"I saw a man with an unsheathed weapon in his hand. It looked like a sword or a hunting-knife. He turned round at once and made three jumps.

". . . He wore a black cloak on one shoulder. I only heard the wounded man say it could not be anyone but Michelangelo da Caravaggio."

26 Agosto, 1605

22. [Ed ecco come finì, se non cavallerescamente, da buon cristiano, come dice l'atto medesimo:]

Fidem facio ego notarius publicus infrascriptus etc. etc. inter D. Marianum Pasqualonum de Accumulo ex una et D. Michaelem Angelum Merisium pictorem in urbe partibus ex altera ortae fuerint quaedam inimicitiae et rixae quarum deinde occatione idem D. Michaelangelus unico uulnere in capite et percussione in bracchio sinistro cum ense siue alio armorum genere eundem D. Marianum sub die 28 Julii proxime preteriti seu alio ueriori die affecerit et curia Ill.mi e R.mi D. Gubernatoris Urbis suo ex officio forsan contra predictum D. Michaelem Angelum processerit et postmodum dictae partes communium amicorum hortatu et suasione ad pacem ut bonos decet Christianos deuenire decreuerint uolentesque super premissis et infrascriptis ualidum edificare instrumentum etc. etc.

"Io Michelangelo Merisio essendo stato iniurato de para de M.° Mariano Notaro del

Vicario et non hauendo di giorno lui uoluto portar spada, mi risolsi a darli doue io l'incontrassi et capitandomi auanti una sera con un altro accompagnato et conosciutolo benissimo in uiso li diedi, del che me ne rincresce assai che se l'hauessi da fare nol faria et ne li domando perdono et la pace, et tengo che detto M.º Mariano con la spada in mano sia huomo da rispondere a me et a qualsiuoglia altra persona. Io Michelangelo Merisi affermo quando di sopra."
Datum 26 agosto 1605, ecc. ecc.

Bertolotti, *op. cit.*, p. 73.   *26 August 1605*

[And here is how the affair was closed, if not in a chivalrous, at any rate, in a Christian manner, as the instrument itself declares:]

I, the undersigned notary public, etc. etc., do hereby certify that between Mr. Mariano Pasqualoni of Accumoli, on one side, and Mr. Michelangelo Merisi, a painter in Rome, on the other, a certain enmity and quarrel had arisen, as a result of which the said Mr. Michelangelo later inflicted on the said Mr. Mariano a single wound in the head and a bruise on the left arm with a sword or other kind of weapon on or about 28 July last, and that the court of the Most Illustrious and Reverend Governor of Rome ex-officio prosecuted the said Mr. Michelangelo, and subsequently the above-named parties, exhorted and persuaded by mutual friends, determined to make peace as befits good Christians, and, upon what precedes and follows, willingly consented to execute this valid instrument, etc. etc.

"I, Michelangelo Merisi, having been insulted by Mr. Mariano, clerk of the Vicar's Court, as he would not wear a sword in the daytime, resolved to strike him wherever I should meet him. One night, having come upon him accompanied by another man and having perfectly recognized his face, I struck him. I am very sorry for what I did, and if I had not done it yet, I would not do it. I beg him for his forgiveness and peace, and I regard the said Mr. Mariano with a sword in his hand as a man fit to stand his ground against me or anybody else. I, Michelangelo Merisi, do affirm all the above."

                                                                  1 settembre 1605

23. [Non mai emendato pochi giorni dopo, cioè a dì 1 settembre 1605, trovo che Prudenzia Bruna romana abitante in Campo Marzio dava querela contro Michelangiolo da Caravaggio pittore, senza dimora fissa.]

"Questa notte pr. p. verso le 5 ore è venuto M. di Car. ed ha tirato molti sassi alla mia gelosia della finestra e me l'ha rotta tutta da una banda come si vede. Dopo è ripassato con suoi compagni. Ha fatto ciò perchè tenendo lui a pigione una mia casa attaccata alla mia, i giorni passati ferì un notaro del Vicario e se partì, e dovendo io esser pagata di sei mesi e di un suffitto mio di detta casa che esso l'ha rotto ed avendo io hauuto un mandato di pigliar le robbe sue restate in casa dando una securtà come feci. E per ciò credo lui per farmi dispetti mi habbia rotto la gelosia."

Bertolotti, *op. cit.*, p. 74.   *1 September 1605*

[He didn't reform, however. A few days later, to wit, on 1 September 1605, we find that Prudenzia Bruna of Rome, living in Campo Marzio, lodged a complaint against Michelangelo da Caravaggio, painter, no residence.]

"Last night about five hours after nightfall [midnight] Michelangelo da Caravaggio came and threw many stones at the Venetian blind of my window completely breaking it on one side, as you can see. Later he again passed by with his companions. He did it because he had leased a house of mine adjoining my home, and a few days ago had wounded a clerk of the Vicar's Court and had left the house. I was his creditor for six months' rent and for a ceiling in the said house which he had damaged, and I had obtained a warrant to take his belongings left in my house, upon giving a bond, as I did. That's why, I believe, he broke my Venetian blind—to annoy me."

MURDER OF RANUCCIO TOMASSONI*

24. Avviso: *1606, Maggio 31*

Successe in Campo Marzo la suddetta sera di domenica una questione assai notabile di 4 per banda, capo di una un tal Ranuccio da Terani che vi restò morto subito dopo lungo contrasto, et dell'altra Michelangolo da Caravaggio, pittore di qualche fama a nostri giorni, che vogliono sia restato ferito, ma però non si trova ove sia, ma bene è restato malamente ferito et prigione uno di suoi compagni, che chiamano capitano, da Bologna, che era soldato di Castello, et vogliono la causa sia stato interessi di gioco et di X scudi, che il morto haveva vinto al pittore.

Orbaan, J. A. F., *Documenti sul Barocco in Roma*, Rome, 1920, p. 73.

31 May 1606

Notice: On the aforesaid Sunday night a serious quarrel took place in the Campo Marzio, with four men on either side. The leader of one side was Ranuccio of Terni, who died immediately after a long fight; and of the other Michelangelo of Caravaggio, a painter of some renown in our day, who reportedly received a wound, but his whereabouts is not known. Severely wounded, however, and taken to prison, was one of his companions whom they call the Captain, from Bologna, and who was a soldier of Castel Sant'Angelo. The incident is alleged to have been caused by a dispute over a game involving 10 scudi which the dead man had won from the painter.

1605-1606

25. [Il notaio de'Malefizi, che lo visitava, mentre era in letto nella casa di Andrea Rufetti, vicino alla piazza Colonna, non potè sapere chi l'avesse ferito nella gola e nell'orecchio sinistro. Le sue risposte furono:]

"Io me so ferito da me con la mia spada che so cascato per queste strade et non so doue se sia stato nè c'è stato nessuno."

[Insistendo l'esaminatore:]

"Io non posso dire altro."

[Allora il notaro della curia gli proibì sotto pena di 500 scudi di multa di partirsi da quella casa.]

Bertolotti, *op. cit.*, p. 75.

* See also docs. 63-67.

1605 or 1606

[The clerk of the Criminal Court, who visited Caravaggio while he lay in bed in Andrea Rufetti's house, near Piazza Colonna, was unable to ascertain who had wounded him in the throat and on the left ear. His replies were:]

"I wounded myself with my sword in falling on these streets. I don't know where it happened, and no one was present."

[As the examiner insisted:]

"I can say no more."

[Then the clerk of the Court forbade him to leave that house under penalty of a 500 scudi fine.]

26. PETITION OF ONORIO LONGHI: *1606*

Beatissimo Padre

Honorio Lungo con ogni humiltà espone a V. B.ne come nel 1606 hebbe il bando da Roma come appare ne' processi dei tribunali del Governatore di questa città et Vicario di V. S. perchè si trouo presente all'homicidio fatto da Michelangielo da Caravaggio in persona di Ranuccio Tomassoni nel qual fatto non hebbe l'oratore colpa, anzi accompagnaua il Caravaggio come suo amoreuole; perchè non occorresse disordine et esshortandolo a far la pace; come buon testimonio è Iddio e la sua propria coscienza. Laonde dalla parte che dell'innocenza sua è rimasa molto ben consapeuole, ha ottenuta la pace et in questo tempo si è trattenuto in Milano in seruitio della M.tà Cesarea e desiderando di ripatriare con la moglie e cinque figli che ha acciocchè possa principalmente seruire sua Chiesa e V.a Beatitudine in quello che si degnerà comandargli, humilmente lo supplica a fargli gratia del detto bando che ne uiuerà con obbligo perpetuo con la sua famiglia di pregar Dio per la lunga uita et salute di V. Stà.

Bertolotti, *op. cit.*, pp. 75-76.

Most Blessed Father: *1606*

Onorio Longo, in all humility, states to Your Holiness that in 1606 he was banished from Rome—as appears from the records of the courts of the Governor of this City and Vicar of Your Holiness—because he happened to be present at the homicide committed by Michelangelo da Caravaggio on the person of Ranuccio Tomassoni. Of this deed your petitioner was not guilty. On the contrary, he was accompanying Caravaggio as a loving friend lest some disturbance should occur, and was exhorting him to make peace, of which God and his own conscience bear witness. Accordingly, he has effected a reconciliation with the injured party, who are perfectly aware of his innocence. During this time he has been dwelling in Milan in the service of His Imperial Majesty. Now, desiring to return to his native city with his wife and five children, chiefly in order that he may serve the Holy Church and Your Holiness in whatever You may deign to order him, he humbly petitions You to grant him remission of the said banishment, and pledges himself and his family that as long as they live they will constantly pray God to give a long life and good health to Your Holiness.

THE ORDER OF MALTA

die xiiii mensis Julii 1608

27. RECEPTIO in fratrem Militem obedientiae pro Magnifico Michaeli Angelo de Caravaggio.

Frater Alofius de Wignacourt Dei gratia Sacrae Domus Hospitalis Sancti Joannis Hierosolymitani, et Militaris Ordinis Sancti Sepulchri Dominici Magister humilis, pauperumque Jesu Christi Custos. Universis et singulis praesentes nostras literas visuris, lecturis, et audituris salutem in Domino. Cum in provehendis hominibus non solum genere, sed aliqua etiam arte, ac disciplina rerum publicarum principes, et Rectores benignos se praebere debeant, ut praemii, et honorum spe mortalium ingenia totis viribus ad praeclara studia incumbant. Cumque Magnificus Michael Angelus Carraca oppido vulgo de Caravaggio in Longobardis natus, hanc Urbem appellens, mox zelo Religionis accensus habitu, ac insignibus Militiae nostrae decorari valde cupere nobis significaverit. Nos eximium pictura Virum sui voti compotem facere volentes ut tandem Melita nostra Insula, ac Religio non minori iactantia illum adoptatum alumnum, ac Civem suum aliquando praedicet, quam Coos etiam nostrae dictionis Insula Apellem suum extollit neve si cum recentioribus nostri saeculi illum conferre velimus, artis excellentiam posthac invideamus alteri hac in re praeclarissimo cuius nomen aeque ac penicillum is [*eius*] refert. Nos inquam illum specialibus gratiis et favoribus prosequi volentes, Ordine nostro donandum, ac insignibus Religionis, et cingulo militiae decorandum duximus. Quapropter dicti Michaelis Angelis optimum desiderium [supply: *probamus*] Omnipotenti Deo, Deiparae Virgini Mariae, ac Divo Joanni Baptistae, auctoritate Apostolica nobis ad hoc speciatim concessa eum recipimus, et cooptamus in gradum fratruum militum obedientiae nuncupatorum. Volumusque insuper atque praescrivimus, ut ubique plenissime gaudeat ac fruatur omnibus, et singulis privilegiis, immunitatibus, gratiis, libertatibus, exemptionibus, commoditatibus, et praerogativis quibus alii fratres milites obedientiae Ordinis nostri potiuntur et gaudent, participemus ex nunc ipsum facimus omnium, et quorumcumque bonorum spiritualium quae ad Dei gloriam, et honorem tam contra fidei Catholicae hostes, quam in pio Hospitalitatis exercitio divinoque cultu. Inhibentes universis et singulis Ordinis nostri fratribus praesentibus et futuris quacunque auctoritate, dignitate, officioque fungentibus ne contra praesentes nostras receptionis gratiae et privilegii literas aliquatenus facere vel venire praesumant, quinimmo eas inviolabiles observent. Non obstantibus quibusvis constitutionibus, statutis, ordinationibus Capitularibus decretis, usibus, et consuetudinibus, caeterisque contrariis quibuscunque; quibus omnibus et singulis hac vice duntaxat ad effectum praesentium specialiter et expresse derogamus. In cuius rei testimonium Bulla nostra Magistralis plumbea praesentibus est appensa. Datum Melitae in Conventu nostro die xiiii mensis Julii 1608.

Liber Bullarum (G. M. Aloph de Wignacourt, 1607-08-09); vol. 456, fol. 282.

14 July 1608

RECEPTION of the Honorable Michael Angelo de Caravaggio as Brother and Knight of Obedience. [Abridged translation]

Brother Alof de Wignacourt, by the grace of God Master of the Sacred Hospital of St. John and Guardian of the Poor of Christ to one and all.

Whereas it behooves the leaders and rulers of commonweals to prove their benevolence by advancing men, not only on account of their noble birth but also on account of their art and science whatever it may be, so that human talent, in hope of reward and honor, may apply itself to praiseworthy studies with all its might;

And whereas the Honorable Michael Angelo, a native of the town Carraca in Lombardy called Caravaggio in the vernacular, having landed in this city and burning with zeal for the Order, has recently communicated to us his fervent wish to be adorned with the habit and insignia of our Knightly Order:

Therefore, we wish to gratify the desire of this excellent painter, so that our island, Malta, and our Order may at last glory in this adopted disciple and citizen with no less pride than the island of Kos (also within our jurisdiction) extols her Apelles; and that, should we compare him to more recent [artists] of our age, we may not afterwards be envious of the artistic excellence of some other man, outstanding in this art, whose name and brush are equally important. Wishing, then, to extend to him special grace and favor, we have decided to induct him into our Order and to adorn him with the insignia of our Order and the Belt of Knighthood. Therefore, [complying with] the pious wish of the aforesaid Michael Angelo, we receive and admit him, by the grace of God Almighty and by a papal authorization especially granted to us for the purpose, to the rank of the Brethren and Knights known as Brethren and Knights of Obedience. . . . We further decree that he enjoy all and sundry of the privileges . . . Enjoining . . . Barring statutory obstacles . . . In witness thereof we have affixed our leaden Magisterial Seal . . . Enacted at Malta, on the fourteenth day of July, sixteen hundred and eight.

28. Commissio Criminalis.   *Die sexta mensis Octobris 1608*

Audita querela Domini fratris Hieronymi Varays Procuratoris fiscalis Religionis facta adversus fratrem Michaelem Angelum Marresi de Caravaggio, qui cum detentus esset in carceribus Castri Sancti Angeli ab eis aufugit et absque licentia Illustrissimi et Reverendissimi Domini Magni Magistri clandestine e Conventu discessit, contra formam statuti 13. de prohibitionibus et poenis. Illustrissimus et Reverendissimus Dominus Magnus Magister, et Venerandum Concilium commiserunt Dominis fratribus Joanni Honoret, et Blasio Suarez, ut vocato praedicto Procuratore fiscali per ministerium Magistri Scutiferi debitas diligentias ad dictum fratrem Michaelem Angelum perquirendum, et citandum adhiberi faciant, et de hujusmodi fuga, et discessu informationes iuxta stylum Religionis capiant, et ad Venerandum Concilium referant.

Liber Conciliorum; vol. 103, folio 13 verso.

Criminal Commission [Abridged translation]   *6 October 1608*

The complaint was heard of Lord Brother Hieronymus Varays, Procurator for the Treasury of the Order, made against brother Michael Angelo Merisi di Caravaggio, who, while detained in the prison of the Castle of St. Angelo, fled from it without permission of the most

illustrious and most Reverend Lord, the Grand Master, and departed secretly from the district, against the form of the statute. 13. concerning prohibitions and penalties:
the most Illustrious and most exalted Lord the Grand Master and Venerable Council commissioned the Lord Brothers Joannes Honoret and Blasius Suarez that, . . . through the agency of the Master Shield-Bearer they should see that all due diligence is shown in searching for the said Brother Michael Angelo and in summoning him to appear, and should gather information about the nature of his flight . . . and should report it to the Venerable Council.

Die vigesima mensis Novembris 1608

29. CONGREGETUR PUBLICA ASSEMBLEA contra fratrem Michaelem Angelum Marresi de Caravaggio.

Visis informationibus captis, habitaque relatione Commissariorum, et constito, qualiter, frater Michael Angelus Marrese de Caravaggio, cum ad instantiam Procuratoris fiscalis detentus esset in carceribus Castri Sancti Angeli ab eis aufugit, et sine licentia Illustrissimi et Reverendissimi Domini Magni Magistri, et contra formam statuti 13 de prohibitionibus et poenis, e Conventu discessit; Et audita instantia praedicti Procuratoris fiscalis Illustrissimus et Reverendissimus Dominus Magnus Magister, et Venerandum Concilium cum scrutinio ballotarum mandaverunt congregari publicam Assembleam ut moris est, et ibi, servata forma statutorum contra dictum fratrem Michaelem Angelum Marrese de Caravaggio procedatur ad privationem habitus.

Liber Conciliorum; fol. 32 verso.

20 November 1608

LET THE PUBLIC ASSEMBLY BE CONVENED against Brother Michael Angelo Merisi di Caravaggio. [Abridged translation]

The information gathered having been established . . . as to how Brother Michael Angelo Merisi di Caravaggio being detained in prison in the Castle of St. Angelo at the instance of the Procurator of the Treasury, did escape without permission . . . and depart from the district. . . . The most Illustrious and most exalted Lord the Grand Master and the Venerable Council have ordered that a General Assembly be summoned as is the custom and that, in accordance with the terms of the statute, proceedings be taken against the said Brother Michael Angelo Merisi di Caravaggio with a view of depriving him of his habit.

30. PRIVATIO HABITUS.   *Die prima mensis Decembris 1608*

Ex decreto et mandato Illustrissimi et Reverendissimi Domini Magni Magistri, et Venerandi Concilii celebrata fuit Publica Assemblea Venerandorum Baiulivorum, Priorum, Preceptorum, et fratruum nostrorum in Ecclesia, et Oratorio Divi Joannis Baptistae Patroni nostri ad sonum campanae, secundum antiquas, et laudabiles consuetudines Sacrae Religionis Hospitalis Hierosolymitani in qua Dominus frater Don Hieronymus de Guevara Magister hospitii, et Procurator prelibati Illustrissimi et Reverendissimi Domini Magni Magistri, et eius nomine fecit plantam adversus fratrem Michaelem Angelum Marrese da Caravaggio. Quare iuxta formam statutorum fuit concessum, et legitime congregatum sgardium in quo repetita dicta planta, et visis, atque perlectis informationibus captis ad instantiam Procuratoris fiscalis contra dictum fratrem Michaelem Angelum Marrese da Caravaggio, et constito, quod cum esset detentus in careribus Castri Sancti Angeli, ab eis aufugit funibus scalando dictum castrum, et sine licentia Illustrissimi et Reverendissimi Domini Magni Magistri et contra formam statuti decimi tertii de prohibitionibus et poenis, iugo Sanctae obedientiae reiecto, e Conventu discessit. Necnon visa, et intellecta relatione Magistri Scutiferi, qui ad eundem fratrem Michaelem Angelum reperiendum fecit consuetas diligentias, citationes, et proclamate per loca publica Conventus, qui denique hodie ipse Magister Scutifer, sive eius locumtenens de mandato Reverendi Sgardii in ipsa publica Assemblea reiteravit alta voce vocando, ut dictus frater Michael Angelus personaliter per primum, secundum, usque ad tertiam, et quartam superabundantem citationem, et non comparuit, nec adhuc comparet, ipse frater Michael Angelus Marresi de Caravaggio per Reverendos Dominos Sgardium celebrantes omnibus bene discussis, et consideratis, servata forma statutorum, cum scrutinio ballotarum nemine discrepante ad privationem habitus condemnatus fuit. Et deinde facta relatione Illustrissimo et Reverendissimo Domino Magno Magistro, sententiam praefatam omnino exequutioni demandari precipienti, in publica Assemblea per Reverendum Dominum Praesidentem dictus frater Michael Angelus Marresi de Caravaggio habitu privatus, et extra Ordinem, et consortium nostrum tanquam membrum putridum, et foetidum eiectus, et separatus fuit.

Liber Conciliorum; fol. 33 verso and 34.

EXPULSION FROM THE ORDER [Abridged translation]   *1 December 1608*

. . . A General Assembly was summoned of the Venerable Bailiffs, the Priors, Preceptors and Brothers in the Church and Oratory of St. John our Patron, at the sound of the bell, according to the ancient and praiseworthy custom of the Holy Order of St. John of Jerusalem . . . the information inspected and carefully read against Michael Angelo Merisi di Caravaggio: And it being determined that he, while detained in the prison of the Castle of St. Angelo, did escape by means of ropes from the said prison and without permission . . . did depart from the district: And moreover the report of the Lord Shield-Bearer being inspected and understood, he having performed the usual observance in seeking out Brother Michael Angelo Merisi di Caravaggio, to wit, summonses and proclamations throughout public places of the district, which summonses the Lord Shield-Bearer himself or his deputy . . . has repeated in a loud voice in the Public Assembly so that the said Brother Michael Angelo di Caravaggio being personally summoned once, twice, thrice and a fourth time, on abundant notice, did not appear nor as yet doth he appear, therefore the same Brother Michael Angelo Merisi di Caravaggio was by the Reverend Lords gathered together, all circumstances being well discussed and determined, according to the terms of the statute, a vote having been taken and no dissentients appearing, condemned to be deprived of his habit.

Thereupon a report was delivered to the Illustrious and exalted Lord, etc., and on his ordering the aforesaid sentence to be put into full execution, the said Brother Michael Angelo Merisi di Caravaggio was in the Public Assembly by the hands of the Reverend Lord President deprived of his habit, and expelled and thrust forth like a rotten and fetid limb from our Order and Community.

See Faith Ashford, "Caravaggio's Stay in Malta," *Burlington Magazine*, Oct. 1935, vol. 67, pp. 168-174.

DEATH OF CARAVAGGIO

31. Avvisi   *1609 ottobre 24*

Si ha di Napoli avviso, che fosse stato ammazzato il Caravaggio, pittore celebre, et altri dicono sfregiato.

24 October 1609

NOTICE: Word has been received from Naples that Caravaggio, the famous painter, has been murdered. Others say disfigured.

32. Avvisi   *1610 luglio 28*

Si è havuto avviso della morte di Michel Angelo Caravaggio, pittore famoso et eccellentissimo nel colorire et ritrarre del naturale, seguita di suo male in Port' Ercole.

28 July 1610

NOTICE: Word has been received of the death of Michelangelo da Caravaggio, the famous painter, excellent in the handling of color and painting from life, following an illness in Port' Ercole.

33. Avvisi   *1610 luglio 31*

È morto Michiel Angelo da Caravaggio, pittore celebre, a Port' Hercole, mentre da Napoli veniva a Roma per la gratia da Sua Santità fattali del bando capitale, che haveva.

31 July 1610

NOTICE: Michelangelo da Caravaggio, the famous painter, died at Port' Ercole, while he was on the way from Naples to Rome because a pardon had been granted him by His Holiness from the sentence of banishment which he was under for a capital crime.

Orbaan, J. A. F., *Documenti sul Barocco a Roma*, Rome, 1920, pp. 157, 175, 176.

34. LETTER in the Segretaria Particolare del Vicere
Auditor de los Presidios de Toscana.

Magco. Señor. Estoy informado q. en Puerto Hercules es muerto Miguel Angelo de Carauaccio, Pintor, y q. en vro. poder ha quedado toda su hazienda, particularmente la que va en el Inuentario q. serà con esta, por hauer hecho espolio d'ella so pretesto q. fuesse del habito de St. Juan, y que tocasse al Prior de Capua, q. ha declarado no tener derecho en este espolio por no ser el defuncto cauallero de Malta, y assi os encargo q. en recibiendo esta, me embieys la dicha ropa con la primera comodidad q. se ofreciere de Faluca, y en particular el quadro de St. Juan Bautista, y si por suerte se huuiesse hecho exito del, o quitadose de la ropa de qualquier suerte, procureys en todas maneras que se halle y cobre para embiarlo bien acondicionado con la demas ropa para entregarla aqui a quien tocare y executareys esto sin replica, auisandome del recibo d'esta.   *Nuestro Escritorio. De Naps. a 19 de Agosto 1610*

To the Judge of Military Affairs in the Garrisons of Tuscany.   *19 August 1610*

Honoured Sir: I have been informed that the painter Michael Angelo di Caravaggio has died at Port' Ercole and that you have in your possession all his property, especially the items indicated in the inventory which accompanies this letter, the property having been taken over as a spolium under the pretext that the deceased was a member of the Order of St. John, and that it belonged to the Prior of Capua who has declared that he has no right to this spolium inasmuch as the deceased was not a Knight of Malta; and thus I charge you that as soon as you receive this letter you send me the aforesaid property by the first felucca available, and especially the painting of *St. John the Baptist*, and if by chance it has been disposed of or removed from the property for whatever reason, you shall endeavour by all means to see that it is found and recovered in order to send it well packed with the other property and deliver it here to the proper authority, and you shall carry this out unconditionally, informing me of the receipt of this letter. From my desk. Naples, August 19, 1610.

[Its date places it in the term of office of Don Pedro Fernandez de Castro, seventh Conde de Lemos, who was Viceroy of Naples from 1610 to 1616.]

From Green, O., *Burlington Magazine*, June 1951, pp. 202-203.

35. Two Epitaphs containing Caravaggio's birth and death

Mich. Angel. Merisius de Caravaggio—eques Hierosolimitanus—naturae aemulator eximius—vix. ann. XXXVI. m. IX D. XX—moritur XVIII Julis MDCX.

Michelangelo Merisi da Caravaggio—Knight of Jerusalem—eminent emulator of nature—lived thirty-six years, nine months and twenty days—died 18 July 1610.

Michaeli Angelo Merisio Firmi F.—de Caravaggio—in picturis jam non pictori—sed naturae prope aequali—obiit in portu Herculis—e Partenope illuc se conferens—Romam repetens—XV Kal. Augusti—Anno Ch. R: MDCX—Vix ann. XXXVI. mens. IX. D. XX—Martius Milesius Jur. Cons.—Amico eximiae indolis—P[osuit].

Michelangelo Merisi, son of Firmo of Caravaggio—in painting not equal to a painter, but to nature itself—died in Port' Ercole—betaking himself hither from Naples—returning to Rome—15th calend of August—In the year of our Lord 1610—He lived thirty-six years, nine months and twenty days—Marzio Milesi, Jurisconsult—Dedicated this to a friend of extraordinary genius.

Inscriptiones et Elogia (Cod. Vat. 7927) composed by Marzio Milesi. Published by Longhi, *Pin*. I, p. 19.

3. DOCUMENTS ON CARAVAGGIO'S WORK

ST. FRANCIS

25 October 1597

36. [TESTAMENT of the Reverend Ruggero Tritonio of Udine, Abbot of Pinerola, concerning a painting of St. Francis by the "famous painter" Caravaggio.]

. . . divi Francisci signum a Caravagio celeberrimo pictori summa cum diligentia affabre pictum, quod mihi d. Octavius Costa civis Ianuensis nobilissimus, mutui amoris incomparabilisque amicitiae ergo donavit, perpetua asservari nec ulli unquam concedi aut alienari iubeo.

Miscellanea di storia veneta (R. Deputazione veneta di storia patria. Monumenti storici. ser. 4). vol. 12, Appendix, p. 41, 1894.

I order that the image of Saint Francis, painted with diligence and skill by the celebrated painter, Caravaggio, which M. Ottavio Costa, a very noble citizen of Genoa, gave me as a token of our mutual affection and incomparable friendship, shall be preserved perpetually and never given or sold to anyone.

THE CONTARELLI CHAPEL*

37. CONTRACT WITH MUZIANO for the Contarelli Chapel   *Die 13 7.bris 1565*

D. Hieronimus Mozanus de Brixia pictor in urbe sponte etc. suscepit in se onus faciendi promisitque facere et pingere unam capellam R.^{do} D. Mattheo Contarello presenti etc. in ecclesia S.^{ti} Alloysii de urbe cum historia Sancti Matthei diuisa in sex partibus cum pactis ac conuentionibus infrascriptis et primo in partibus inferioribus in una quando Dominus noster Jesus Christus uocauit e Theloneo Sanctum Mattheum et cooptauit in numerum apostolorum. In alia parte inferiori idem S. Mattheus occisus sacrificando in tabula autem altaris in medio constituenda S.^{tus} Mattheus scribens Evangelium cum angelo; in apside uero, siue volta diuidenda pariter tribus partibus. In quarum media cum futura sit maior erit S. Mattheus baptizans Regem et Reginam Aetiopie cum universo populo, in reliquis uero duabus partibus historiae et uisa de miraculis eiusdem S.^{ti} Matthej ad bene placitum supradicti R. D. Matthej Contarelli. Item quatuor prophetas in quatuor angulis apsidis. Que quidem omnes Historiae fient ut uulgo dicitur affresco excepta tabula altaris quae fiet ut etiam uulgo et secundum artem pictorum dicitur a oglio. Cuius capelle ornamentum in circuitu et pro magnitudine altaris erit opere, tectorio siue vulgariter loquendo de stucco quod uero reliquum erit operis ac diuisionum siue compartimentum intus in capitibus ingressus, etiam facie fiet siue pingeretur claro obscuro uel alijs coloribus arbitro dictorum R. D. Matthej et Hier. Qui quidem D. Hyeronimus teneri et obligatum esse uoluit et promisit perficere totum hoc opus suis sumptibus et inpensis ac manu propria exceptis illis quae erunt necessaria pro muro pontibus et clausura omnesque historias et ceteras picturas absoluere accurate et diligenter et

---

* Only the documents pertinent to Caravaggio's work are reproduced here. For fuller discussion of the Contarelli Chapel, see Denis Mahon, *Burlington Magazine*, January, 1952.

ad magnitudinem quam ratio loci postulabit et ad satisfactionem R. D. Matthej predicti infra tempus annorum trium ad plus ab hac die inchoand. et ut sequitur finiend. pro pretio et nomine pretii scutorum 300 monete ad rationem juliorum x (omissis) eidem D. Hier. promisit dare fideiussorem pro dicta summa. . . . D. Johannem bap. Sorgiati florent. Actum Rom. regione Parionis in domo R. D. Mattheij . . . presentibus D. Diomede De Leonibus clerico . . . et Cesare Falopio laico Mutinense.

Bertolotti, *Artisti Lombardi a Roma*, I 1881, p. 119 f.

On the 13th day of September 1565

[ABRIDGED TRANSLATION] Master Girolamo Muziano of Brescia, a painter in this city, by his own free will, etc., has undertaken the task of making and has promised to make and paint a chapel for the Reverend Sir Matteo Contarelli, himself present, etc., in the church of S. Luigi in this city, with the story of St. Matthew divided into six parts, with the agreements and stipulations stated below: first, in the lower parts, in one, when our Lord Jesus Christ called St. Matthew from the toll house and elected him among the number of his apostles. In another lower part the same St. Matthew is killed while administering the sacrament. And on the panel to be placed in the middle of the altar, St. Matthew writing the gospel with his angel. The apse or vault is likewise to be divided into three parts. In the middle one of these, as it is to be the larger one, shall be St. Matthew baptizing the King and Queen of Ethiopia with all the populace; and in the other two parts, stories and scenes of the miracles of the same St. Matthew, as is pleasing to the above mentioned Reverend Sir Matteo Contarelli. Item, four prophets in the four corners of the apse. All of these stories are to be made, as is commonly said, "in fresco," except the panel of the altar which is to be made, as is commonly and according to the painter's craft, called, "in oil." . . . and to carry out all the stories and other pictures accurately and diligently and to the magnitude which the nature of the place demands, and to the satisfaction of the aforementioned Reverend Sir Matteo within the time of three years at most beginning from this day and to be concluded as follows for the price and denomination of 300 scudi, at the rate of 10 giulios [per scudo]. . . .

THE CONTARELLI CHAPEL
SAN LUIGI DEI FRANCESI

38. CONTRACT between Jacob Cobaert, the Fleming, and the heir of Cardinal Contarelli.

Jacobus Cobàrt flandrus scultore abitante a S. Pietro—atto notariale del 25 Ottobre 1587. Egli prometteva all' erede del Cardinale di S. Stefano di "fare per se stesso doi statue di marmoro, una di San Matteo ed altra dell' Angelo gia sbozzati da lui, poste nel giardino di detta heredità vicino a Campo Santo, quale statue hanno da servire per la capella che sta nella chiesa di San Luigi nominato San Matteo quale si fa e si orna per il detto bo. mem. cardinale a farne quel tanto che piacerà al detto Ill° Sign° herede . . . promette farle lui proprio bene secondo l'arte e da diligenzia e accurato maestro . . . et darle perfette in pottere di detto herede fra quatro anni per scudi 1000 d'oro e più scudi 70 ogni anno per le spese di chi l'aiuterà a sbozzare dette statue. Et il detto herede. . . . volendo in ciò adempire la mente detto bo. mem. del detto cardinale dà et concede l'usufrutto della casa che esso Mre Jacomo vicino a Campo Santo reserverebbe però a esso erede il giardino di detta casa . . ."

Bertolotti, *Artisti Belgi ed Olandesi a Roma*, Florence, 1880, p. 381.

Jacob Cobaert, the Flemish sculptor living at St. Peter's—notarized act of *October 25, 1587*. [The above-named promises to the heir of the Cardinal of St. Stefano] "to execute by himself two marble statues, one of St. Matthew and the other of the angel, which he has already blocked out and which have been placed in the garden of the said estate near the Campo Santo. These statues are destined for the St. Matthew chapel in the church of San Luigi, which is being made and decorated for the said Cardinal. They shall be made in a manner which will satisfy the said heir. . . . He [Cobaert] promises to execute them himself in accordance with the art and industry of a careful master . . . and he will deliver the completed statues to the said heir within four years for one thousand gold scudi plus an additional seventy scudi per annum for the expense of assistants to work on the statues. And the said heir . . . wishing to carry out in this way the will of the said Cardinal, gives and concedes the usufruct of the house near the Campo Santo, etc."

39. INSCRIPTION in pavement of the chapel.   *1596*

D. O. M.

MATTHAEO   CONTARELLO

TIT   S.   STEPHANI

S.R.E.   PRESB.   CARD.

HUIUS   SACELLI   FUNDATORI

VIRGILIUS   CRESCENTIVS

EX.   TEST .   HAERES .   POS .

M . D . X . C .

Forcella, *Inscrizioni*, III, p. 28, n. 70.

D. O. M.

Virgilio Crescenzi, heir by testament, has placed [this inscription] to Matteo Contarelli, Priest of the sacred Roman Church, titular cardinal of St. Stephen, founder of this chapel.

1590

40. PETITION to Pope Clement VIII from the clergy of S. Luigi dei Francesi.

Beatissimo Padre, La natione francese della Chiesa di San Luigi di Roma divoti oratori di V.S. espongono humilmente come la capella di San Matteo in essa chiesa fondata, e dotata di scudi cento d'oro l'anno per doi capellani dalla bo. me. il Cardinale San Stefano, è stata più di XXV anni, et è ancora al presente serrata, et se la Stà V. non interpone la sua autorità, va a pericolo che la non si finisca mai poichè il Signor Abbate Giacomo Crescentio essecutore del testamento

del sudetto Card., surrogato dal padre di lui Vergilio Crescentio dopo anni XI (et passa) che
morì detto Card. non l'ha mai finita scusandosi or' su'l scultore, or su'l pittore ora sopra una
cosa ora sopra un'altra, et così l'anima del defunto viene ad esser fraudata del suffragio ch'ivi
si dee fare, et la Chiesa di S. Luigi similmente fraudata del emolumento, ad esser capella
assignato. Il che torna in gran pregiuditio del culto divino, et vergogna della natione, stimando
gl'esteri che da loro provenga tal difetto, poichè la vedono continuamente serrata di tavole
mentre che diverse Chiese si sono fabricate in Roma interamente da fondamenti in manco
tempo che quella capella è stata serrata, la qual cosa si crede provenire, per conto d'un legato
che fece il Card. nel suo testamento di scudi otto mila da pagarsi à suoi poveri parenti in
partibus doppo che sarebbe finita essa capella, et così non finendo la capella non si pagarà il
legato a'poveri parenti. A tal che in questo tempo di XI anni li heredi, et figlioli del Crescentio,
cumulando anno per anno, et dì per dì hanno comprato molti, et diversi uffitii in cancellaria,
Casali, et altre cose, senza effettuare cosa alcuna relevante della volontà del testatore, et senza
far dire pure un anniversario per l'anima del defunto. Però detta natione ricorre humilmente
a Sua Stà. supplicandola che si degni commettere questo negotio con tutte le sue dependentie
alla Visita Apostolica, ch'ella veda, d'onde procede tanta negligentia, con autorità di con-
stringere detto Abbate, et suoi fratelli arrichiti con quella heredità, a restituire tutto ciò
ch'hanno havuto in mano fatto per la Chiesa di S. Luigi, et a far il debito secondo la volontà
del testatore, et fondatore, sotto pene, et con tal essecutione ch'a loro parrà in forma di raggione,
et in ogni miglior modo che vedranno esser espediente, et tutta la natione pregherà il Sor Dio
per la longa et prospera vita di V. Beatitudine. Quam Deus, etc.
Archives, liasse 13. From Hess, J. *Burl. Mag.*, June 1951. p. 191, note 44.

Most Blessed Father, the French community of the Church of San Luigi in Rome . . .
humbly represents that the chapel of St. Matthew, founded in this church by the late cardinal
San Stefano and provided by him with one hundred gold scudi per annum for two chaplains,
has been closed for more than twenty-five years and is at present still closed. And if Your
Holiness does not bring His authority to bear in the matter, there is a danger that the chapel
will never be completed, because Signor Abbate Giacomo Crescenzi, the executor of the will
of the above-named Cardinal since the retirement of his father Virgilio Crescenzi, eleven or
more years after the death of the Cardinal, has not finished it and excuses himself on the
grounds of difficulties with the sculptor, the painter and other things. Thus the soul of the
deceased has been cheated of its masses and the church of San Luigi similarly cheated of the
endowment which was destined for the chapel. All of this is a discredit to the divine service
and a shame for the community, and it leads people to believe that the neglect is the fault of
the community when they see the chapel continually boarded-up and closed while various
other churches in Rome are constructed from their foundations up. This seems to be the
result of a legacy which the Cardinal made in his testament of eight thousand scudi to be
paid to his poor relatives only after the completion of the chapel, and thus as long as the
chapel is unfinished, the legacy is not paid to the poor relatives. Thus in these eleven years
the heirs and sons of the Crescenzi, accumulating [revenues] year after year and day after day,

have bought many and various offices in the Cancelleria, real estate and other things without doing anything which relates to the will of the testator and without even having anniversary services said for the soul of the deceased. Therefore the above-named community humbly has recourse to Your Holiness and asks that he deign to subject this affair and all which is therein involved to an Apostolic Investigation so that the reasons for such negligence might be discovered and authority given [to the investigating body] to constrain the above-named Abbot and his brothers, who grow rich from this inheritance, to restore everything which they have obtained at the expense of San Luigi and to carry out their commitments according to the will of the testator and founder, under penalty, and to do whatever seems reasonable to them [the investigators], and the whole community will pray to the Lord for the long and prosperous life of Your Blessed Self etc.

Die 8 Julij 1597

41. STATEMENT of the case of the sons and heirs of the late Virgilio Crescenzi, made by their representative in litigation against the venerable Fabbrica di San Pietro.

"Quo vero ad Constructionem Cappellae ex ipsamet visione quae maior est caeteris probationibus, manifeste constat, multis abhinc annis absolutam fuisse cu[m] impe[n]sa⊿tor circiter 4m. Et qua[m]vis a duobus t[antu]m lateribus pingenda remaneat, no[n] est, quod dictis eius plibus [principalibus?] imputari possit, aut debeat, sed ipsimet Pictori, qui licet sub die 27 Maij anni 1591 di[ct]um opus picturae conduxerit finiendum infra duos annos tunc proximos, prout apud acta d Augustini Amabutij [or: Amatutij] Notarij Capitolini videri pot[est], et pecuniae fere totae fueri[n]t ei solutae, Nihil [ominu]s ob opera, et impedime[n]ta, quae ei sup[er] veneru[n]t (ut creditur) adhuc di[ct]am picturam non absolvit. Cum aut[em] per di[ct]os [?] eius ples [principales?] no[n] steterit, neq[ue] stet, quin di[ct]a pictura perficiatur, et o[mn]ia pro parte ipsor[um] adimplenda adimpleverint, non debet eis alicuius negligentiae aut defectus vitio imputari."

Mahon, D., *Burl. Mag.*, January, 1952, p. 21, Doc. no. XIII.

IN FACT, as far as the construction of the chapel is concerned, one can verify by looking at it, which is the best proof, that it was finished many years ago at a cost of about 4000 scudi. The fact that it [the chapel] still remains to be painted on two sides cannot and must not be blamed upon the executor but rather upon the painter himself. He had agreed on the 27th of May, 1591, to finish the above-mentioned job of painting within the following two years, as can be seen in the acts of Don Augustino Amabuzio, Capitoline Notary; and almost all the money had been paid to him. Nevertheless, because of commissions and other hindrances which came up (at least as one believes) he has not until now executed the aforementioned painting. And since the completion of the said job of painting does not depend upon the said executors, and since they have done all that they were meant to do, they must not be accused of any negligence or default.

Di Roma li XII di Luglio 1597

42. Avviso: La causa che verteva tra la Chiesa di San Luigi de Francesi con gli heredi del s.r. Virgilio Crescentio sopra l'heredità del già Cardinal Contarelli che importa oltre 100 mila

scudi dicesi essere stata decisa da N. S.re il quale per levar ogni differenza ha applicata tutta la heredità alla fabrica di S. Pietro.

Vat. Lib. ms. Urbs. Lat. 1065. From Mahon, *Burl. Mag.*, January 1952. p. 21. Doc. no. XII.

Rome, 12 July 1597

NOTICE: The case which has been pending between the church of San Luigi and the heirs of Virgilio Crescenzi concerning the inheritance of the late Cardinal Contarelli, amounting to over 100,000 scudi, is said to have been settled by His Holiness who, in order to remove all the differences, has assigned the entire inheritance to the Fabrica di San Pietro.

43. PROMISSORY NOTE for payment of four hundred scudi to Giuseppe d'Arpino.

Io Tiberio del q[uondam] Girolamo Ceuoli p[er] la p[rese]nte p[ro]metto pagare libera-mente e senza ecettione alcuna al m.ᶜᵒ m. Gioseppe d'Arpino Pittore ad ogni mandato delli Ill.ᵐⁱ sig.ʳⁱ Deputati della R.ᵈᵃ fabrica di san Pietro di Roma Δ.ᵈⁱ quattrocento di m.ᵗᵃ di Giulij dieci p[er] scudo, e la p[rese]nte faccio ad istantia et d'ordine delli Ill.ʳⁱ sig.ʳⁱ figli et [eredi] del s.ʳ Vergilio Crescentio di bo: me: dalli quali havero da rivalerme di quello che paghero, dissero essere p[er] resto et intiero pagam.ᵗᵒ della pittura che fa nella capella di san Matteo del Ill.ᵐᵒ s.ʳ Cardinale Contarello bo: me: nella Chiesa di san Luigi della Natione franzese, e la p[rese]nte duri p[er] un año p[ro]ssimo poi resti di niun valore, e In fede si e fatto la p[rese]nte quale sara sottoscritta di mano del nostro mag.ᶜᵒ s.ʳ Tiberio In Roma qu.ᵗᵒ di VI di 9bre 159[7]

Mahon, D. *Burl. Mag.* January 1952, p. 21, Doc. no. XVI.

6 November 1597

I, TIBERIUS, son of Girolamo Cevoli, herewith promise to pay . . to the excellent Master Giuseppe d'Arpino, the painter, on the order of the . . deputies of the Fabrica di San Pietro, 400 scudi . . The present note is made on the request and order of the . . sons and [heirs] of the late Sr. Virgilio Crescenzi, by whom I am to be reimbursed for what I pay. They have informed me that this is for the remainder of the full payment for the paintings which he [Arpino] is doing in the chapel of St. Matthew of the late Cardinal Contarelli in the Church of San Luigi of the French nation. The present note is valid for one year and after that it will be no longer valid. The present note is made in good faith and is to bear the signature of . . Tiberio in Rome, the 6th of November, 1597.

44. RESOLUTION of the governing body of San Luigi dei Francesi concerning the opening of the Contarelli Chapel:

Die Sabbato prima Maij 1599

Fuit facta Cong.º gñlis et ordinaria Dnoru[m] Rectoru[m] et officialu[m] ecclesiae et hospitalis S.ᵗⁱ Ludovici nationis gallicae de Urbe In loco solito In qua interfuerunt Infra[scri]pti. . . . Qui Dñi congregati decreverunt quod capella bo: mem: Card: Contarelli aperiatur, ad off[ici]um celebrandi missas, et deputaverunt Dnos Claudiu[m] Vinceiu[m] et Andrea[m] Bergeriu[m] ad facien[dum] aperire di[ct]a[m] capella[m] dans illis facultates hoc facie[ndi] o[mn]i mel[iori] modo. Quibus peractis R. D. Carolus curatus recitavit orationes solitas sup[rascrip]tis congregatis r[espo]ndentibus Amen. Amedeus Millietus Not.ˢ rogatus.

The first of May, 1599

A general meeting of the congregation, the rectors, and officers of the church and hospital of San Luigi dei Francesi was held . . . these assembled members decreed that the chapel of the late Cardinal Contarelli be opened for the official celebration of masses, and they designated . . . Claudio Vincy and Andrea Berger to have the said chapel opened, giving them power to carry this out in the most suitable manner. This done, the curate Carolus recited the customary prayers and the assembled Reverend members mentioned above responded: Amen. Amedeo Millet, notary.

Mahon, *Burl. Mag.*, January, 1952, p. 22, Doc. no. xx. See also Chéramy, H. *Rassegna d'arte*, 1922, v. 9, p. 170, n. 2.

CARPENTER'S REPORTS CONCERNING THE CONTARELLI CHAPEL

44A. [this document is not precisely dated, but the preceding date is December 13.]

1600

In sopradetto mese, per havere foderato li dua cuadri che sonno di qua e di la della cappella [between the lines is written: di cardinale] del Contarello, che sonno lungi e largi tutti dua P[almi] 14½, largi P.15; incastrattoci le piane [here the word travicelli has been written and crossed out], in nello muro per potere inciodare le tavole, messone tre per cuadro, sonno lungi P., e divisato le tavole di abetto numero cinquanta, di tutta robba mia, monta: Scudi 20 Baiochi 50. Per havere fatto le cornice alli detti quadri di mio legname di albuccio, monta: Sc.20 B.20.

In the aforesaid month [December 1600] for lining the two pictures which are on either side of the chapel of Cardinal Contarelli, which are both 14½ palms broad and 15 palms long; for fixing the laths [the word "joists" is crossed out] in the wall so that the boards may be nailed, for putting three [laths] for each picture—they are ___ palms long, and for dividing the fir-wood boards, by 50, all of my own material—it amounts to 20 scudi and 50 baiocchi.

For making the frames of the said pictures of my own white-poplar timber—it amounts to 20 scudi and 20 baiocchi.

Jacques Bousquet, "Documents inédits sur Caravage," *La Revue des Arts*. Vol. III, 1953, no. 2, p. 104.

44B.   *22 March 1602*

Per havere fatto uno telaro per il paliotto di altaro della cappella di Santo Matteo, fatto di bona grossezza, fatto largi li regoli largi L. mezzo palmo, lungo P.10, largo P.5, di mio legname di albuccio. Sc.1. B.50.

For making a stretcher for the antependium of the altar of the chapel of St. Matthew, made of a good thickness, for making the mullions half a palm broad [the stretcher being] 10 palms long and 5 palms broad, of my own white-poplar timber—1 scudo, 50 baiocchi.

44C.   *5 October 1602*

Per havere fatto una telaro di grossezza di piane di castagno, lavoratto et dirigatto le tavole per mettere drento al detto telaro di legname della ciesa, ciodi di mio, lungo P.13, largo P.9, questo s'è fatto per conservare la pittura del cuadro di Xzn Matteo, dove si dice la messa in Santo Louigi, monta Sc.3 B.50. In detta cappella, per havere fatto le cornice intorno a detto cuadro di mio legname, monta Sc.1 B.20.

For making a stretcher of thick chestnut staves, for working and straightening the boards to put inside the said stretcher [some] wood belonging to the church, with my own nails [the stretcher being] 13 palms long and 9 palms broad—this has been done in order to preserve the painting of the picture of St. Matthew, where mass is said in San Luigi—it amounts to 3 scudi, 50 baiocchi.

In the said chapel, for making the frame around the said picture of my own timber—it amounts to 1 scudo, 20 baicchi.

44D.   *February 1603*

Per havere fatto le cornice al cuadro de l'altare di Santo Matteo di mio legname, lunga P.—, larga P.—, monta Sc.1 B.10.

For making the frames of the picture of the altar of St. Matthew of my own timber __ palms long and __ palms broad—it amounts to 1 scudo, 10 baiocchi.

CERASI CHAPEL
SANTA MARIA DEL POPOLO

45. INSCRIPTION in left wall:

D. O. M.
Tiberio Cerasio Romano
Primum in Rom. Curia inde Fisci
Et Sacrae Aulae Consistorialis
Advocato

.   .   .   .   .

.   .   .   .   .

Virtutisq Meritis Erecto
Xenodochium Consolationis
Heres Ex Asse
In Hoc Sacello Ab Ipso Ante Obitum
Constructo Atque Exornato
In Quod Parentum Ac Fratris Ossa
Transferri Seq In Eodem Humari
Ex Testamento Jussit
Custodibus Curatoribus P.
Obiit An. Aet. LVII Salutis MDCI
V NON MAII

Forcella, *Inscrizioni*, 1, p. 373, no. 1439.

46. CONTRACT FOR CERASI CHAPEL   *Dei XXIIIIᵃ mensis Septembris 1600*

[Ob]ligatio pingendi duo quadra. . . . Dominus Michael Angelus Merisius de Caravagio Mediolanensis Diocesis egregius in Urbe Pictor sponte omnibus promisit Illustrissimo et Reverendissimo Domino Tiberio Cerasio, Suae B[eatitudin]is et Camerae Apostolicae Thaesaurario generali p[raese]nti pingere duo quadra cupressus longitudinis palmorum decem et latitudinis octo pro quol[ibe]t, in altero u[er]o misterium Conversionis Sanctorum Pauli et in altero martyrium Petri Apostolorum, eaque infra octo menses prox[ime] futuros ab hodie persoluere et absolutos reddere et consignare in manibus ip[siu]s Illustrissimi Domini cum omnibus et quibuscumque figuris, imaginibus et ornamentis ipsi Domino Pictori bene uisis ad satisfactionem tamen D[omi]n[ati]onis Suae Illustrissimae cui ipse Pictor teneatur, prout promisit, ante dictarum picturarum confectionem exhibere specimina et design[atione]s figurarum et aliorum, quibus ipse Pictor ex sui Inuent[ion]e et ingenio dicta misterium et martyrium decorare intendit. Hanc autem promissionem dictus Dominus Pictor fecit pro mercede, et precio scutorum quadringentorum m[oneta]e ad quorum bonum conmutum, et diminutionem nunc coram in[fra] d[ic]tis testibus meque habuit ab eodem Illustrissimo Domino Scuta quinquaginta mon[et]ae mediante ordine Illustrissimo Vinc[enti]o Just[inia]no mer[cato]ri in Urbe negot[ian]ti directo et ips[ius] Illustrissimi D[omini] manu subscripto, de quo et scutis quinguaginta in eo contentis exnunc protunc et quando illa receperit et habuerit a d[ict]o Illustrissimo D[omino] Vincentio, eumdem Illustrissimum D[ominum] Thaesaurarium quietavit per pactum. Residuum uero idem Illustrissimus Dominus Tyberius sponte promisit eidem Domino Pictori p[raese]nti soluere, et exbursare seu solui et exbursari facere statim ac dictas picturas modo et forma praem[issi]s compleuerit et persoluerit eid[em]q[ue] Illustrissimo D[omino] tradiderit et consig[naue]rit in . . . hic Romae libere alias. Pro quibus sese, haeredes et bona in amp[lissim]ae eiusdem Camere Apostolice forma cum cla[usul]is invicem obligarunt, renunciarunt app[ellatio]ni, consentientes unica, et tactis per Illustrissimum Dominum Thaesaurarium pectore more Praelatorum et per dictum Dominum Michaelem Angelum scripturis resp[ecti]ue [?] Jurarunt, Rogarunt. Actum Romae in Aedibus solit[is] residentiae ipsius Illustrissimi Domini Thaesaurarii praesentibus ibid[em] Per Ill[ustrissimo] et Reverendissimo Domino Alexandro Ludouisio Bononiense Sacri Palatii Apostolici Aud[itore] ac Per Ill[ustrissimo] Domino Com[it]e Horatio eius fratre germano testibus.

Mahon, D., *Burl. Mag.*, July, 1951, Pl. 17.

24 September 1600

CONTRACT to paint two pictures. . . . Michael Angelo Merisi of Caravaggio in the diocese of Milan, the distinguished painter in Rome, has promised, entirely of his own free will, to the Very Reverend Tiberio Cerasi, Treasurer General to His Holiness and the Camera Apostolica, in his presence, to paint two pictures on cypress wood, each 10 palms long and 8 palms wide: one representing the *Mystery of the Conversion of St. Paul* and the other the *Martyrdom of St. Peter,* and to have them ready and deliver them, within the next eight months from this date, into the hands of the said nobleman, with all and sundry figures, persons and ornaments which seem fit to the Painter, to the satisfaction however of his Lordship [Cerasi]. The painter shall also be obliged, as he has promised, to submit, before executing the said pictures, specimens and designs of the figures and other objects with which according to his invention and genius he intends to beautify the said mystery and martyrdom.

This promise the said painter has made for a honorarium and price of 400 scudi in cash, for the correct computation and reduction of which he has now received, in the presence of the below-mentioned witnesses and the notary [me] from the said gentleman 50 scudi in the form of a money order directed to the Most Illustrious Vincenzo Giustiniani merchant operating in Rome and signed by the same nobleman [Cerasi]. For this [money order] and the 50 scudi conveyed therein, the painter has given a receipt by pact [handclasp ?] to the illustrious Lord Treasurer [Cerasi] for the present as well as the future when he will have received them [the 50 scudi] from the illustrious Lord Vincenzo. As for the rest [Cerasio] has promised, of his own free will, to the painter to make, or cause to be made, payment as soon as the latter has finished the said pictures in the aforesaid manner and form and delivered them to the said nobleman and consigned them to . . . here in Rome, or differently if desired.

For [all] this [the parties] have pledged themselves, their heirs and belongings according to the formula used by the Amplissima Camera Apostolica, with the [usual] clauses. They have renounced to the right of appeal [in case of disagreement], in perfect consent and have taken their oaths respectively: the Prelate according to the custom of his rank, by touching his breast; Mr. Michel Angelo by touching the Bible; and have requested [the notary to certify the contract by a public instrument].

Done in Rome in the permanent residence of the Treasurer, in presence of the Very Illustrious and Very Reverend Alessandro Ludovisi of Bologna . . . and the Very Illustrious Count Orazio, his brother.

Di Roma li 5 di Maggio 1601

47. Avviso: Mercordi notte Monsr. Cerasio, Tesauriero Generale di S.ta Chiesa passò all' altra vita, et datoli sepultura nella sua bellissima Capella, che faceva fare nella Madonna della Consolatione, per mano del famosissimo pittore Michel Angelo da Caravaggio; prima che morisse, intendesi habbia giunto un codicillo al suo testamento, fatto un pezzo fà, lasciando Herede delle sue facultà li Padri della Mad.na della Consolatione, con obligo che debbino far finire la sudetta Capella.

Rome, 5 May 1601

NOTICE: On Wednesday night Monsignor Cerasi, Treasurer General of the Holy Church, passed away and was buried in the beautiful chapel which he had made in the Madonna della Consolatione [actually Sta. Maria del Popolo] by the hand of the most famous painter Michael Angelo of Caravaggio; before he died he is understood to have added a codicil to his will, which was made some time ago, making the Fathers of the Madonna della Consolatione the heirs of his estate with the obligation of completing the above-mentioned chapel.

Mahon, *Burl. Mag.*, July, 1951, p. 227, note 41.

DEPOSITION OF CHRIST

9 January 1602

48. ALLA CAPPELLA della Pietà era stato concesso l'altare privilegiato. Or essendo venuto il patrono della medesima nella determinazione di cambiarvi il quadro facendo dipingere quella meravigliosa tela uscita dal pennello di Michelangelo Caravaggio riputato il capolavoro di lui, non vi si poteva in questo tempo più celebrare messa e lucrare le concesse indulgenze. Perciò fu risoluto dai nostri Padri d'interporre il card. Baronio presso il papa perchè esse in altro altare interinamente si conseguissero.

Che il P. Prometheo [Peregrini] tratti col Sig. Cardinal Baronio che S. S. ne dia licentia di dir la messa a un altro altare sin che si accomada il privilegiato.

To the Chapel of the Pietà had been conceded the right to a privileged altar. Now, when the patron of this chapel reached the decision to replace the altarpiece, ordering the wonderful painting from the brush of Michelangelo da Caravaggio which is reputed to be his masterpiece, mass could not be celebrated on this altar and the conceded indulgences could not be obtained at this time. Thus it was resolved by our Fathers that Cardinal Baronio should intervene with the Pope so that the indulgences could temporarily be given at another altar.

Father Prometheo . . . will negotiate with Cardinal Baronio for His Holiness' permission to say mass at another altar until the privileged altar is ready for service.

6 September 1604

49. SI DIA AL NEPOTE del Sig. Pietro Vittrici il quadro della Pietà con il suo ornamento di legno, che dimanda havendo di sua cortesia fatto fare il quadro nuovo del Caravaggio al quale non serve il sop. detto ornamento di legno.

THE PAINTING OF THE PIETA, with its ornamented wooden frame, shall be given to the nephew of Signor Pietro Vittrice who has asked for it, since it was through his generosity that the new painting by Caravaggio was made; the said wooden ornament is of no use to this [new] painting.

Information from the *Libro dei Decreti*, S. Maria in Vallicella. Lopresti, L., *L'Arte*, 1922, v. 25, p. 116 (quoting Generoso Galenzio, *La Vita e gli Scritti del Cardinal Cesare Baronio, ecc.*, Roma, 1907).

MADONNA DI LORETO
S. AGOSTINO, CAPELLA CAVALLETTI

50. CONTRACT between the Fathers of S. Agostino and the Cavalletti for the acquisition of the Cavalletti Chapel.

. . . quondam Ermete Cavalletti Bononiensis in suo ultimo quod condidit testamento [lasciasse obbligo ai suoi eredi, Pietro Paolo e Agostino Cavalletti, di usare la somma di cinquecento scudi] "in fabricanda et ornanda quedam (*sic*) cappella existente in Ecclesia Sancti Augustini di Urbe . . . prope portam eiusdem ecclesiae magnam intrando primam (*sic*) videlicet in ordine versus altare majus tendendo, ad praesens sub invocatione nuncupato B. Mariae Magdalene. . . ."

[Il testatore] "voluit et mandavit fieri inscriptionem ipsius quondam domini Ermetis, uti fundatoris pro se suisque heredibus et successoribus, et in ea erigi altare in pittura, et ad honorem Beat.^me Marie de Laureto sub cuius invocatione nuncupari voluit. . . ."
Lopresti, Lucia, *L'Arte*, 1922, v. 25, p. 176.

THE LATE Hermes Cavalletti of Bologna, in his last testament, ordered his heirs, Pietro Paolo and Agostino Cavalletti, to employ the sum of 500 scudi "to build and decorate a certain chapel in the church of S. Agostino in Rome . . . , the first chapel near the main entrance of the church, . . . which is now dedicated to the Blessed Mary Magdalene. . . ."

The deceased, as founder, "wished and ordered that an inscription be made for himself and his heirs and successors, and that an altarpiece be erected in honor of the Most Blessed Mary of Loreto. . . ."

51. EXCERPT FROM PASSERI [not included in the edition of 1772]

Quando egli (il Caravaggio) dipinse il Quadro che stà nella Chiesa di So. Agostino in Roma nella prima Cappella a sinistra dell' ingresso, nel quale è dipinta, al suo costume, Maria Vergine col Figlio in braccio, e due Perregrini che stanno in atto di adorarla, stava egli di Casa agl' otto Cantoni in quelli vicoli, che sono dietro al Mausoleo d'Augusto. Vicino a lui abitava una Donna con una sua figliola zitella, la quale non era discara nelle sembianze; gente povera; ma onorata, e Michel' Angelo procurò d'havere questa Giovinetta per esemplare della Madre di Dio, che deveva dipingere in quel suo Quadro, e gli riuscì l'haverla havendogli offerta una tal ricognizione, che fu bastante, per la loro povertà, di farlo rimaner sodisfatto di questo suo desiderio come l'eseguì. Questa Putta veniva amoreggiata da un giovane di professione Notaro, e l'haveva più volte fatta chiedere alla Madre per Moglie dalla quale sempre ne ottenne una continua negativa; havendo quella, come Donna semplice, et innocente, rimbrezzo di dare la sua figliola a Notari delli quali (diceva) è sicura la dannazione. Questo Giovane stando sdegnato di questa repulsa, e non perdendo mai di traccia quella sua Diletta, s'avvide, che più volte andò in Casa del Caravaggio nella quale si tratteneva qualche spazio di tempo per cagione che quegli la dipingeva. Punto da gelosia, et adirato sommamente incontrando, a bello studio, la Madre un giorno le disse: "buona Donna, che siete così scrupolosa, e guardinga, tenetevi pure quella buona zitella di vostra figliola, che havete negato a me per moglie, e dopo l'havete condotta da quel pittoraccio a farne quello che gl'è piaciuto. Veramente havete fatto un'ottima elezione degna del vostro grado, negarla ad un mio pari per isposa, per concederla ad uno scomunicato, e maledetto per concubina; tentevela pure, che buon prò vi facci," e voltandole la schiena, lasciolla in grandissima confusione con estremo ramarico. Pareva a quella donna d'haver errato, senza haver comessa colpa nessuna, in haver condotta la figlia da Michel Angelo, benche con ogni innocenza, e che quel Notaro havesse havuto ragione, quanto all'apparenza, di trattarla male, et imediatamente andò a trovare il Caravaggio facendo seco una lacrimosa doglianza di quello che gl'era avenuto per sua caggione. Sorridendo amaramente egli di questa accusa, le chiese chi l'haveva, con tanto torto, così mal trattata, et ella gli significò la persona, della quale ne venne facilmente in cognizione per la frequenza di lui del passaggio per quella strada, e racconsolandola con parole amorevoli, la mandò a Casa. Alteratosi di questo accidente, e per esser'egli assai iracondo, e feroce la mattina seguente, mettendosi sotto un'accetta, uscì di Casa per andare in traccia di questo Giovane, et essendo quel giorno il Mercordì giorno di mercato, portò il caso, che se gli fece avanti giusto in piazza Navona dove è per l'appunto la fiera in quella giornata, e fu avanti la Chiesa di San Giacomo degli Spagnuoli vicino alla fontana delli Tritoni. Avicinatosi a lui, gli diede sul capo si smisurato colpo con quella accetta, dicendogli, "O impara a procedere se tu nol sai" che di fatto cadde per terra mal concio, e tutto lordo nel proprio sangue. Salvatosi egli, doppo il misfatto, in San Luigi de Francesi vi dimoro molto tempo, e volle la sua sorte che quel Notaro, benche assai mal concio, non morì di quella ferita; ma lungamente ne stette infermo; et avanti ch'egli agiustasse l'inimicizia, e il Fisco, vi corse qualche anno.

Hess, Jacob, "Nuovo Contributo alla Vita del Caravaggio," *Bollettino d'Arte*, Anno 26, Ser. 3, July, 1932, pp. 42-44.

IN THE first chapel to the left of the entrance in S. Agostino, Caravaggio painted the Holy Virgin with the Child in her arms and two pilgrims adoring her. At that time he lived in the House of the Eight Corners, in one of the little streets behind the Mausoleum of Augustus. Nearby lived a lady with her young daughter, who was not at all unattractive; they were poor but honest people. Michelangelo wished to have the young girl as a model for the Mother of God which he was to paint in this work, and he succeeded in this by offering them a sum of money which was large enough, considering their poverty, to enable him to carry out his wish. This girl was being courted by a young man who was a notary by profession and who had asked the mother for her daughter's hand in marriage. However, he had always received a negative answer because this simple and naïve woman was unwilling to give her daughter to a notary since, as she said, all notaries are surely bound for damnation. The young man was indignant at this refusal, but he nevertheless did not lose track of his beloved. Thus he found out that she frequently went to the house of Caravaggio and remained there for long periods of time posing for him. Full of jealousy and totally enraged, he contrived to meet the mother one day and said to her, "My good woman, you're so scrupulous and such a good guardian, and here your lovely daughter, whom you refused to let me marry, goes to this miserable painter so that he can do anything he likes with her. Really, you have made a wise choice and one which is worthy of your class, refusing to let her marry a man like me so that you can make her the concubine of this excommunicated scoundrel. Now you can just keep her and I hope it will do you a lot of good." Then turning his back, he left her confused and completely upset. It seemed to this lady that she had inadvertently done the wrong thing by taking her daughter to Michelangelo, even though she had done so in perfectly good faith, and it also seemed that this notary had had good reason, at least from his point of view, for treating her so badly. She went immediately to Caravaggio in tears and complained about what had happened on his account. He smiled bitterly at this accusation and asked her who it was that had so unjustly mistreated her. From her description he easily recognized him as a person whom he frequently met in the street. He consoled the lady with gentle words and sent her home.

He was upset by this incident and being by nature irritable and violent, the next morning he put a hatchet under his coat and went out to look for this young man. This being Wednesday, market day, he carried the affair right into Piazza Navona, just when a fair was being held there. It took place in front of the church of S. Giacomo degli Spagnoli, near the Triton Fountain. He went up to the notary and gave him such a terrific blow on the head with the hatchet that he fell to the ground unconscious and covered with his own blood. And Michelangelo said, "Now learn to behave yourself if you don't know how." After this misdeed he took refuge at San Luigi dei Francesi and remained there for a long time. Fortunately for Caravaggio, the notary did not die from the blow, even though he was unconscious and for a long time remained ill. It was some years before they settled their feud and the indemnity.

DEATH OF THE VIRGIN

52. Giovanni Magno ad Annibale Chieppio   *Di Roma, il di 17 feb[io] 1607*

. . . Si vide Domenica passata il quadro del Caravaggio proposto dal Sr Piet° Pauolo Rubens quale riveduto da esso Rubens ne prese anco maggior sodisfatione, come fu tenuto per opera buona anco dal Fachetti, che a parte mi ha detto il suo parere. Io ne presi quel gusto che conveniva al giuditio concorde di huomini della professione, ma perchè li poco periti desiderano certi allettamenti grati all'occhio, restai però piu captivato dal testimonio d'altri che dal proprio senso mio, non bastando a comprendere bene certi artificii occulti che mettano quella pittura in consideratione e stima. Il pittore però è dei più famosi di quelli che habbino cose moderne in Roma, et questa tavola è tenuta delle meglio opere che habbi fatto, onde la presuntione sta a favor del quadro per molti rispetti, et realmente vi si osservano certe parti molto esquisite. Ne m'estenderò più oltre, perchè credo che il Sr Pietro Paolo havera dato intero conto dell'historia, grandezza et altre circonstanze, quanto al prezzo è tuttavia incerto, perchè non si vorrià stringer in disavantaggio con segno di troppo voluntà, ma starà di sopra delli dugenti scudi, et s'accostarà forse alli trecento et di questo ne lascio la cura al d[to] Rubens sin che vi si habbi a mettere l'ultima mano. . . .

Di V. S. M[to] Illma

Prontis[mo] et obb[mo] ser[re],

Giovanni Magno

Ruelens, Ch., *Correspondance de Rubens* . . . Tome I 1600-1608. Anvers, 1887, p. 362.

Letter to Annibale Chieppio   *Rome, 17 February 1607*

. . . Last Sunday I saw the painting by Caravaggio, proposed by Signor Peter Paul Rubens who, when he saw it again, was still more satisfied by it. Also, Fachetti, who had given me his opinion privately, held it to be a good work. It pleased me to a degree corresponding to the concordant judgment of the professionals. However, because people of little experience desire some pleasure to the eyes, I was more impressed by the testimony of the others than by my own feeling which is not sufficient to understand well certain occult artificialities which place this picture in such high esteem. The painter, however, is one of the most famous for the collectors of modern things in Rome, and the picture is held to be one of the best paintings he has ever made. Thus, presumption is in favor of this painting in many respects, and really one can observe in it certain very exquisite parts. I will not digress because I think Sr. Peter Paul has already related the essence of the whole story, size and other circumstances. The price, however, is uncertain because one does not wish to fall into disadvantage by showing too much eagerness. But the price will be over two hundred scudi and will perhaps be close to three hundred. I leave this to Rubens until we have to close the deal. . . .

Y^{rs}, etc.
Giovanni Magno

53. GIOVANNI MAGNO AD ANNIBALE CHIEPPIO   *Di Roma, il 24 feb^{io} 1607*

Mi era uscito di memoria di dar conto che il quadro proposto dal Sr Piet^o Pauolo sia accordato in dogento ottanta scudi di moneta, essendosi fatto quanto si è potuto col Padrone, acciò si migliorasse de conditione, ma egli non ha voluto sentir de perdere pur un giulio del prezzo pagato. Il che può anco esser argomento della qualità del quadro, perchè non resta punto discreditato per esser fuori delle mani del Pittore et rifiutato dalla chiesa a quale era stato donato. Appresso si doverà la mancia ad un pittore che con molto incommodo è stato mezano di questo contratto, onde credo che restarà poco meno che assorbita tutta la lettera de credito che mi è stata mandata di 300 scudi, massime computandovi quanto bisognarà per inviarlo costi. Di che ho voluto avisar V. S. per l'ordine che mi da di non levar se non il danaro necessario per d^{ta} compra. . . .

Gio. Magno

LETTER to the same   *Rome, 24 February 1607*

It slipped my mind to mention that the price for the painting proposed by Sr. Peter Paul has been set at two hundred and eighty scudi. We have done as much as possible with the patron to persuade him to lower his conditions, but he did not want to lose even a penny of the price. One might also argue about the quality of the painting, whether it is not discredited by being out of the painter's hands and in having been refused by the church to which it was donated. Furthermore, a gratuity is due to a painter who, with much trouble, has been mediator in this contract so I believe that there will be very little left of the letter of credit for 300 scudi which you sent me, calculating therein whatever is necessary to send it there. I wanted to report this to your Lordship in view of your order not to spend more than is necessary to buy it. . . .

Gio. Magno

54. GIOVANNI MAGNO AL CONS^{re} CHIEPPIO   *Di Roma, il di ultimo Marzo 1607*

. . . Finalmente il quadro comparato per S. A. s'è ridotto in casa mia con molto stento, perchè non si sapea trovar la via di consegnarmelo, onde essendomi caduto in pensiero che non se ne facesse copia, vi feci applicar la dovuta provisione col mezzo di Monsr della Cam^a. Hora non restarò d'inviarlo quanto prima secondo l'ordine di S. A. . . .

Giovanni Magno

Ruelens, p. 365.

LETTER to the same   *Rome, 31 March 1607*

. . . Finally, the picture purchased for Your Highness has been taken to my house with great delay because they were not able to find a way to consign it to me. I wondered, therefore, whether they were not making a copy of it, and so I applied the due provisions with the help of the Treasurer. Now nothing remains but to send it to you as soon as possible in accordance with Your Highness' orders.

                                                           Giovanni Magni

55. LETTERA AL CHIEPPIO, consigliere del Duca di Mantova   *Di Roma, il 7 Aprile 1607*

. . . Mi è stato necessario per sodisfare all'università delli Pittori lasciar veder per tutta questa settimana il quadro comparato, essendovi concorsi molti et delli più famosi con molta curiosità, attesochè era in molto grido essa tavola, ma quasi a nessuno si concedeva il vederla, et certo che m'è stato di sodisfattione il lasciarla goder à satietà, perchè è stata commendata di singolar arte et la prossima settimana s'invierà.

                                                           Giovanni Magni
Ruelens, p. 366.

LETTER to Chieppio, Councillor of the Duke of Mantua   *Rome, 7 April 1607*

. . . I found it necessary, in order to gratify the Painters' Guild, to let the purchased picture be seen all this week long. Many of the most famous painters have been flocking there with a good deal of curiosity because this panel was the talk of the town, but scarcely anybody had been allowed to see it. It has certainly been a great satisfaction to me to let it be enjoyed by the public because it has been commended for the exceptional art with which it is done. It will be forwarded next week.

                                                           Giovanni Magni

56. LETTERA come sopra   *Di Roma, il di 14 Aprile 1607*

. . . Il quadro comperato sta a dispositione del S.ᵣ Pietro Pauolo, quanto all'esser inviato, ma egli per assicurlarlo da patimento fa lavorar non so che cassa, che farà tardar necessariamente sin doppo le feste il metterlo in via.

                                                           Giovanni Magni
Ruelens, p. 367.

LETTER to the same   *Rome, 14 April 1607*

. . . The purchased picture is at Sr. Peter Paul Rubens' disposal, ready to be forwarded. But he, in order to preserve it from injuries, is having I know not what sort of case constructed, which will necessarily delay the shipment until after the holidays.

                                                           Giovanni Magni

57. LETTERA come sopra   *Di Roma, il di 28 aprile 1607*

. . . Intanto dirò a V. S. che giovedi s'incamina a cotesta volta il quadro, le candele benedette et li tre volumi della continuata opera del Sʳ Cardᶫᵉ Tosco in tre cassette, essendosi qui sodisfatto alla condotta sin nella città di Mantova per dove hanno i suoi ricapiti, et pigliano robbe con diligente transmissione questi mercanti o condottieri nominati gli Antonii. Mando con questo la spesa fatta che batte a punto nelli trecento scudi manco uno, onde resta fuori il danaro della lettera che mi si rimise a questo effetto di comperare il dᵗᵒ quadro.

                                                           Gio. Magno

LETTER to the same   *Rome, 28 April 1607*

. . . Meanwhile I shall tell your Lordship that Thursday the picture started on its way to Mantua, etc.

Giovanni Magni

MADONNA OF THE ROSARY

Documents from the R. Archivio di Stato in Modena. Cancelleria ducale. Correspondence of the Ambassadors of the Este family in Rome.
From L. Venturi, *L'Arte*, 1910, vol. 13, pp. 281-284.

58. LETTERA al conte Gio. Batt. Laderchi   *Di Roma il di 6 agosto 1605*

Sarà cosa impossibile l'hauer i quadri per la Capella alla Madonna di settembre perchè il Caravaggio è in contumacia della Corte per alcune ferite ch'egli diede a un sustituto del Spada Notar del Vicario et com'intendo si ritroua a Genoua. . . .

Fabio Masetti

LETTER to Count Giovan Battista Laderchi   *Rome, 6 August 1605*

It will be impossible to get the pictures for the Chapel by the day of the Nativity of the Virgin [September 8] because Caravaggio is a fugitive from justice on account of some wounds which he inflicted upon a substitute of Spada, the clerk of the Vicar's Court, and, as I hear, is now in Genoa. . . .

Your Most Illustrious and Excellent Lordship's Most Devoted and Obliged Servant.

Fabio Masetti

59. LETTERA come sopra   *Di Roma il di 17 Agosto 1605*

. . . Il Caravaggio è in contumacia della Corte e si troua a Genoua. . . .

Fabio Masetti

LETTER to the same   *Rome, 17 August 1605*

. . . Caravaggio is a fugitive from justice and is now in Genoa. . . .

Fabio Masetti

60. LETTERA come sopra   *Di Roma il di 24 Agosto 1605.*

. . . et hauendo inteso che il Carauaggio è comparso a Roma per la speranza della pace, sono ricorso all'Ill.mo del Monte che faccia comandargli l'ispeditione del Quadro di S. A. che me l'ha con molta prontezza promesso anchorchè s'assicura poco di lui, dicendo che è uno ceruello strauagantissimo et che pure era stato ricercato dal Principe Doria a dipingergli una loggia, che voleua dargli sei millia scudi et non ha voluto accettar il partito, se bene hauesse quasi promesso, onde a me era uenuto in pensier di farlo tastare se in questa congiuntura di contumaccia si fosse contentato di trasferirsi costà, oue haurebbe potuto dar ogni gusto a S. A. ma iscoprendo tanto instabilità non ho fatto altro.

Fabio Masetti

LETTER to the same   *Rome, 24 August 1605*

... and having heard that Caravaggio has turned up in Rome in the hope of a reconciliation, I have appealed to the Most Illustrious Cardinal Del Monte to send him orders to forward
His Highness' picture. The Cardinal very promptly promised to do so, although he has little
confidence in him, for he says that Caravaggio is an extremely capricious sort of man, and
that he has also been requested by Prince Doria to paint a loggia for him with the offer of
six thousand scudi, but he has chosen to reject the proposal, although he had almost promised.
Wherefore, I had thoughts of having him sounded out as to whether, at this juncture of his
being a fugitive, he would consent to move to Modena, where he would be in a position to
give full satisfaction to His Highness. But on discovering so much instability, I did nothing. ...

                                                          Fabio Masetti

61. LETTERA come sopra   *Di Roma il di 12 Ottobre 1605*

Michel Angelo Caravaggio questa sera m'ha ricercato dargli dodece scudi a buon conto del
quadro che fa per S. A. promettendomelo presto finito ond' io prontissimamente glieli ho
fatto sborsare per un ordine al Corsiani et dicendogli che desiderarei saper quello pretendesse
di quest'opera per poter s'avisar costà, m'ha risposto ch'io mi faccia mandar sin a 50 o 60 scudi
se bene non contradirà a quello che comanderà S. A.
                                                          Fabio Masetti

LETTER to the same   *Rome, 12 October 1605*

... Michelangelo da Caravaggio this evening has requested me to give him twelve scudi
as an advance payment for the picture he is painting for His Highness, and has promised
that it will soon be finished. I had them disbursed to him immediately through an order to
Corsiani. Upon my telling him that I should like to know what he is going to charge for
this work, so that I might inform Modena, he replied that I should send for as much as
50 or 60 scudi, although he will make no objection to whatever His Highness may command. ...
                                                          Fabio Masetti

62. LETTERA come sopra   *Di Roma il di 16 Novembre 1605*

Mi fu hier sera a ritrovar il Caravaggio pregandomi di novo a dargli 20 scudi perchè il
quadro sarebbe finito la presente settimana et me lo portarebbe et per raccomandarmesi con
tante effetto io glieli diedi et con protesta che m'havesse a portar detto quadro, et subito che
me lo consegnerà aviserò V. S. Ill.^me il giudicio che ne faranno persone intelligenti.
                                                          Fabio Masetti

                                                          Rome, 16 November 1605

Last night Caravaggio came to see me, again begging me to give him 20 scudi, inasmuch
as the picture would be finished within the current week and he would bring it to me. He
pleaded so earnestly that I gave them to him, on his solemn promise that he would bring me

the said picture. As soon as he delivers it to me, I shall advise Your Serene Highness what estimate competent critics form of it.

Fabio Masetti

63. LETTERA come sopra   *Di Roma l'ultimo Maggio 1606*

. . . Il Caravaggio Pittor s'è partito da Roma malamente ferito havendo egli Domenica sera amazzato un'altro che lo provocò a far seco questione, et mi vien detto che s'è inviato alla volta di Firenza et forse anco verrà a Modena.

Fabio Masetti

LETTER to the same   *Rome, 31 May 1606*

. . . Caravaggio, the painter, left Rome badly wounded, having killed on Sunday night a man who had provoked him to a quarrel. I am told that he set out in the direction of Florence, and that possibly he may proceed to Modena.

Fabio Masetti

64. LETTERA non contenente l'indirizzo   *Di Roma il di ultimo Maggio 1606*

. . . Due sere sono Il Caravaggio Pittor celebre accompagnato da un certo Cap.º Antonio Bolognese affrontò Ranuccio da Terni et doppo breve menar di mano il Pittor restò su la testa mortalmente ferito et gli altri due morti. La rissa fu per giuditio dato sopra un fallo, mentre si giocava alla racchetta, verso l'Ambasciator del Gran Duca.

Pellegrino Bertacchi

LETTER bearing no address   *Rome, 31 May 1606*

. . . Two nights ago Caravaggio, the famous painter, accompanied by a certain Captain Antonio, of Bologna, started a fight with Ranuccio of Terni. After a short exchange of blows, the painter received a mortal wound in the head and the other two were killed. The brawl was over a decision given upon a fault while they were playing tennis near the palace of the Tuscan Ambassador.

Your Most Illustrious and Reverend
Lordship's Most Humble and Devoted
Servant
Pellegrino Bertacchi

65. LETTERA al conte Gio. Batt. Laderchi   *Di Roma il di 15 Luglio 1606*

Al Pittore ho fatto sapere se mi manderà il quadro finito per tutta la prossima settimana ch'io lo pigliarò, altrimenti non occorre, che più vi si affatica perchè pur troppo s'è aspettato.

Fabio Masetti

LETTER to Count Giovan Battista Laderchi   *Rome, 15 July 1606*

I have informed the painter that if he sends me the finished picture by the end of next week, I shall take it. Otherwise, he need not labor at it any longer, for we have been waiting too long as it is.

Fabio Masetti

66. Lettera come sopra   *Di Roma il di 23 Settembre 1606*

. . . Comesse il Caravaggio l'homicidio già scritto et si trattiene a Pagliano con disegno di dover esser presto rimesso; procurerò da lui recuperar 32 scudi ch'io gli diedi come per sue recevute ch'io mandai in mano del Milani che le mostrasse a V. S. Ill.ma

Fabio Masetti

Letter to the same   *Rome, 23 September 1606*

. . . Caravaggio committed the homicide I have already written you about and is now staying at Paliano with a view to obtaining a reprieve soon. I shall endeavor to recover the 32 scudi which I gave him, as appears from his receipts, which I have had put into the hands of Milani, who was to show them to Your Lordship.

Fabio Masetti

67. Lettera come sopra   *Di Roma il di 26 Maggio 1607*

. . . Altre volte significai a V. S. Ill.ma che al Carauaggio Pittor s'erono dati scudi 32 et mandai le ricevute del detto al S.or Milani che le mostrò a V. S. Ill.ma ne si sono potuti recuperar per un'homicidio comesso dal detto per il qual è stato bandito, ma perchè il detto homicidio fu casuale et restò anch'egli malamente ferito, si tratta della sua remissione et si spera la gratia, che quando ritorna non mancarò di ricuperar i detti 32 scudi.

Fabio Masetti

Letter to the same   *Rome, 26 May 1607*

. . . I have previously informed your Most Illustrious Lordship that 32 scudi had been given to Caravaggio the painter, and I sent the latter's receipts to Mr. Milani, who showed them to Your Lordship. It has not been possible to recover the money because of a homicide committed by the said painter, on account of which he has been banished. However, as the said homicide was accidental, and the painter was badly wounded too, a reprieve is being negotiated and a pardon is hoped for. So, when he is back, I shall not fail to recover the said 32 scudi.

Fabio Masetti

68. Lettera come sopra   *Di Roma il di 2 giugno 1607*

. . . Al Carauaggio Pittore ho scritto una mia per la restitutione delli 32 scudi sebene non è la prima et egli non mi hà altra uolta data altra risposta, et mentre si trattiene bandito dubito non cauarne altro profitto ma comparendo a Roma non gliela perdonarò spiacendomi infinitamente il mal termine usato in ricompensa della humanità et benignità che s'è compiacciuta S. A. che gli faccia.

Fabio Masetti

Letter to the same   *Rome, 2 June 1607*

. . . I have written a letter to Caravaggio the painter for the restitution of the 32 scudi, although it was not the first one, and the other time he failed to send a reply. So long as he remains in exile, I am afraid we shall get no further profit of him, but if he shows up in Rome, I shall not forgive him, because I resent infinitely the bad behavior with which he has requited the kindness and benevolence which His Highness was pleased to have us show him. . . .

Fabio Masetti

69. LETTERA come sopra *Di Roma il di 20 Agosto 1607*

Quanto è maggior il desiderio che dimostra S. A. delli quadri tanto è maggiore il dispiacere che comprendo dal ueder ch'egli è impossibile ch'habbia effetto il detto desiderio perche a quello di Michel Angelo non occorre pensarci, all'altro del Caraccio. . . .

Hora si tratta la pace per il Caravaggio, che subito conclusa, ritornerà, et io ui sarò al pelo.

Fabio Masetti

LETTER to the same *Rome, 20 August 1607*

The greater the desire His Highness shows for the pictures, the deeper the regret I feel in seeing that it is impossible that this desire should be fulfilled, since Michelangelo's picture is out of the question, and Carracci's. . . .

A reconciliation is now being negotiated for Caravaggio. As soon as it is concluded, he will return and I shall keep hounding him.

Fabio Masetti

MADONNA OF THE ROSARY and JUDITH AND HOLOFERNES

70. LETTERA da Pourbus al Duca di Mantua *Di Napoli, il 15 Settembre 1607*

. . . Ho visto ancora qualche cosa di buono di Michelangelo Caravaggio che ha fatto qui che si venderanno. . . .

Ho visto qui doi quadri bellissimi di mano de M. Angelo da Caravaggio: l'uno è d'un rosario et era fatto per un'ancona et è grande da 18 palmi et non vogliono manco di 400 ducati; l'altro è un quadro mezzano da camera di mezze figure et è un Oliferno con Giuditta et non lo dariano a manco di 300 ducati. Non ho voluto fare alcuna proferta, non sapendo l'intentione di V. A., me hanno però promesso di non darli via sin tanto che saranno avisati del piacere di V. A.

LETTER from Pourbus to the Duke of Mantua *Naples, 15 September 1607*

. . . I have also seen something very good by Caravaggio which he has made here and which is for sale. . . .

I have seen here two most beautiful paintings from the hand of Michelangelo da Caravaggio. One is a *Rosary* and was made as an altar piece; it is 18 palmi high and they are asking no less than 400 ducats for it. The other is a painting of medium size with half-figures and is a *Judith and Holofernes*; they will not let it go for less than 300 ducats. I did not want to make an offer because I did not know the intentions of Your Highness; however, they have promised me not to let the painting go until they have been informed of the wishes of Your Highness.

From Luzio, A., *La Galleria dei Gonzaga*, Milan, 1913, pp. 277-278.

INDEX

PLATES

PLATE 1. Basket of Fruit. Milan, Ambrosiana

(See Catalogue Raisonné, No. 1B)

PLATE 2. Boy Peeling Fruit, copy. Hampton Court
(See Catalogue Raisonné, No. 2)

PLATE 3. Boy with a Basket of Fruit (Fruttaiuolo). Rome, Galleria Borghese
(See Catalogue Raisonné, No. 3)

3A

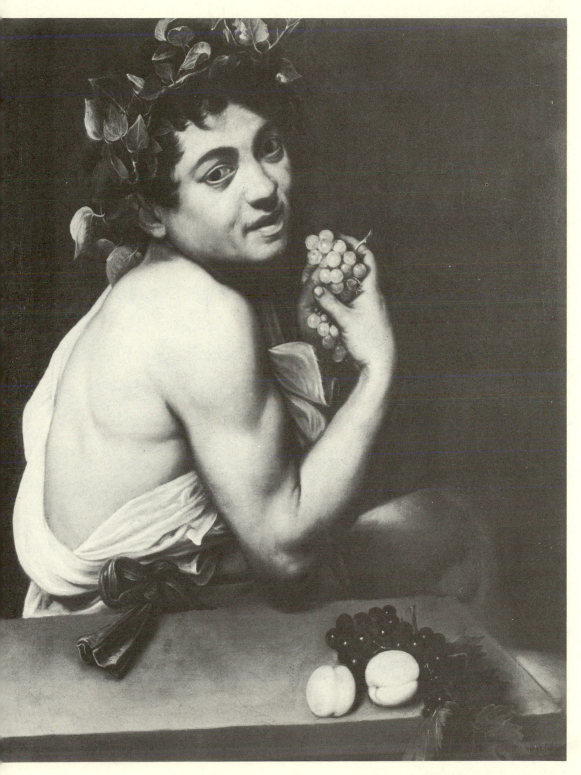

PLATE 4. Boy with Fruit (Bacchino Malato). Rome, Galleria Borghese

(See Catalogue Raisonné, No. 4B)

PLATE 5. Concert of Youths (Musica). New York, Metropolitan Museum
(See Catalogue Raisonné, No. 5)

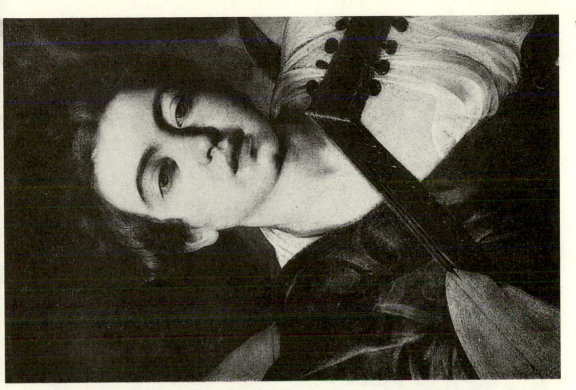

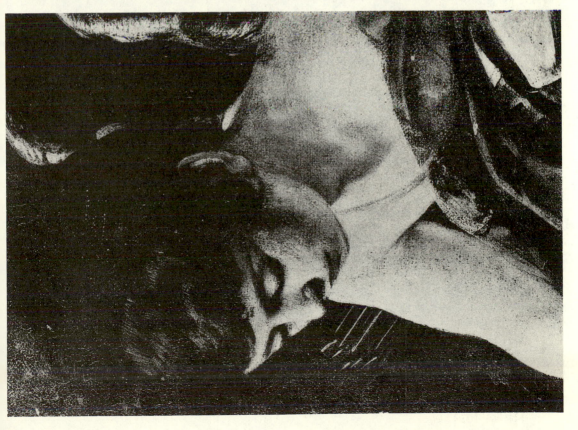

PLATE 6. St. Francis in Ecstasy. Hartford, Wadsworth Atheneum
(See Catalogue Raisonné, No. 6A)

PLATE 7. Bacchus. Florence, Uffizi

(See Catalogue Raisonné, No. 4A)

7A

7в

PLATE 8. Rest on the Flight to Egypt. Rome, Galleria Doria-Pamphili
(See Catalogue Raisonné, No. 7)

8B

8c

8D

PLATE 9. Boy Bitten by a Lizard. Florence, Collection Roberto Longhi

(See Catalogue Raisonné, No. 10A)

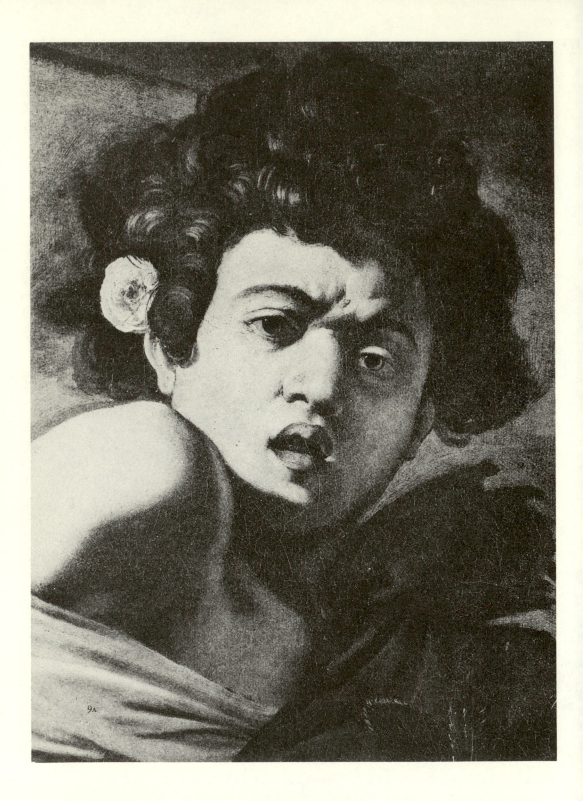

9A

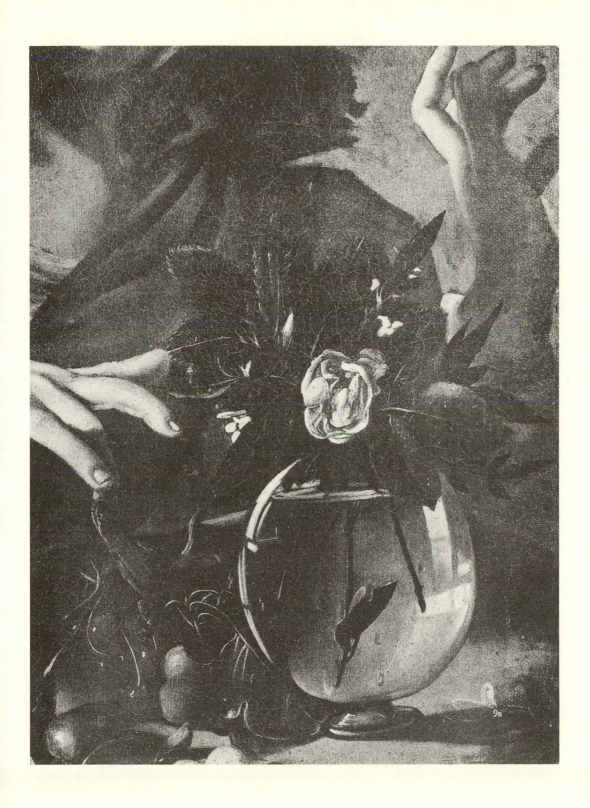

Plate 10. Fortune Teller. Paris, Louvre

PLATE 11. Fortune Teller. Rome, Pinacoteca Capitolina

(See Catalogue Raisonné, No. 9B)

PLATE 12. The Cardsharps (I Bari). Formerly Rome, Galleria Sciarra
(See Catalogue Raisonné, No. 10)

12A

12B

PLATE 13. Lute Player. Leningrad, Hermitage
(See Catalogue Raisonné, No. 11)

PLATE 14. Head of Medusa. Florence, Uffizi
(See Catalogue Raisonné, No. 12)

PLATE 15. Magdalene. Rome, Galleria Doria-Pamphili
(See Catalogue Raisonné, No. 13)

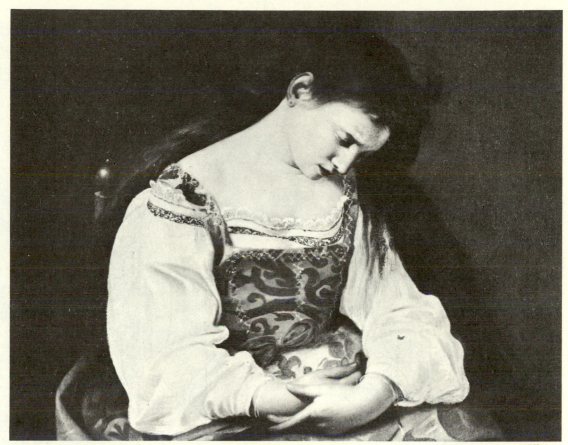

15а

15в

PLATE 16. Portrait of a Young Woman. Formerly Berlin, Kaiser Friedrich Museum
(See Catalogue Raisonné, No. 44A)

42.

PLATE 17. Portrait of Maffeo Barberini. Florence, Collection Principe Corsini
(See Catalogue Raisonné, No. 44B)

PLATE 18. St. Catherine. Lugano, Thyssen Collection
(See Catalogue Raisonné, No. 14)

18a

19a

PLATE 19. Judith and Holofernes. Rome, Casa Coppi

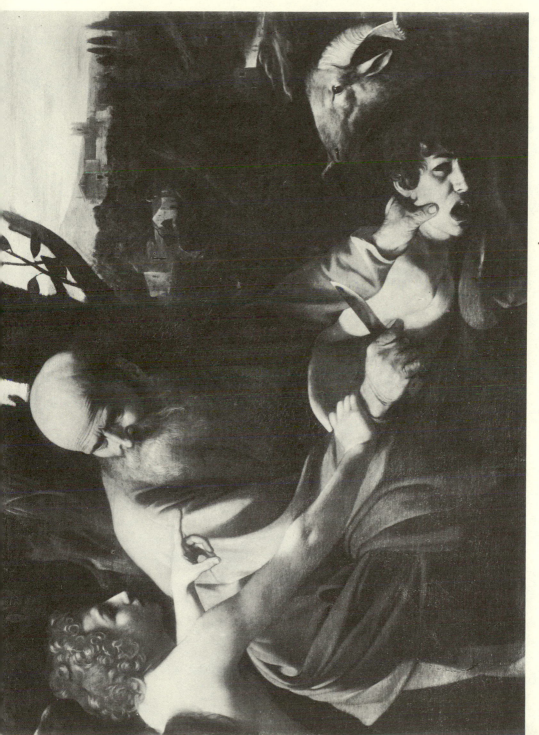

Plate 20. Sacrifice of Isaac. Florence, Uffizi

(See Catalogue Raisonné, No. 16)

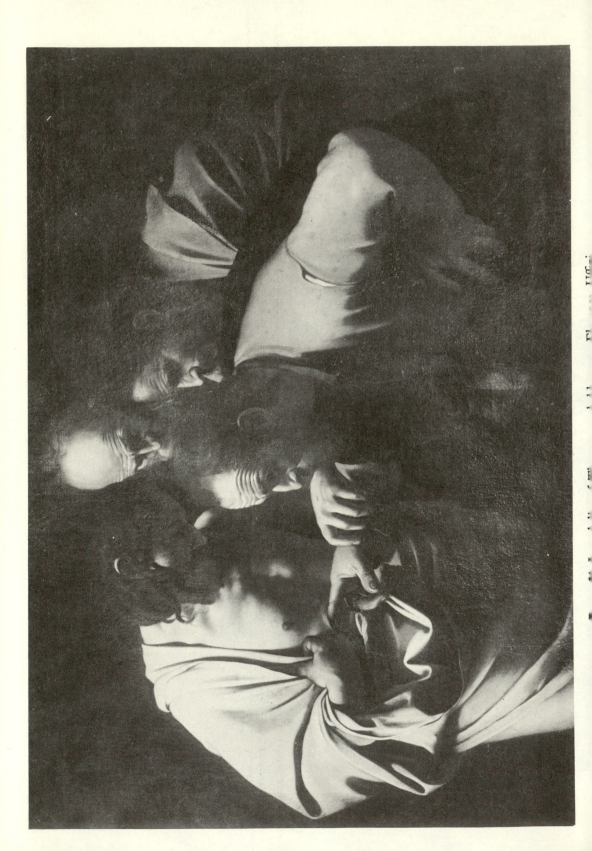

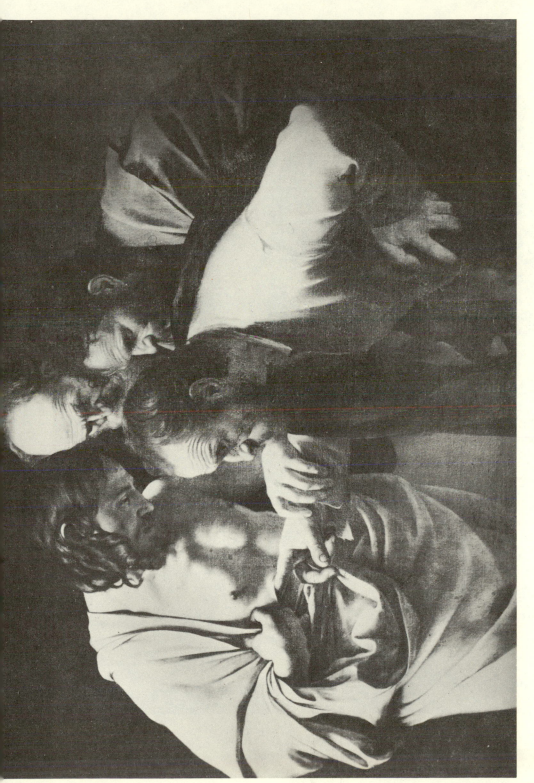

PLATE 22. Incredulity of Thomas. Formerly Potsdam, Neues Palast

(See Catalogue Raisonné, No. 17A)

PLATE 23. Walk to Emmaus, copy. Hampton Court

(See Catalogue Raisonné, No. 19)

Plate 24. Supper at Emmaus. London, National Gallery

(See Catalogue Raisonné, No. 18a)

23в

23а

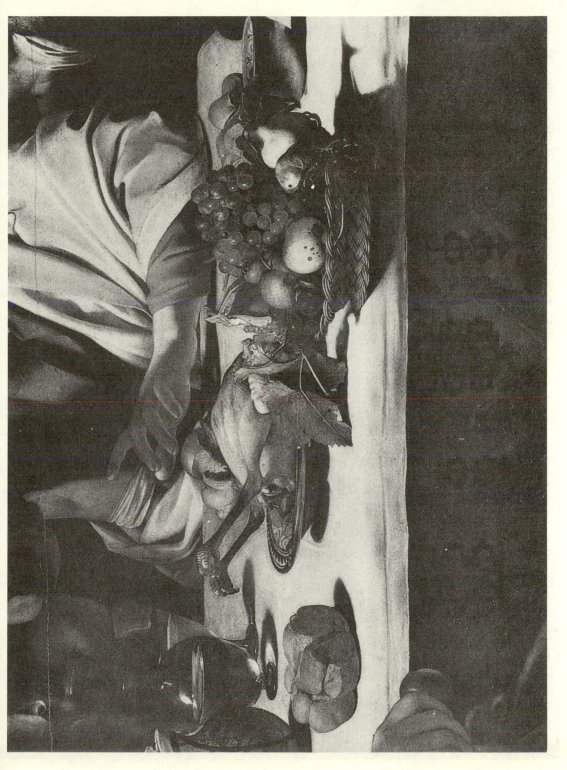

PLATE 25. St. John with a Ram. Rome, Galleria Doria-Pamphili
(See Catalogue Raisonné, No. 20A)

PLATE 26. St. John with a Ram. Rome, Capitoline Collections

(See Catalogue Raisonné, No. 20B)

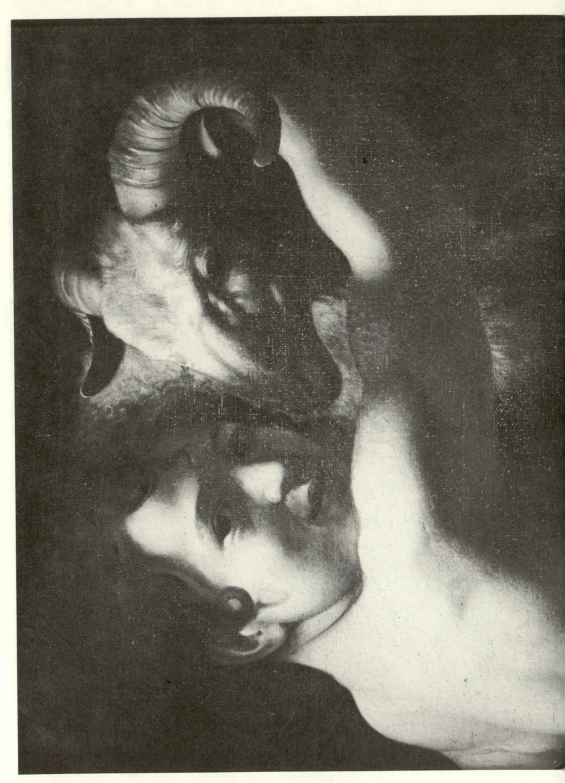

PLATE 27. Taking of Christ, copy. Florence, private collection

(See Catalogue Raisonné, No. 21)

PLATE 28. First St. Matthew (destroyed). Formerly Berlin, Kaiser Friedrich Museum
(See Catalogue Raisonné, No. 22A)

PLATE 29. Calling of St. Matthew. Rome, S. Luigi dei Francesi
(See Catalogue Raisonné, No. 22B)

29D

29в

29c

29F

29ᴇ

PLATE 30. Martyrdom of St. Matthew. Rome, S. Luigi dei Francesi
(See Catalogue Raisonné, No. 22c)

30A

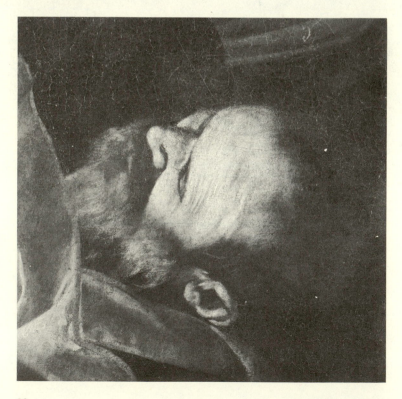

30B

30c

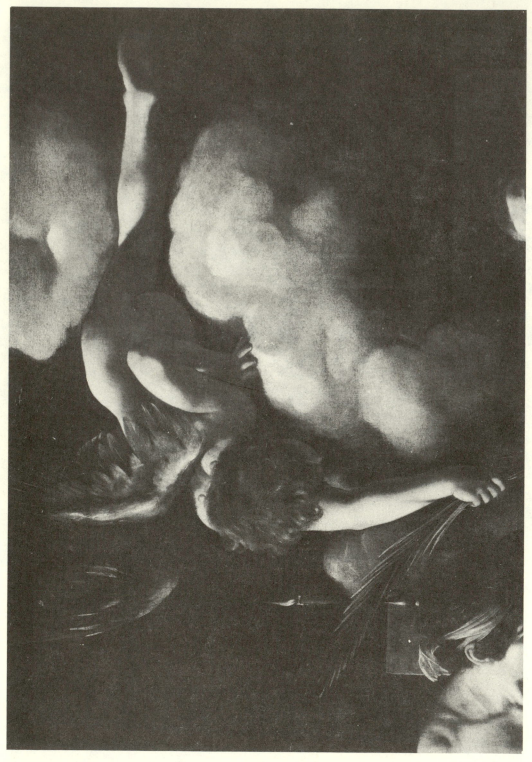

30b

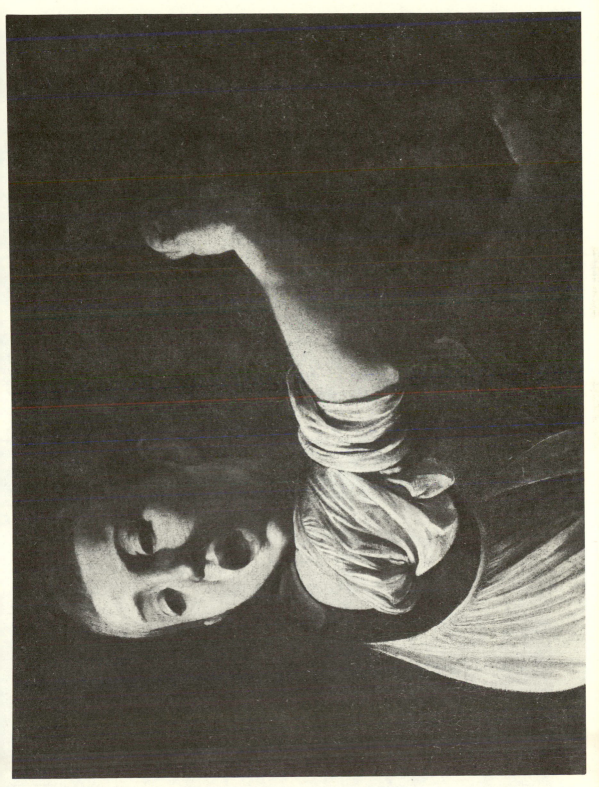

30f

30G

PLATE 31. Second St. Matthew. Rome, S. Luigi dei Francesi
(See Catalogue Raisonné, No. 22D)

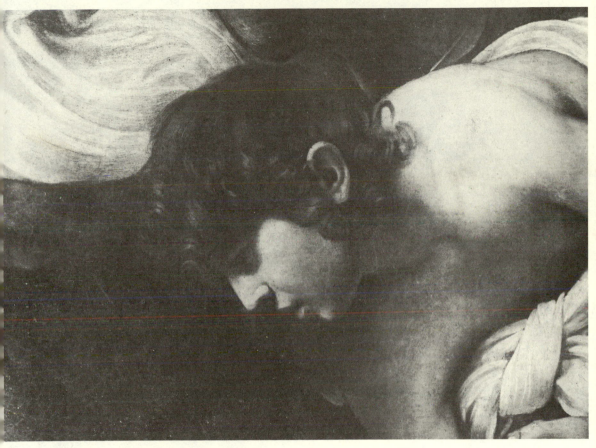

31A

32л

PLATE 32. Amor Victorious. Berlin, Kaiser Friedrich Museum
(See Catalogue Raisonné, No. 23)

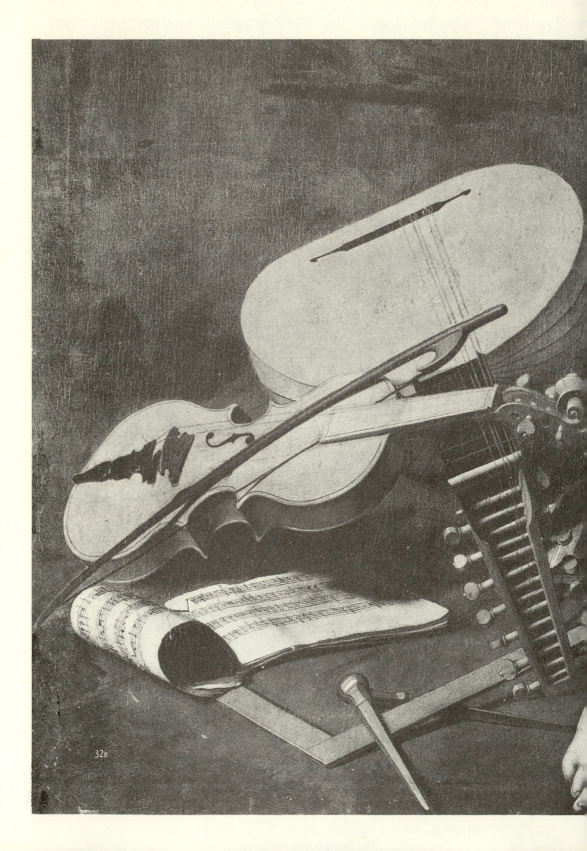

32в

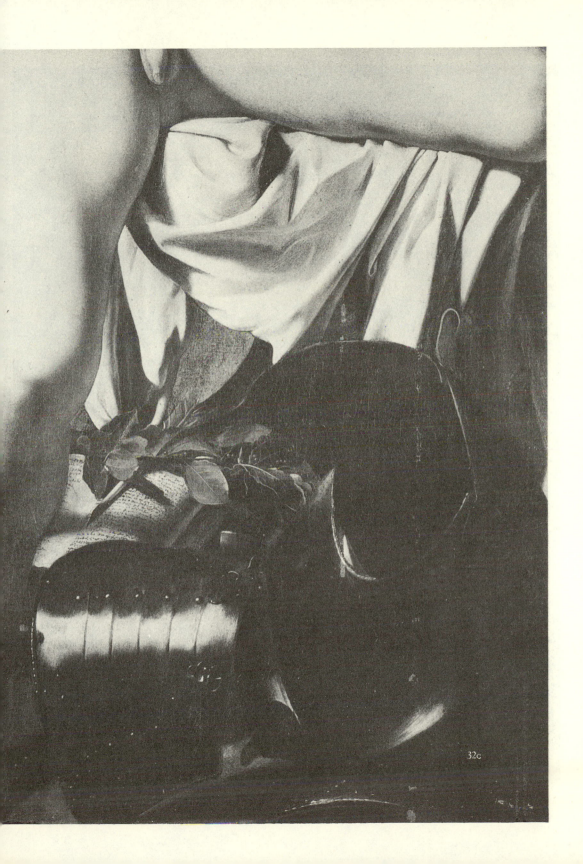

32c

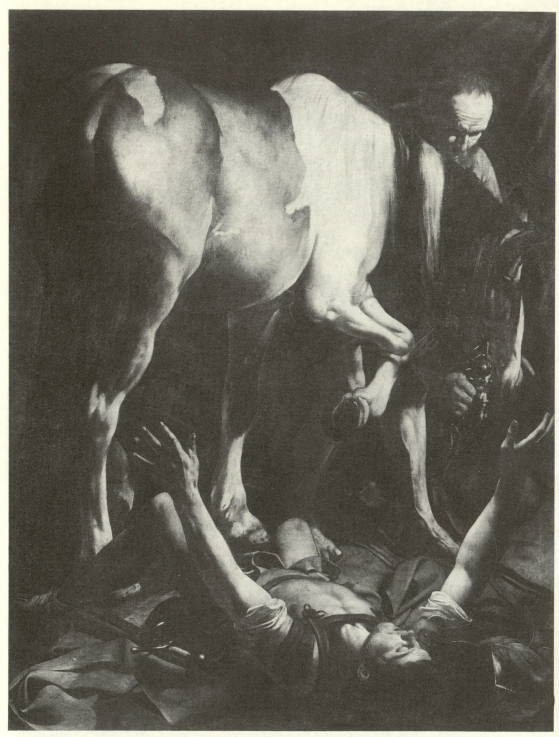

PLATE 33. Conversion of St. Paul. Rome, Sta. Maria del Popolo

(See Catalogue Raisonné, No. 24c)

PLATE 34. Crucifixion of St. Peter. Rome, Sta. Maria del Popolo

(See Catalogue Raisonné, No. 24D)

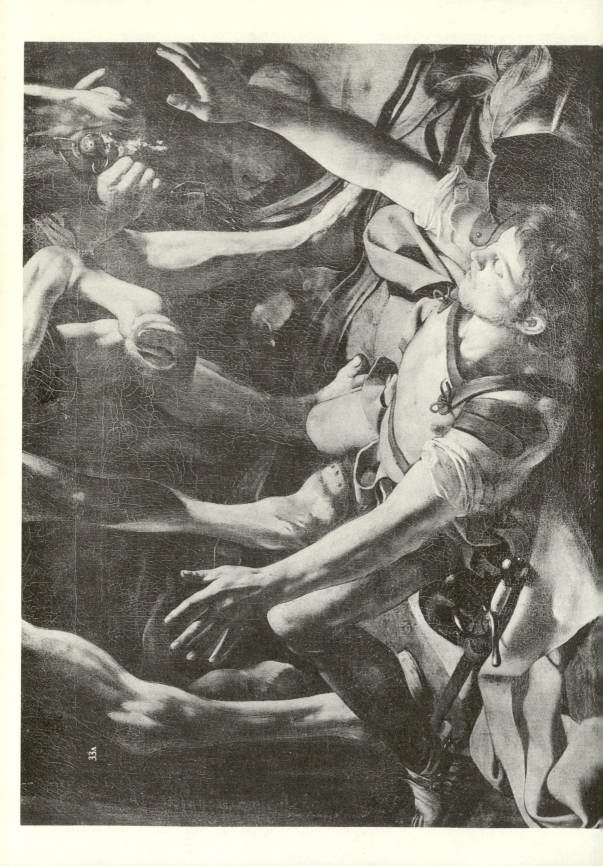

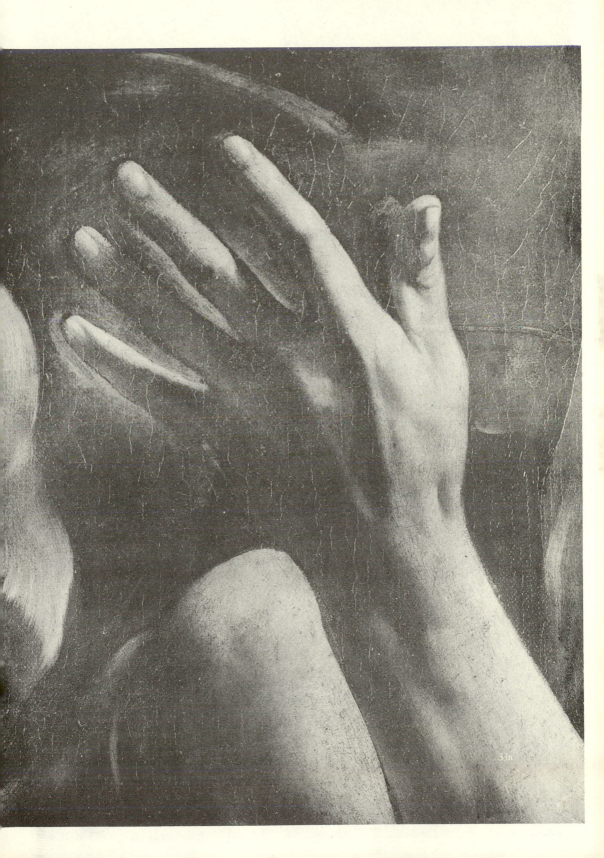

33B

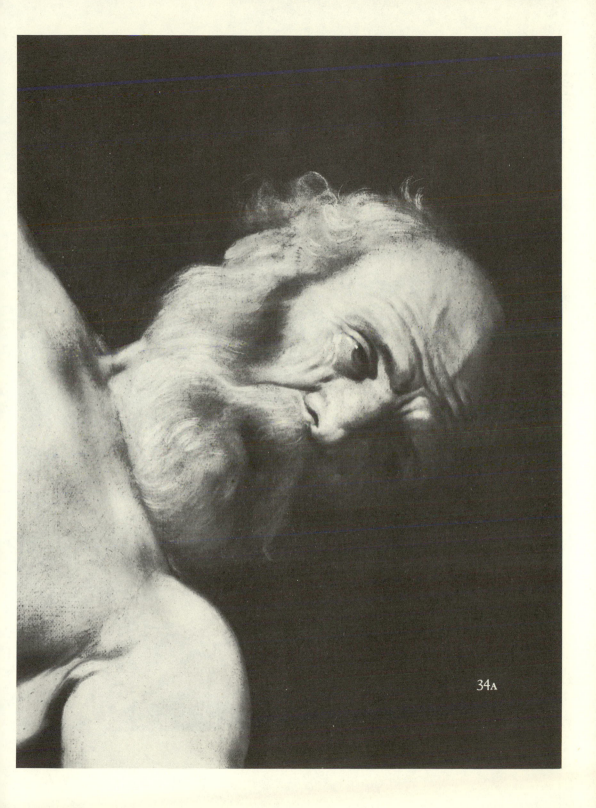

34A

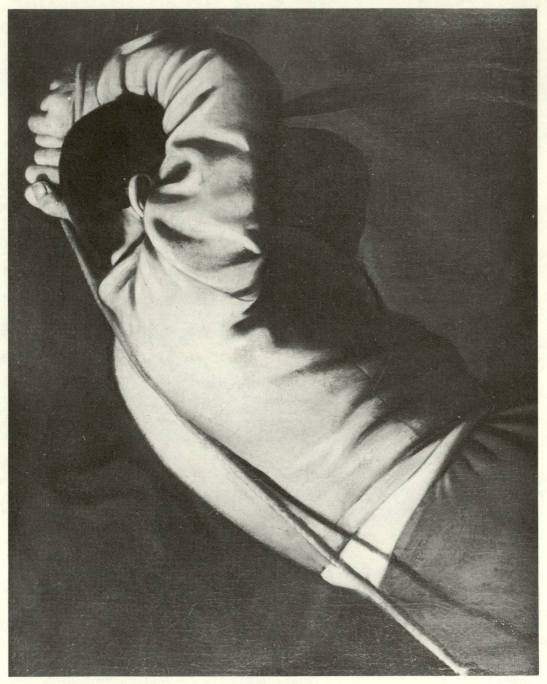

34B

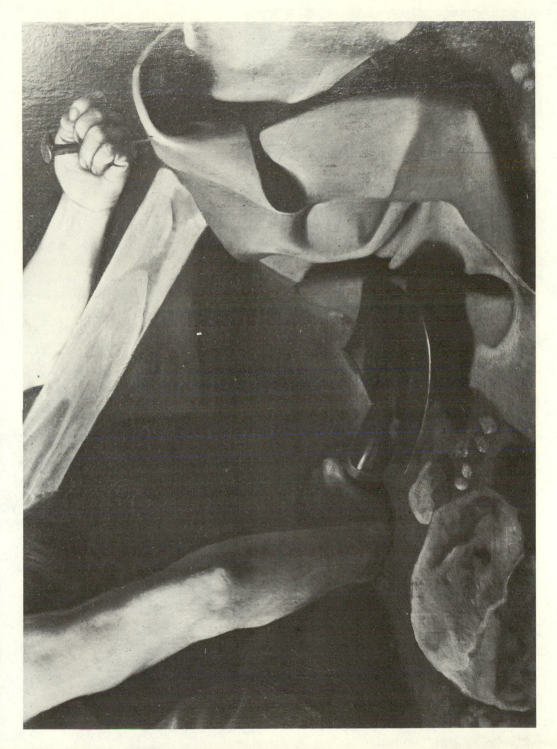

34c

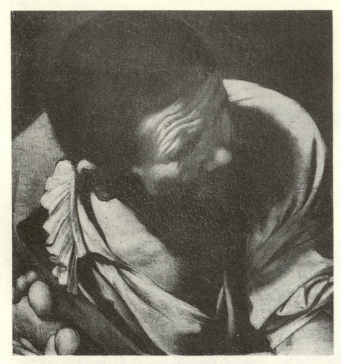

34E

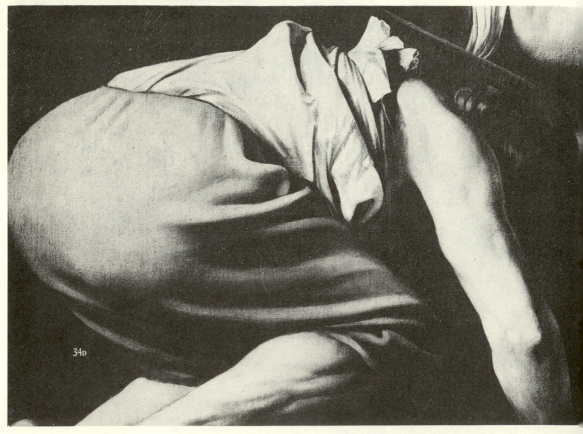

34D

PLATE 35. Deposition of Christ. Rome, Vatican

(See Catalogue Raisonné, No. 25)

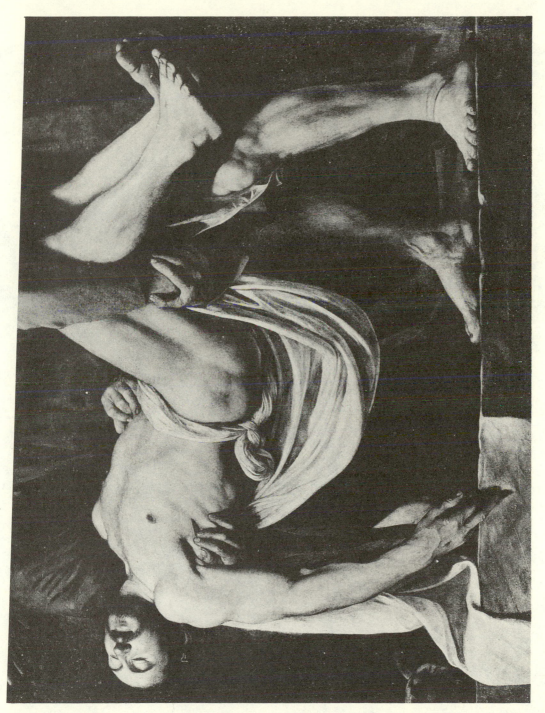

35c

PLATE 36. Madonna di Loreto. Rome, Cavalletti Chapel, S. Agostino

(See Catalogue Raisonné, No. 26)

36a

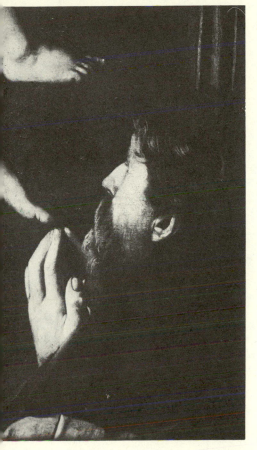

36b

36c

36d

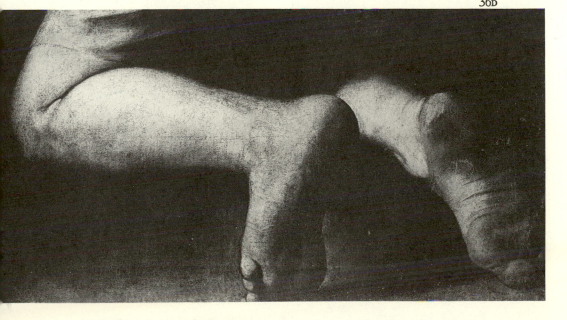

PLATE 37. Madonna and Child with St. Anne (Madonna del Serpe). Rome, Galleria Borghese
(See Catalogue Raisonné, No. 27)

37A

37в

37c

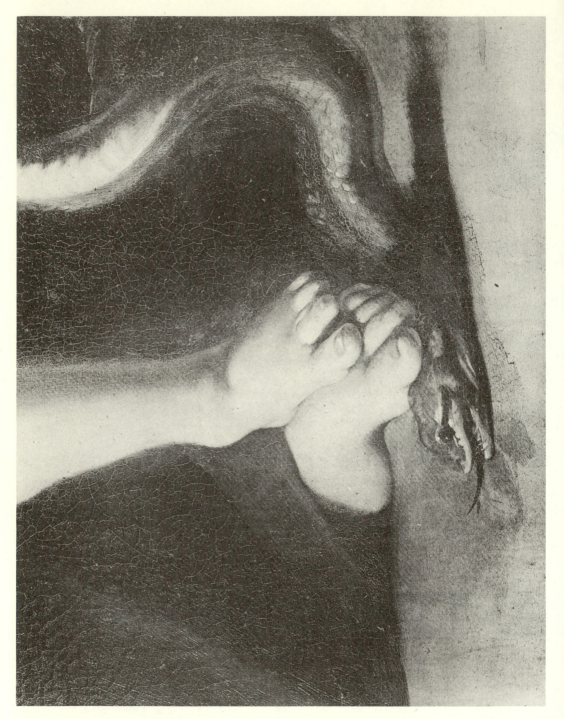

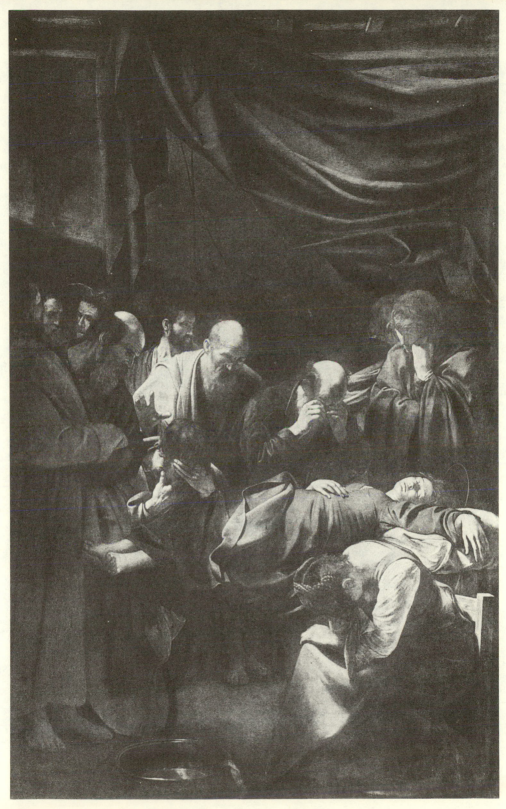

PLATE 38. Death of the Virgin. Paris, Louvre
(See Catalogue Raisonné, No. 28)

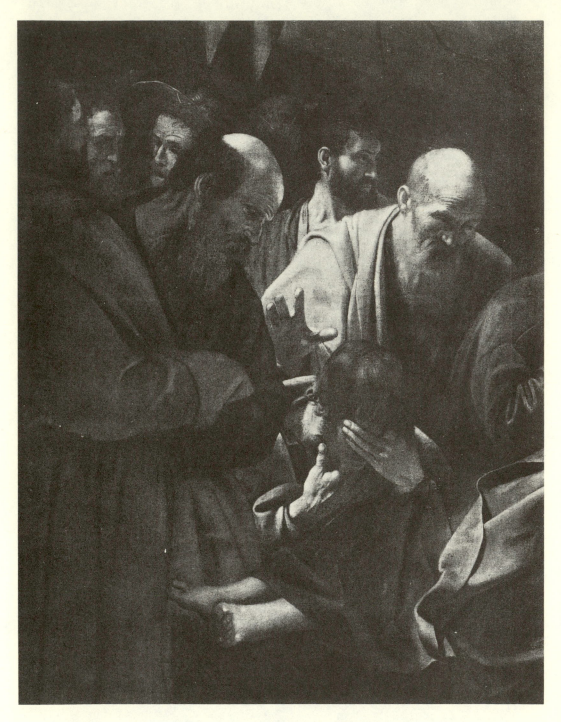

38a

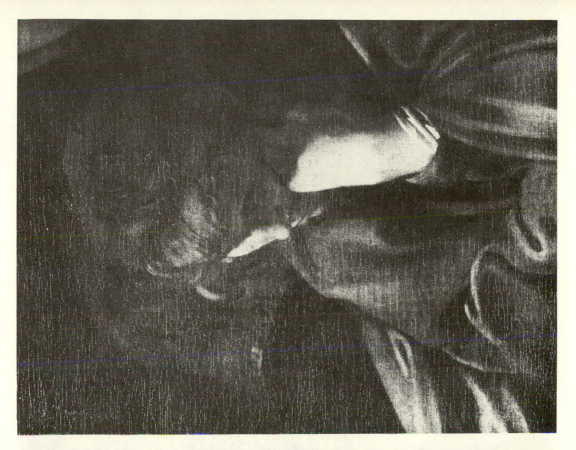

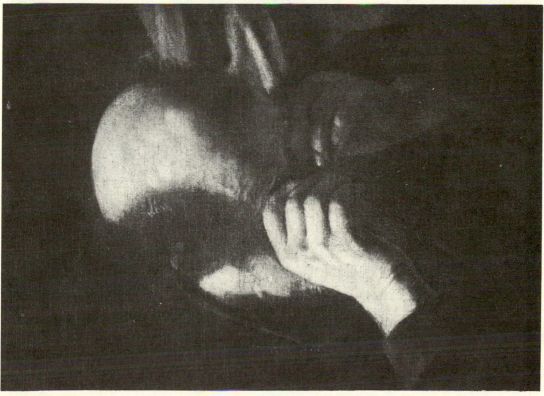

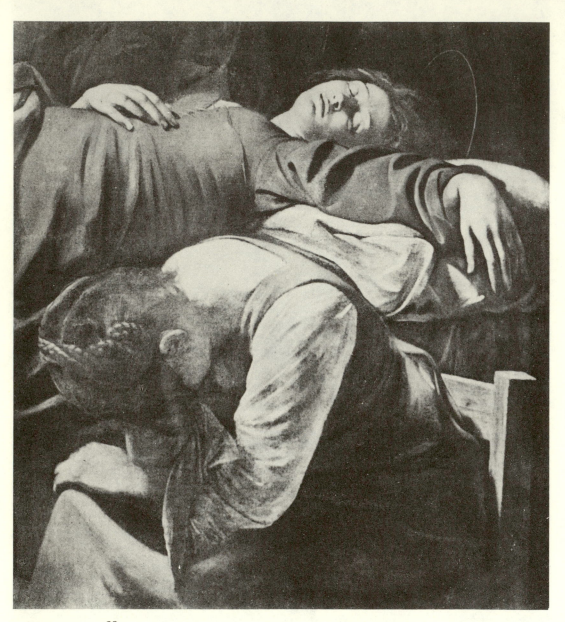

38c

PLATE 39. Madonna of the Rosary. Vienna, Kunsthistorisches Museum

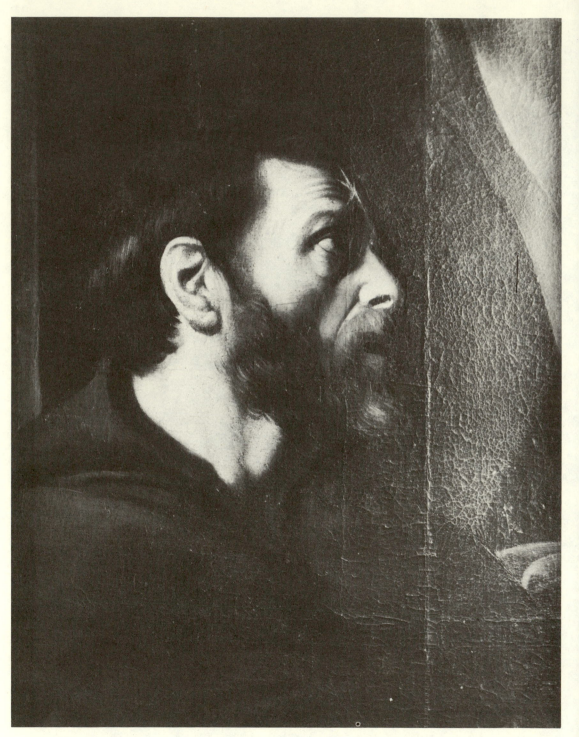

39c

PLATE 40. Portrait of Paul V. Rome, Palazzo Borghese

(See Catalogue Raisonné, No. 44B)

PLATE 41. David with the Head of Goliath. Rome, Galleria Borghese
(See Catalogue Raisonné, No. 30)

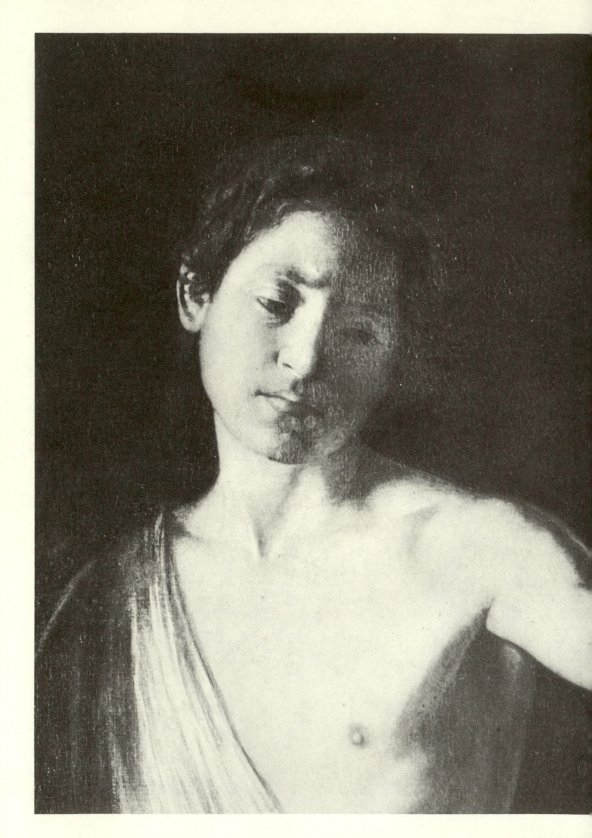

41A

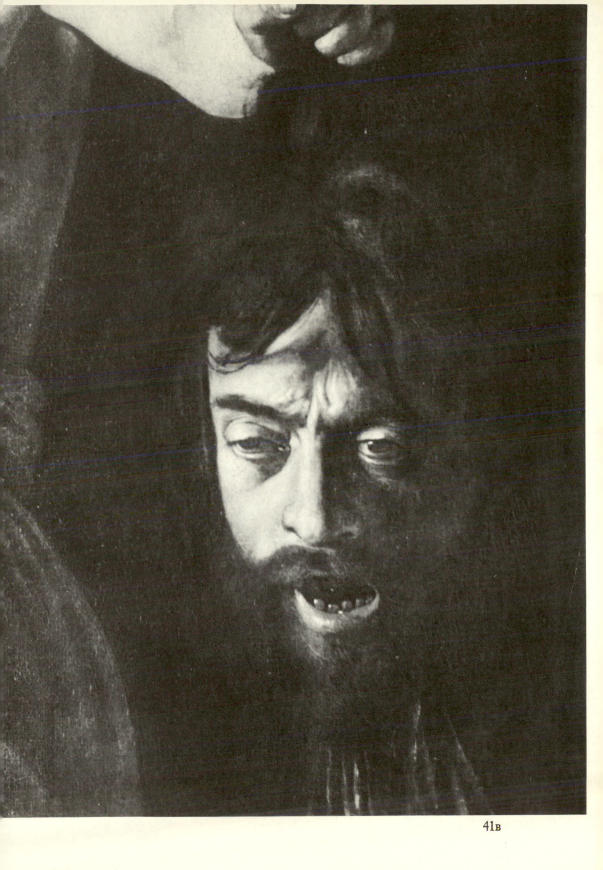

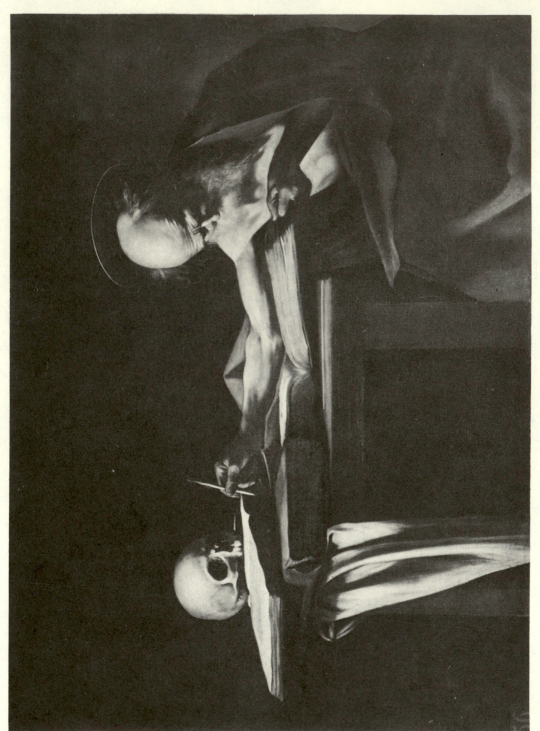

PLATE 42. St. Jerome Writing. Rome, Galleria Borghese
(See Catalogue Raisonné, No. 31A)

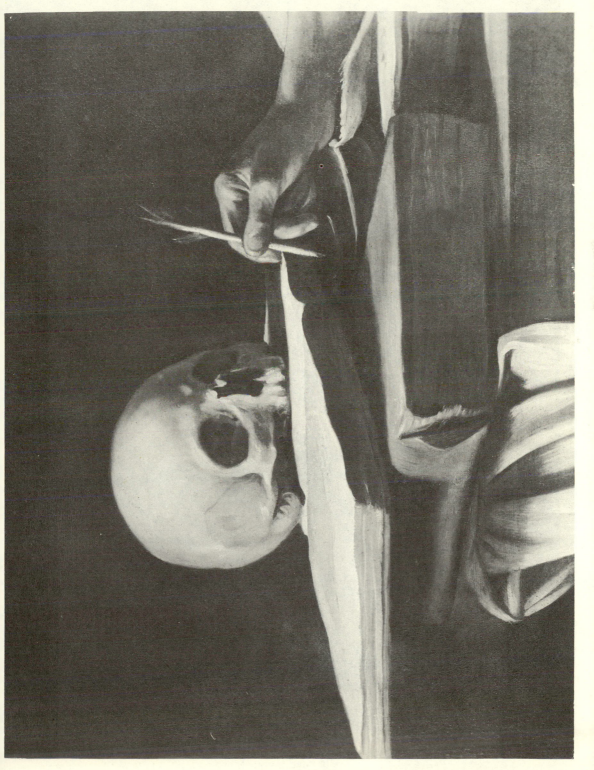

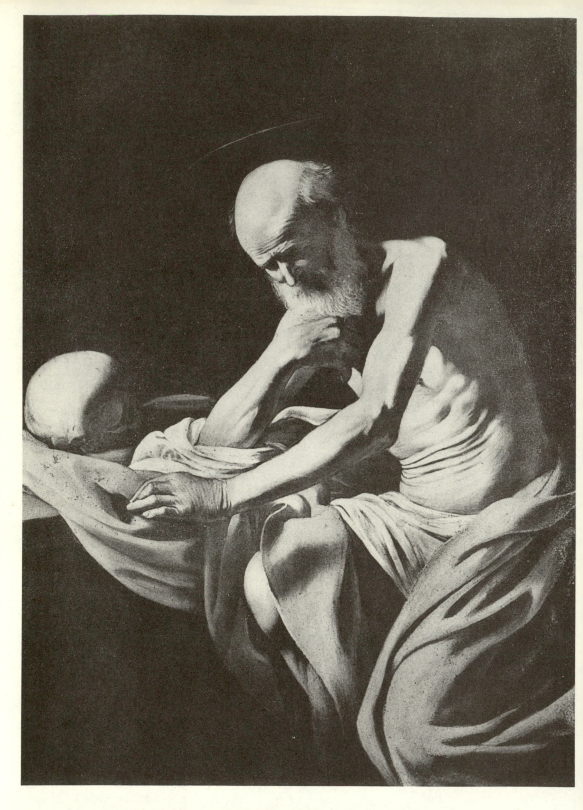

PLATE 43. St. Jerome in Meditation. Montserrat, Monastery
(See Catalogue Raisonné, No. 31B)

PLATE 44. St. John the Baptist. Kansas City, Nelson Gallery

(See Catalogue Raisonné, No. 20D)

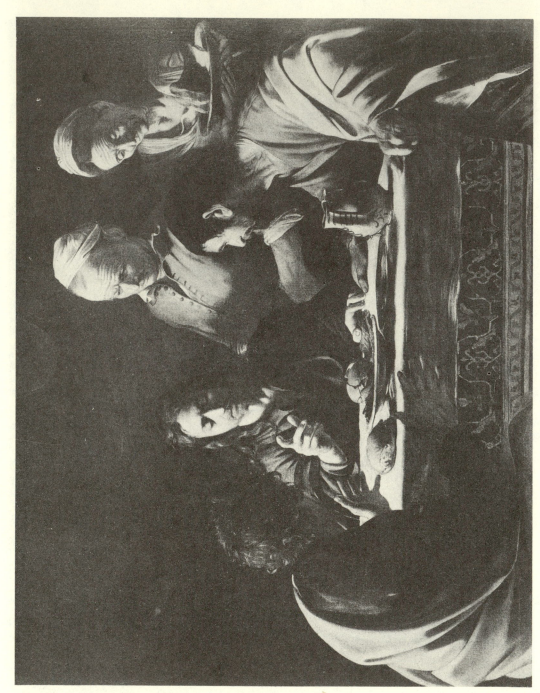

PLATE 45. Supper at Emmaus. Milan, Brera
(See Catalogue Raisonné, No. 18b)

PLATE 47. Fainting Magdalene, copy. Marseilles Museum
(See Catalogue Raisonné, No. 32B)

PLATE 46. Fainting Magdalene, copy. Barcelona, Collection Alorda
(See Catalogue Raisonné, No. 32A)

PLATE 48. Flagellation of Christ. Naples, San Domenico Maggiore
(See Catalogue Raisonné, No. 33)

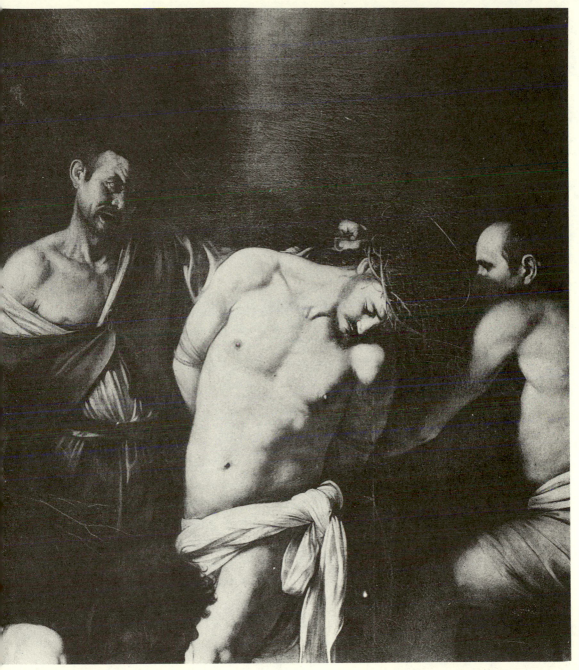

48A

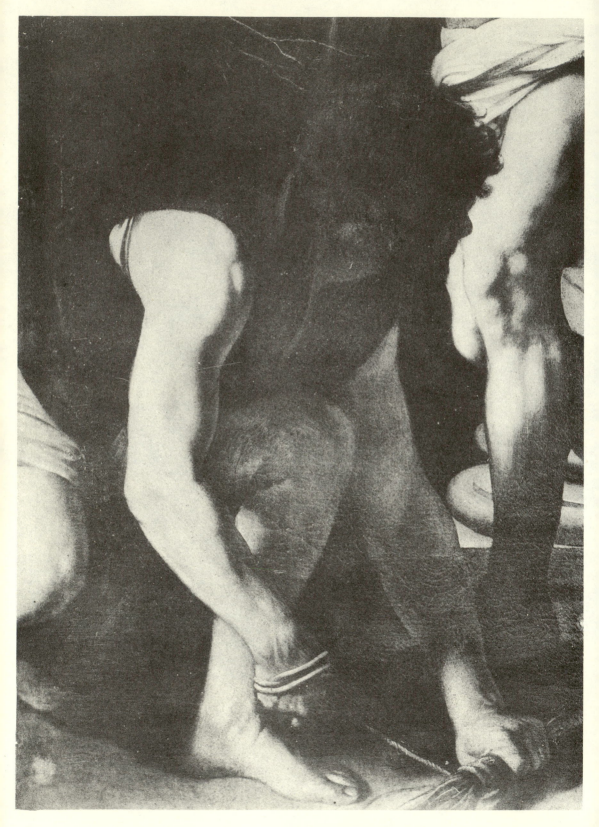

PLATE 49. Seven Acts of Mercy. Naples, Chiesa del Monte della Misericordia
(See Catalogue Raisonné, No. 34)

49A

49в

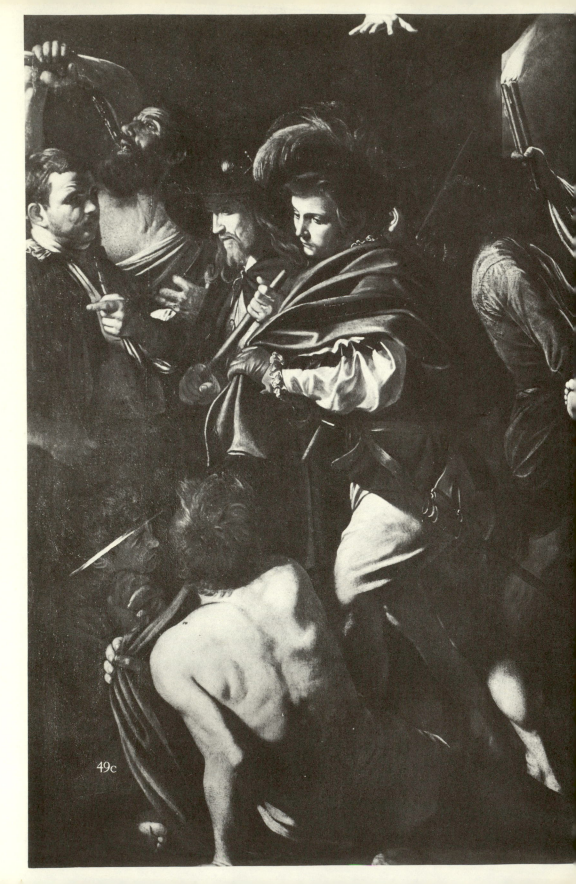

49c

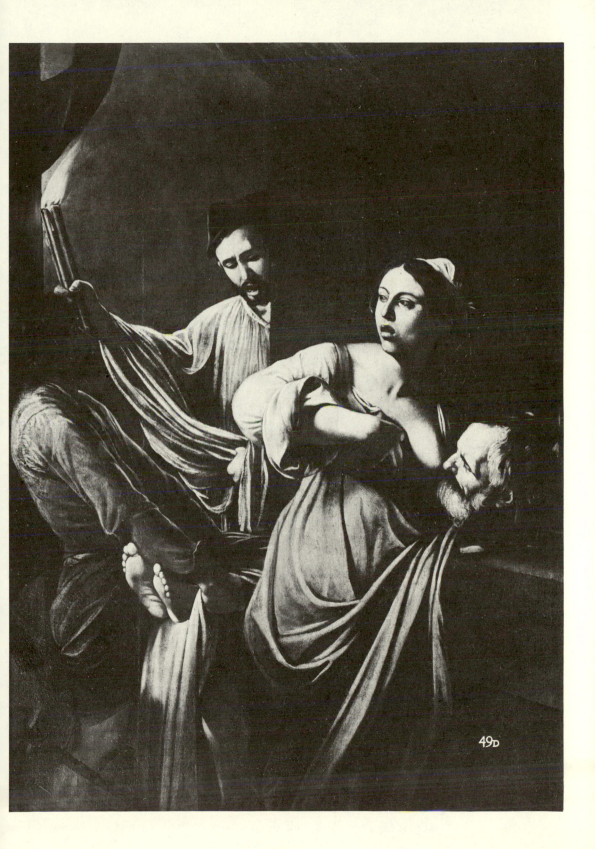

49D

PLATE 50. Portrait of Alof de Wignacourt. Paris, Louvre

PLATE 51. Beheading of St. John the Baptist. Malta, La Valletta Cathedral

PLATE 52. St. Jerome Writing. Malta, La Valletta, Church of S. Giovanni
(See Catalogue Raisonné, No. 37)

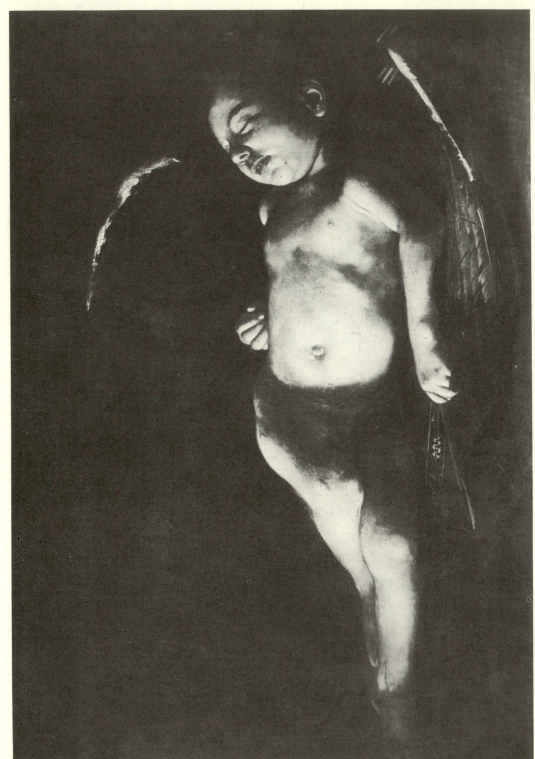

PLATE 53. Sleeping Cupid. Florence, Pitti Palace
(See Catalogue Raisonné, No. 38A)

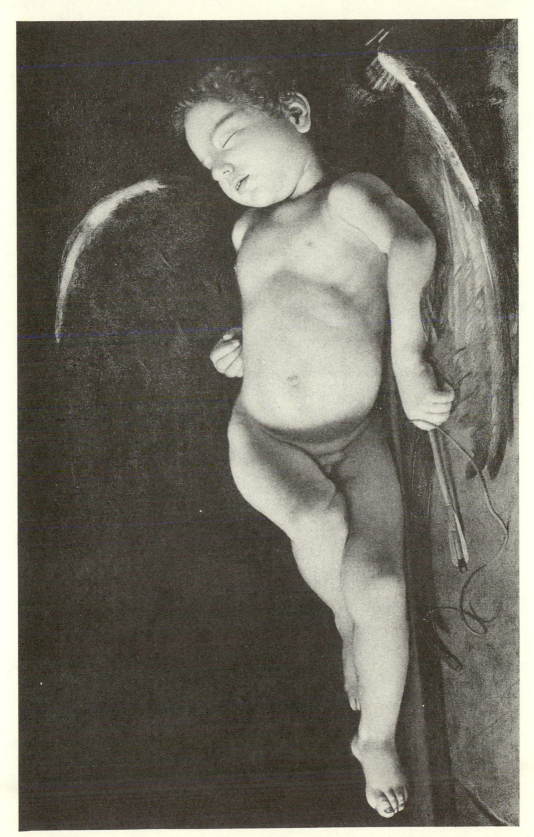

PLATE 54. Sleeping Cupid. Indianapolis, private collection

(See Catalogue Raisonné, No. 38B)

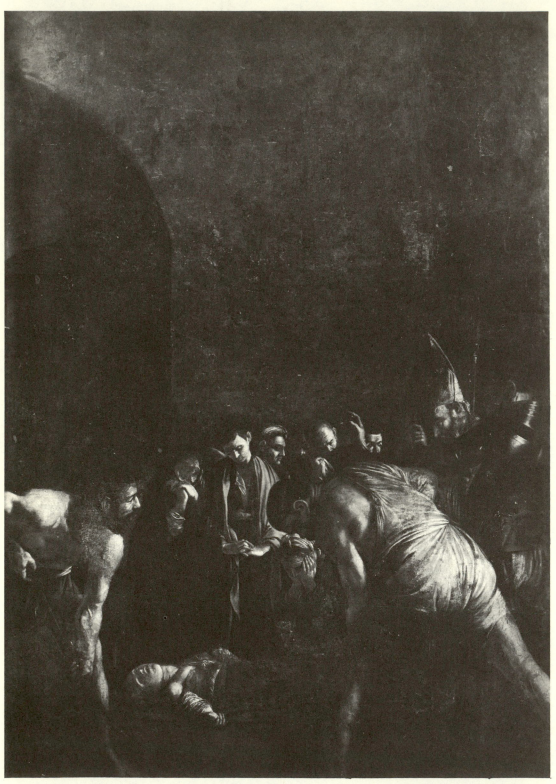

PLATE 55. Martyrdom of St. Lucy. Syracuse, Church of St. Lucy

(See Catalogue Raisonné, No. 39)

55A

55B

5

55D

PLATE 56. Nativity. Messina, Museo Nazionale
(See Catalogue Raisonné, No. 41)

56A

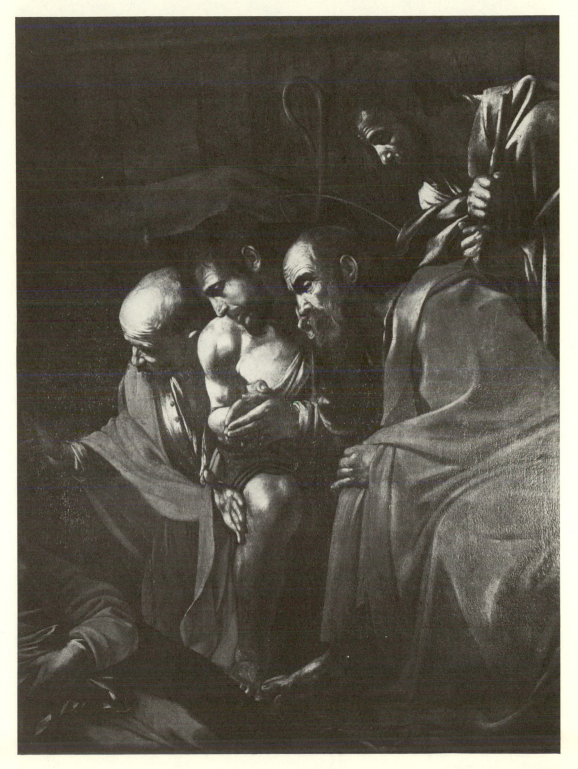

PLATE 57. Resurrection of Lazarus. Messina, Museo Nazionale

(See Catalogue Raisonné, No. 40)

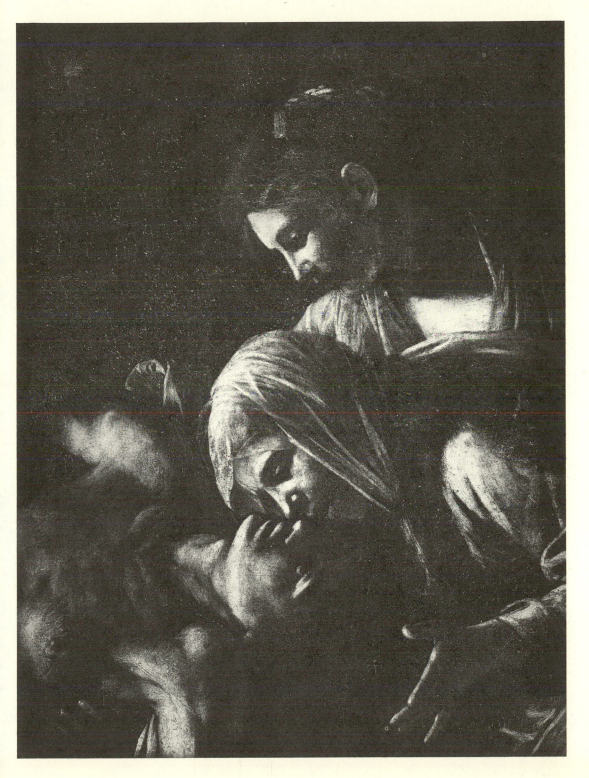

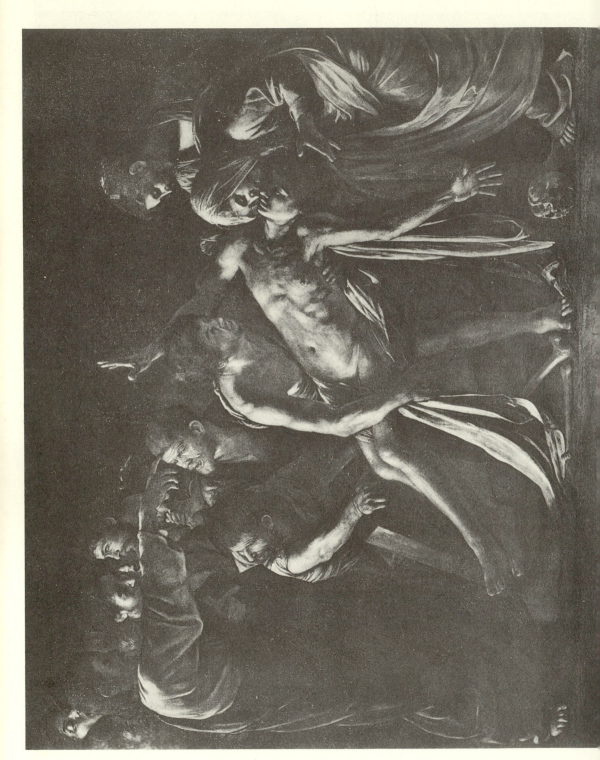

57в

PLATE 58. Adoration with St. Francis and St. Lawrence. Palermo, Oratorio di San Lorenzo
(See Catalogue Raisonné, No. 42)

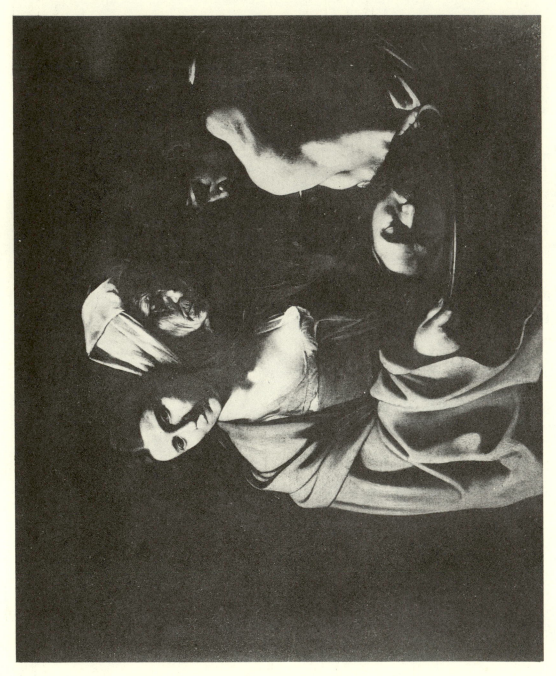

PLATE 59. Salome with the Head of St. John. Escorial, Casita del Principe

APPENDIX

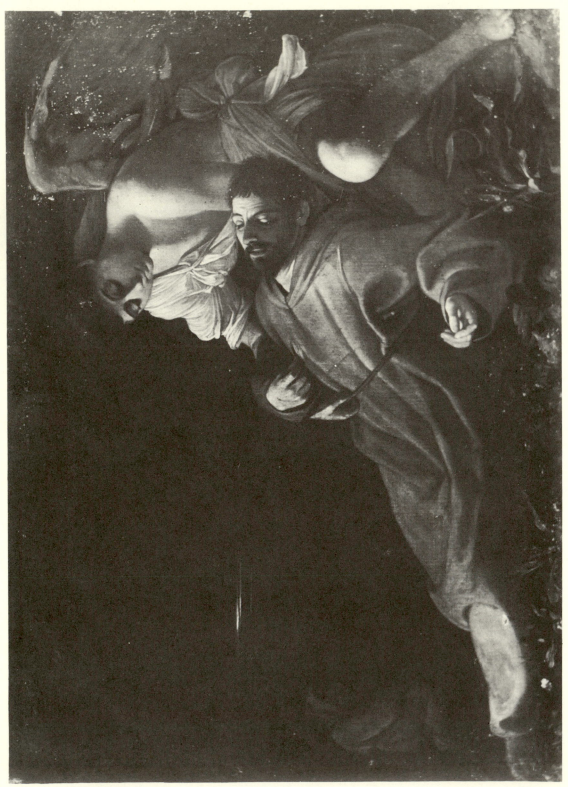

PLATE 60. St. Francis. Udine, Museo Civico

PLATE 61. St. John the Baptist. Rome, Galleria Borghese

(See Catalogue Raisonné, No. 20c)

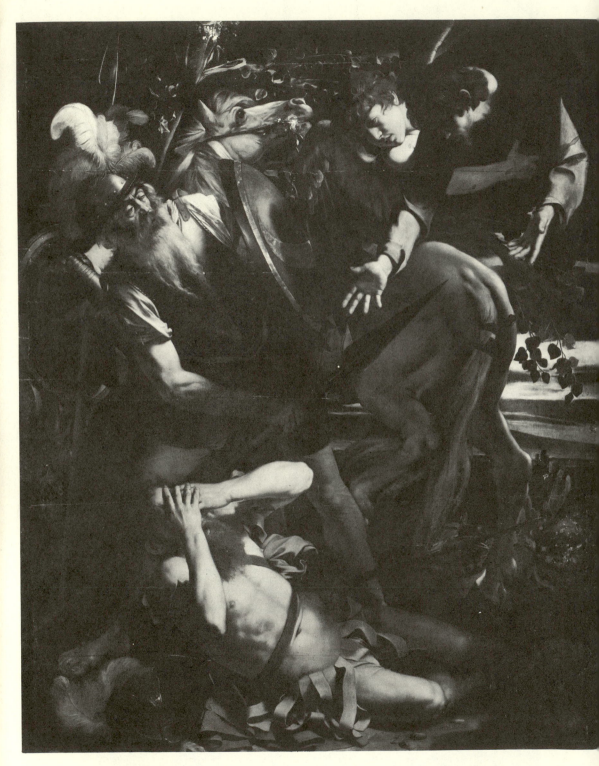

PLATE 62. Conversion of St. Paul. Rome, Collection Odescalchi-Balbi

(See Catalogue Raisonné, No. 24A)

PLATE 63. Crucifixion of St. Peter. Leningrad, Hermitage
(See Catalogue Raisonné, No. 24B)

PLATE 64. Crucifixion of St. Andrew, copy. Barcelona, Museo del Arte
(See Catalogue Raisonné, No. 35)

PLATE 65. Crowning with Thorns, copy. Vienna, Kunsthistorisches Museum
(See Catalogue Raisonné, No. 46)

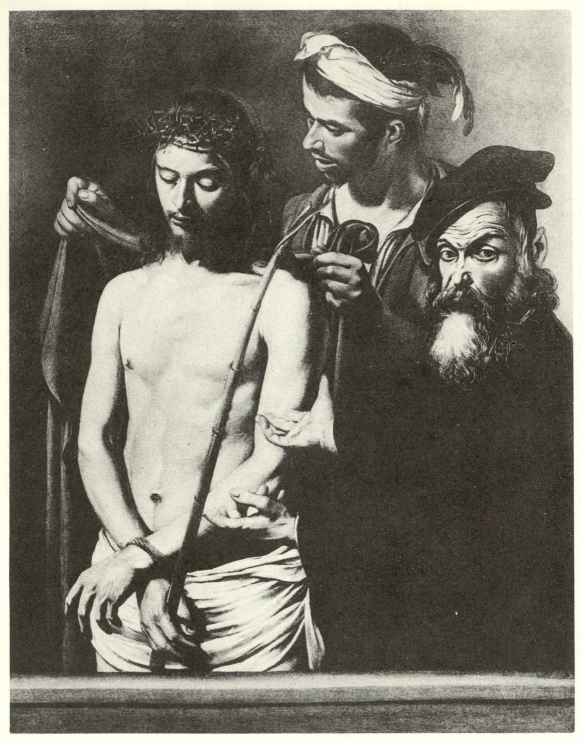

PLATE 66. Ecce Homo. Genoa, Palazzo Communale
(See Catalogue Raisonné, No. 47)